POSITIVE PSYCHOLOGY

in the

ELEMENTARY

SCHOOL

CLASSROOM

Norton Books in Education

POSITIVE PSYCHOLOGY

in the

ELEMENTARY SCHOOL CLASSROOM

Patty O'Grady, PhD

W. W. Norton & Company

New York • London

For information about permission to reproduce selections from this book, write to Permissions, W. W. Norton & Company, Inc., 500 Fifth Avenue, New York, NY 10110

For information about special discounts for bulk purchases, please contact W. W. Norton Special Sales at specialsales@wwnorton.com or 800-233-4830

Manufacturing by R. R. Donnelley, Harrisonburg
Production manager: Leeann Graham

Library of Congress Cataloging-in-Publication Data

O'Grady, Patty.
    Positive psychology in the elementary school classroom / Patty O'Grady, PhD.
        p.   cm. — (Norton books in education)
    Includes bibliographical references and index.
    ISBN 978-0-393-70758-8 (pbk.)
1. Educational psychology. 2. Positive psychology. 3. Education, Elementary.
I. Title.
LB1060.O37 2013
370.15—dc23   2012037355

ISBN: 978-0-393-70758-8 (pbk.)

W. W. Norton & Company, Inc.
500 Fifth Avenue, New York, N.Y. 10110
www.wwnorton.com

W. W. Norton & Company Ltd.
Castle House, 75/76 Wells Street, London W1T 3QT

1 2 3 4 5 6 7 8 9 0

I dedicate this book to Amanda, who is my unofficial coauthor and who mastered the gift of positive psychology when she was 3 years old and gives it freely to everyone she meets.

CONTENTS

EXPANDED CONTENTS

ACKNOWLEDGMENTS

There is truth in wine and children.

—Plato

Thank you to my daughter, Amanda, who is the most virtuous person I know and who added to her 18-hour lawyer workday by reading chapters and saying, "You can do it." Amanda, your keen intellect got me refocused when I needed it most, and you taught me grace under pressure. Thank you to my son, Eamonn, who is the strongest person I know and who has overcome enormous obstacles to become an accomplished musician, golfer, tennis player, accountant, and educator. The example of his courage motivated me when I faltered. Eamonn, you taught me to be brave. Thank you to my husband, a former Vietnam prisoner of war who knows something about trauma recovery, for reading every page and commenting, "Why didn't they have this when I was in school?" He taught me that there is resilience to muster even in a POW camp. Thank you to my friends and colleagues for forgiving all the missed phone calls, lunch dates, office parties, and meetings, and for teaching me patience. Thank you to the thousands of aspiring and veteran teachers who have been my students over the past 25 years. Everything I needed to know about positive psychology, I learned from them. My students have asked hard questions, taught me about flow, and have inspired me to find new and better answers. Thank you to all teachers everywhere for all you do every day to help all children flourish because you understand the importance of your legacy.

I offer a toast to my family, friends, students, and teachers everywhere. Cheers!

INTRODUCTION

Excellence is not a gift, but a skill that takes practice. We do not
act rightly because we are excellent; in fact we achieve
excellence by acting rightly.

—Plato

As I write this book, I am sitting in a chair with my laptop looking out
my window that overlooks the Seddon Channel in Tampa, Florida,
where the dragon boats are assembling for the 2011 Tenth Annual International Dragon Boat Federation (IDBF) World Championship Dragon
Boat Races. This is the highest level of competition in the sport of dragon
boat racing and is hosted every two years in cities across the globe from
Yue Yang, China ('95), to Nottingham ('99) to Shanghai ('04). The competitors will race five different courses at 18 different competition levels.

While I write, dragon boat crews arrive from 27 different nations,
from Australia and Brazil to India and Macau to Trinidad and Tobago.
About 2,000 competitors paddle graceful boats that skim the water
under my window. I am distracted, watching the boats and the crews.
They revel in the pleasures of my pretty city. They cheer each other down
the river, use their strong arms to move the boats effortlessly through
the water, paddle together in perfect unison to the rhythm of the dragon
boat drumbeat. They enjoy simply being a part of it all whether they win
the race or not. Surely, this is the pleasant, good, connected, meaningful,
and accomplished life floating on colorful display beneath my gaze.

There are 20 paddlers in each dragon boat, including a lead pair of
paddlers who are called pacers or timers. All other paddlers synchronize
their strokes with the pacer on the opposite side of the boat from where
they sit—not with the pace paddler in front of them—because the direction of the boat is propelled not by individual paddlers but by the crew's
sweep or momentum. The most important consideration in the cycle
of the stroke is taking the paddle in and out of the water and keeping it

straight up. A vertical orientation is the only way to maintain optimal paddle attitude. Properly executed, this upright move uses the gravitational weight of the paddler herself to generate an enormous impulse power that is not otherwise achievable. Upward and onward: similar to how aspects of positive psychology are related, the paddlers do not look ahead to compete but look to their partners to coordinate. They keep their paddles upright in the wind or in rough water to maintain optimal flow, and they work together to maintain forward momentum.

The paddlers also depend on the drummer, who sits at the front of the boat and calls the stroke—he is the boat's heartbeat. The paddler needs the drummer's beat to work together rhythmically. The paddlers also need the sweep standing in the stern to call the directions and steer the boat down the center of the lane. In a positive psychology classroom, the children are the paddlers, the teacher is the sweep, and the lessons are the drum.

The spiritual and mystical history of the dragon boats lends itself to teaching the good life. Dragon boat makers construct a long boat, often of teak, decorated with a dragonhead at the front and a dragon tail at the back. The first boats date back 2,500 years when they raced on the Yangtze River in southern central China. Dragon boat racing is a happy part of the many Chinese water rituals and festivals that celebrate the venerable Asian water dragon. Annual dragon boat festivals are part of ancient ceremonial religious traditions that honor the mythical Asian dragon deities who, in Chinese culture, represent a spirit of strength and vitality. Dragons are regarded as wholesome and beneficent, and they are thus worthy of loyalty and celebration.

Among the dragon boat crews outside my window are teams of cancer survivors, inner-city children, and corporate executives. They are all friends, athletes, and competitors. They, and the families who applaud from the shoreline, are all happy and joyful, emanating a sense of physical and mental well-being. I am tempted to abandon my work and rush down to hand out well-being questionnaires in order to quantify what I observe.

Outside my window, the sun is shining brilliantly on the sparkling blue water and there is a flotilla of dragon boats in an array of strikingly different colors and patterns but all in the same shape. The teams are lively and spirited; they shout to each other, laugh, create a flow down the river, and enjoy the exhilarating emotions they feel, the signature strength they bring, the contribution they make to their team, the meaning of the festival, and the accomplishment of paddling as fast as they can down the course offering their personal best—win or lose.

As the teacher in me watches from my window, I construct a positive psychology dragon boat curriculum in my head. From kindergarten to sixth grade, with just a little creative elbow grease, the dragon boats can easily teach children about history, art, music, philosophy, geography, mathematics, physics, biology, ecology, and more, with positive psychology at the core of it all. We can research the boats, write about them, build model replicas, measure them, decorate them, drum the rhythms, and learn the history of the countries that race them. The class will consider the positive emotion that paddlers must evoke to compete by appreciating the blue sky above and the calm sea below. The children can assess their signature strength by striving to become a lead paddler someday. They will understand how every paddler in the boat helps or hinders the race over the water and they know it matters to all the others how well each one performs in synchronicity. Lastly, the children will understand that the accomplishment is in crossing the finish line. Whether they win or lose, they figure out how to inspire the paddlers, drummer, and sweep to be excited to try again next year in some other wonderful part of the world as part of a festival that everyone enjoys. Surely, positive psychology is everywhere if we only know where to look for it and share it. This book intends to help teachers understand it, value it, and learn to use it with passion and proficiency. My ideas as to how to do it will end where yours begin: This book is meant to stimulate your ideas.

Building on children's capacity to flourish in the classroom and throughout their lifetime must begin with a cohesive approach to teaching positive psychology. While the research and practice of social emotional learning begin the process, they bifurcate emotional learning and social skills rather than conceptualizing them across a continuum. To the extent that children develop neuroscientifically validated emotional strength, they are better equipped to apply these to the art of friendship and the pursuit of fulfillment in the quest for accomplishment. The focus of positive psychology is the cultivation of emotional strength. Those positive emotions and strengths can build relationships into true friendships and can imbue all learning activities with meaning.

My book's starting point is Martin Seligman's positive psychology principles. I translate them into positive psychology practices for elementary school teachers. These practices are the tenets of Positive Emotion, Engagement through Strength, Relationships, Meaning, and

Accomplishment. I begin with an overview of affective learning, including its philosophical and psychological roots, from finding the golden mean of emotional regulation to finding a child's potencies and golden self. The conversation then continues to connect the core concepts in educational neuroscience to the principles of positive psychology. Core concepts help to explain how feelings permeate the brain, affecting children's thoughts and actions, how insular neurons make us feel empathy and help us learn by observation, and how the frontal cortex is the brain's hall monitor. Neuroscience teaches us that there is no bad behavior, only poorly regulated emotions and underdeveloped strengths. This foundation shapes the positive psychology teaching taxonomy that identifies standards, indicators, methods, and techniques for veteran and novice teachers alike to use in the elementary school classroom. I hope that this book will validate some of the positive psychology methods and techniques that teachers may already use. For others, it may introduce a new approach to teaching the whole child.

After I introduce the positive psychology teaching taxonomy, each chapter will consider the best techniques to teach children how to generate positive emotion, identify and use their emotional strengths, make and keep friends, recognize the meaningful aspects of what they do, and accomplish goals. The book is full of unique and interactive teacher resources, from a comprehensive positive psychology curriculum to simple games, and presents the following 12 techniques:

1. *Class greetings*—how to use the language of positive psychology to get the day off to a good start and how to end the day with positive affirmations and reflections.
2. *Class meetings*—how to conduct various kinds of classroom interactions from friendship circles to goal-setting meetings.
3. *Class pledges, creeds, and agreements*—how to use positive psychology pledges to ensure that children commit to the aims and intentions of positive psychology and a promise to live the good life.
4. *Reflective journals*—how to use journal writing to create more positive self-talk.
5. *Clubs and teams*—how to organize clubs and teams to teach academics and positive psychology simultaneously.
6. *Learning centers*—how to develop learning centers that teach feelings, strengths, friendships, flow, and scaffold accomplishments.

7. *Service learning*—how to help others while helping to practice your own signature strengths.
8. *E-learning*—how to use digital tools to engage thoughts and feelings in flow learning.
9. *Art, dance, drama, and music*— how to use the arts to teach children emotional strengths.
10. *Visualization and observation*—how to help children envision and imitate their strengths.
11. *Self-assessment and self-awareness*—how to help children reflect and reconsider actions.
12. *Self-talk*—how to help children tell a positive story to themselves through self-narratives.

Twenty years ago, while traveling in the most remote parts of North Vietnam into the mountain village of Don Hoa in Minh Hoa district, my young children, my husband, and I encountered a large group of more than 100 children who did not speak English and who had never met an American. We were traveling as a family in a dangerous area under central government protection. The crowd pressed forward into our heavily protected, barbed-wire encampment, curious to see and greet us. The energy was high and the local officials used switches to chase the children away. As the scene became more chaotic, my teacher instincts took over. I stood up in the open jeep where we were sitting and began to chant and gesture: "1-2-3 . . . A-B-C." After each chant, I clapped for the crowd and they imitated me by clapping along. Children and their parents stopped pushing and shoving and now happily chanted along with me with big smiles on their faces. This impromptu lesson went on for about 15 minutes until the crowd easily dispersed, waving good-bye and lifting their fingers to count. At nightfall in that faraway village, two little brown-eyed boys slipped past the compound guards, past the barbed wire, and tapped on my window. Smiling, they chanted, "1-2-3 . . . A-B-C" and clapped. Then they scurried away a few steps ahead of the guards chasing them.

Positive psychology recognizes universal feelings and strengths, creates meaningful interactions with others, and offers a sense of satisfaction and joy. Teaching positive psychology trades the negative for the positive in a guarded compound, invites engagement by sharing strength far from home, connects new friends even across insurmountable language and cultural barriers, encourages collective action that all can enjoy, and leaves everyone feeling a little more accomplished. Teachers send children into their future while hoping they remember the most important lessons. A. A. Milne, the author of Winnie the Pooh's adventures, sums up my book with these words: "If ever there is tomorrow when we're not together, there is something you must always remember. You are braver than you believe, stronger than you seem, and smarter than you think."

POSITIVE PSYCHOLOGY

in the

ELEMENTARY SCHOOL

CLASSROOM

CHAPTER 1

THE PROMISE OF POSITIVE PSYCHOLOGY IN THE ELEMENTARY SCHOOL CLASSROOM

The beginning is the most important part of the work.
—Plato

Positive psychology is the scientific study of optimal functioning associated with physical, mental, social, and emotional well-being, along with the "strengths and virtues that enable individuals and communities to thrive."[1] With the advent of positive psychology, psychologists shifted their focus from helping those with emotional deficits to lead functional lives to helping ordinary people to improve their lives.

Positive psychology makes the good even better. Positive psychology considers how all people can cultivate positive attitudes, build their personal strengths, and find deeper happiness in their lives and communities. Yet this ability to thrive and to flourish depends on the individual's unique emotional strengths that underpin positive psychological and personal adjustment in all areas of learning and life.

In the elementary classroom, integrating positive psychology into the academic curriculum has the power to dramatically improve children's academic achievement by helping them to stay optimistic, delay gratification, strengthen willpower, increase resiliency, build meaningful social relationships, and find greater meaning and satisfaction. There can be no more important academic or life lesson for children to learn and there is no more important lesson for the teacher to teach them. Children who develop those qualities are more likely to succeed in their lifelong endeavors, large and small, because they are equipped to over-come the adversity, failure, and difficulties that are inevitable in life. What's more, they develop a lasting happiness, have a deeper apprecia-tion for life, earn better grades, and live more accomplished lives.

Adopting a positive psychology worldview, the teacher abandons the deficiency model in education and her attention shifts from what is wrong in education to what is right in education, and how to replicate it. Positive psychology in the classroom and the ways that the teacher shapes the lesson to be consistent with neuroscience principles of learn-ing facilitate achievement and accomplishment. The hallmark of posi-tive psychology is the emotional strength that self-actualizes well-being.

Positive psychology experiences, whether the experience is a field trip, sharing a sandwich with a friend, picking up trash on the beach, or acting out emotions in a school play, enrich life and teach important life lessons. When the teacher implements positive psychology in the classroom, the expected learning outcomes are increased engagement and strength, increased positive emotions and emotional regulation, increased positive relations, and increased positive intentions. The by-product of this learning is an associated increase in confidence.

Teachers sometimes forget the courage it takes to learn and the risks inherent in the learning. To do well in school, children risk embarrass-ment and rejection by exposing their most vulnerable fragile selves to insecurity and failure. Some teachers unintentionally condition anxiety, timidity, and compliance in children, and these learned reactions can interfere with academic, social, and emotional learning and can inhibit optimal functioning.

Teaching Positive Psychology in the Classroom

There is no clear definition as to what constitutes teaching positive psy-chology in the classroom. The focus is most often on the somewhat ran-dom implementation of it. For the most part, there are numerous descrip-tions of positive psychology strategies and activities, but no cohesive and coherent framework exists. What does exist is a large body of evidence that confirms that positive psychology is highly correlated with academic achievement.

From the existing body of work, a definition emerges that ensures a clearer understanding of the essential principles proposed as to the teaching of positive psychology in schools. Positive psychology in education is the systematic application of its principles and practices in order to facilitate intrapersonal and interpersonal learning to increase academic, social, and emotional well-being. Positive psychology in the classroom focuses on the correlates of optimal learning, particularly the social emotional component of learning, resulting in increased positive emotion, strengths, relationships, purpose, and accomplishment. Students will obtain the learned and skillful ability to turn negative emotion inside-out, to find and use strengths to engage and persist, to apply those strengths for friendship and service, and to live lives of accomplishment.

The PERMA model proposes five components of positive psychology extrapolated to teaching positive psychology: *positive emotions, engagement* using strengths, *relationships, meaning,* and *accomplishment* (see Table 1.1). Martin Seligman, a founding father of positive psychology, reengineered his model, elaborating it to include the pursuit of a pleasant, good, connected, meaningful, and accomplished life. The PERMA model, applied explicitly to education, teaches children how to rally *positive* emotion, *engage* through strength, develop *relationships,* find *meaning,* and self-actualize through *accomplishment.*

How does the teacher explain positive psychology? How does the teacher create a pleasant life, an engaged or good life, a connected life, a purposeful life, and a contented life in the elementary classroom? She specifically teaches children how to act and interact in their personal and public school lives. Children learn to execute the lessons of positive psychology in order to regulate their emotions, marshal strengths, make and keep friends, be helpful, and accomplish goals. Children learn the positive psychology of learning and life so that they are more prepared for the joys and sorrows and the successes and failures.

Table 1.1. PERMA for Elementary School

Positive Psychology Principles	Positive Psychology Practices	Positive Psychology Lessons for Success
Positive Emotions (P)	Teaching the Pleasant Life	Feelings
Positive Engagement (E)	Teaching the Good Life	Strengths
Positive Relationships (R)	Teaching the Connected Life	Friendship
Positive Meaning (M)	Teaching the Purposeful Life	Contribution
Positive Accomplishment (A)	Teaching the Contented Life	Satisfaction

The cognitive aspect of learning addresses mental functions such as memory and organization of ideas. The affective aspect of learning addresses emotional functions such as gratitude and resiliency. The conative aspect of learning involves self-awareness of thought and feeling— and the subsequent arousal to a particular action for better or for worse. Children utilize their conative learning skills in order to guide how they *act* on their thoughts and feelings. To teach conative skills, the teacher can give examples of ways that children can act to emotionally protect themselves and preserve their dignity without harming others.

With positive psychology, the teacher advises that the coalescence of thought and emotion directs actions. She ensures that children are able to strategically self-monitor and self-manage to the greatest extent possible. Children will learn that anger is not bad behavior, just mismanaged emotion. The ability to identify and manage those emotions well enables them to act accordingly. Positive psychology teaches children the conative skill of acting in their own best emotional interests and in the best interests of others. For example, when one child ignores another, the anger of the ignored child flares. The ignored child can learn to respond without escalating by saying, "You hurt my feelings and are unkind. I will not say anything to hurt you because you don't deserve it either."

The teacher trains children to manage their anger toward another by learning to substitute a positive emotion for a negative emotion. Children learn to engage the strength of empathy to think about how the other child feels, to remember their past positive relationship with that child, and to consider that positive heroes in life are the people who are able to control their anger. The teacher reminds all the children of the story about young Chief Joseph of the Nez Perces and his tragic journey on the Lo Lo Trail, remembering his brave words, "I will fight no more forever."[2]

Combining cognitive, affective, and conative skills, children learn to self-scaffold to more reflective and reasonable action. From being hurt and angry to understanding and forgiving, positive psychology is emotional first aid. Confronted with peer conflict, Eric says to himself, "I remember when Mike and I had a great time building that volcano together. Maybe Mike is just having a bad day. I will just let it go and try to talk to him tomorrow. No matter how it turns out, I know that I have been a good friend to him and I still have many other friends."

When children practice positive psychology techniques, the restraint is self-reinforcing and makes it more likely that children will take the same approach the next time, or in other circumstances, when confronted with stressful feelings. Eventually children achieve social emotional automaticity of action. Through neurological practice and habituation, children learn to immediately trade the negative emotion for a positive one. The teacher has taught them, when confronted with a distressful event, to first identify the negative emotion, pause to process it, and immediately replace it with a positive emotion. As a result, children are not codependent on external structure or teacher control. The teacher gives the children tools to self-manage emotion and self-moderate behavior. Children acquire emotional literacy in the same deliberate and sequential manner they learn to read and to write—often while they read and write.

The teacher also explains to children that feelings do not just happen or change like the weather. Emotional life is not sunny or cloudy depending on the Gulf Stream breeze. Emotional moods do not just arrive like an unexpected storm completely outside of any personal control. Children learn to choose emotions like they choose a thick sweater to wear when it is chilly or yellow boots when it is raining. They learn that feelings are like the weather and there are predictive factors and confounding variables to identify and consider.

Positive psychology mobilizes mindfulness of emotion as the starting point and personal control over the emotion as the endpoint. In between, children learn a repertoire of positive psychology strategies, through carefully crafted positive learning lessons that increase self-awareness, self-knowledge, self-regulation, self-motivation, self-direction, and self-mastery. Positive lessons leverage positive emotion for positive purpose and result. Children understand how emotional currents—both positive and negative—can enhance or inhibit learning. They learn to self-regulate so that life is not only manageable but also more enjoyable.

When children acquire positive psychology knowledge and skills, the teacher hears them speak differently about their experiences at school: their feelings, their comfort level, their sense of belonging, their contribution, and their success experienced as gladness.

"I am so glad to be here. This is such a fun place to learn."

"I returned the money I found on the playground. Honesty makes me feel glad."

"I am so glad that you are my friend. I could not have done this without you."

"I am so glad I got to help clean up the beach. This is important work."

"I am so glad I learned to name the planets. I just kept trying."

"I am so glad I read that book. The book was long but worth the effort."

"I am so glad that I accomplished so much today."

Whether a teacher has "five minutes, five hours, five days, or five weeks"[3] to invest in positive psychology in the classroom, every formal and informal effort guided by the principles of positive psychology adds considerable value to the academic, social, and emotional learning process. The teacher who is well versed in positive psychology serves children well.

Philosophical, Psychological, and Educational Roots of Positive Psychology

The principles of positive psychology evolved from the philosophical and psychological tenets of happiness and well-being as espoused across the ages. More than two thousand years ago, Aristotle (384–322 BCE) wrote that happiness comes to those who live the good life. Eudamonia (eudaimonia) is the word that he used for happiness and its literal translation is "good spirit." The teacher brings good spirits to children by helping them to reach their fullest potential congruent with their own highest ideals of self or the ideal self that all strive to attain. Children learn to use their virtue and reason to their utmost capacity, and the teacher helps children learn to use their best judgment to take care of themselves and others emotionally, to identify their virtues, and so to enjoy the good spirits that create their own happiness.

Aristotle proposes 12 virtues that contribute to the good life—a life that strives toward excellence and finds happiness despite personal adversity. These virtues include courage, liberality or fairness, dignity or self-respect, friendliness or hospitality, wit or good humor, justice, temperance, generosity or magnificence, good temper, truthfulness, regret, and honor. In the elementary classroom, children identify their own virtues and rank the top three virtues, or their "signature strengths."[4] Each week the children pick the virtue that they intend to practice that week and the teacher makes colorful tags for children to wear with the name of the virtue on it. Whenever a child practices the virtue, he adds a star to his weekly virtue and strengths chart. The star is not a reward for practicing the virtue; instead, it is a monitoring device to help increase it.

Children practice balancing their virtues as the ancient philosophers encourage.[5] They learn not to exhibit either a deficit or an excess of virtue. Too little courage becomes timidity and too much courage becomes recklessness. Virtue can be "tamed, by rigorous self-discipline to accept the dictates of reason."[6] The teacher explains the connection between balanced thought and action. The balance between the excess and deficit of virtue is the ideal or the golden mean.[7] The golden mean is the equilibrium found in the ecology of science, in the harmony of music, in the mindfulness of measure, in the balance of nature, and in the ebb and the flow of life. The golden mean is the symmetry of well-being. One of the most important lessons to teach children is the lesson of the golden mean.

The primary teacher can collect children's literature and stories, such as *Goldilocks and the Three Bears*,[8] to emphasize the theme of "just right." The teacher uses the key words "just right" to comment on young children's actions throughout the school day. For example, when children share materials or ideas, the teacher can respond, "That is just right." The intermediate teacher explains the concept of virtue relative to the study of antonyms, with children giving examples of the deficits of virtue. They contrast courage and fear, compare fairness and favoritism, and consider justice and injustice. They study synonyms with different interpretations such as rashness and courage or generous and ostentatious.

All children learn to find the sweet spot in life: the quantitative and physical center of gravity found in the sports of tennis and baseball, in the acoustics of percussion, and in the phonetics of language. When children find their sweet spot, they find their happy, golden self.[9] In the positive psychology classroom, children do not just earn gold stars but they learn to find their golden selves. Positive psychology teaches children to use virtue to seek the right answers to do the right thing and to take balanced action based on balanced emotion to achieve excellence.[10]

Doing the right thing in the right way in the right moment is what Aristotle referred to as phronesis, which is practical wisdom and it is the basis for his *arete*, or excellence.[11] High grades on a test, neat notebooks, or complete homework do not necessarily define excellence. Typical and ordinary compliance tasks do not require any measure of extraordinary balance or action. For this reason, children too often confuse conformance, completion, and perfectionism with excellence. Positive psychology teaches more than the mechanics of achievement by teaching the dynamics of accomplishment.

When working with older children, one way to teach excellence is to actually teach philosophy. Learning philosophy helps them understand how virtue is related to balanced, purposeful action and how enjoyable or fulfilling it is to consider and choose the correct, or balanced, action. The teacher who teaches philosophy helps children to learn how to make good decisions based on thoughtfulness, reflection, and time-honored wisdom. Philosophy gives children a knowledge base in the study of excellence and practical wisdom so they learn to examine personal perspectives using a wider philosophical lens.

While teaching philosophy to elementary-aged children might seem impractical, philosophy lessons are everywhere. An urban teacher may use rap songs to teach about Western philosophy. There are also traditional philosophies deeply enmeshed in the fabric of Harry Potter's story. In the book *Philosophy for Kids*, middle schoolers can read a child-friendly summary of an ancient philosopher's main idea and then answer fun and practical questions based on the philosophy studied. The questions increase self-awareness and self-knowledge and make children "wonder about everything."[12]

If positivity depends on a wider lens, the study of philosophy in elementary school is the wide-lens camera. Children read a simple summary of Aristotle's philosophy of friendship and answer the question, "How do you know who your friends are?"

The ensuing discussion revolves around the virtues and strengths that sustain happy friendship. Children learn to notice and applaud virtues and strengths in themselves and others. This is integral to teaching the philosophy and practice of the good life, the golden mean, and the sweet spot that brings the philosophy of arete and eudaimonia to life and learning.

Psychologists of the early nineteenth century added psychological understandings to the philosophy of happiness and many wrote about it extensively. William James, America's first positive psychologist, wrote that happiness is life's chief concern and that the humanistic and existential psychologists all deemed happiness as central to mental health and well-being.[13]

Carl Rogers reminded us that to be happy is hard work. He stated that an easy or comfortable life is no guarantee of happiness, and he cautioned that happiness is not for the faint-hearted. Happiness requires courage—the courage to live up to one's potentialities and to live life fully.[14] He was the first to explain that for children to be happy they must be taught to be brave, to face failure with resolve, and to show true grit. Happiness involves the courage to be who you are today and it means launching yourself "fully into the stream of life."[15] Children are able to launch into that stream against the tide if needed.

To launch their learning, children muster the courage to take risks and the spirit needed to try again. How does the teacher impart courage and spirit? She develops creative curricula, lessons, and activities to explicitly teach it, in order to ensure that children understand concepts and develop skills needed. For example, children play the "Try Again Lottery" game. If they do not earn the grade that they expected on an assignment or test, they try it again. Children earn a lottery ticket for trying again and each time they try again, they earn another lottery ticket. While only one child wins the prize, all win because they are all learning to fail, renew, and redo. Even children who produce A-grade work try again to expand on and enrich their work.

Learning to self-improve and self-enrich is of lasting value because learning to fail up, or to get up when you are down, is a prerequisite for self-actualization. The term "positive psychology" was coined by Abraham Maslow and is quite appropriate given that his theory focused almost exclusively on how to self-actualize. Self-actualization is fulfilling the biological drive toward the realization of full potential.[16] The flip side of the self-actualization coin is peak experience that occurs each time children reach their full potential or fail to do so while trying to achieve a peak experience by recognizing that the peak experience is often embedded in the pursuit of it.

As Maslow and colleagues have written, "Without effort, without persistence, there is no joyful esthetic experience, creative experience, love experience, mystic experience, insight experience, or the perfect flow found at the pinnacle of all peak experiences."[17] Children climb to the top of the tree, hit the highest note, offer a helping hand, or figure out long division in order to find their joy, and teachers can help them recognize and savor the joy. Children learn that success after failure feels good, and they revel in it and enjoy it. The more roadblocks and potholes that children encounter on the road to their destination, the more joyful their arrival will be. Every instructional unit, lesson, activity, and game must teach positive psychology at every opportunity. The teacher uses guided visualization so children imagine themselves climbing moun-

tains, swimming seas, and overcoming frustrations about multiplication. Happy people feel more intentionally and think more intently.

There is no criticism or punishment in the positive psychology classroom and children accept failure as a stepping-stone to accomplishment.
Positive psychology teaches a simple theorem: "This is life and we are all
in it together to help each other when we struggle." The keeper of the positive psychology flame, the teacher, teaches engagement through strength
so she reaches out and teaches children to "try out powers . . . reach out
. . . be absorbed, be fascinated, be interested . . . play . . . wonder."[18]

Beyond the biological drive, what influences children's persistence
toward a goal and how can we teach it? The interpersonal happiness
psychologist Albert Bandura proposed that biology interacts with psychology to excite or inhibit persistence toward peak experience, and he
described the phenomena as self-efficacy: the belief in self or an internal
locus of control.

Self-efficacy is intrinsic motivation that convinces children to do well
for the sake of doing well and this echoes Aristotle's *arete*—excellence for
the sake of excellence. Children understand that what they do matters—
or will matter—in some way or on some day to themselves and others,
and so they try. Positive observational experience builds self-efficacy by
helping children to self-organize, self-regulate, and self-assure through
imitation. According to Bandura, children who observe an action performed by a positive role model believe they can do likewise by imitating that person's actions.[19] They watch and get mentally organized and
emotionally ready to replicate the action because observing the success
of others triggers confidence.

Children learn from all experiential observation and the learning is
most powerful when children can connect to it emotionally. Learning to
apply emotional learning to positive action is life's primary psychosocial
learning task. Social learning morphs into self-learning because of the
interactive nature of emotion and experience, and observational learning self-actualizes potential.[20] Children acquire strengths through imitation and inspiration.

The teacher ensures that children also can understand themselves as
observers and as role models. Young children play Simon Says, discussing how carefully watching the leader can help you win the game, lose
the game, take the wrong action, or take the correct action. Older children volunteer to teach classmates how to juggle, make French toast, use
a graphing calculator, or remember the state capitals while playing the

Watch How I Do It game. The teacher makes children mindful that all observation is learning and expects them to demonstrate what they know.

Erik Erikson's ego development theory identified life's eight psychosocial tasks that cultivate a particular virtue or strength. He proposed that, at each stage of development, a psychosocial task shapes a basic virtue that is affiliated with a secondary virtue, and both virtues work in concert. At each stage of life, children face an emotional learning task: to learn to trust, be independent, take the initiative, and be industrious. No matter the degree of the challenge, it is crucial to resolve these tasks; as a result, a lifelong adaptive strength emerges.

> The teacher knows that Ellie, a fourth grader, is unmotivated and disinterested in her work. When asked, Ellie says she just does not think that she can do it—so why should she try? The teacher suggests she just try to complete one problem of her choice and that is good enough. She tells her she can use whatever materials she wants and can ask any other student in class for help. Ellie smiles: "Really? Can I use the computer and can Jinni help me after I am done with the computer?" The teacher helps Ellie become more hopeful about her chance for success, and hopefulness motivates her to action. The next day, Ellie gives her teacher the completed assignment with all the problems finished. Ellie told the teacher, "After we talked I knew I could do it."

In Erikson's model, hopefulness becomes motivation, and motivation transforms into the adaptive strength of trust in self and others.[21] Ellie's motivation brings trust in her own ability to do the task and her hopeful emotions, and her affiliated actions, motivated by increased optimism, empower her to trust that she can do the task. Optimism energizes children so they can get started, work independently, and stay busy on the task. The teacher uses positive psychology to help Ellie change her mind-set by using self-talk to shift her feelings from negative to positive and to use her emotional strength to persevere. Ellie changes her feelings of discouragement to hopefulness and from fear to courage. Ellie has joined the positive psychology I Think I Can club.

Each day, the K–2 I Think I Can club reads selected children's literature about trying hard. After the story *I Knew You Could*,[22] children choose a difficult task that they are not sure they can do. If they accomplish the task, they wear a button that says "I Did It." Children in grades

3–5 write three weekly goals in their goal journal and then assess progress. They list the virtues and strengths, such as grit, gratitude, and calm, that helped them accomplish the task or achieve the goal.

Adaptive strengths are Erikson's potencies, Aristotle's optimal virtues, and Seligman's signature strengths. These are the prerequisites for joyful self-actualization and peak experience (see Table 1.2). Howard Gardner claims the greatest potencies in the classroom are truth, beauty, and goodness, and he discusses the importance of teaching truth, beauty, and goodness to schoolchildren as the correlates of happiness.[23] He argues persuasively that education must be reframed to promote well-being and recommends that children explore and evaluate truth, beauty, and goodness, as these are understood in their own lives.

The teacher asks children to describe the constructs of truth, beauty, and goodness and what those mean. One child describes beauty as his grandmother's garden, and the children draw pictures of flowers. Another child finds goodness in fishing and writes a story about a happy fishing day. A third child states that there is truth in math and history, and she lists five indisputable mathematics formulas and ten interesting history facts. Everyone plays the Truth Told game, and they guess whether a statement is true. A child makes three statements and one is not true. The other children give a thumbs-up if they think the statement is true. Is it a correct mathematics answer, a correct date in history, or the true reason she did not do her homework?

Children also play the I Spy Beauty and the I Spy Goodness games. "I spy a rain cloud outside." "I spy a really neat desk." "I spy someone acting patient." When children describe truth, beauty, and goodness with examples found in their own lives—both happy and poignant—they learn

Table 1.2. Ego Development Adaptive Strengths

Primary Basic Virtue	Secondary Virtue	Adaptive Strength
Hope	Motivation	Trust
Determination	Self-Control	Autonomy
Purpose	Direction	Initiative
Competence	Productivity	Industry
Fidelity	Devotion	Identity
Love	Affiliation	Intimacy
Care	Contribution	Generativity
Wisdom	Contentment	Integrity

to be more mindful of the counterbalancing weights in a hard life.[24] The construction of a portfolio, scrapbook, or other compilation is another good way to help children examine and illustrate their personal ideas, impressions, and certainties about truth, beauty, goodness, and happiness. Traditional parchment paper or e-scrapbooks preserve a variety of artifacts that are mental representations of children's feelings and thoughts.

Children expand and elaborate their ideas by using writings, drawings, photographs, poetry, music, and diaries to create an interpretive collection that translates their ideas of truth, beauty, goodness, and happiness. A fifth-grade girl, who had recently lost her mother, drew a rose in her happiness scrapbook. Next to the rose, she wrote, "My mother loved me and she was like a rose. Losing her was like thorns sticking me." The teacher suggested she find a song or poem about a rose to add to her scrapbook. She also suggested that she create a special scrapbook to honor her mother. The child channeled her sad feelings about the loss of her mother into positive feelings to honor her.

Portfolios are also a good way for children to document changes relating to their feelings, strengths, friendships, and accomplished tasks in concrete and meaningful ways. They have a record to show that their patience and persistence helped them improve. They have a record showing the results of their efforts.

Journal writing and scrapbooking is important to the process of self-exploration and is the basis for Carl Jung's version of happiness and well-being. In the 19th century, he enumerated six happiness factors: physical health, mental health, positive intimate relationships, appreciation of art and nature, philosophical or spiritual perspective, and satisfaction of basic survival needs.[25] These ideas ground happiness theory in the 21st century. Jung considered happiness as both a project and a process toward potentiality and potency.

As part of the process, one of his lesser-known ideas—quite accessible to children in the classroom setting—is coloring mandalas. Mandalas are symmetrical, geometric designs usually enclosed within a circle, square, or a rectangle that seem to have movement or purposeful form. Throughout history, the mandala—the Sanskrit word for circle—was a symbol of unity and the universe; it also was a focus for meditation in religious ceremonies.[26] Young children color mandalas as a relaxing transition activity that improves their attention. Mandalas teach older children geometry. Jung believed that mandalas, given their universal patterns of line and form, elicited automatic positive emotions with effects similar to meditation. He believed that coloring or studying mandalas calmed and focused the brain in order to create flow. This claim is somewhat validated by advances in the science of fractals[27] and by Wolfram's brain complexity theory.[28] Many cultures believe that the universal complexity of the mandala generates positive energy and children do seem to respond to the designs. Jung believed that coloring, drawing, or studying a mandala had a healing power and could reduce tension and boredom while increasing cognition and positive emotion.[29] Mandalas seem to trigger conjoint cognitive, affective, and conative activity.

Positive energy, positive education, positive discipline, assertive discipline, positive classroom management, positive behavioral supports, positive teaching, joyful teaching, and joyful learning are all ideas gaining more visibility and momentum in education. Now the principles and practices of positive psychology subsume, organize, and synthesize these related ideas and proposals. Positive psychology teaches Rogers's potentiality, Maslow's self-actualization, Bandura's self-efficacy, Erikson's adaptive potencies, Gardner's appreciation, and Jung's spiritual virtues, and all of these methods help children contend with challenges in life by cultivating emotional strengths. All of these comingle with the science of social emotional learning.

Positive psychology is closely aligned with social emotional learning, and it offers a blueprint for teaching emotional strength. Current work in the area of social emotional learning is highly compatible with positive psychology. The Collaborative for Academic, Social, and Emotional Learning (CASEL) constructs learning around five social emotional learning core competencies: (1) self-awareness; (2) self-assessment of emotions, strengths, and virtues; (3) self-management; (4) relationship; and (5) decision-making skills.[30]

The PERMA[31] model for educators (Table 1.1) provides the schema for positive education that also emphasizes social emotional learning. In doing so, the model also delineates the goals and the expected student outcomes associated with teaching positive psychology that ensures emotional learning: (1) increased positive emotion, (2) increased engagement, (3) increased positive relations, (4) increased service, and (5) increased accomplishment. Alignment between the program goals published by collaborative and program goals of positive psychology as published by the Center for Positive Psychology (CPP) is almost perfect.[32] The positive psychology goals and intentions incorporate, organize, and detail the social emotional goals that build the adaptive development assets associated with children who flourish.

The U.S. Department of Education's Blueprint of Education,[33] developed by the Partnership for 21st Century Skills,[34] publishes and details the common core skills necessary for success in learning and in life. The Partnership for 21st Century Skills (P21) is a national group of representatives from corporations, professional associations, and the U. S. Department of Education who work to shift the national education focus from a standards-based to a skills-based model. The P21 Blueprint includes three categories of skills for education: academic or content (the 3Rs), learning or processing (the 4Cs), and technology. Positive psychology aligns nicely with the emerging national model of education of common core skills.

The 3Rs are reading, writing, and arithmetic across the study of world languages, arts, mathematics, economics, science, geography, history, government, and civics. The 4Cs are collaboration, communication, creativity, and critical thinking. While there is no explicit reference to positive psychology outcomes or social and emotional competencies, these are congruent with the practice of the 4Cs of learning and innovation: collaboration, communication, and critical thinking. All of the P21 skills are dependent on a positive emotional outlook and the ability to improve social outcomes.

Teaching positive psychology complements the teaching of both the 3Rs and the 4Cs of learning. Proponents of positive psychology would argue that it is not possible to teach the 3Rs or the 4Cs without having positive psychology as a prerequisite. For example, to participate in a discussion on astronomy, children need knowledge of the subject, communication skills, and empathy. Positive psychology goals, social emotional competency, and P21 skills combine to offer a cohesive approach that goes beyond the traditional academic curriculum.

Positive psychology is at the core of the curriculum that teaches children to tolerate frustration and persist, make and keep friends, resolve conflicts and seek consensus, reach out and help others, and make ethical and safe choices. As a result, academic performance increases. The teacher can adopt the positive psychology curriculum by taking one of two approaches. First, the teacher delivers positive psychology as a discrete subject in a stand-alone unit that parallels the academic content. Second, the teacher implements positive psychology fully infused in the academic curriculum. For example, the positive psychology lesson

Table 1.3. PERMA Schema and Outcomes, CASEL Competencies, and P21 Skills

PERMA Schema	CASEL Competencies	P21 Skills	PERMA Outcomes
The Pleasant Life	Self-Awareness	Communication	Positive Emotions
The Good Life	Self-Assessment	Critical Thinking	Positive Engagement (Positive Strengths)
The Connected Life	Relationships	Collaboration	Positive Relationships
The Meaningful Life	Self-Management	Creativity	Positive Meaning
The Satisfied Life	Responsible Decisions	Achievement	Positive Accomplishments

teaches resiliency as the subject itself and academic instruction is secondary. In the infused model, the teacher identifies a positive psychology lesson that he can intermingle with the academic instruction that is primary.

Positive psychology proponents work toward full integration of the PERMA schema and outcomes into all curricular, cocurricular, and extracurricular learning. Teaching positive psychology does not divert from the academic mission—it advances it. There are many proven educational models that are compatible with teaching positive psychology.

All of the educational models address the social, emotional, and psychological well-being necessary for learning.[35] They are consistent with the principles and practices of positive psychology, and teaching positive psychology, either formally or informally, is the common denominator. Each program acknowledges the significant emotional component in all learning and the importance of strengths training. The teacher galvanizes children to use these acknowledgments to improve relationships, value service, and enjoy accomplishment. Some are historical models and others are contemporary models: the democratic school, the humanistic model, the Montessori model, progressive education, synergistic teaching, and the whole child.

Democratic Model—Democratic education values personal self-determination and opportunity for participation in democratic processes. Teachers and learners work together as equals. A democratic school is one in which students are free citizens of the school, in charge of their own educational lives. They participate in decisions that affect everyone with an emphasis on a free and expressive dialogue with no rules or conventions imposed.[36] Democratic education weighs respect, tolerance, and love equally with the academic curriculum.

Humanistic Model—The humanistic model encompasses four main approaches: (1) content curricula that teach topics directly relevant to the students' lives (e.g., drug awareness), (2) process curricula that focus on the whole student and include life skills (e.g., assertiveness training), (3) teachers as facilitators, and (4) flexible timetables and environments.[37]

Montessori Model—The Montessori model understands the pervasive effect of experience on children and prepares the environment for learning. This method emphasizes play as intrinsically motivating and desirable in lessons in order to increase absorption in the learning process. The principles are (1) intrinsic motivation; (2) choice and control in learning; (3) education for peace; (4) no competition; (5) self-regulation and independence; and (6) positive experiences and learning.[38] As Maria Montessori said, "Children form a love of humanity, a cognizance of self, and appreciation for others . . . for the constructive work that the human soul is called to do, and to bring it to fruition, a work of formation which brings out the immense potentialities with which children . . . are endowed."[39]

Progressive Education Model—The progressive education model has a long history of advocating for constructivist education. The model proposes eight defining principles held steadfast by progressive educators since the early nineteenth century. These principles are as follows: (1) a focus on social, emotional, academic, cognitive, and physical development equally; (2) the liberal arts; (3) nurturing natural curiosity and innate desire to learn; (4) the fostering of internal motivation; (5) active participation in learning; (6) the activation of prior positive learning and experience; (7) respectful relationships; and (8) the preparation of children to participate in a democratic society. The progressive principles intersect with the principles and practices of positive psychology.[40]

Synergistic Teaching Model—The synergistic model emphasizes positive interactions between children and peers and between children and their teachers. The model describes nine elements of teaching: (1) ethical teaching, (2) mutual trust, (3) personal charisma, (4) passion for learning, (5) communication, (6) class agreements, (7) coopetition (cooperation/

competition), (8) human relations, and (9) problem resolution. Synergistic teaching abandons the spare model of education and supports an abundant model. The teacher is generous in giving children whatever they need to be successful. She eliminates contingency management and does not withhold any support, assistance, or tools that children need to learn. She does not require children to earn learning advantages. If a child needs a shorter assignment, she gets a shorter assignment. If a child needs a calculator to solve mathematics problems, he gets one to use. No coercion is used and the teacher eliminates all negative responses, especially punishment. The teacher strives to create a synergy of cooperative and joyful effort between the class as family and community.[41]

Whole Child—The whole child initiative model stresses that children learn best when teachers are able to meet their academic, emotional, physical, and social needs. This is a multiyear initiative of the Association for Supervision and Curriculum Development (ASCD). The developmental model advocates for a broader definition of educational achievement that measures success across all developmental areas: physical, emotional, and social. The whole child model claims that academic success depends on overall well-being, and this model mirrors the proven principles of positive psychology. The proponents of the model work to guarantee that all children learn in an emotionally safe classroom, have access to active learning, and flourish as students, family members, friends, neighbors, and citizens.[42]

The Penn Resilience Program (PRP) and the Strath Haven Program (SHP) exemplify two groundbreaking, evidence-based programs derived from the principles and practices of positive psychology labeled positive education. Both programs use signature strengths as a thematic and curricular approach. The central focus of these programs is identifying and growing students' strengths. Students read, write, and discuss how to use their strengths, how to change automatic reactions, and how to develop healthy social relationships. Students assess themselves on how well they use their signature strengths to manage emotions, improve relations, and find meaning in school. They complete homework assignments and journal reflections that facilitate the positive psychology learning process.[43]

In 2009, the Geelong Grammar School Positive Psychology Project (Geelong), a whole school K–12 program, was piloted at the Geelong Grammar School in Australia, with promising field results. Stand-alone courses as well as integrated subject units present the crucial topics: resilience, gratitude, signature strengths, meaning, flow, relationships, and positive emotion.

Lessons fuse across all subjects and extracurricular activities from sports to music.[44] Positive psychology exercises, some of which were initially developed and tested in these pioneering programs and adopted in programs across the world, include affirmations, visualization, relaxation, movement, meditation, creative thinking, journal writing, class meetings, and more.

Positive psychology games are also a quick and simple way to teach the principles. For example, children play the I Accept game, which was inspired by other positive psychology program activities. Each day children track how many times they say "I accept." Younger children get tokens each time they say it; tokens can be exchanged for time in a classroom learning center, such as the happiness center discussed in a later chapter. Older children track and graph the number of times they hear the words. "I accept that it will rain today so no outside recess." "I accept that today I am going to have to clean my desk before I can join my group." "I accept that I cannot be first in line today." "I accept the apology."

When teaching positive psychology is concurrent with academic content, the cognitive, affective, and conative domains of learning merge. At the same time that children learn positive psychology concepts and skills, they learn academic concepts and skills. While learning academic concepts and skills, children also learn positive psychology concepts and skills. Children simultaneously practice their knowledge and skills in both the academic and emotional learning spheres because when all pistons fire together, the engine hums. Any lesson that bifurcates academic and emotional learning suppresses optimal academic performance.

The teacher teaches academic and emotional learning together, first identifying the academic or affective concept or skill that he wants to teach. For example, the teacher plans a lesson that enables him to teach both science and positive psychology conjointly.

Teaching a subject area and social emotional mastery are not mutually exclusive. The K–2 academic concept to teach is metamorphosis and the academic skill is being able to tell, draw, dance, and write the stages of metamorphosis. Younger children learn about change as physical and emotional transformation by using the e-curriculum Journey North.[45] The 3–5 concept is migration, and the skill is being able to research and write about it. Older children learn about change as movement from one point to another whether it is movement from place to place or from one perspective to another. They watch the video program *Who Moved My Cheese?*[46] and discuss the strengths that are needed for physical and emotional migration. They also watch a science video about migration and decide what strengths and adaptations the various migrating animals need.

The affective concept that permeates the science lesson is change as a natural process and how children can adapt to it, whether adapting to changing seasons or changing moods. In the process, children build the skills needed to manage the demands and stress of change. Positive psychology assures that the learning conversation occurs around the academic content with attention to the emotional content.

The academic curriculum is not just the textbook, the tests, and the homework that teaches the traditional academic lesson. Positive psychology education rejects segregation of learning by discipline and a focus on narrow content standards. The pedagogy is not static or rigid, and academic boundaries are flexible. When conceiving the lesson, the teacher should always begin with the end in mind. The teacher decides what she wants the children to know and to do. She decides to teach mood regulation and emotional balance, engaged and committed effort, and positive strength, inspired service, intrinsic meaning, and accomplishment. What is the expected end result that guides a teacher's planning? Greater well-being that enhances learning and positive mood produces broader attention, more creative thinking, and more holistic thinking.

While discussing Native American history, a teacher might use the positive psychology subjects of gratitude optimism, resiliency, or peacemaking. The study of Native American history and culture lends itself to lessons in geography, literature, language, economics, mathematics, and political science as well as honesty, courage, and tolerance. Children learn to read so they can read stories about strengths, they learn to write so they can express emotions, and they learn to do mathematics so they can be of service someday whether building bridges or making pizza. Children learn to rally their strengths to help themselves and their friends in meaningful and important ways that go beyond sharing cupcakes and party days.

A teacher helps children to use positive emotion to displace negative emotion, self-regulate when upset, and use their strengths to get the job done. The teacher says, "Remember when you felt excited about the mathematics competition last week? Use that feeling now to help you solve harder problems. Once you get finished, I would be grateful if you could help Jennie." Children who use their emotional strengths to help friends and share accomplishments are happier. Happy children are the specialty of positive psychology.

As Seligman has said, "I believe we have finally arrived at an era in which more creative thinking . . . and yes, even more enjoyment . . . will succeed better. . . . I believe that what every parent wants for their children is more well-being than they themselves had."[47] The closest thing that educators have to an elixir for well-being is to increase happiness.[48]

Principles and Practices of Positive Psychology in the Classroom

Flow—In the elementary classroom, emotions flow in every direction. They can either stimulate the flow of learning or block it. Emotions sustain focus or prevent it. Without flow, it is very difficult to concentrate on the task. Positive psychology teaches the positive emotions and engaged strengths that increase flow. With flow, the task is easier and more enjoyable.

The definition of flow is "the way people describe their state of mind when consciousness is harmoniously ordered, and they want to pursue whatever they are doing for its own sake."[49] This fluid state of being occurs when emotions, strengths, relations, interests, and intentions are perfectly aligned with the task so that there is complete absorption without effort. Positive psychology capitalizes on children's innate curiosity about themselves and their world. When the teacher presents a real problem or an interesting project to complete, interest activates attention. The teacher should plan a flow class or period during which time children choose what creates flow for them: they can read a book, work on a puzzle, or exercise, learning to stimulate intrinsic motivation and experience contented accomplishment.

When children persist in being fully engaged in the learning process by working to find the solution or finish the project, there is learning flow. The flow emanates from the convergence of attention and persistence and is crucial to engagement in learning. When the task also requires children to overcome a fear or insecurity, finding flow in the task is even more important. Flow comes to the classroom where children know how to use their strengths to increase their engagement in learning, commitment to learning, and persistence for learning even when the task is difficult or the barrier is high.

Facing a challenging test, children learn to self-calm. They breathe the fresh air deeply and plan to call a friend to study together every day until the test occurs. The rush of negativity that interferes with the flow of learning subsides. The teacher helps children develop the resilience that maintains the flow, especially when the task is formidable. She teaches them to deploy positive emotional assets to neutralize negative learning experiences that interfere with concentration and perseverance. Children learn to connect the learning to some aspect of their own lives—what they feel, what they know, what they can do, what they want to do. Children learn to identify the signature strength to use to make learning as effortless and effective as possible. When children are able to invest their emotions and individual strengths within the learning process, learning flows.

The collection of strengths needed—flow, focus, and fortitude—is often labeled as grit, defined as "persistence of motivation and effort or as passion for a long-term goal and perseverance."[50] Children withstand learning challenges that tempt them to disengage from the learning process and instead maintain flow. With grit, children are able to defer immediate gratification, exercise more impulse control, and focus on the long-term goal. In a classic Stanford University study, researchers told children that if they waited to eat the marshmallow given to them, they would then receive two marshmallows.[51] When left alone in the room with the one tempting marshmallow, only about one-third of kindergarten-aged children would wait for the greater reward. The majority opted for immediate gratification at a higher long-term cost. Resiliency, determination, and grit help postpone the short-term benefit for the long-term gain. Children with grit did not eat the marshmallow.

How do children learn about grit? They learn it in the same way that they learn about the ocean: They learn to recognize it, understand it, value it, and use it. Teachers plan lessons to teach both subjects in exactly the same way: "What is the ocean. What is resiliency? What do you know about it? What is the value of it to you and others? How do you use it as a resource for greater benefit and well-being? What facts are interesting to you? What ideas inspire you?"

The teacher helps children learn to defer gratification by committing to the long-term benefit over the short-term sacrifice. Given the opportunity to earn play money to use to purchase simple gifts for others, children with grit are not easily tempted to short-term spending, and they save up the money until they can buy a more valuable prize. The Savings Account game uses play money to pay children for well-done academic, social, and emotional work. The teacher posts the compensation for various tasks. The children bank their money and keep a record of it. At the end of the week, children use their savings to buy raffle tickets for others—not themselves—in order to win simple gifts for friends, family, and peers.

The commercially produced Stock Market Game, available for fourth and fifth grade, encourages savings, investment, and long-term gain over short-term profit.[52] At the same time, it teaches mathematics and economics while also informing about cost-benefit analysis, resilience, and flow.

Emotional Balance—In the positive psychology classroom, emotional learning is a central feature of the curriculum and the primary task is to teach the balance of emotion. To achieve emotional balance children learn to activate positive emotion and deactivate negative emotion in the pursuit of learning. Positive psychology teaches positive emotion by constructing positive experience that evokes positive thoughts, memories, and feelings. Positive emotions mobilize to replace negative emotions that emerge throughout the school day and are the antidote to negativity: "Jimmy, you seemed really happy when you were working on the computer earlier. Get that happy going for history today, too."

Positive experiences create positive psychology teaching moments. A positive experience is a simple, daily activity that is inherently pleasant, such as assigning children a friendly work partner or inviting the whole class to listen to a favorite song, calling specific attention to the emotion generated. To help children to be aware of positive feelings, the teacher provokes them. She may ask a child who loves words to write a poem for a classmate's birthday, or she may ask a strong reader to read to a younger student. The teacher assigns a group of children to research a classmate's pet, one to collect school supplies for homeless children, and another to learn to play chess. Children are taught to become mindful of the positive emotion engendered as their reference points when negative emotion surfaces. One important metric of the teacher's success is the positive emotion reported by children in the classroom and their ability to make note of it.

Shared positive experiences that generate positive emotions and cultivate strengths serve to solidify friendships, offer service, accomplish a task, or achieve a goal. Most important, children are able to consciously evoke positive emotions that comfort when there is a negative event. Positive emotion is like a warm blanket turning cold anger to warm kindness.

Positive Outlook—Where there is flow and emotional balance, a positive outlook is the fuel of learning. Children learn to presume the virtue and expect the good. Positive psychology learning activities and exercises may recall or imagine a positive experience past or future that is joyful. Older children plan a cross-country dream trip. They develop a detailed travel plan, itinerary, route, transportation, and budget. They include all the places that they will go and all the things they will do. They conduct Internet research and submit a written proposal. Simply imagining the trip excites positive emotions because they anticipate the happiness.[53]

Sharon Salzberg, in her book *Lovingkindness*, explains that you open up the mind and the heart through Metta Bhavana—the lovingkindness that brings joy.[54] The teacher opens up the minds and hearts of children by cultivating—and celebrating—the joy in learning. When children finish the assignment, the teacher leads the children in a cheer for themselves to celebrate their learning as if they were at a sporting event. One example is when children are excited about an upcoming book festival their class will host. They look forward to dressing up like characters, performing play acts, and reading outside with friends sharing a picnic lunch. They read books on the Storyline[55] website and learn about the authors.[56] After identifying the feelings and strengths of the characters, children can also research the authors' lives. They often discover that the authors had to work hard and suffer rejection before they found success. When learning is personalized and reflects children's own feelings, strengths, friends, and purpose, the lessons ensure that children do not want to miss even a single day of school.

A child may enjoy caring for the class fish, and he feels happy when he is feeding it and changing its water. When he looks forward all morning to caring for the class fish later that day, he feels excited anticipation. Later that afternoon while preparing to do the job, he feels optimistic that he will do the job well. When he finishes this important task, he feels a sense of accomplishment and satisfaction.

A teacher can connect the child's responsibility to positive psychology by using the Fish! Philosophy lessons.[57] This series of fun fish-themed activities for children in grades K–5 teaches children to be mindful, playful, helpful, and thoughtful by asking, "Is this working for me?" The Fishful Thinking[58] website offers online lessons in positive psychology such as the Favorite Things game, which directs children to make a list of their favorite things. In another exercise, children retrieve or imagine positive experiences using sentence completion exercises: "Children anticipate positive experiences. Imagine that . . ."; "Children plan positive interactions. Think about . . ."; "Children participate with positive emotion. That will feel . . ."

At every opportunity, the teacher accentuates the positive and prompts exploration of positive emotional experience. Positive reflection, visualization, planning, and experiences orient children to positive learning. Reading, discussion, and journal writing about positive experiences contribute to children's eagerness and readiness to learn. Positive psychology trains the emotional capacities necessary to constrain the negative emotion that intrudes on learning. Accumulation of the positive experiences and emotions builds a more positive outlook. Children do not necessarily know what to do when confronted with overpowering feelings of anger, sadness, disappointment, hurt, or other negative emotions. One of the most important insulating emotional skills that children learn is affective regulation using positive outlook.

The ability to know how to adopt a positive outlook is even more important when the task or situation is overwhelming or when there are other stressors involved. The most vulnerable children are the ones who derive the greatest benefit from positive psychology because they have fewer resources at their disposal and more stress in their lives. They benefit greatly when they learn to automatically focus on their virtues and strengths in order to counter external negative input.

The teacher helps children to accept themselves unconditionally, no matter how others treat them. One of the most effective positive psychology techniques that children learn to use to regulate emotion is self-talk or private speech.[59] Private speech helps children to balance emotion and, in doing so, reduce stress, tension, and anxiety so they can try again. Positive self talk is more likely to produce a positive outcome.

Cindy struggles with her handwriting and is afraid to show her new teacher her work. Last year a substitute teacher marked a grade of F in red pen for handwriting on her paper and the other children laughed at her. However, if Cindy does not learn resiliency, if she does not learn to cultivate the strength to take learning risks again, she cannot improve. Using the private speech technique taught to her, Cindy gives herself praise: "I have worked really hard to improve. I think my new teacher will recognize my effort." She balances perspective: "Even if the teacher is not happy with my work, I still have many friends who encourage and play with me." She encourages herself: "No matter what happens I can handle this matter. I will be brave. Besides, I am great at texting, really good at mathematics, and just finished my second Harry Potter book." She turns in her paper to the teacher with feelings of calmness and optimism.

Children learn that past disappointment is not prologue to future failure. They do not expect too little or too much of themselves and are not too hard or too easy on themselves.

As long as children are doing their best, they accept their best efforts as important accomplishments, no matter the outcome. They learn to stop focusing on winning, stop blaming themselves, and start encouraging themselves. The teacher knows that emotional strength is the best protection when threatened, and he can teach children how to use their signature strength to change a negative reaction to a positive one.

Children learn to fail expertly because failure is inherent in the learning process. Children begin to understand failure as a step toward success. In the positive psychology classroom failure is not a source of stress, it is a source of strength. Children learn to pick themselves up with dignity and a positive outlook. They learn there is no shame in failure.

Teachers know that when there is less stress, there is more learning flow and positive emotional and academic engagement. Teaching a positive outlook teaches stress management. Stress is a negative emotion and there is indisputable cross-disciplinary research that documents that stress is physically, mentally, and emotionally debilitating. There is no disagreement that stress hinders cognitive processing and adversely impacts working memory and other critical learning functions. No one disputes that stress stunts emotional processing and hijacks learning. Children under stress are more likely to be inattentive, defensive, and resistant to the learning process.[60] Positive psychology teaches children to ease the hyperintensity of frustration, the hypervigilance of fear, and the paralysis of hyperreflection so that children feel more emotionally relaxed and psychologically safe.[61] The teacher uses, and teaches, positive psychology techniques to decrease stress and reduce its contrary effect.

Schools can incubate stress or inoculate children against it. The teacher's highest priority in the classroom—his or her foremost goal—is to help children learn to manage the stress that interrupts learning. Positive psychology teaches ways to manage the stress of negative emotion and yield increased academic achievement. There is substantial evidence from well-controlled studies that schools can teach positive emotions such as kindness and strengths such as resilience in order to reduce stress, increase engagement, and foster meaning.[62] As Seligman has stated, "I want you to imagine that schools could, without compromising either, teach both the skills of well-being and the skills of achievement. I want you to imagine positive education."[63]

Every day in the elementary classroom, children manage difficult emotions, conflicting virtues, problematic relationships, unclear purposes, and varying degrees of competency across various academic subjects. Positive psychology promises to harness positive flow, balance, and outlook to make it easier for children to meet the emotional, social, and academic challenges they encounter so that all children can thrive and flourish under every condition and given any demand. Positive psychology classrooms prioritize the emotionality of learning so that all children benefit from self-comfort and momentum.

Benefits of Teaching Positive Psychology in the Classroom

To understand the promise of positive psychology is to understand the transformative power of teaching it. When the teacher creates a positive school climate, it predicts both teacher and student satisfaction and a more optimistic outlook.[64] Numerous studies prove that positive psychology abilities and skills, such as positive emotion, engagement, relationships, and meaning, can be infused into academics and taught to schoolchildren.[65] If the teacher invests in positive psychology, she will have children in class who have a positive outlook, try hard, help others, and earn higher grades.[66]

The research unquestionably concludes that teaching positive psychology has both short-term and long-term benefits. Positive psychology research reports immediate positive effects on relationships, conflict, mental health, and academic achievement. Both in-class and after-school programs are effective as recent meta-analyses have documented and are particularly effective with racially and ethnically diverse children and with all children who lack emotional resources, across all grades and demographics.[67] Studies also found that happiness and success are reciprocal—happiness is what most likely causes the success, and then success amplifies the happiness.[68] Happiness and academic success are cocurricular variables.

Programs that self-identify as positive psychology programs, positive education programs, social emotional learning programs, social emotional skills training programs, youth development programs, or character education programs all conduct efficacy studies, and most report impressive results. Each type of program identifies at least one of the principles of positive psychology as a guiding or implementing principle in the program: teaching positive emotion, virtue or strength, relations, service, or accomplishment. All programs share the conviction that social and emotional well-being underlies overall well-being and success.

One difference is the degree of academic emphasis. Positive psychology programs are definitively concerned with overall well-being as a means to increased academic achievement. Youth development programs such as 4-H[69] and character education programs such as Character Counts[70] give secondary attention to academic achievement. Either way, various positive psychology programs increase children's readiness, willingness, ability to learn, and overall well-being. Regardless of the type or form of program, teaching positive psychology is effective across divergent demographic variables and diverse programmatic formats.

Programs that foster school engagement reduce problem behaviors[71] such as drug use, student misconduct, suspensions, expulsions, and rebellious behavior.[72] Long-standing research confirms that when students report feelings of attachment to school, to prosocial teachers, and to peers, they are more likely to behave in prosocial ways and avoid high-risk behaviors.[73] Children who are emotionally connected with peers, who positively bond with adults, and who value academic performance develop a positive academic orientation[74] and increased achievement.[75] Social emotional learning also increased standardized test scores by 11 to 17 percentile points.[76]

Children will develop a more prosocial disposition. A student's positive perceptions of a teacher's warmth and support, and of the teacher as a caretaker of respectful emotional and social interactions, is a significant predictor of her academic motivations, engagement, and performance.[77] A large-scale study extrapolated the findings of 61 independent researchers, 91 meta-analyses, and 179 summaries from textbook chapters, which confirmed the value of positive psychology. Overall, positive psychology programs increase positive attitudes about self and others, increase school affiliation, increase positive social behavior, and reduce conflict.[78]

Literacy-based programs are particularly effective as a means to teach positive psychology through academics[79] and are among the most common academic curricula that teach the positive psychology of social emotional learning. A four-year programmatic follow-up study reported that a pioneering social emotional literacy program positively affected children's attitudes, motives, and ethical values. The children also outperformed comparison groups based on achievement tests and grade point averages. The emotional content in literature is a powerful way to teach positive psychology, and it also improves academic results.[80] Positive psychology programs often use literature in the curriculum and the teacher selects from many excellent books and workbooks to build lessons.

Pioneering research in positive psychology evaluated the Penn Resiliency Program (PRP) finding that positive psychology interventions prevent symptoms of depression, reduce and prevent anxiety, decrease feelings of hopelessness, increase optimism, and improve well-being.[81] PRP research concluded that positive psychology programs decrease the prevalence of high-risk behaviors that interfere with academic learning.[82] Positive psychology teaches social emotional learning skills that change how much—and how well—students learn by changing how they feel.[83] When positive psychology lessons are part of the learning plan, performance in the content area improves.[84] The preponderance of the evidence, based on the aggregated results of more than 200 strong studies of school-based social emotional learning programs, confirms the value of positive psychology in the classroom. Children receiving high-quality instruction in positive psychology benefited significantly across a number of variables:[85]

1. Better academic performance, earning achievement test scores an average of 11 percentile points higher than students who did not receive such instruction.
2. Improved attitudes with greater motivation to learn, deeper commitment to school, increased time devoted to schoolwork, more positive behavior, and better attendance.

3. Fewer negative behaviors such as disruptive class behavior, noncompliance, delinquent acts, aggression, and disciplinary referrals.
4. Less emotional distress, depression, anxiety, stress, and social withdrawal.

The research confirms that positive psychology programs are most effective when taught in comprehensive, systematic, sequential, developmentally appropriate ways, when taught by a teacher who has positive relationships with the children, and when taught as part of, or in tangent with, the academic curriculum.[86] This compilation of data should give impetus to the positive psychology movement in elementary education.

Across the nation, and the world, 50 groups of scientists at 50 major universities, including Harvard University, the University of Pennsylvania, Princeton University, Cambridge University, and others, are conducting ongoing research that highlights the benefits of positive psychology in education.[87] The debate as to the value of positive psychology in education is over. The time has come "for social and emotional learning to be recognized as an important component of education reform and for politicians to stop ignoring the data."[88]

Overall, teaching positive psychology by teaching social emotional skills increases academic indicators, including motivation and persistence; engagement indicators, including attendance and cooperation; and performance indicators, such as grades and test scores.[89] There is significant empirical evidence that documents the efficacy of positive psychology programs and activities. The best result is found in programs that develop the emotional resiliency and the social capacity to manage negative emotions that interfere with concentration and perseverance essential to learning. These programs reduce stress, and increase flow so the children are able to learn in a more pleasant, good, connected, and meaningful ways with greater accomplishments.[90]

Summary and Conclusion

The philosophical, psychological, and educational wisdom of the ages intersects with the principles and practices of positive psychology of the 21st century. Large-scale implementation of these ideas has the potential to improve the well-being of all children. Positive psychology activates and motivates well-being and facilitates achievement and accomplishment. "Positive psychology is the scientific study of what makes life most worth living."[91] Every teacher works every day to deliver lessons that prioritize emotional learning and teach children how to live a pleasant, good, connected, meaningful, and contented life, resulting in the accomplishments and achievements that make life worth living.

The promise of positive psychology is the enduring benefit of the emotional competence that prepares children to activate their strengths, manage their relationships, find their purpose, and accomplish their goals. They learn to do their personal best as good enough and so they are free to explore and pursue what is most meaningful and enjoyable. They also learn that positive experiences do not guarantee, and are not sufficient for, happiness. Children learn that a happy and productive life is not always an easy life, failure is expected, and learning to overcome difficulty is part of the learning and growing process. Positive psychology fills their emotional reservoir.

Children will learn to invoke positive emotion at will with skill, ask for help and support in relationships, be of service to others, and extract meaning from life circumstances no matter their trials and tribulations. Positive psychology promises that children will leave elementary school curious rather than apathetic, and confident instead of fearful. They can learn to change themselves and increase well-being. They will leave educated, not schooled, and will be free to continue to participate, cultivate, relate, dedicate, celebrate, thrive, and flourish in learning and in life. Positive psychology has the potential to radically change the learning dynamics in any classroom. The potential of this research-based and value-based approach to education is not only the promise of positive psychology but also the gift of positive psychology.

Guiding Question Exercise

Do you remember your favorite teacher in elementary school? Do you remember any of his or her personality traits or signature strengths? Did he or she address emotional learning in the classroom? Did he or she recognize or encourage any of your strengths? When you reflect on your favorite teacher, consider to what extent the teacher infused positive psychology into your schooling. Did he or she teach positive emotion, strengths, or friendship? How was this done?

Guiding Question Discussion

The memory of a favorite teacher likely evokes positive emotions. He or she likely practiced some of the principles of positive psychology: focusing on your emotional development, teaching you how to replace negative feelings with positive ones, engaging you by noticing your strengths, facilitating friendships, helping you find intrinsic meaning in all your efforts, and applauding your accomplishments. A favorite teacher probably taught you important emotional skills such as honesty and how to use those skills to help yourself and others. Perhaps he or she taught life lessons embedded in the curriculum or enrichment activities that taught you positive psychology.

Web Resources for Children

The Mandala Project, http://www.mandalaproject.org/.
Philosophy for Children, http://www.mtholyoke.edu/omc/kidsphil/.
Smilebox, http://www.smilebox.com/.
Storyline, http://www.storylineonline.net/.
Who Moved My Cheese? for Kids, http://redtree.enstore.com/item/ wmmc-for-kids-book/.

Web Resources for Teachers

The Center for Positive Psychology, http://www.ppc.sas.upenn.edu/.
Collaborative for Academic, Social, and Emotional Learning (CASEL), http://casel.org/.
Flourishing Schools, http://www.flourishingschools.org/.
National School Climate Center, http://www.schoolclimate.org/ climate/.
The Safe and Caring Schools Society, http://www.sacsc.ca/.

CHAPTER 2

THE NEUROSCIENCE OF POSITIVE PSYCHOLOGY IN THE ELEMENTARY SCHOOL CLASSROOM

Human behavior flows from three main sources: desire, emotion, and knowledge.

—Plato

The principles of neuroscience inform positive psychology goals, methods, and efficacy. Positive psychology is a tool that teachers can use in the elementary classroom. The biology of neuroscience validates the social science of positive psychology, explaining how strengths emerge and why the use of strengths to direct attention and focus is important in both cognitive and emotional learning. Understanding how both cognitive and emotional strengths develop is one of the primary intentions of both neuroscience and positive psychology. Yet, despite the neuroscience evidence, there is still insufficient effort to mobilize the promise and power of emotional learning. Too often teachers disconnect academic learning from emotional learning and segment these two pillars of learning contrary to the neuroscience of learning.

Neuroscience proves that academic and emotional learning are not separate and must wholly integrate into educational practice. Educators refer to the importance of teaching the whole child while neuroscientists specify the need for whole-brain teaching strategies. Teaching to the whole child by using the neuroscience of learning evokes the strengths that enable children to thrive and flourish. An educational taxonomy and pedagogy derived from the cross-fertilization of neuroscience and positive psychology that weighs cognitive and emotional components of learning equally changes the current elementary education paradigm completely. As a result, teachers must understand the basics of brain structure and function, and particularly, how these build the strengths that nurture friendships, extract meanings, and motivate accomplishments.

Neuroscience is the study of the nervous system and it advances the understanding of human thought, emotion, and behavior.[1] A mature, interdisciplinary science, it combines the study of brain anatomy, physiology, chemistry, molecular biology and neurobiology, evolutionary biology and neurology, and evolutionary, developmental, and cognitive psychology. Neuroscientists study the spongy, pinkish, beige brain that has a working surface composed primarily of specialized fat cells that protect the brain's vital communication system. Neuroscientists also study the one billion nerve cells, or neurons, that the brain grows, organizes, and connects into massive, interstellar-like constellations of neural networks.

The research emphasis in neuroscience is on brain structure, function, and connectivity, including research as to the origins and dynamics of cognition, affect, and conation. "The knowledge that brain mapping is delivering is not only enlightening, it is of immense practical and social importance because it paves the way for us to recreate ourselves in a way that has previously been described only in science fiction . . . and control brain activity in a precise and radical way."[2] The neuroscience findings explain how environmental experience arouses the brain's emotional networks, filters emotion through the cognitive networks to make decisions, and prompts the conative network to decide on an action. The brain watches a shooting star, holds a child's hand, and remembers a mother's birthday. Within its vast labyrinth live the cells that make us human and that shape and shelter our hopes, dreams, wonders, passions, and fancies.

Every new idea, profound experience, emotional epiphany, poignant memory, social contract, and physical performance begins in the brain. No one yet knows the full capabilities of the brain. What do scientists know? They know that the brain is the most complex structure in the body and one of the most complex in the universe. "The smell of a flower—the memory of a walk in the park—the pain of stepping on a nail: these experiences are made possible by three pounds of tissue in our heads."[3]

An understanding of the brain offers a scientific prototype for teaching because all thoughts, feelings, and observable actions are the direct results of neural communication. The teacher, who masters the fundamentals of neuroscience and applies these core concepts to educational practice, is better equipped to ensure that optimal learning occurs. However, in many teacher-training programs, there is a tendency to emphasize behavioral theory so even veteran teachers have a unilateral focus on isolated behaviors. They may not consider the neurobiological genesis of the behavior within the brain's intricate networks and may fail to account for the environmental milieu that changes those networks. Absent an understanding of the neuroscience of learning, the teacher may not fully grasp the intricacies of the learning process that involve both academic and emotional networks that are ever changing, communicating, coordinating, and compounding.

The teacher may not have the necessary neuroscience background to know how to guide children's learning from action potential to accomplishment. According to the neuroscience, a simplistic stimulus-response contrivance does not determine children's actions; instead, dynamic, complicated, and mutually reciprocal interactions between cognition and affect—between ideas and feelings—prompt them. The importance of neuroscience is that it describes the actions of children within the rich context of brain science and explains why children's actions are not unilaterally cognitive. Increasing the teacher's knowledge about neuroscience increases his or her academic and emotional teaching repertoire.

Brain networks govern all thought and emotion and children's actions are the result of a coalescence of thought and emotion. The brain's networks are primed to build the strengths of positive psychology, and the teacher is in an ideal position to reinforce strengths such as optimism, empathy, and moderation.

Academic and Emotional Learning in the Classroom

Interacting subsystems or modules organize and manage the activity of the brain. Brain cells connect and build structures in particular areas of the brain that have a standardized function (e.g., moving muscles). However, even cells within its subsystems and modules themselves are highly differentiated by function. Some cells are so specialized that, in some areas of the frontal neural cortex, they respond only to musical notes.[4]

The brain's prefrontal cortex processes academic learning while the limbic system processes emotional learning. These two modular systems function in highly cohesive ways with the neural circuits of both systems crisscrossing all brain systems, networks, modules, regions, and hemispheres. As a result, neuroscientists have mapped a thinking brain and a feeling brain that work closely together as a synergistic whole as the ying and yang of the brain: "We do have more than one brain although it is not the right and the left. It is the primitive emotional brain and the advanced cognitive brain . . . one thinks in music and one thinks in lyrics . . . the left brain can talk while the right brain is asleep, but it cannot sing."[5]

Neurons communicate with each other by electrical signals that travel long distances and then release chemicals that activate thoughts, emotions, and actions. The neurons perform by firing their cells together, creating an action potential. An action potential is an electrical charge that can incite or inhibit action; all actions actually performed are the result of the neural communication that incites it. Neurotransmitters act as communication couriers and release chemicals such as endorphins that produce a runner's high, amino acids such as serotonin that regulate sleep, and cortisol that is a hormonal response to stress.[6] There are different types of neurons that are receptive to different kinds of neurotransmitters that switch the brain's stress signals on and off depending on experiential input.[7]

Trillions of specialized neurons, each with tens of thousands of synaptic terminals acting as a functional whole, shape the brain's ecological system. The brain's systems, and its subsystems, are mutually interdependent so all electrical activity flows between, and among, all parts. Neural activity operates across the many codependent brain systems, or modules, that are interspersed throughout it. Neurons transmit electrical signals along the axons of the neurons. When a signal reaches the end of an axon, it triggers the release of neurotransmitters that bind to receptor molecules on the adjacent neuron. The point of contact is the synapse; a single axon generates thousands of synaptic connections that innervate multiple parts of the brain. The growth of new synapses turns on the genes that improve academic and emotional learning.[8]

The brain is a living, breathing, learning organism that adapts to experience, and that adaptation is a result of constant communication between the regions of the brain via neural transit. When the neurons talk to each other, the executive learning functions of the brain transmit information fluently and fluidly between the brain's cells and modules. *Executive learning function* is the term for the neurologically advanced, higher-order thinking skills that are involved in the mental focus, activity, and regulation essential to learning.[9] Primarily the work of the prefrontal cortex, executive functions include cognitive operations, such as perception, organization, and working memory, that enable children to shift perspective, modulate emotion, inhibit or initiate action, remember prior learning, manage demands, prioritize tasks, and self-monitor.

Here is an example of how executive functions occur in the classroom. A teacher gives the class 15 minutes to answer three history questions. She hears Johnny sigh and notices that he does not shift his attention to the task. Instead, he is staring at the clock, unable to inhibit his unfocused attention or to initiate focused action to begin the assignment. Johnny takes a little blue car out of his pocket.

The teacher walks over to Johnny but she does not take the car away. She tells him kindly to put it back in his pocket and reminds him that he has only 15 minutes to do the work. She tells him to use his book to help answer the questions. She also tells him if he finishes his work early, he can then play quietly with his car.

The teacher guides Johnny to focus, self-manage, inhibit, initiate, prioritize, and establish a positive goal. The teacher knows taking away the toy teaches him nothing. Simply telling him to do the task again, or punishing him, does not redirect learning. Simply collecting contraband toys misses the opportunity to activate executive functions and re-route learning by using means compatible with the neuroscience of learning. Little blue cars can have a place in school.

Executive function is crucial to both academic learning and emotional learning. Skillful integration of the executive functions is necessary for children if they want to decide to complete all assigned homework before playing a videogame or to fondly remember last summer's vacation. The prefrontal cortex is where a child can shift his perception of a negative event to a positive one and calm his angry reaction. This area of the brain translates emotional experience in such a way as to cause children to either walk away from a fight or take the first punch.

As children explore the world, and aggregate their learning experiences, they exchange and test their ideas and emotions. Positive psychology theory aligns with the neuroscience of executive function, and the teacher's lessons aim to rewire children's brains—to think, to feel, and to act differently—for improved academic, social, and emotional learning.

The structure, chemistry, and function of the child's brain can influence readiness and the ability to learn. Thus, there are three ideas that are central to the neuroscience of learning: (1) the brain constructs all learning; (2) academic performance and emotional health cannot be bifurcated; and (3) positive psychology advances optimal learning.

Discoveries in neuroscience offer teachers a new 21st-century pedagogy that focuses equally on mental, physical, and psychological well-being. Many of the early proponents of the neuroscience of learning understood the value of brain-based research to teachers and worked to transcribe the neuroscience literature for them.[10] Early adopters reported the benefit of neuroscience in education and their shared vision dramatically increased educators' interest in applying brain research to teaching. Now it is possible to connect the neuroscience of learning to the positive psychology of learning by promoting a strengths-based approach to education. Strengths training can help change children's counterproductive emotional anxieties, assumptions, attitudes, dispositions, habits, moods, and regrets that otherwise stagnate brain growth.

Brain Basics: Understanding How the Brain Changes and Learns in the Classroom

The brain changes because of the characteristics of neuroplasticity and through the process of neurogenesis. Neuroplasticity describes the adaptive change that occurs in the brain in response to environmental input; brains will grow new neurons and pathways in an ongoing process of neurogenesis. The most exciting aspect is how new learning propagates new neurons that increase learning capacity. All available sensory information stimulates the neurons to communicate, connect, and coordinate actions based on the sensory input and environmental experience. The input is then processed across multiple brain regions and modules, and the result is the growth of new learning, ideas, perspectives, and performance.

New neural circuits energize themselves as the brain converts sensory stimuli to chemical and electric signals that it uses to communicate, connect, and grow new neurons that build the brain's complex neural super highway. The electrical charge travels along the axon to the terminal to release neurotransmitters called action potentials because each signal is able to produce an action when it crosses the synapse.

Synapses are chemical or electrical junctions that transfer the electrical message from neuron to neuron or to another specialized cell. Changes in stimulation intensity or frequency of activity at a synaptic junction can incite or inhibit resultant action (similar to traffic lights on a highway).

As one researcher has found, "Every millisecond of every day, a remarkable string of events occurs in the brain: billions of brain cells called neurons, that are central to all aspects of learning, transmit signals to each other across trillions of synapses."[11] The signals sent between, and among, the hundreds of billions of neurons—all of which are in use at any given time—are strengthened or weakened by environmental input. If children learn how to manage the stimulation, and thereby the signals, they can learn to calm agitated nerves that are overstimulated and to modulate their thoughts, feelings, and actions.

The simplest neural circuit produces a reflexive response. A more complex action occurs when the brain amalgamates experiential information collected across many circuits. While simple, reflexive reactions may occur within milliseconds, complex responses may take months to produce. Children may be quick to anger, while learning patience takes more time and practice.

Positive experience readies the brain for neural growth; however, it does not necessarily create new learning and so is not sufficient for neurogenesis.[12] Toys in the dream playroom and visits to the museum alone are not sufficient to grow children's brains. Deliberative teaching and intentional learning are necessary catalysts for the new learning that triggers neurogenesis. When toys connect children to new concepts, when the playroom tests new skills, and when the field trip connects to prior learning, then children learn and flourish. All children need direct instruction to learn to ride a bike because simultaneous control of balance and movement is a highly complex motor action requiring practice with a coach.

Emotional learning is even more complex and requires even more observation of, and systematic practice with, a proficient tutor. Neuroscience research has shown that a positive psychology strengths-based approach elongates children's abilities to use positive feelings, thoughts, and language.

The cerebral cortex, the outermost layer of the cerebral hemispheres of the brain, is largely responsible for all forms of conscious experience and learning, including perception, thought, emotion, and planning. However, other structures, modules, and networks—especially the hippocampus—contribute to this process. A seahorse-shaped structure, the hippocampus is part of the brain's limbic system and is a complex set of multiple structures located on both sides of the thalamus below the cerebrum deep in the primitive brain. The hippocampus is a structure where learning, memory, and emotion converge, and it seems to be the most active area for neurogenesis.[13] The hippocampus produces thousands of new cells each day. As more learning occurs, new neurons grow because emotional memory is the nucleus of learning.

The limbic system forms the emotional infrastructure of the brain; embedded in it is the memory system that records both positive and negative emotional events. Neural arousal of positive and negative emotion occurs in the brain's emotional memory network and reminds us to wave to a friend or avert our eyes. The brain makes sense of the world by using all available information, including senses, instincts, emotions, and especially remembered experiences.

Research suggests that the hippocampus is both a memory and prediction terminal that shapes future thoughts, actions, and imaginings.[14] The hippocampus stores experiences and uses them as the basis for decisions about future actions and the remembered information it stores predicts what might happen in the near and far term.[15] The hippocampus learns from prior experience and, in a microsecond, makes predictions about the best course of action in response to a present challenge.

If the brain is stimulated to expect failure, it is more likely to accept failure. This leads scientists to believe that the hippocampus encodes learned helplessness—and learned optimism. When the reasoning frontal cortex communicates with the emoting amygdala, channeling the information through the predictive filter of the hippocampus, it visualizes outcomes even more vividly.[16]

Different brain structures and areas manage different kinds of memory. The hippocampus, parahippocampal region, and some areas of the cerebral cortex compose a system that supports declarative, or cognitive, memory. Nondeclarative memory, including autobiographical memory, is the infrastructure of emotional memory supported by the amygdala, striatum, and cerebellum. These two interdependent memory systems work together to connect and use the recollection of cognitive memory and the recall of emotional memory in decision making. As the Society for Neuroscience has found, "Emotions are based on the value judgments made by our brains and manifested as feelings as basic as love and anger and as complex as empathy and hate."[17]

The brain generates some of these emotions consciously as part of normal brain activity while others are the result of unconscious brain chatter, or a running internal chronicle, that is highly personal and idiosyncratic.[18] The brain writes an "internal coherent self-narrative" and seeks to interpret its autobiography through the production of autogenesis—or self-knowledge—as a result of the free flow and integration of information and energy between the two brain hemispheres.[19] The memory system of the brain catalogues and consolidates all the physical and psychological changes that occur as the whole brain organizes and reorganizes the incoming information, often creating an indelible memory. When experience becomes a permanent part of children's long-term memory, they essentially deposit it into a memory bank from which it is difficult to make a withdrawal.

For example, conditioned fear responses are imprinted permanently in the memory system and they create a lasting negative memory or an "indelible fear, that if not completely indelible, is hard to erase."[20] Children do not forget how to swim, or the day their dog died. While the brain organizes to recognize sensations, store, and access lifetime memories—and initiate behavior based on its memory bank—it does not mean original memories cannot be rerouted or supplanted.

Positive psychology has developed evidence-based ways for teachers to help. Because of neuroplasticity and neurogenesis, children are able to recalibrate emotion and redirect thought by creating new learning around old experiences. The teacher uses this process to influence the development of emotional intelligence, which improves academic and emotional learning and performance. The teacher intervenes in ways that optimize the neurology involved in decoding imprinted sensory patterns enabling children to remember, generalize, and apply information, anticipate outcome, predict consequences, and make better decisions.

Non-neuronal cells, such as glial cells, also play an important supporting role in this process of learning and relearning in the brain. The glial cell is the most abundant cell in the nervous system: It outnumbers neurons at about nine to one. These fibrous cells do not conduct electrical impulses and, instead, provide insulating support for the surrounding neurons, and without glial cells in tow, some neurons even shrivel and die.[21] So it is the job of glial cells to keep their partner neurons alive, well, and communicating.

Glial cells are also capable of extensive signaling and are always in bilateral communication with other kinds of cells, including neurons. The glial cells act as communicator cells, compacting learning and memory into intelligence. These chattering cells connect what we feel to what we know to what we understand to what we do.

In this decision-making process, the neurons collect information and the glial cells collate it before sending it back to a partner neuron to use to build learning connections that facilitate problem solving and decision making. The more glial cell involvement there is in learning, the more new learning, intelligent connections, and practical wisdom emerge. There is more neurogenesis when there is more communication between neurons and glial cells, and between the neural and fibrous networks. These networks intertwine in a spiraling double helix of learning. As the Society for Neuroscience has also written, "To live and become part of the working brain, a new neuron needs . . . support from the communicator glial cells and nutrients from blood, but most importantly, connections with other neurons."[22]

The number and type of cells involved in neurogenesis is important because general neural connections contribute to overall mental, social, and emotional development. Specific neural connections in certain brain structures, or regions, predict the increase of specific strengths such as motor coordination or optimism. However, the brain does "not act or think in rigidly separated compartments but can relate different contents."[23]

Cognition is the process of thinking that generates children's conscious thought by the firing of neurons that cross all brain networks and modules. Most often, the teacher associates it with academic thinking, comprehension, and problem solving although it crosses the cognitive, affective, and conative domains of learning and is best understood in relationship to the whole child as the process of acquiring, comprehending, and using both academic and emotional knowledge and skills. Neuroscience of learning research has documented that children do not think only about ideas, they also think about feelings and actions, and "deployment [of reasoning strategies] probably depends, to a considerable extent, on a continued ability to experience feelings."[24] Neuroscience-based cognition is three-dimensional: thinking about ideas, about feelings, and about feeling-based actions.

Positive psychology is the only educational taxonomy that addresses this 3-D learning: academic, social, and emotional processes. Intelligence materializes as children learn to generalize increasingly complex and abstract thoughts and feelings, including emotional thoughts and feelings, to novel events using past and current information to anticipate possible outcomes and solve future problems. Intelligence is not only a function of academic knowledge or cognitive ability: rather, it is heavily dependent on emotional intuition, skill, and strength. Connections to self, others, and the world will mold intelligence.

Applying Neuroscience Principles and Practices in the Classroom

The Society of Neuroscience works to translate the insights of neuroscience for teachers and has developed core concepts, and essential principles, of neuroscience to guide educators.[25] The society publishes four mega concepts of neuroscience, and eight associated core concepts, that have "broad application for K–12 teachers offering the most important insights gathered through decades of brain research."[26]

These four mega concepts explain why neuroscience is the key to optimal learning and well-being. These include (1) the nervous system controls direct body functions and all other actions; (2) the nervous system structure and function are determined by genes and environment; (3) the brain is the foundation of the mind; and (4) research addresses healthy development as well as therapies for disorders and disease.[27]

Elaborating the mega concepts of neuroscience, eight neuroscience core concepts further condense the neuroscientific data by notating the essential principles associated with the core concepts in ways that are useful to teachers. Eight neuroscience core concepts provide a prescription and template for teaching positive psychology that is consistent with the neuroscience research.[28]

These core concepts parallel the principles of positive psychology and form the basis for best practices in the classroom through an understanding and mastery of (1) brain complexity, (2) neural communication, (3) genetically formed circuitry, (4) adaptive change, (5) intelligence, (6) language, (7) curiosity, and (8) well-being. Recently, the core concepts were reformulated and embedded as basic brain facts and now summarize research about neuroanatomy, neural network function, cell communication, evolution, and brain development. Basic neuroscientific understandings provide a framework for a new approach to education that emphasizes the importance of teaching emotional and academic competence and mastery simultaneously. Together the neuroscience concepts help to explain both intrapersonal and interpersonal change and growth in academic, emotional, and social areas.

The core concepts show that positive psychology teaches children essential knowledge and skills, and children will benefit from early and thorough instruction. Each core concept explains an important, preprogrammed characteristic of the brain that describes how to better help children adapt to their environments by cultivating brain strengths. For example, improved neural communication builds broader and deeper connections, enlarges cognitive options, invites optimism, and mediates frustration.

One of the eight core concepts, well-being, is allied very closely with the positive psychology literature. Well-being relates to the development and growth of the brain as it systematically broadens and deepens in every area of human endeavor across the life span. Teaching based on both neuroscience concepts and positive psychology principles develops the brain in ways that bring more learning and enjoyment to the classroom. The teacher must help children understand their temperament, recognize their feelings, and identify their signature strengths to enhance learning. As Seligman has written, "Well-being enhances learning, the traditional goal of education . . . I believe we have finally arrived at an era in which . . . enjoyment [of learning] . . . will succeed better."[29]

The first neuroscience concept states that children have an idiosyncratic brain print and will respond differently to the same learning experience. Therefore, children always bring different emotions and strengths to learning. The brain is highly complex, possessing infinite potential for difference because of the interaction of genes and environments, or epigenetics, that make each brain unique.

Second, communication between, and among, neurons is essential to brain function and structure. Neurons communicate by using electrical and chemical signals and the messages travel across initial circuitry that is genetically determined. As the neurons communicate and connect, they proliferate, and brain networks expand to accommodate the new connections. These new connections are the result of new neural learning, and a teacher is in a key position to build new neural connections. When new learning experiences nurture broad and deep connections, especially between cognition and emotion, children learn how to flourish academically, socially, and emotionally.

Third, early neural circuits form during embryonic development based on a genetic code imprinted on every cell. These genetically established circuits survive a lifetime and interactions with the internal and external environment modify them over time. Life experiences change the brain's neural communication and connective circuitry, ever deconstructing and reconstructing prior learning. As a result, children have different and changing neural profiles, different ways and rates of learning, different cognitive and emotional intelligences, and different strengths. For this reason, it is essential to customize both academic and emotional learning.

Fourth, life experiences change the nervous system at the level of gene expression. Children are not the sole products of their genetic prototypes because experiences also change them biologically, as proven in epigenetic studies of the brain. As the brain's frontal neural cortex learns and changes in response to positive experience, it manages complexity and nuance of ideas better.

The strategic education of the whole brain amplifies cognitive abilities and stretches emotional range. Genetics program the brain with natural curiosity, novelty responsiveness, the ability to learn, and a proclivity to adapt. Neurological evaluation and assimilation of experience enable children to develop cognitive strengths such as creativity and emotional strengths such as generosity. The brain is able to frame an issue in a habitual and narrow way or open it up to a larger conceptualization, whether considering the speed of sound or the need for forgiveness. Guiding the whole brain to positive emotional attention, focus, and activity helps children to use their strengths to react and respond in ways that are more conducive to learning. Otherwise, the proclivity moves in the opposite direction toward the manufacture of negative reactions.

Fifth, neural learning evolves from the brain's adaptive response to experience and materializes as intelligence—or the ability to reason, to plan, and to solve both academic and emotional problems. Intelligence is not only of the cognitive or academic variety. Daniel Goleman coined the term *emotional quotient* to describe emotional intelligence as the ability to self-soothe, take initiative, persist on a task, and cooperate with others.[30] Emotional intelligence "is not fixed at birth"[31], is not only bestowed by blessing or birth, and can be taught. The lessons of positive psychology teach children to improve their emotional quotient, physical health, and mental hygiene. Neglecting the emotional core of learning fragments academic learning and may even fracture it completely. Teachers work to increase both emotional and academic intelligence.

Sixth, the brain's innate ability to learn language makes it possible to share acquired knowledge and emotional experience. Children learn language early in development, facilitating information exchange, emotional relationships, and creative thought throughout life. The linguistic system embeds itself in the brain, working with specialized lingual centers to relay thoughts and feelings to every region and module of the brain.

Most of the linguistic system traverses the right and left cerebral hemispheres in the frontal cortex. However, billions of linguistic fibers branch into all parts of the brain and consume enormous neural resources across the brain's linguistic system. Human language, both expressive and receptive, is one of the most pervasive, complex tasks of the brain emanating from the language web.[32] The language web connects to the cognitive, affective, and conative systems of the brain, enabling children to think, read, write, and talk not only about academic knowledge, but also personal feelings. Language is the basis for all human relations, and frames many of the most pressing classroom problems.

Seventh, the human brain endows children with a natural curiosity to understand how the world works from birth onward. Novel stimulus causes neurons to fire across many regions and systems and it self-propels learning.[33] Curiosity constructs the neural connections that arouse interest in learning and it is what initially compels children to attend, concentrate, and persist in learning. The teacher recognizes that children are naturally curious about what makes the moon shine, why the Liberty Bell is cracked, and how sinkholes are created. She also knows that they are equally, if not more curious, about what makes them feel sad, what makes heroes brave, and how to make friends. They are curious about how to get over a bad mood, say they are sorry when they are wrong, and offer congratulations when someone else wins the race they expected to win.

Eighth, neuroscience findings promote healthy living and emphasize the inextricable mind-body connection. What affects children's thoughts and feelings affects their physical health and what affects their physical health affects their thoughts and feelings. The overall well-being of children depends on learning experiences that expand, extend, and connect the cognitive, emotional, and conative networks of the brain because neural connection and communication is strengthened, or weakened, by an individual's experiential learning activities.

To learn is to grow, and the process of neural renewal enables the brain to not only generate new neural pathways, but also regenerate damaged ones throughout a life so children can recover from disease, injury, stress, and more. Equally important, neuroscience also guides optimal development, making emotionally healthy children even more emotionally proficient.

Teaching to the Brain: A Strengths-Based Approach

Strengths that bring attention and focus to the brain systems and that have the potential to help children envision opportunities, embrace compassion, bridle emotions, and show fortitude are the teacher's most important tools. Discovering and cultivating children's brain strengths is the work of positive psychology.

Optimism: Envisioning Possibilities. Optimism is a brain-based function, and greater numbers of neural connections in the left prefrontal cortex are associated with more optimism.[34] The science of optimism proposes three ideas relevant to teachers: (1) memories are inaccurate because memory systems are better able to envision the future than reconstruct the past, (2) there is a clear optimistic bias in predicting a personal future, and (3) positive imagination is the companion of optimism.[35] Building a broader and deeper neuronal network gives children a greater capacity for predicting and imagining good outcomes. When children reassess an actual outcome, they typically discard the alternative, unlikely, outcomes as undesirable.[36] Children's brains activate positive expectations that reduce distress and restore the homeostasis of well-being. In other words, unless overwhelmed, the brain self-protects its own mental health.

Just as Rumpelstiltskin spun straw into gold, the brain spins positive memories into optimism. In other words, even if an event is not good, the brain is capable of deconstructing it and reconstructing it in a more favorable light. Contemplating rival outcomes, whether positive or negative, the brain works to persuade you that whatever happens is the best possible outcome.

The brain works hard to decrease conflict and avoid what psychologists term the cognitive dissonance between the rival options. Whenever possible, the optimistic brain works to reduce tension by remaking the actual outcome and persuading itself that it was the best choice or result. "Our brain . . . enables us to bounce back to normal levels of well-being . . . it is wired to place high value on the [positive] events we encounter."[37]

Children are capable of reframing any outcome as a good outcome through practiced reappraisal. The healthy brain is able to exchange the bad for the good, increasing beneficial levels of optimism that correlate with greater physical, emotional, and social well-being. The brain is biologically predisposed to wear rose-colored glasses and wired to try to live happily ever after. Of course, optimism is a more difficult task when children must reconcile extreme or repeated hardship. Yet the neurological tendency is to build optimism and its corollary resiliency, even in extraordinary circumstances, such as a natural disaster.

Another neural mechanism that increases optimism is the brain's ability to remember a past result as well as to anticipate a future reward. Memory alerts to an expected good experience by tracking, recording, and reporting past events and using that data to predict the future. Within the caudate nucleus in the striatum, there is a cluster of nerves that announces a reward is pending and then broadcasts to expect something good.[38] The more good that is anticipated, the more brain activity is found in this area. The less good that is anticipated, the less brain activity in the area.

Those same neurons, faithfully encoding positive memories, do not encode discouraging information with the same reliability. The hippocampus has a bad memory for negative experiences.[39] Feelings of satisfaction and disappointment are both neural processes; however, the brain is biased against negative feelings and acts to shield from disappointment by installing selective memory as a protective sentry. Essentially, the hippocampus acts as a positive fortune-teller by forecasting future events as positively as possible.

If children reassess negative events, especially with past positive experiences as the reference point, the brain is inclined to accentuate the positive and diminish the negative. When exposed to two contrary outcomes, brain activity usually biases toward a good result. Practice with adversity has the potential to perfect positivity because the more opportunity there is to learn to rehabilitate a negative event, the better.

A teacher can demonstrate optimism by asking children to choose positive perceptions, thoughts, emotions, and actions and thereby tapping children's natural optimism. Children learn to positively reassess and reconsider events, then turn a positive perspective to learning advantage. To himself, Timothy says, "This chapter on bugs is not very interesting to me. However, after three pages, I can work with my friend and look at some bugs under the microscope. I am not sure I want to do that either. However, what if it is fun to see them get bigger? I am going to try to enjoy it."

Children can learn to widen their emotional viewpoint so that they are better able to envision, expect, and capture a more positive outcome even when confronted with a difficult situation. Children's well-being depends on their ability to look to a positive future. Victor Frankl, who survived a Holocaust concentration camp, wrote that everything can be taken from a man or a woman but one thing: "the last of human freedoms to choose one's attitude . . . to choose one's own way."[40] Children choose optimism and the teacher offers opportunity for the practice of it. Barbara Frederickson's broaden-and-build theory proposes that the practice of positivity widens children's field of vision and builds a more positive view.[41] "Positivity whether it blooms as joy, serenity, or any other hue on your positivity palette, literally gives you a new outlook on life."[42] A new outlook correlates with the ability to be optimistic. Optimism is a gateway emotion that opens the door to other positive emotions such as joy, which is the pinnacle of positive emotions. From hopeful to joyful is only a short leap of faith. Interpretation matters.

Children have faith that making mistakes, and learning from those mistakes, is a part of the learning process. This conviction increases children's optimism because they believe that they will eventually succeed or, at least, learn from and enjoy the attempt. Optimism reshapes learning brains so that they are able to produce a more cheerful neurological reaction to academic, emotional, and social demands and difficulties.

Empathy: Exponential Caring. Empathy is a brain-based function that is dependent on the actions of the mirror neurons. Mirror neurons look like ordinary motor neurons but have an extraordinary function. Mirror neurons are defined as "neurons that discharge when an individual performs an action, as well as when he/she observes a similar action done by another individual."[43] The relatively recent discovery of mirror neurons and how they function confirms what teachers have long believed to be true: demonstration and imitation are powerful learning tools. Mirror neurons form the cortical mirror neural system found in four regions of the brain. These connect the cortical region to the limbic system: (1) the superior temporal sulcus, (2) the ventral premotor cortex, (3) the rostral part of the inferior or posterior parietal lobe, and (4) the anterior sector of the insular lobe.[44] These specialized, smart neurons are not motor neurons and are designed for communication only. They transfer observational learning to the rest of the brain so the whole brain can initiate cognitive, emotional, and motor action in response. Children say, "Let *me* try."

Children learn by watching because their brain circuitry is hard-wired to learn by observation. Infants as young as a few minutes old will stick out their tongues at an adult doing the same to them.[45] The cortical mirror neuron system is the reason that children can reproduce emotions and actions after observation only. The mirror neurons cognitively map the action so children can mimic it and then emotionally connect them to the action so they want to do it.[46]

While learning by doing has been a mantra of educators for many years, neuroscience now suggests that it is only effective if children are learning by duplication. Children are more ready to learn to ride a bicycle after watching a big brother ride it. Children learn by discerning and the mirror neurons make a detailed mental note to copy later. Mirror neurons are visual learners, endowing children with the ability to simulate action and emotion in their brain. Children have the innate ability to reproduce both motor actions and emotional responses.

A teacher can show children how to do addition by showing them how to make a pizza: Add two olives, take away three peppers, and add one anchovy. Children usually have positive pizza reactions and happily imitate it. When attending a sporting event, children react physically and emotionally as if they are in the game themselves, just by watching the players run the bases and hit the home run.

The mirror neurons can clone others' feelings and actions and are intensely embroiled in emotional learning. Children do not only mimic others' feelings and repeat others' actions; they are also able to neurologically recreate the experience and feel another's joy or pain. The same neurons fire whether children are watching or experiencing an event because children are vicarious learners of emotion and action. They can imagine, intend, anticipate, and emotionally reconstruct what they observe without taking any overt action or actually having the experience themselves.

Children's mirror neurons fire exactly the same way whether they cry or see another child cry. This phenomenon explains what preschool teachers already know: emotion is neurologically contagious. If one child cries, others will cry. The feeling travels by way of the mirror neuron network not only from one neuron to the next, but also from one child to another. Children observe another child fall down on the playground and cringe in sympathy. A boy observes another child look surprised and then looks surprised, too. Mirror neurons enable children to recognize and reproduce emotions they observe.

Scientists speculate that this amazing ability to replicate emotion, as well as action, by observation evolved as a means of social survival: "We are exquisitely social creatures and our survival depends on understanding the actions, intentions, and emotions of others."[47] Empathy seems to be the currency of social survival and an evolutionary adaptation that allows us to live and work successfully in groups. Children recognize sadness in another's facial expressions, and a teacher can encourage a child to reflect the emotion back to the sad child in words. Children recognize happiness in another child's face, and everyone begins to smile. They not only see but also feel others' emotions.

Children learn to understand their family, friends, and neighbors through shared emotions and actions toward others by using emotional acumen and not by using reasoning ability. Mirror neurons communicate the intentions and emotions of others to children so that they are able to respond in kind. When a friend smiles, mirror neurons fire, and children smile back: "You don't have to think about what the other person intends by smiling. You experience the meaning of the smile immediately and effortlessly."[48] The strengths of kindness, generosity, forgiveness, and compassion are learned by feeling them —and not by thinking about them.[49] In this way, children share emotions almost telepathically.

The ability to share the emotions of others appears intimately linked to the functioning of mirror neurons.[50] In particular, neurons in the apple-sized insula respond to all observed emotion, including social emotions like guilt and embarrassment. Children with more neurons in this area feel their own pain, and the pain of others, more acutely. This may explain why sensitive children suffer higher levels of social anxiety. If children see another child being teased, their own mirror neurons fire and they feel the same self-consciousness, guilt, or discomfort. Social pain activates the same neurons as physical pain, so the humiliation of a public scolding hurts every child who hears it, especially the most empathetic children.[51]

Emotion: Empowering Change. Emotion is a pervasive brain function that originates in the amygdala and, when mediated by the prefrontal cortex, regulates effectively and expresses constructively. Neural reaction to a threatening experience is self-protective, visceral, immediate, and automatic while neural reaction to a favorable experience is not automatic—sometimes requiring conscious effort. A stressful task often prompts a corresponding negative fight reaction such as defiance: "No, I won't do it." A negative flight response might take the form of procrastination: "I will do it later." Whatever the form of negative reaction, the teacher's job is to diffuse it and then reconstitute it. In the classroom, children frequently try to avoid distress by either actively refusing to cooperate or by passively resisting cooperation. Children who lack the ability to self-regulate their feelings are not prepared to contend with situations that might make them feel afraid or ashamed. Negative experiences can create a neural storm of negative emotion that overwhelms them and jeopardizes learning because where there is stress there is minimal learning.

Learning depends on optimal working memory that is, in part, a function of the degree of active neurogenesis in the brain and the intensity of the stress that obstructs it. New brain cell production is necessary for academic achievement and emotional well-being; negative emotions provoke the release of stress hormones known to hinder neurogenesis and learning.[52] These stress hormones, such as cortisol, adversely affect the executive functions of academic and emotional learning, and they derail attention, memory, focus, organization, motivation, and more.[53]

Pioneering research, using electroencephalography (EEG) scores, establishes firm correlations between levels of stress hormones and self-reports of susceptibility to anxiety and depression.[54] Exposure to stress hormones causes connections between brain cells to shrivel up and disconnect, especially in the hippocampus, which is the central circuit board for memory.[55] High levels of cortisol alter brain functioning so dramatically that severe, prolonged stress can cause permanent brain cell damage.[56]

Neuroscience brings the teacher ever closer to understanding how they need to activate positive emotion and to deactivate negative emotion in order to advance the neurogenesis of learning closer to teaching positive psychology. Neural connections between the frontal cortex and the limbic system are crucial to emotional regulation, and the orbital prefrontal cortex is at the crossroads of emotion and thought. Negative events interrupt neural contact between the limbic system and the frontal cortex so that emotion and cognition are disconnected. When this happens, neural disruptions caused by negative experiences and emotion interfere with learning.[57] Cognition and emotion intertwine so that stress unravels emotions and diminishes the ability to self-regulate. Negative emotions overwhelm the neural system and severely interfere with the rational thought that manages reactions to physical and emotional threats in more moderate and stable ways.

Negative emotions interfere with reasoned response so a teacher must help children learn to deconstruct the habitual negative response and reconstruct a more positive response.[58] Reason mediates emotion and serves to either invigorate or depress it in response to environmental stimuli: "Feelings may not be intruders in the bastion of reason at all, they may be enmeshed in its networks for worse and for better."[59] In some children, it is for the worst because self-regulation of negative emotion is even more difficult when it reoccurs frequently. When a fear trigger occurs, the brain recognizes it from prior experience, expects the same outcome, and automatically initiates a negative reaction that originates in the amygdala and then spreads quickly throughout the limbic system. Each time the fear is retriggered, children reexperience the past trauma as if for the first time. As a result, sometimes children will react to a past event that was upsetting to them and not to the current situation.

The current stressor may simply precipitate a habitual response mired in the brain's circuitry, creating ever-greater levels of stress. Some neurological systems have a lower threshold to stress tolerance; others have a higher level. However, every system can reorganize to reroute around the disruption.

Children bring varying levels of stress reaction, and stress management skills, to the classroom. Nonetheless, all children can learn to deliberately conjure a positive emotion in response to negative arousal so that a new neural pattern organizes and reorganizes the brain's emotional networks. The more children practice summoning positive emotions to mind, the better they become at processing and reprocessing negative energy into positive energy because adaptive neural connections get stronger with repetition. The deliberate and purposeful recall of positive experiences helps children manage threats with equanimity and they get better and better at doing it under increasingly stressful conditions.[60]

The antidote for the negative emotion, aggravated by stress, is positive emotion. The plasticity of the brain enables it to retool to affect a positive response to a negative experience. A negative memory, and the ensuing emotion, causes neurons to automatically fire against the threat or perceived threat. The brain works to shield itself from attack in one way or another, so children learn the best way to protect themselves—change the perception, thought, memory—and choose a different way to feel and act. Neurological alteration and mediation change the initial emotional reaction, and subsequent action, so it is more balanced.[61]

The advanced forebrain is the center of advanced learning and solves algebra problems, composes musical scores, and softens anger. Together with the anterior cingulate gyrus, a fibrous bundle overlapping the corpus callosum, the prefrontal cortex synergistically blends the thought and feeling needed for academic and emotional well-being.[62]

If children are emotionally skillful, they are able to quickly pair a negative feeling with a positive emotion, defuse a negative thought with a positive thought, and counter a negative memory with a positive one. If children supercharge positive emotion, the emotion or memory change is more permanent, making the residual effect more lasting.[63]

Optimal learning requires children to learn to summon positive replacement emotions and substitute them for negative ones. The structure, circuitry, and chemistry of the brain can change over the course of days and even hours. "In this way, the brain adjusts its performance and control of behavior in response to a changing environment."[64] Neuroscience researchers are clear in their belief that when children focus on positive emotions, this effort curtails the adverse learning effect of negative emotion.

Resilience: Finding Fortitude. Resilience is a brain strength associated with optimal learning and well-being that transforms courage and determination into grit. Children learn to turn off the neurological stress switch by clearing numerous biological pathways using their strengths to positively adapt. Children's brains endow them with a predisposition to optimism that minimizes negative experience and increases their ability to discard negative memories. The positive psychology teacher capitalizes on the ability to generate a positive outlook and develops lessons that teach fortitude.

In his work, Victor Frankl wrote that man needs a brave spirit to transcend the "fears and frailties of ordinary life."[65] When children are emotionally resilient, they are better able to stop the rush of negativity and replace it with courage, determination, and a resolute commitment to their personal best.[66] Children who can self-manage negative emotions and self-generate positive emotions will then bolster their resilience through neural reengineering. They find the inner fortitude to endure and to prevail over pain. As it turns out, children's brave spirits are found in the miraculous mechanisms of the brain.

The prefrontal cortex is the brain's transcendence center, able to forge resilience from discouragement using eight strengths. Children learn to (1) control the autonomic nervous system and stay calm until fear runs its course; (2) regulate emotions and not stifle grit with anger, guilt, or sadness; (3) remember that others have suffered and survived; (4) know that others understand; (5) rest, reflect, reassess, and regroup; (6) gain self-knowledge through insight; (7) use intuition to heal feelings; and (8) maintain integrity.[67] Using these strengths is the means to happiness because teaching positive psychology is like putting a learning life vest on children. Every time a flood of negative emotion drowns a child's neurological coping mechanisms, he can get his head above water and keep swimming toward the shore that he sees in his mind's eye.

Communicating Hopefulness, Compassion, Balance, and Grit. Language may be the brain's greatest strength, and it involves more than teaching children to spell words correctly or to conjugate verbs. Language is necessary to navigate academic, social, and emotional learning because no academic or emotional interaction or transaction can occur without it. Specialized lingual centers act as relay stations for feelings and thoughts, which are infused throughout the brain's linguistic system.[68]

Children communicate emotions mediated by their thoughts through their actions. A quick laugh, long talk, loud whistle, happy dance, or an angry tantrum all express emotion via thought to action. Without the brain's ability to produce the sophisticated language needed to communicate what children know and feel—and to mobilize actions around that knowledge and emotion—there is no collegiality, companionship, or friendship. There is no learning because language is the basis for all conceptual development. Children express what they know, do not know, and want to know with their verbal and nonverbal language. They write a poem, tell a story, dance, or draw a picture.

Language enables children to offer each other support and comfort in learning and in life. Language is the bridge to friendship. Having friends, and a sense of connectedness to school, reliably predicts school happiness and pleasure.[69] Lacking adequate language skills for expressing emotion, empathetic children cannot communicate feelings of caring, forgiveness, and generosity. Without language, children cannot share what they know about asteroids, what they understand about politics, how they feel about their best friend, or where to meet for lunch to resolve a conflict.

The teacher models for them the language of positive psychology. Grounded in neuroscience, language is one of the most important methods used to teach positive psychology. The teacher can use words that remind and redirect children's attention and focus toward positive emotions and strengths and away from a negative and critical landscape. She uses words carefully to convey positive emotions—and strengths—to scaffold children to the moderation of emotion and the practice of strength. Language elevates children to peak learning or deescalates learning by subduing their strengths. The teacher uses the language of positive psychology to teach children what they need to do to put disappointment behind them and look forward to a happier tomorrow. She uses that same language to teach them the self-talk, the private speech, that gives voice to an inner coach that speaks gently and firmly, and she banishes self-defeating talk.

Summary and Conclusion

Medicine, psychiatry, and psychology have long directed research and practice to reducing illness rather than improving mental health. Adopting this deficiency model, education uses high-stakes test data to punish shortcomings and thereby fails to acknowledge strengths and gains. Positive psychology offers educators a new and different option and is most concerned with the neuroscience-driven well-being data and is less concerned with software-driven test data.

For decades, scientists have known that the brain develops into specific subsystems or modules that perform standardized functions. However, from that point forward, the brain differentiates itself: it grows new cells, establishes connections, breaks them, and reestablishes them in an infinite, unique loop of learning and adaptation in response to experience. Positive neuroscience and positive psychology overlap: Both explain the biological and psychological development of positive cognitive and emotional strengths from simple to complex.

Teachers organize emotional and strengths learning from simple to complex as a feature of both positive psychology strength theory and neuroscience complexity theory. These theories state that the brain moves from less complex to more complex learning across all neural networks; some of these form quickly and easily, and some coalesce laboriously over time with much effort and practice. The brain's networks aggregate thresholds of strengths such as optimism, empathy, resilience, and more, to maximize flow and engagement with self and others in daily work and play. Neurobiology suggests that the highly complex cognitive function of practical wisdom evolves as cognitive and affective neural brain pathways increase over time.

Children are born to be wise; however, they must learn how to act wise. Wisdom is not something children ought to have—it is something all children *must* have to flourish.[70] Positive psychology teaches the will, or desire, to be more balanced and stronger in order to improve relationships, find meaning, and enjoy accomplishment. Positive psychology also teaches the skills to know exactly how to do so. Children learn how to animate cognitive, affective, and conative strengths that enable them to balance emotions, cultivate strengths, make friends, restore meaning, and accomplish tasks as well as contribute to the well-being of themselves, others, and the community. Strengths-based teaching remodels negative brain states so children believe that they can make change in their lives and assures that they have the tools necessary to achieve a sense of purpose and accomplishment.

Guiding Question Exercise

What do you think is the most important neuroscience concept in education? How does your experience in the classroom validate the importance of it? Do you think this concept confirms the importance of teaching positive psychology in the classroom? Give an example. What one general teaching method are you currently using that you could change to be more consistent with this neuroscience concept? Is there a specific method that you already use in your classroom that you could extend to the teaching of neuroscience of positive psychology? Do you deliver any lessons that teach the neuroscience of positive psychology? If you could tell other teachers to change a practice that is contrary to the neuroscience of positive psychology, what would it be? What are your reasons? What positive psychology benchmark would you teach: feeling, strength, friendship, or meaning, or would you embed them all? Is it helpful to teach children more about their brains? How would you plan to teach children about their brains? How do you think the children would respond and would they benefit? How would they benefit?

Guiding Question Discussion

The neuroscience concepts should inform teachers how and why to change long-standing practice that may not be compatible with the most recent and important neuroscience research. There are many educational practices that neuroscience suggests are, at best, not helpful and are, at worst, harmful to learning. There are misunderstandings about how children learn; the current neuroscience counters misinformation so that teachers can rely on 21st-century science.

Teachers strive to align new teaching methods and techniques with the most current, scientific knowledge. In the process, teachers should consider that elementary-aged children might benefit from learning about their brains, how they work, and how to take good care of the most important organ in the body. Children are always fascinated to learn about the body and if they understand their brain structure, they understand themselves and their own well-being better. There is excellent curriculum available that teaches children of all ages about the brain. Children can work online to complete research projects about brain facts, neurons, brain modules, and more. Children can create posters, view real brain scans, generate questions to ask online experts, enter an art contest, color pages with pictures of the brain, read a newsletter, watch videos, take a 3D tour of the brain, and play interactive games. The teacher shares the principles of positive psychology by using brain-based techniques, and he or she then invites the study of neuroscience.

Web Resources for Children

BBC Human Body and Mind, http://www.bbc.co.uk/science/human body/.

Discovery Channel Brain Anatomy, http://www.yourdiscovery.com/anatomiesof/brain/.

Exploratorium Minds, http://www.exploratorium.edu/explore/mind/.

Kids Health: Brain and Nervous System, http://kidshealth.org/kid/htbw/htbw_main_page.html

The Secret Life of the Brain, PBS video, http://www.pbs.org/wnet/brain/.

Web Resources for Teachers

BrainFacts, http://www.brainfacts.org.

Learning and the Brain, http://www.learningandthebrain.com/.

International Mind, Brain, and Education Society, http://www.imbes. org/.

Mind Matters, http://patwolfe.com/?pid=94/.

Neuroscience Educational Resources and Virtual Encyclopedia http://www.ndgo.net/sfn/nerve/ New Horizons for Learning, http://education.jhu.edu/newhorizons/

CHAPTER 3

THE TAXONOMY OF POSITIVE PSYCHOLOGY IN THE ELEMENTARY SCHOOL CLASSROOM

We do not act rightly because we are excellent—we achieve excellence by acting rightly.

—Plato

Children learn much more in school than long division and state capitals. They learn to make friends, to resolve disputes, to manage time, to look forward to summer vacations, to play soccer, to work as a team, to give compliments, to give insults, to give up, to keep trying, to forgive, to forget, to feel grateful, to feel embarrassed, and to find courage. They learn from all of the everyday experiences that occur within a classroom's walls. Children's learning is formal and informal, intentional and random, and deliberate and incidental. Given children's potential to learn to achieve their personal best or not, and to learn all things well or poorly, what are the teacher's goals in the classroom? What does the teacher want the children to learn? Positive psychology answers this question by offering a teaching taxonomy that is consistent with neuroscience facts and that focuses on the social emotional learning crucial to both academic and overall success.

Taxonomy is the science of categorizing related concepts; education taxonomies classify the content—or the subject taught. Defining and developing an educational taxonomy is the first step in building learning structure and content. Before the teacher can teach effectively, he must determine what to teach. Educational taxonomies that identify categories of learning and instructional goals generate a curricular map for the teacher to follow. While traditional educational taxonomies are primarily concerned with how to best teach subject-area content and how to build a child's academic knowledge—reading, writing, and 'rithmatic taxonomies also need to address what else to teach so as to develop well-rounded children who learn to thrive in school and throughout their adult lives.

Teachers understand that education must address more than the accumulation of subject-area knowledge only, and yet few taxonomies address the emotional variables of learning. A few teaching taxonomies do incorporate emotional education into the more traditional education taxonomy. However, these are often ad hoc efforts and almost always compartmentalize the cognitive and emotional aspects of learning.

The first affective learning taxonomy to consider emotional development as an educational goal was proposed as part of Benjamin Bloom's pioneering work describing the essential domains or types of learning: (1) cognitive or mental abilities; (2) affective or emotional attitudes; and (3) psychomotor or physical skills.[1] His taxonomy described affective education as emotionality in learning, and it included content, general methods, and specific techniques that emphasized the emotional ingredients of learning. "We use affect as a generic term to describe such phenomena as emotions, attitudes, beliefs, and moods."[2]

This affective taxonomy teaches the stages along a continuum from the simplest level to the most complex—from primary to intermediate. At the primary level, children simply receive the emotional content such as when they read positive stories or watch positive videos that teach general life lessons (but not specific techniques for well-being). This taxonomy suggests that visual, observational learning techniques, such as modeling, demonstration, and imitation, help children learn to recognize and sort out their feelings and strengths. At the more advanced level, children learn to actually analyze emotions and strengths and to consider how all of these impact behaviors and relationships. However, there is little information about the teaching approaches that transform emotion into strength. Too often, the emphasis is on simply teaching children what is socially acceptable and expected behavior. The teacher tries to motivate them to maintain the acceptable behavior—a narrow focus at best.

Thinking Actively in a Social Context (TASC) is a newer affective taxonomy that is consistent with a neuroeducational approach.[3] TASC goes beyond earlier taxonomies that only identify and analyze emotions emphasizing the development of the skills that underpin successful learning so that children are explicitly taught to listen actively, work with purpose and optimism, focus on others, react more thoughtfully, interact more cooperatively, and be more persistent. The TASC taxonomy points educators in the direction of an improved teaching taxonomy that addresses some aspects of social emotional learning. However, it also confirms the need for a taxonomy that goes much further to identify in much greater detail not only what to teach but also how to teach social emotional learning. For this reason, a positive psychology teaching taxonomy is the educational taxonomy of the future. Found at the intersection of neuroscience research and positive psychology theory, a positive psychology teaching taxonomy provides the instructional manual for teaching social emotional learning in ways that change children's responses at the biological level. A positive psychology taxonomy goes beyond identifying and processing emotion and strength in general terms to teach specific emotional self-help so children can triage emotions and apply emotional first aid to their emotional nicks and wounds, therefore promoting both healing and well-being.

The positive psychology principles are used as the basis to develop the positive psychology teaching taxonomy, and the taxonomy organizes an emotional literacy curriculum that benchmarks the five positive psychology principles, summarized in the acronym PERMA (Positive Emotions, Engagement Through Strengths, Relationships, Meaning, and Accomplishment—see Table 1.1).[4] Children learn to appreciate and use their positive emotional power to generate self-inflicted good.

When children learn positive emotions, outlooks, and attitudes, they can build strengths that insulate them from failure and defeat; deconstruct negative emotions that may impede learning, social relationships, or personal well-being; and manufacture their own happiness, no matter the circumstances. Using specific techniques, positive psychology teaches the inner strength needed to overcome obstacles with confidence and so to progress academically and socially. The use of individual strengths in learning is like building a sturdy structure with the blocks of emotional competence. Just as children put one block on top of the other to build a tall tower, they become the architects of their own emotional infrastructure.

Teaching friendship builds a foundation that allows children to make and maintain the social support systems that are essential to their own happiness and development by thinking about others' thoughts and feelings, developing kindness and empathy, and growing a rewarding connection to their classroom community and beyond. Friendship is the proving ground of strength, and it accelerates emotional maturation by making children stronger in every way.

Teaching meaning transforms a classroom from a place of dull chores and rote learning to a place where children may learn the same academic material but feel fulfilled having learned it, because they were taught to draw connections with the material and to apply those connections to their own lives, especially their emotional lives. Children remember best what they learn by heart.

Finally, teaching accomplishment teaches pride in both the work product and the work ethic, so children will value the process as much as the result. Even when children fail, having put forth the effort, they learn to create a reservoir of positive emotion and strength that they call upon when faced with a new challenge or adversity: "No matter what happens I will feel proud that I tried." The joy of accomplishment is the high-watermark in positive psychology, whether it emanates from the pursuit or attainment of the goal.

The Benchmarks of the Positive Psychology Teaching Taxonomy

Teaching Positive Emotion and the Pleasant Life. The first benchmark in the taxonomy is positive emotion. Children learn to take control of their emotional states by consciously choosing whether or not to employ strategies to replace negative emotions with positive ones. They learn to connect their good and bad moods to their positive and negative emotions, and they begin to readily exchange one for the other as with baseball trading cards. Younger children become self-aware of their emotions and the emotions of others, and they change their moods accordingly. Older children acquire a deeper self-understanding of emotion and learn to deliberatively assess, monitor, and alter their emotions. Children learn to feel caring, not angry; grateful, not resentful; brave, not afraid; determined, not discouraged; hopeful, not apathetic; and relaxed, not stressed. They learn to appreciate the power of a positive feeling to supplant a negative one and learn that what they think determines how they feel. They learn that they can change the way that they feel by changing what they think and tell themselves.

Teaching Positive Engagement Through Strength and the Good Life. The second benchmark of the taxonomy is the virtue that helps children to identify and practice strength as the basis for engagement in learning and life. Positive emotions emerge over time as a signature or adaptive strength and such emotions help children to fully engage in learning despite any impediments. The ability to engage through strength is emotional capital that children can earn and spend in the pursuit of a good and ethical life. Daniel Goleman writes that children must learn to find, cultivate, and rely on their inner strength—their empathy, grit, or calm.[5] "The good life is hard work and there are no shortcuts to sustained happiness."[6] Happiness depends on engagement through strength.

Teaching Positive Relationships and the Connected Life. The third benchmark is the friendship that invites children to use positive emotions and strengths to make and keep friends. Children who share their positive emotions and signature strengths with others are better equipped to develop and sustain positive relationships over time. Those friendships, in turn, build foundation skills that not only provide children with the social support systems that they need to succeed but also require them to think about others' thoughts and feelings, develop kindness and empathy, and grow a fulfilling connection to others that goes beyond superficial interactions. Children with friends go to school with anticipation and enthusiasm, and while at school, they use positive emotions and strengths to demonstrate forgiveness, appreciation, loyalty, commitment, support, and enjoyment. They learn that they do not have to always be the most right, the best dressed, the first, the smartest, or the richest to be a good friend, and they learn that the value of true friendship is priceless.

Teaching Positive Meaning and the Purposeful Life. The fourth benchmark is meaningful learning so that children invest emotionally, and more fully, in the learning process. Children use their emotions and strengths to connect to their studies in a purposeful way that transforms a classroom from a place of dull chores and rote learning to a place where children may learn the same academic material, but they feel energized learning it because they make emotional connections with the material. Most important, children learn to apply what they learn to their own lives, especially their emotional lives, to generate meaning. Positive psychology teaches meaning as synonymous with practical wisdom or the "will and the skill" to do well.[7] The will of practical wisdom is the desire to do well because we connect what we learn to our own feelings, strengths, relationships, and goals.

The skill of practical wisdom is the ability to recognize and accept failure as the only path to success, and children learn to reflect on why they failed and decide what they can do differently the next time. They vest disappointment and failure with meaning and grow up to be more emotionally rugged and durable. They do not take action based on a failed past and instead they take action based on a resolve to create a different future and create new meaning. As a result of learned wisdom, children discover that it is a worthy purpose in itself to be tolerant, helpful, respected and to show fortitude, maintain balance, and share inspiration not only when they succeed, but also especially when they fail. Practical wisdom is using their will to make a difference in their lives and the lives of others, as well as using their skills or strengths, such as optimism or grit, to succeed.

Teaching Positive Accomplishments and the Contented Life. The final benchmark considers the seminal accomplishment of positive psychology as the ability to tame emotion and elicit the strengths that result in cooperation, contentment, confidence, resiliency, joy, and peacefulness in learning and life. Accomplishment can be intra-individual, culminating in the pleasure of playing the piano, or it can be inter-individual, resulting in the satisfaction of helping others get the project done on time. Accomplished children must develop strength of both mind and heart because the emotional strengths of the heart, such as determination, are even more important to success than are the cognitive virtues of the mind such as creativity.[8] The flow of optimal emotional experience invigorates accomplishment[9] and teaching the art of Metta Bhavana,[10] or lovingkindness, cultivates the joy of living and celebrates the joy of learning. Lovingkindness predicts optimal emotional flow that is the emotional current of accomplishment, because whatever children do out of lovingkindness they do willingly and skillfully.

A Positive Psychology Teaching Taxonomy Matrix: Benchmarks and Indicators

What does it mean to teach positive psychology? What does positive psychology teach? The five benchmarks of positive psychology are the core knowledge of the taxonomy. The taxonomy identifies the common methods and specific techniques used to teach the five benchmarks so that students learn to live a pleasant life, a good life, a connected life, a meaningful life, and an accomplished life. The taxonomy delineates the positive emotions and strengths needed to foster friendship, engender meaning, and support accomplishment as the capstone outcomes of positive psychology.

The benchmarks have worthy outcomes that not only are likely to increase academic performance and well-being but also bring children more satisfaction so that their school days are happier. If the positive psychology emotions and strength lessons are well learned, children are able to better listen to themselves and others, be a good friend, understand all lessons as life lessons, cooperate more with the teacher, take tests more confidently, try harder to earn better grades, and emerge as more contented, peaceful, and joyful learners.

The Positive Psychology Teaching Taxonomy Matrix (see Table 3.1) summarizes the core knowledge, using the taxonomy implemented across the full learning spectrum. The taxonomy identifies essential emotions and strengths across five taxonomy benchmarks and associated indicators across a continuum delineating the expected strengths-based outcomes so the teacher is able to identify what to teach. The teacher uses the matrix as the basis to plan lessons that teach the posi-

Table 3.1. Positive Psychology Teaching Taxonomy Matrix: Benchmarks and Indicators

Positive Emotion	Engagement Strengths	Relationships Friendship	Meaning Contribution	Accomplish Success
Feeling Indicators	Strength Indicators	Friendship Indicators	Contribution Indicators	Success Indicators
Feel Caring/Kindly Not Angry	Demonstrate Empathy	Offer Forgiveness	Value Tolerance	Embrace Cooperation
Feel Grateful Not Selfish	Demonstrate Generosity	Offer Gratitude	Value Helpfulness	Embrace Contentment
Feel Brave Not Afraid	Demonstrate Courage	Offer Honesty	Value Fairness	Embrace Confidence
Feel Determined Not Unsure	Demonstrate Grit	Offer Commitment	Value Resilience	Embrace Fortitude
Feel Calm/Relaxed Not Frustrated	Demonstrate Patience	Offer Support	Value Peace	Embrace Serenity
Feel Hopeful Not Discouraged	Demonstrate Optimism	Offer Enthusiasm	Value Anticipation	Embrace Inspiration
Feel Happy Not Sad	Demonstrate Good Cheer	Offer Gladness	Value Enjoyment	Embrace Joy

tive psychology benchmarks, and indicators, discretely or as connected units that scaffold children from positive feeling to accomplishment in a systematic way.

Some teachers choose to teach the benchmarks, and associated indicators, of positive emotion, engaged strength, friendship skills, meaningful outcomes, and capstone accomplishments horizontally across the teaching taxonomy while others teach vertically down it. The teacher uses the benchmarks and indicators to teach children the positive emotions that prompt enduring strength, which invites friendship and meaning to life. The taxonomy aggregates into cooperation, contentment, confidence, fortitude, serenity, inspiration, and joy of accomplishment, all of which make life worthwhile.

In this way, the teacher who begins by teaching children about their feelings ends with children who demonstrate significant emotional accomplishment. The six feelings identified in the teaching taxonomy matrix are the ones most often found in the positive psychology literature. The research suggests that children who are able to feel more caring, more grateful, more determined, more relaxed, more hopeful, and more confident are better able to fully engage in learning and achieve more academic success.[11] However, for these positive emotions to manifest themselves, especially when children are under demand and stress, they must displace the opposite negative emotion. Children who are uninterested in completing assignments must decide to be more determined; children who are angry waiting their turn must decide to be more caring; and children who are afraid to give a speech must decide to be more brave. Osmosis does not enable children to simply absorb strength, although watching successful performances and imitating role models definitely helps. Still, there is no magical day when children just wake up being more hopeful, grateful, and patient.

There is magic in strengths training because emotions that are managed and practiced well morph into adaptive and, eventually, enduring strengths. Just as some children can carry a tune, some can read with prosody, and some can do math in their heads, children have different signature emotional strengths. While some children will always be the best readers, all children can learn to read; while some children will start off singing a song without missing a note, all children can learn to sing. This same positive psychology principle applies to emotional strengths. While some children are naturally more caring, all children can be taught to be more empathetic and show more forgiveness to their friends.

As with singing and reading, practice causes the strength to take root and become a more automatic response and deliberate action. If children can transform an occasional feeling of hopefulness into the persistent strength of optimism, they can rehearse their way to a greater sense of determination and enjoyment of learning and life. Strengths-based teaching yields exponential results, and learned strengths ripple into all areas of the classroom and change every interaction and transaction in the classroom for the better.

Positive psychology teaches that when emotion fuses with strength, it is transgenic and emerges as an accomplishment that changes lives. Emotional strength is a developmental trait that is transformative when it is tested in the classroom. Positive psychology explains how a particular strength positively affects relationships. For example, children who are more empathetic are more forgiving. Empathy breeds forgiveness and eventually translates to a larger, and more complete, understanding of self and others.

> Jake insulted Mike and wanted to shout back at him. Then he reminded himself that Jake had told him at the start of the week that his dad had just lost his job. Mike understood that Jake might feel very angry and afraid and that the name-calling might have nothing to do with him. Mike just walked away and decided that tomorrow he would ask Jake how his dad was doing. The next day when he did express his concern, Jake looked grateful and apologized to Mike for the name-calling.

A larger understanding of an event invites different interpretations of the event, and this enlarged perspective creates more tolerance for all people. The enlarged vision changes how children treat others and how they think about themselves. As they develop more tolerance, they find intrinsic meaning in the act itself and they find something that is larger than the self, that improves relationships, and that imparts authentic meaning.

A Positive Psychology Teaching Taxonomy: Methods and Techniques

Once a teacher determines what to teach, she or he turns to methods of teaching it. After identifying the core knowledge of the taxonomy, the pedagogy that delivers the lessons and activities is considered. Four general educational methods serve as the blueprint for teaching positive psychology: (1) language of emotions and strengths; (2) infused academics; (3) visual and performing arts; and (4) strengths training exercises. Within these general categories of educational methods, whether using all or some of them, there are endless possibilities for teaching the benchmarks and indicators.

Each of these four methods is associated with specific techniques that integrate positive psychology into the classroom curriculum. The 12 specific techniques that are in the Teacher's Toolbox prescribe how to teach the taxonomy. They include (1) class greetings; (2) class meetings; (3) class pledges, creeds, and agreements; (4) reflective journals; (5) clubs and teams; (6) learning centers; (7) service learning; (8) e-learning; (9) art, dance, drama, and music; (10) visualization and observation; (11) self-assessment and self-awareness; and (12) self-talk and stress reduction. In the following chapters, the teacher learns how to use these techniques as the best means to teach the positive psychology taxonomy and its benchmarks.

Method 1—Language of Emotions and Strengths

Language is the basis for everything the teacher does. Language permeates all learning and all interaction in the class, whether the subject is art or math or social studies, and it is one of the most powerful tools for modeling and introducing the benchmarks. Yet language is one of the most underexamined aspects of a teacher's interaction with students. A teacher may devote many hours in carefully developing lesson plans to teach long division, but no time to thinking about how his or her own attitudes are revealed and imparted.

A teacher may make an offhand comment to a student like, "You never pay attention" or "You're so much better at reading than fractions." She may forget it immediately. However, the message to the child and the others listening—that the child never pays attention and cannot learn to get better at fractions—will remain ever-present. On the other hand, the power of language harnesses positive emotion to encourage and motivate children's abilities. The teacher models language of virtue so that children learn to know, describe, and encourage a feeling or a virtue when they see it: "You were very helpful to let Cindy go ahead of you in line. You are a caring friend." Even when used to make a strength correction, negative language either explicit or implicit is not used. Instead, children focus on the strength: "Do you think that was a patient response?"

The language of emotions and strengths goes well beyond positive praise. Positive psychology strategically uses language to identify, explain, and share emotions and strengths as the bridge to friendship, meaning, and accomplishment. When teaching positive psychology, the teacher consistently and constantly uses words that remind and redirect children rather than criticize them.[12] "You must not feel very hopeful if you stopped trying to finish the work." "You really seem to care about her feelings and you showed empathy for her situation." "You seem grateful that you did well on the test and I noticed that you showed appreciation for your own math talent by helping those who did not do as well."

Using carefully selected words to convey a message of positive emotion and strength, and to correct a negative emotion or action, is a crucial aspect of positive psychology. The teacher models the language of emotion and strength so children learn how to express and describe a feeling or strength when they see it. Both the teacher and children use precise language that articulates emotion, strength, friendship, and meaning in ways that share emotional knowledge and understandings about themselves and others.

The four primary techniques that teach the language of positive psychology to children are class greetings; class meetings; class pledges, creeds, and agreements; and reflective journals. Each of these techniques helps children to learn to think about their actions differently: they see their actions not as bad or good but as evidence of a positive emotion or strength—or not. These techniques offer children the opportunity to hear, imitate, practice, and exchange the language of emotions and strengths in the classroom. They greet each other by acknowledging emotions, meet with each other discussing how to manage those emotions, pledge to balance their emotions, and write about how their efforts made their friends happy, made them feel proud, or helped win the race.

1. Class Greetings

Class greetings offer an opportunity to set the tone for the day. The teacher meets and greets children at the door at the start of the school day and bids goodnight at the end of the day. Rather than just make casual comments, she uses greetings as an opportunity to model positive emotions and to connect positive psychology principles directly to children's lives. In the good morning ritual, she comments on children's emotions, virtues, friendships, contributions, and accomplishments.

The teacher greets a child by saying, "Good morning, Sarah. I noticed you were helpful making good suggestions to your group last week. It shows that you really appreciate their effort on the food pyramid project. Your team seems more confident about the work now." Her words convey empathy by showing the teacher is thinking about how the child feels and her work by noticing the child's effort. In the afternoon, the teacher may customize the good-bye with personal details of a child's out-of-classroom life. In this way, the teacher builds rapport with the child, convinces the child that the teacher is paying special attention to her, and models how a child might use personal attentiveness to initiate and maintain close relationships.

The teacher may tell an individual child, "Please tell your grandmother that I am grateful that she is home from the hospital now. When you told the class about her trip to the hospital, I felt sad, but it made me feel better to hear you share your story and know that the rest of the class was there to offer reassurance and share their own stories with you. Maybe tomorrow you can tell everyone how much better she is doing." Teaching children how to connect matters.

The teacher may greet the entire class by telling them, "Wow, you all made it to school through the pouring rain! You must have really wanted to come to read the last chapter of Harry Potter together. *Harry Potter and the Sorcerer's Stone* is my favorite, too. My car had trouble starting this morning. I almost didn't make it here either, but then I thought about how disappointed you would all be if I was not here to read you the rest of the story, so I tried again."

At the close of the day, the teacher tells the class, "I truly appreciate how hard you all worked on collecting canned goods for the food kitchen as part of your food pyramid projects. I feel satisfied knowing that so many people will be able to enjoy a better Thanksgiving because of your work. I am reminded of how grateful I am for my favorite foods and favorite students, too!" The teacher begins and ends the class by reminding children of how to use the language of positive psychology. She notes children's emotions, strengths, relationships, contributions, and accomplishments. The teacher sets the tone at the beginning of the day and provides closure at the day's end. In the hours in between, the teacher uses the toolbox to teach positive psychology.

2. Class Meetings

Teachers structure class or group meetings as stand-alone meetings to address emotional learning topics or to teach academic subjects while promoting social relationships among students. The teacher conducts class meetings that invite children to actively participate in building shared trust, responsibility, and governance in the classroom.

Glasser suggested classroom meetings in concert with his school choice theory[13] and they are a perfect vehicle to teach the principles and practices of positive psychology. There are many different types of classroom meetings. Glasser described three types of class meetings: the sharing meeting, the problem-solving meeting, and the curricular meeting. However, there are endless varieties and applications. A thorough review of the academic literature describes ten types of classroom meetings: (1) open circle sharing meetings, (2) problem-solving meetings, (3) conflict-resolution meetings, (4) interview meetings, (5) curricular meetings, (6) literature circles, (7) recognition and appreciation meetings, (8) game meetings, (9) suggestion-box meetings, and (10) goal-setting meetings.

A classroom meeting is a flexible tool tailored to the needs of the class or the teacher's individual style. A teacher may utilize a structured or unstructured meeting style and may adjust the purpose of the meetings to meet the class's needs, either by using a meeting as a stand-alone platform to discuss emotions or by using it as part of the academic curriculum. A teacher may organize a structured meeting in which the teacher or the children identify a goal, activities, and expected outcomes, creating a mini-circle lesson. For example, the teacher may bring the first-grade class together to read a story in the circle. The teacher engages the children in the story by asking questions about the character's feelings, strengths, and dilemmas. In every instance, the teacher processes children's understandings of emotions and strength at every chance.

In contrast to a structured academic meeting, the meeting may simply invite children to share whatever is on their minds. The intention of the more unstructured, open-ended meeting is to share thoughts, feelings, and any other general matters of individual or mutual interest or concern. The meeting focuses on increasing self-awareness and knowledge of feelings, strengths, and connections between self and others rather than academic knowledge or skill.

Class meetings are a collaborative and systematic way of teaching positive psychology and exploring children's feelings, strengths, friendships, service, and mastery. Meeting structure, intentions, times, formats, activities, and purposes vary widely, depending on many different variables including the age of children, type of meeting, and frequency of the meeting. The meeting is often a daily circle meeting held at a fixed time, and it ranges from 15 minutes to an hour. Many teachers conduct morning meetings and some conduct short meetings at both the start and end of the school day. Regardless of the frequency or duration of the meeting, consistency is crucial. Occasional or sporadic meetings do not work well. Most important, the teacher conceives the meeting as being a circle of friends teaching each other how to understand and help each other.

3. Class Pledges, Creeds, and Agreements

Pledges, creeds, and agreements are ways in which children can set goals, plan actions, pursue objectives, and achieve results, all while building a connection and cohesiveness with the class or group that has made the same pledge. A pledge is often a narrative, sometimes a poem, found or written by the class. A pledge is collaboratively developed and replaces classroom rules, encouraging children to articulate positive intentions and dedicate themselves to the collective good rather than to simply comply with regulations.

In the positive psychology classroom, a pledge is a formal class goal that contains a summary of best intentions that codifies and practices the language of positive psychology so that children become personally and emotionally invested in the pledge's ritual and goals. The public pronouncement of expectation strengthens children's devotion to the goal and introduces engagement as a formal process.

Pledges or agreements promote a child's sense of control over his own behavior and so are intrinsically motivating. By agreeing to do something, children are implicitly acknowledging that they can do it. By agreeing as a class, the children develop an instant support system consisting of others with common goals so they are more likely to work together to achieve goals and support each other. A pledge may mean the difference between seeing a goal through to the end and giving up midway. Writing a pledge encourages children to work together to develop their own goals. By asking children to identify and verbalize what they want to accomplish by the end of the year, the end of the month, the end of the week, or on a daily basis, children learn emotional and academic planning and communication skills. They learn to think ahead about what they can actually accomplish in a week or a month and what might take longer.

The teacher uses the pledge to direct the children to develop plans for accomplishing the goal within the time frame—what should children do by the end of this week? What do the children need to do by next month? Teaching the children how to break down a goal into smaller steps builds invaluable planning skills that children apply to other aspects of their education. Finally, the fulfillment of the pledge links directly to children's day-to-day accomplishments, providing a valuable lesson about the interrelations among commitment, effort, and success. The failure to fulfill the pledge is also a key learning opportunity.

The best pledges also include goals that are not entirely results-oriented but include goals that are entirely within a child's control—give a compliment to another child, replace a negative thought with a positive thought, or finish the science fair project. With these types of pledges, even if the child fails to offer a compliment on a particular day, the teacher emphasizes that there is always another opportunity to do it tomorrow. The teacher offers all children a fresh start daily.

The pledge occurs as part of a morning or afternoon ceremony or celebration that acknowledges children's efforts to uphold the pledge, and this also involves singing the class song or cheering on the class mascot. Children can measure their accomplishments against the ideals that the children pledge to uphold, and this is the most important standard to teach. It is a standard of emotional reaction and strengths action that is self-imposed.

4. Reflective Journals

Children can use reflective journals to develop an understanding of, and control over, their emotional lives as well as to use as a good example of how to infuse academic learning with positive psychology education. They provide a good opportunity for children to explore how they feel and to record events from their own lives—a topic that is always interesting to children—and the journals also can be used in language arts practice for organizing thoughts, expressing written ideas clearly, and penmanship or word processing.

The teacher provides children with journals to make daily, reflective entries, and each child uses it to write about feelings, strengths, family, friends, trials, tribulations, and joys. When children enter the classroom each morning or at the end of the day, they spend at least 15 minutes writing in their reflective journals. When using the journals, the teacher has great latitude and may create structured lessons or may simply allow children to write what they feel.

Young children might complete simple sentences the teacher prompts, such as "The time I was most afraid was when _____". "Once my friend made me angry because _____". Older children may write a longer narrative in response: "If I were to describe my favorite day it would be _____". Once children have expressed their thoughts, the teacher can lead them to discuss their entries. Children practice oral and written communication skills and articulate insights they acquire about their own and others' emotional lives.

Alternatively, the teacher can read the entries and ask children to explore what they have written in more depth. "I understand how you felt that time when you were most afraid because you got lost in the mall because I get afraid when I'm lost, too, especially when I'm driving alone at night. How did you get through it? What did you tell yourself when you realized you were lost? Now that it is over, what would you do if you got lost again? Do you think you would be as scared? What would you tell me to do if I got lost?"

Reflective journal writing also quiets children's thoughts and teaches them to use writing for the primary purpose of meaningful communication. Children use journal writing as a springboard for the contemplation of feelings and strengths and the effect these have on their relationships, efforts, and accomplishments. The language of positive psychology flows through the journal and offers the teacher an opportunity to expand and extend the ideas and dialogue in important ways. Whether it is a traditional paperbound journal or an e-journal, reflective writing gives children the opportunity to chronicle feelings, strengths, setbacks, and accomplishments. Children process, report, consider, assess, imagine, and publish their thoughts and feelings regarding how they feel, how they are strong, how they help friends, what matters to them, and what they have accomplished. They learn to listen to their inner narratives. Children also use the journal process to address positive psychology benchmarks.

Children write about the pleasant life by describing a favorite toy, the good life by drawing a favorite park, the connected life by introducing a favorite person, the meaningful life by reviewing a favorite book, and the accomplished life by analyzing a poem. Journals contain words, notes, lists, essays, letters, doodles, drawings, stickers, mementos, such as pressed leaves and old tickets, favorite quotes, and affirmations: they contain the best and worst of experiences, imaginings, and unique interpretations. A journal is a personal and emotional account of what is important and valued.

Method 2—Infused Academics

Positive psychology techniques do not segment academic and emotional learning; instead, the teacher uses an academic subject and topic to teach the benchmarks of positive psychology in an integrated way. In literature, history, science, geography, and even mathematics, there are rich opportunities to teach about the emotional life. Fifth-grade students read the narrative poem "The Midnight Ride of Paul Revere"[14] and write a report about the emotions they would have felt riding through the dark at night to warn friends of impending danger. They discuss the strengths that Revere demonstrated, such as courage and grit. Younger children read and discuss the book *The Good in Me from A–Z*[15] and make a class mural that illustrates the good in each of them by filling the mural with words and drawings about their signature strengths.

Unfortunately, traditional academic taxonomies often neglect or short-change academic and emotional learning even though emotions and strengths taught along with academic content yield great benefit. Academic teaching does not limit the study of emotions and strengths; it enhances it because emotional memory is more permanent and children are most curious about themselves, others, and their place in the world.

Young children write poems about their happiest or saddest day to enter in a poetry contest. Older children plan a week's menu of healthy, low-cost meals for a local shelter nearby. As they write, they consider their own gratefulness for the food they eat, and they cultivate a sensibility of gratitude. They learn nutrition, mathematics, problem solving and planning, and the ability to express appreciation for the gifts in their lives by repaying their good fortune. Increased academic achievement is the objective of all education, and social emotional learning contributes to it greatly. At every academic juncture, the teacher can take an emotional learning turn and begin an expedition that teaches about emotion and strength.

There are many techniques used to teach academic subjects and the positive psychology teaching taxonomy benchmarks conjointly.

Whether organized as cooperative, interactive learning groups or as independent, self-directed learning, the techniques promote authentic, interdisciplinary, meaningful, and project-based learning. They include clubs and teams, learning centers, service learning, and e-learning.

5. Clubs and Teams

The teacher creates a menu of clubs and the subjects taught in the club that teach both academic and emotional content, which encourage the practice of emotions and strengths in a social setting. There is no limit to the nature, purpose, type, and organization of clubs. The most successful are linked to academic standards and children's assessed interests. Some popular clubs concentrate on, but are by no means limited to, math, weather, music, art, dinosaurs, space, chess, sports, nutrition, travel, coins, stamps, nature, insects, exercise, Legos, cooking, and pets.

The ideal cooperative learning group is the classroom club. The mathematics and chess clubs can tackle hard problems and prove their persistence. Later club members can teach other children how to play chess. Immersed in the study of weather disasters around the globe, the weather club can discuss how survivors of a tornado must feel and what could be done to keep safe during a tornado.

Some clubs are organized around emotional themes such as the happiness club, where the children read books about happiness, discuss what makes people happy, learn happy songs to hum to themselves when in a bad mood, and create a happiness scrapbook with drawings of their favorite memories to recall when they need a morale boost. They can blow bubbles and make a wish before the bubble pops.

Older children can be in the heroes club and read about heroes in myths, legends, fables, and fairy tales. All the children especially love stories about animal heroes, and they read the newspaper every week to find local community heroes such as firefighters, soldiers, and police officers. The club also plans a bulletin board about heroes and a class hero's day when they will invite local heroes to visit. They make certificates to give to a family hero and consider what strengths they themselves need to be an everyday hero. As one of the club members said, "I figured out that heroes are people who sometimes do what they don't really want to do, what they are afraid to do, or simply the right thing. They are not just brave. They are caring about others."

In the book club, children study the emotions and strengths of heroes and villains by reading books with themes of interest to them, discussing the books, writing about the characters' emotions, and talking about how they handle similar events in their own lives. They write stories about an imaginary surprise party planned for a friend or what they would do if they found a $100 bill.

All clubs provide opportunities for intrapersonal and interpersonal accomplishments. The club members are excited be a like-minded group pursuing a common interest. The children select one club for the entire year. They rotate monthly through the other elective clubs. One student tells everyone, "I love my math, book, and art clubs. In the clubs, we learn our subjects, we talk about important problems, and solve them together. My art club taught me to be a calmer person because I used to have an anger problem. I am excited to choose my new clubs for next month. I love coming to school now and I am learning a lot more in my clubs than I did before."

The teacher helps children to process the emotional content of what they study and to connect emotionally to what they learn. Working with others in clubs shifts their perspective and enlarges their vision while having fun and learning to read, write, draw, think, calculate, and problem solve. Children do not have to sit in rows and fill out worksheets in order to learn academically.

6. Learning Centers

A learning center is a designated, multipurpose area of the classroom where children engage in self-organized and self-directed learning independently or in small groups. A learning center may be an acceleration center or an enrichment center that facilitates deep learning either in small groups or autonomously. "Deep learning is learning that takes root in our apparatus of understanding and in the embedded meanings that define us and that we use to define the world."[16] The teacher may use the center as a formal and central part of the curriculum by constructing learning centers that encompass academic subjects, like a science center. The teacher may structure the class so that all children move from center to center in small groups on a schedule, or the teacher may use the centers as a supplement to formal classes for enrichment or remediation as needed.

A learning center may also work as a positive psychology center to teach children how to manage intense emotions and as an effective alternative to a punitive timeout. Children can use a relaxation center to learn how to use strengths to manage emotions. Younger children may use the center to make button art: they make "angry" buttons and "calm" buttons to put on their desks. The next time they have an angry feeling, they can push the "calm" button. One little boy said, "I really need to push the calm button when someone pushes my angry button."

An older child may use the center to write a letter of remorse apologizing for hurt feelings caused by an angry incident or dispute. She can then deliver the letter personally with a heartfelt verbal apology, too. All the children use the center to reflect on, and correct, impulsive actions. They read books about anger and learn how others manage it calmly, use charts to track it, and complete exercises that help them learn to replace anger with caring. At the intermediate level, the teacher might use the center to teach conflict resolution and negotiation skills.

In every center, there should be a sign-in and sign-out form, a timer, and a checklist of activities to complete. Each child should have a plastic bin in which to keep any materials that he or she uses, collects, or creates. No matter how the teacher conceives or uses them, the centers are always workstations where children learn to be more optimistic or empathetic. Learning centers are one of the most efficient ways to teach all of the benchmarks of positive psychology.

7. Service Learning

The National Clearinghouse for Service Learning defines service learning as when young people—from kindergarteners to college students—learn to use the knowledge and skills acquired in the classroom to solve real-life problems.[17] Service learning teaches children to practically apply their studies and become active community helpers. The practical application of knowledge and skill through service learning demonstrates competency and accomplishment, teaching children how to build strengths through service.

First-grade children get to know their bus drivers and then plan ways to show appreciation for the drivers' work. The second grade works on a school beautification project. The third grade considers how to improve playground safety, the fourth grade writes to elders at a nearby nursing home, and the fifth grade plants a community garden. Children benefit from working with role models and mentors who assist them as they develop the strengths and skills needed to contribute in real, meaningful ways to the welfare of others while increasing their own academic knowledge and emotional well-being. Service learning is a personal and powerful way to teach the benchmarks of positive psychology, and it is relatively easy to implement in the elementary classroom. There is a growing body of evidence that children's happiness and well-being tend to increase after they help and support others.[18] Service to classmates and the school is a good place to start.

Service learning has the greatest benefit in school when it is directly connected to the academic curriculum, meets a real need, requires reflection, matches the abilities and skills of the children to the project, and recognizes children's service-learning accomplishments in formal ways. "It seems clear that a hallmark of the positive psychology approach is active student engagement both in the classroom and in the community."[19]

Some students had the following observations. "I felt like I was really helping my school by picking up the trash with my friends every day and it was amazing to chart the amount and different kinds of trash we found." "I used my allowance to buy stickers for the first grader I am tutoring. She was so happy when I gave her a sticker for reading all the new words correctly." "When I go to the animal shelter, I play with a little kitty who jumped out of a window and broke both of her front legs. She has these little casts on her legs, and if I ever break a bone, I will try to be as brave as that little kitty."

During another project, children plan a whole-school hallway sale and sell toys, clothes, books, games, and more that they no longer need. They organize, inventory, price, advertise, account, and manage all aspects of the sale. All of the proceeds go to children in the school who need help and write mini-grants to receive it.

Positive psychology emphasizes learning with a purpose and learning as a search for personal meaning that is encouraged, facilitated, and supported by the teacher who invites children to brainstorm service-learning ideas, develop purposeful goals, plan the implementation schedule, evaluate their success, and reflect on how the experience changed them and others.

8. E-learning

E-learning offers new ways to teach positive emotions and strengths in ways that are colorful and intrinsically motivating. There is an e-curriculum that includes formal lessons as well as informal activities and games that teach children how to manage emotions, build their strengths for friendship, plan service projects, and more.

Second-grade children can use the Journey North: Tracking the Migration of Butterflies[20] curriculum website where they track butterflies and discuss transformation, survival, and resiliency. The group focuses on the science of metamorphosis; as they study Monarch butterflies, the children apply the concept of metamorphosis to their own development. They write about how to learn, shed their old emotional selves, and build new, stronger ones in a never-ending process of personal discovery.

Older children learn human anatomy and physiology from the Discovery Channel by using the Human Body's Learning Experience curriculum website and working together to complete a puzzle that depicts the heart and lungs working at full power in order to escape a fire.[21] After they complete the puzzle, they discuss how the body reacts to stress.

The teacher can use e-learning lessons and games as stand-alone curricula with individual children or with children working in pairs or in a group. On a weekly basis, children get a menu of web-based emotional learning activities, exercises, and games. Throughout the week, they complete as many of the e-learning tasks as possible. They also complete evaluation checklists rating and commenting on the lessons and activities. Younger children use stickers to rate the activity, and older children produce written reviews about what they learned and how they benefited. Every Friday is designated positive psychology e-learning day: The younger children work online by using a Sneetches Writing activity[22] and then drawing and writing about a favorite picnic or outdoor party. They can share their work at a picnic lunch and learn more about each other's favorite memories of picnics and outdoor parties.

Older children complete a Harry Potter character analysis and have a long list of games to play, starting with the Repel a Dementor game on the Scholastic Harry Potter website.[23] The children list the strengths that they would need to repel a dementor, with much joking.

All children can participate in emotional learning games that the teacher has planned for the whole class by using a smartboard. The teacher's job is to identify and teach e-lessons about emotion, strength, and friendship and then to process those lessons with the children.

Method 3—Visual and Performing Arts

Too often, children learn the arts as compartmentalized subjects and focus only on formal artistic lessons intended to teach them to paint or play the trumpet. Sometimes, the children do not study art at all because budget cuts do not allow for the proper materials. However, this does not preclude an elementary teacher from introducing art, dance, drama, and music into the classroom. The arts teach and reinforce positive psychology lessons as well as academic lessons. The visual and performing arts are a very effective way to infuse the positive psychology teaching taxonomy into the curriculum and to meet the benchmarks and standards. Art, dance, drama, and music are the elixir of well-being.

9. Art, Dance, Drama, and Music

Children engage in art, dance, drama, and music naturally and happily. Integrating these activities into the general classroom improves academic learning, and studies show that the patterns of art, the freedom of dance, the vibrancy of drama, and the melodies of music have a powerful, positive impact on overall learning and well-being.[24] These activities imprint universal patterns on the brain that are similar to the patterns found in language, reading, literature, mathematics, science, and more.[25] These activities also express universal emotions and strengths, and the teacher can help children to process the emotional content.

Children study and create art that expresses their emotions; by doing this they connect the emotional messages found in art, dance, drama, and music to their personal experiences. They find museum photographs that represent particular emotions and they listen to a thundering symphony play. Transforming reading into drama, children can act out emotional scenes that portray complex emotions and strengths. They can dance folk dances from around the world.

Younger children can take a virtual trip to an art museum and find paintings that evoke how they feel today and explain why they feel those emotions when they see the paintings. An older child can research an artist's life and create a brochure about the artist's work, emotions, special talents, and strengths. Children explore and evaluate truth, beauty, and goodness through personal engagement with the visual and performing arts.

Art can also serve as a release for emotions, transfiguring them along the way so children are better able to share emotions that are hard to verbalize. The healing found in music, the comfort found in a favorite film, the joy found in dance, and the beauty found in art are essential to helping children understand and connect to their positive and negative emotional lives. A happy classroom is full of children who are drawing, singing, dancing, and acting every day.

In his most recent work, Howard Gardner discusses the importance of teaching truth, beauty, and goodness as the means to earned success and a life of accomplishment and well-being.[26] He recommends that each child should create a life-long portfolio to showcase his or her interpretations of truth, beauty, and goodness. Children can interpret these by using the arts and cutting, clipping, pasting, gluing, and stapling a collage of what they value and appreciate. The classroom is then full of the children's artwork and the teacher captures their performances to exemplify their sense of truth, beauty, and goodness. They have weekly art shows, plays, film festivals, dances, concerts, and more, in order to teach the positive psychology teaching taxonomy benchmarks.

Method 4—Strengths Training

Emotional and social strengths training is a fundamental component of the positive psychology teaching taxonomy of signature strength. Positive psychology cultivates the strengths that children need to flourish by using positive psychology teaching techniques of visualization and observation, self-assessment, self-awareness, self-talk, and stress reduction.

10. Observation and Visualization

The teacher uses visualization and observation techniques in the classroom to teach children how to respond by observing others and imagining possibilities within the construct of their personal narratives. Every lesson can utilize one or both of these techniques to teach strengths and adaptation. One of the best ways to promote observational learning is through video and film study. Films and videos illustrate new points of view, preview new approaches, and demonstrate different ways to respond, widening children's emotional field of vision. In a similar way, watching plays, skits, role plays, and simulations exposes children to different points of view that they assimilate into a new emotional schema. The teacher processes what the children watch on film or in real time, and the children discuss what they learned about the emotions, strengths, friendships, and contributions that were observed.

The most effective type of role modeling is direct person-to-person observation—a stage play is more influential than a television show. In the classroom, children can observe the teacher and each other, and personal observation has a direct and immediate impact. They can also observe each other processing their own emotions and strengths filtered through observational learning. The teacher helps children notice their own emotions and strengths, and those of others every day, all day long, both good and bad. "How did Cindy handle the dispute over who is first in line? What did you see? Kindness? Could she have done anything differently? What would you do?"

Children learn the causes and consequences of the feelings and strengths, both positive and negative, just like they learn about the pull of gravity: they observe the teacher drop an apple to the floor, process their observations, and talk about it. Ongoing observational emotional learning exercises help children recognize emotion, label it, express it, classify it as positive or negative, consider it, and correct or enhance it in real life and real time. In the process, children acquire a rich emotional vocabulary that expresses a full range of feelings and the causes and consequences of emotions and strengths observed.

Young children can play the Pantomime game by acting out different emotional scenarios presented in books, songs, and films during the normal course of the day. Older children record their television viewing and identify positive and negative emotions and strengths observed on their favorite shows by reflecting on the causes, consequences, and alternatives. All children learn the skill of keen observation so that they notice the emotions of others and how those emotions affect decisions and actions for better or worse. They sharpen their emotional insights so that they can offer others kindness, empathy, and support when it is needed. By consciously noticing others' emotions, and talking about them, children become aware of their own.

Visualization exercises also help children to become more aware of emotions, strengths, and actions. Moreover, they learn to use visualization to imagine the steps needed to be successful. They mentally preview their success and envision the emotions and strengths needed to activate the vision. They resist adversity by envisioning the best instead of the worst and by looking forward and not back. Visualization is mental practice that plans for success and prepares for failure as another step on a steep climb to accomplishment. Young children can play the Rubber Duck game by keeping a little rubber duck at their desks. When they are struggling, they look at their ducks and visualize stress rolling off them like water rolls off a duck's back.

Older children can play the Worry Jar game and write a paragraph about a disappointment or failure, read it to a friend or the teacher, and then put it in the worry jar. They then imagine that the worry disappears when set aside and they turn their attention to the positives in their lives. Teaching children observational and visualization skills enables them to turn their emotions inside out, take the long-term view, and defer immediate gratification by observing others' successes and failures and by imagining better results. The teacher can use observational learning and visualization once a day, or 10 times a day, to teach the positive psychology benchmarks.

11. Self-Assessments and Self-Awareness

Self-assessment is an important aspect of teaching the positive psychology teaching taxonomy. Children enjoy completing questionnaires, inventories, and checklists that help them assess their emotional states and signature strengths. Informal assessment gives children a clearer picture of how they feel, what they think, and why they might act the way that they do. The book *Psychology for Kids: 40 Fun Tests That Help You Learn about Yourself* contains simple, interesting surveys that help children quantify their positive traits and strengths.[27] Some of the surveys include "Are You an Optimist or a Pessimist?" "Choose Your Superpowers," and "What Do You See?" All are fun and engaging exercises.

Children score, collate, discuss, report, compare, and graph their results. The teacher uses the results to prompt discussion and then guides them to larger awareness and greater personal insight. If children learn how to self-evaluate the impact of their emotions and strengths in their lives, they can use the data to alter their emotions in mindful and purposeful ways consistent with the benchmarks of positive psychology. Playing strength games also serves as a means of informal assessment in the elementary school classroom. The games enable children to better discern how they feel and become more conscious of emotions and strengths.

Playing games requires children to informally self-assess their emotional literacy and their signature strengths. If they can assess their emotions, then they can evaluate the impact emotions have on their successes and failures. Part of the self-assessment process is self-monitoring and recording the benchmarks that they accomplished.

A young child can use a personal sticker chart on her desk and can put a sticker on the chart each time she shows a positive emotion or a strength. She can measure her emotional reactions by using this metaphor: Is her anger as big as an elephant or as small as a mouse? Older children can rate their intensity of feeling on an ordinal scale from 1–10 and then use graphing calculators to record and analyze emotion and strength data on themselves individually and for the class collectively. They use the data to generate reports about their emotions and strengths and how these affect their friendships, motivation to service, and accomplishments.

Younger children can play the Helpful Friend game. They collect coupons that they give to each another every time someone helps out. Older children can participate in the Pay It Forward game. They get coupons to hand out when they do a good deed that they want another child to pass on. All the children keep track of how many coupons they get or they give them away, making them more aware of how often they use positive emotions and signature strengths to help others.

At the start of the school day, all children can play the Guess Who game by writing down compliments about other children on index cards, and then picking the cards at random. Everyone matches the compliment to a child until each child has a compliment card. The cards serve as assessment data of how others perceive them. The process of self-assessment of emotions and strengths makes children more aware of it and able to leverage it to change it for the better. The teacher helps children to quantify how they are doing. "How many times did you forgive someone who hurt you this week?" "How many times did you wait your turn patiently?"

12. Self-Talk and Stress Reduction

Children learn positive private speech[28] so that they can talk to themselves in a positive way, quiet their inner critics, and tell themselves it will turn out okay. To reduce stress, children are taught not to expect too much of themselves or to be too hard on themselves. They remind themselves that they are doing the best that they can under the circumstances. They learn to forgive themselves first. They then extend that forgiveness to others and try to be patient with themselves, understanding that they are "works in progress and not able to do everything perfectly every time."[29] They learn to stop self-blaming and instead encourage themselves with positive self-talk.

Children learn to cheer a failure as a step in the right direction and as life's natural teacher. They also try to eliminate negative emotions in response to stress and to balance their thinking about the stressful incident with positive recalibration by literally telling themselves a positive story with a positive outcome. "I know I failed this test the last time. However, I did not study with a friend. This time I studied hard with my friend and now I will just do my best because that is all I can ask of myself. I feel brave and I promise myself that I will stay relaxed during the test, no matter how hard it seems."

Young children stop before a test to tell themselves, "One good thing about me is _____". Older children learn to actively coach themselves by using favorite affirmations, such as " Practice strength and overcome adversity." Children learn to shed their regrets and stop asking, "What if?" They learn to ask themselves, "What now?" Each child learns to take care of her inner child before she grows up scared and pessimistic. In the process, she discovers that her inner child likes to laugh. She learns to find the inner humor in every situation and to laugh more and worry less.

Children learn not to obsess about the last time and to look forward to the next time. They can flip a negative emotion like a pancake and then put the brakes on the amygdala with screeching tires. They can chase away a bad mood as if it is a monster under the bed, and they learn to literally talk themselves into their own well-being. Self-talk builds new neurons that wind their way past old habits, wiring new hopes and, thereby, reducing stress.

Stress is an inescapable aspect of life, and the classroom is no exception. Children who suffer from unmanaged stress experience physiological changes that impede comprehension and memory. Every teacher knows a child who is distracted by outside stressors and is unable to absorb information. She knows firsthand the disabling effect of stress on learning; while she knows she cannot eliminate it from children's lives, she knows she can teach them to handle it.

The teacher can demonstrate stress-reduction exercises as frequently as she teaches reading. Young children practice their breathing exercises once an hour; twice a day they practice simple yoga exercises such as the tree pose while they think about the different kinds of trees that they are studying in science. Older children practice 15 minutes of meditation twice a day and do 10 jumping jacks every hour. Stress-management exercises release the fear and anxiety that are a major source of stress and also teach children how to find their own serenity in an increasingly rushed and harried world. Self-talk and other stress-reduction techniques are important ways to teach the positive psychology benchmarks in the classroom: "I will not feel sad today even though I miss my dad."

"I am going to get this done if it is the last thing I do." "I know she takes dance lessons. I am going to ask her to show me a step." "I am not sure why I need to memorize that information but at least I can practice my memory skills." "I was thinking I was the best at jump rope and now I just think it is really fun to play with friends."

Summary and Conclusion

Teaching the benchmarks of the positive psychology teaching taxonomy changes how much children like school and how well they do in school. The core knowledge, the general methods, and the specific techniques of the taxonomy increase children's enthusiasm for learning and their enjoyment of school. Children learn to anticipate the joys of a pleasant, good, connected, meaningful, and accomplished life at school. "I cannot wait to go to school today." They look forward to practicing their strengths, making friends, playing with others, helping classmates to remember their own good fortunes, and accomplishing what matters to them. The taxonomy teaches optimism and brings joy to the elementary classroom: "I know I will find something to enjoy at school today."

The benchmarks teach an outer calm and an inner peace. As a fifth-grade student explains, "I love my science teacher. If I can just make it to science, she teaches me how to stay calm and not feel overwhelmed. She is my oasis teacher." Positive psychology makes every teacher an oasis teacher.

Four general educational methods, and the 12 associated techniques, teach the five benchmarks of the taxonomy. These organize the programs, curriculum, units, lessons, activities, exercises, and games that teach social emotional learning knowledge and skills. One approach is to teach the positive psychology teaching taxonomy horizontally and to address a different benchmark monthly or at each grade level. Teach kindergarten and first-grade children feelings and emotion, second-grade children engagement and strengths, third-grade children relationship and friendships, fourth-grade children meaning and purpose, and fifth-grade children accomplishment as the capstone before they move to middle school.

Another approach is to teach the taxonomy by addressing the benchmarks down the matrix of the taxonomy, vertically. In each grade, the teacher selects one particular feeling and teaches it across all the benchmarks. Regardless of the approach, the teacher develops programs, curriculum, units, lessons, activities, and games with the goal of teaching the benchmarks using the four methods, and the 12 associated techniques, derived from the taxonomy. A teacher can teach all of the benchmarks of the teaching taxonomy by using the Teacher's Toolbox, selecting the positive psychology teaching techniques that best match academic standards and teacher style.

Table 3.2. Positive Psychology Teaching Taxonomy: Teacher's Toolbox

Language	Academics	Visual and Performing Arts	Strengths Training
Class Greetings	Clubs/Teams	Art	Visualization and Observation
Class Meetings	Learning Centers	Dance	Self/Social Awareness
Class Pledges	Service Learning	Drama	Self-Talk/Stress Reduction
Reflective Journals	E-Learning	Music	

The next chapters train the teacher to use the positive psychology teaching taxonomy techniques. Each chapter details one of the benchmarks and describes how to develop the positive psychology programs, curriculum, units, lessons, activities, exercises, and games for both primary-aged and intermediate-aged children. Each chapter also recommends unique interactive resources. Teachers choose from the menu of options by using some or all of the techniques.

Finally, the taxonomy formulates 25 strengths-based standards for elementary school children. The standards of the taxonomy are below.

Positive Psychology Teaching Taxonomy—25 Strengths Standards

Teach Positive Emotion (Pleasant Life)

Teach Feelings: Kind/Caring, Grateful, Brave, Determined, Calm, and Hopeful

1. Teach children to be kind in their thoughts and feelings toward the self and others.
2. Teach children to act enthusiastically upbeat and grateful to enjoy laughter, fun, and humor.

3. Teach children to smile often, be brave, and carry themselves with confidence.
4. Teach children to keep trying even when they want to give up.
5. Teach children to stay calm and stay hopeful by knowing that the situation will improve.

Teach Engagement Through Strengths (Good Life/Ethical Life)

Engage Strengths: Empathy, Appreciation, Courage, Grit, Relaxation, and Optimism

6. Teach children to preserve their dignity, show empathy, and treat all with sensitivity.
7. Teach children to appreciate their potential for success.
8. Teach children to make each other feel safe and secure and to find their courage.
9. Teach children to combine their appreciation and courage by exhibiting grit and tenacity.
10. Teach children to relax, to look forward, not backward, without regret and with optimism.

Teach Relationships (Connected Life)

Show Friends: Forgiveness, Gratitude, Loyalty, Commitment, Support, and Enjoyment

11. Teach children to befriend every child they meet and to forgive those who hurt them.
12. Teach children to show gratitude to those who help them.
13. Teach children to be forever helpful, accepting, and loyal to themselves and others.
14. Teach children to chat with each other in glad, interested, and committed ways.
15. Teach children to be supportive and enjoy friendships.

Teach Meaning (Purposeful Life)

Value Meaning: Tolerance, Helpfulness, Respect, Fortitude, Serenity, and Inspiration

16. Teach children to chat purposefully with each other and to learn tolerance from each other.
17. Teach children to show genuine concern and care for others and to help each other.
18. Teach children to share personal information in appropriate ways and to respect each other.
19. Teach children to develop conflict-resolution skills and to use them with fortitude and serenity.
20. Teach children to congratulate each other and inspire notable accomplishment.

Teach Accomplishment (Contented Life/Accomplished Life)

Embrace Achievement: Cooperation, Contentment, Confidence, Resilience, Peace, and Joy

21. Teach children to act to take positive actions with others that set them apart.
22. Teach children to exercise their competence and to find contentment in all learning.
23. Teach children to try to give up old habits, confidently try new ways, and stay open to ideas.
24. Teach children "coopetition" that combines group cooperation, competition, and resilience.
25. Teach children to accomplish tasks with gentleness, quiet assurance, peacefulness, and joy.

Guiding Question Exercise

What do you think is the most important part of the positive psychology teaching taxonomy? Would you be inclined to teach the benchmarks across or down the continuum? What benchmark do you think is most important? What positive psychology method do you use? What technique do you think is the best one to teach the taxonomy? Is there a technique that you already use in the classroom that teaches positive psychology? Do you prefer to infuse the taxonomy into the academic curriculum or the academic curriculum into the taxonomy? Is there a particular curriculum that interests you? Activity? Game? Create a positive psychology lesson by using the positive psychology teaching taxonomy and techniques.

Guiding Question Discussion

To begin teaching the taxonomy of positive psychology, the teacher decides what to teach. She may choose to teach the taxonomy vertically by focusing on teaching emotions, strengths, or friendships independently or she may choose to teach the taxonomy horizontally by teaching how a particular emotion builds an associated strength, affects a relationship, imparts meaning, and results in a capstone accomplishment. The teacher identifies the general methods to use to teach the taxonomy by using the best techniques to meet the benchmarks, given the age of her students and her academic goals for the class. She might also select one of the 25 standards and decide what general methods and specific techniques lend themselves to teaching that standard. She integrates one, or all, of the benchmarks into every subject every day.

Web Resources for Children

> Children's Favorite Writers, http://people.ucalgary.ca/~dkbrown/
> authors.html.
> Fishful Thinking, http://www.fishfulthinking.com/.
> 4H Youth Development Programs, http://www.4-h.org/.
> Harry Potter Scholastic, http://dsc.discovery.com/tv/human-body/
> puzzles/puzzles.html.
> Talk Blocks, http://www.talkblocks.com/.
> Thumball, http://thumball.com/.

Web Resources for Teachers

> Blooms' Affective Taxonomy, http://www.nwlink.com/~donclark/
> hrd/bloom.html
> Howard Gardner, http://www.howardgardner.com/.
> Positivity, http://www.positivityratio.com/.
> Thinking Active in a Social Context (TASC) Model,
> http://www.tascwheel.com/.
> University of Pennsylvania Positive Psychology Center,
> http://www.ppc.sas.upenn.edu/.

CHAPTER 4

TEACHING POSITIVE EMOTIONS AND THE PLEASANT LIFE: FEELINGS

All learning has an emotional base.

—Plato

Education often overlooks the importance of emotion in the classroom and the fact that emotional attunement improves a child's ability to learn. The positive psychology benchmark of positive emotion teaches children how to modulate, balance, and recalibrate emotions in the same way that they learn to spell the words *happy* and *sad*. When children understand their feelings and those of others better, they are able to keep trudging up the hill and keep their footing along the way. Children learn to identify their emotions, reflect on why they are feeling a particular way, and then recognize what effect it has on them. Then, to achieve the end result, children learn to either change or embrace a particular emotional state.

Children find it easy to respond positively to the material pleasures in life—a pizza party, a favorite toy, or a gold star—that arouse excitement or bring immediate comfort or gratification. The teacher's challenge is to help children find deeper and more lasting happiness in everyday classroom learning experiences so that they leave school with a feeling of peace and contentment. On extra special days, they leave feeling a sense of gladness.

Positive psychology teaches children how to take an active role in emotional management so that they are empowered to choose how to feel and whether to allow their emotions to affect them positively or negatively. They use their emotional understandings as a guide to thinking about the next best step and course of action. Children need to learn how to probe complex feelings and to understand how their emotions contribute or detract from a caring, calm, and confident response.

Teachers and children alike learn to stop focusing on what is wrong and to take delight in what is right. They turn learned helplessness to learned hopefulness and negative feelings to positive ones. A classroom full of children who can recognize and successfully manage their emotions is the intention of positive psychology.

In the positive psychology classroom, there are no children stomping and no teachers scolding. There are no stony looks of defiance, gloomy clouds of pouting, long sighs of boredom, irritable voices, rolling eyes, impatient mutterings, or hidden fears. There is less negative behavioral enforcement and more positive emotional initiative. All effort turns negative energy into positive result, making self and others feel happy.

These changes do not come to the classroom magically. They are the direct result of the efforts of the teacher, who commits to emotional learning with expertise and energy. She organizes her lessons to guarantee that children learn as much about their emotions as they would about any other subject. The teacher uses the positive psychology teaching taxonomy, and its benchmarks, to determine what emotional learning must occur so children can manage their emotions in ways that build strengths, friendships, meaning, and accomplishments.

To teach emotional competence the teacher begins with the end in mind and focuses on accomplished children as the goal. She teaches children to develop the prerequisite knowledge and skills needed to meet the positive psychology benchmark of positive emotion. She guides children to success knowing exactly what she wants them to know and to do. What she most wants for them to do is to use emotional cognizance to turn negative emotion into positive feelings. If the teacher wants children who embrace cooperation, contentment, confidence, fortitude, serenity, inspiration, and joy, she gets back to the emotional basics.

The Importance of Emotional Learning in Positive Psychology

Teachers sometimes confuse the expression of negative emotion, and the inability to properly regulate it, with bad behavior that they reprimand or punish. Teachers spend a great deal of time trying to suppress negative emotions in favor of compliant behavior and to repress positive ones in favor of quiet accommodation. The positive psychology teaching taxonomy suggests a neuroeducational approach because children are better served when they learn how to decrease negative emotions and to increase positive ones.

The teacher adopts the four-branch model of emotional intelligence: (1) teach reliable emotional awareness and perception, (2) teach honest expression, (3) teach cognitive mediation of emotion, and (4) teach emotional understanding and management.[1] In the process, children learn to identify their feelings so that they can assess how their feelings affect their actions. Then they can decide how to manage them by either changing them or enjoying them. These are the basics of emotional intelligence.

The first step toward emotional intelligence is the ability to accurately recognize emotions and automatically acknowledge them. The teacher trains children to become more aware of their emotions and to accurately identify them. Children cry, laugh, skip, shout, stomp, withdraw, shake, sweat, yell, ignore, dance, and sigh with emotion, and the teacher makes certain that they understand that their actions are outward manifestations of their inner emotional states. The teacher guides them in recognizing emotions and connecting them to their moods, thoughts, and actions. "I feel sad because my grandmother's visit is over and so I am acting unenthusiastic today." "I feel angry I did not get a part in the play and so I am acting very unforgiving today." "I feel discouraged because it is hard to make new friends and I am not acting very hopeful today." "I feel afraid today because I am not good at reading and I am acting fearful today."

The teacher helps children to identify their emotions in the context of opposite emotions because children must be able to consider a great range of feelings in order to make good decisions about balancing them. Children learn to identify seven emotional antonym pairs and the underlying moods associated with each of them. Significant emotional states that affect learning and performance are caring/angry, grateful/selfish, brave/afraid, determined/unsure, calm/frustrated, hopeful/discouraged, and happy/sad.[2]

Because negative emotions severely hinder learning and positive emotions enhance it, it is incumbent on the teacher to make emotional learning a priority in the classroom. Children who are cognizant of their feelings are aware of when they feel caring and not angry; hopeful, not discouraged; calm, not anxious; or happy, not sad. Children's accurate emotional perceptions and mindfulness make the classroom a more tranquil and pleasant place to learn.

After children are able to detect and characterize their emotions, they learn to connect covert feelings to overt moods, recognize their emotional states as good and bad moods, and identify the source of the emotion. Most important, they are then able to assess how emotion affects them. "Does my fear or anxiety keep me from trying new things?" "Does my selfishness keep me from enjoying time with friends?" "Does my discouragement cause me to give up too easily?" "Does my sadness cause me to withdraw?" "Does my anger cause me to lash out?" Children also learn how to assess their positive feelings. "How is being caring and kind toward others helping me, too?" "Why does staying calm when frightened benefit me?" "When I stay hopeful, does it make the effort more enjoyable?" "When do I feel most happy?" "What do I feel grateful to have in my life?" In all emotional appraisal, the most important question that children learn to ask themselves is, "How is this feeling working for me?" Children learn to assess their emotions in terms of intensity, duration, frequency, and aptness.

An angry child evaluates her anger and realizes it is always disproportionate to the provocation and it causes her to lose friends. A sad child considers his unhappy feelings and understands that it lasts longer than warranted and causes him to overlook many enjoyable experiences. Children learn whether a particular emotion makes life more pleasant or unpleasant. When there is careful assessment, children tend to distort their feelings less and to understand them more. They tend to overreact less and balance their emotions more often. Children who can conduct an emotional self-appraisal can make informed, thoughtful decisions regarding how to make emotions work for them and not against them. As a little girl said to another, "Sandy, don't worry. This is a good thing." Once children master emotional assessment, they are able to make better decisions regarding what to do about their feelings.

With knowledge about their feelings comes the ability to purposefully decide what to do about them. If children understand their good and bad moods, and positive and negative emotions, they can decide to make a change or not. "I feel discouraged because I am not doing well in math. Now I can decide to just give up or I can ask Kelly to help me. She is good at math." This decision point is at the crossroads of positive psychology.

Teachers remind children that they can choose a feeling just as they choose a book to read. With good instruction, time, and practice, children learn to expertly assess and express emotional states and think about how to alter their affiliated actions. "I do not have to feel unsure about the school play. I can decide to learn my lines really well."

The teacher advises children that they cannot always control what happens to them but they can always choose their emotional reactions. Children learn that life is sometimes random, arbitrary, and unfair. Despite their best intentions and plans, it will rain and they will get wet. Children cannot change the rainy day—they can only change their feelings about it.

Does the rainy day make me feel gloomy or happy to splash through puddles? Do I see the dark clouds behind the storm or the flowers the rain will refresh? Is a rainy day an adventure or a dreary trudge to school? If a feeling is positive and serving a positive purpose, children decide to further amplify it and make it work for them to an even greater extent. If the feeling is negative and hindering a positive purpose, they decide to change it in the same way that they may change their socks.

Every action is an expression of a feeling and the crosscurrents of emotion are turbulent. The only way that children learn to self-manage emotional states and fluctuations is if they learn to recognize the emotions, understand the source of the emotion, express them, assess the effect of the emotion on their learning and life, and decide to change their feelings. Children can effectively regulate their emotion only if they can master the nuance of it so that they can moderate their reaction to it. They use their understanding of emotion to make choices about how to change or intensify their feelings as needed. Emotional wellness is a function of the ability to balance its polarities.

Accomplished children learn to be emotionally flexible and fluent and to exchange one feeling for another at will, and they display a wide array of emotional options. If children learn how to replace a negative emotion with a positive one, or sustain a positive one, it changes everything, including how the brain processes both positive and negative input in the future.

"I am angry at you because you called me a name. However, we have been friends since kindergarten so I decided to act kinder toward you because I care about you and when I feel caring it is easier to be kind." The ability to moderate emotion is the basis for learned accomplishment affiliated with success: satisfaction, cooperation, contentment, confidence, fortitude, serenity, inspiration, and joy.

The teacher's lessons *connect children's positive moods to their positive emotions* so that they are better able to choose their thoughts, attitudes, and actions. "I feel afraid to raise my hand in class. However, I know that when my friends encourage me it is easier to be brave." "I feel unsure about the math problem. However, I am determined to give it a try." "I feel sad when other children ignore me. However, I am happy to have one best friend who smiles whenever she sees me." The positive psychology of emotional understanding and regulation directs teachers to explicitly train emotional proficiency in children or they may never learn it. The degree to which children recognize, assess, and make positive emotional decisions well predicts the degree to which they can moderate their feelings. Negative emotion filtered through positivity is repurposed as positive emotion in a continuous bio-emotional experiential feedback loop. Children learn to interrupt or maintain their emotions by changing or augmenting their feelings about experiences. They process the experience, assess it, choose how to respond, and balance their actions with thoughtful consideration.

A sense of entitlement transforms to a sense of humble helpfulness, short-term fear runs its course without long-term damage, and failure becomes success turned inside out when children capably manage feelings. For this to occur, the teacher plans with the positive psychology benchmark of positive emotion in mind. He helps young children practice emotional perception, expression, and cognitive mediation.

"I felt sad because my grandmother's visit was over and so I was not in a good mood because I miss her. However, if I concentrate on all the fun that we had during her visit, it cheers me up." Older children learn a deeper emotional understanding that gives them the knowledge and skill they need to manage their emotions under the best and worst of conditions. They practice emotional regulation to complete their homework even when they feel sad, forgive a friend even when they feel disappointed, and stay calm even when they feel anxious.

The teacher strengthens children's ability to recognize, recall, and express emotion as easily as they read their ABCs. The teacher ensures that children acquire the knowledge and skills they need to identify and share their feelings accurately, understand the origins and effect of them, and learn to regulate them.[3] Children race to the emotional finish line.

Table 4.1. Teaching Positive Emotion Planning

Positive Emotion	Polar Emotion	Accomplishment
Feel Caring/Kind	Not Angry	Cooperation
Feel Grateful	Not Selfish	Contentment
Feel Brave	Not Afraid	Confidence
Feel Determined	Not Apathetic	Fortitude
Feel Calm/Relaxed	Not Frustrated	Serenity
Feel Hopeful	Not Discouraged	Inspiration
Feel Happy	Not Sad	Joy

Children learn emotional empowerment that is rooted in emotional awareness, assessment, choice, and balanced expression. In time, emotionally empowered children learn to help themselves and others by transforming the power of positive emotion into reliable emotional strength.

The Positive Psychology Teacher's Toolbox: Emotional Learning

The academic curriculum is not just the textbook, the tests, and the homework. A comprehensive academic curriculum always considers the ecology of learning. The ecology of learning includes the general educational methods previously discussed: (1) language of emotions and strengths, (2) infused academics, (3) visual and performing arts, and (4) strengths training. The teacher fuses these with the techniques recommended to teach the positive psychology taxonomy benchmark of positive emotion within the academic curriculum. Emotions energize learning, so the academic curriculum must incorporate it.

To teach emotional learning, the teacher plans effective ways to teach the four pillars of positive emotion: (1) keen emotional awareness and recognition, (2) careful emotional assessment and appraisal, (3) thoughtful emotional processing and decision making, and (4) balanced emotional expression and empowerment. All of these create the emotional insight needed for children to be able to self-regulate emotion. The teacher focuses on teaching these by using the Positive Psychology Teacher's Emotions Toolbox techniques. Children can then learn to recognize and become more aware of their emotions, assess and gain more insight about them, choose them mindfully, and empower themselves to nurture a feeling or discard it.

The toolbox provides specific techniques the teacher uses to teach emotional learning and integrate it into the traditional academic curriculum. The techniques help younger children become aware of feelings, identify them correctly, express them easily, and connect them to their thinking and actions. Older children learn to understand their emotions at a deeper level and regulate them skillfully. All children express their emotions in poised and well-composed ways based on emotional learning. Teaching emotional awareness for the purpose of emotional management is the foundation of the positive psychology teaching taxonomy.

The teacher may use the recommended techniques in the toolbox as part of a larger program, within a comprehensive curriculum, as a themed unit, as stand-alone lessons, as enrichment activities, or in learning games that children play. Positive psychology programs may include a fully developed curriculum that teaches all the benchmarks, a themed unit that teaches one, a series of lessons to assess one, a weekly activity to process one, a daily exercise to practice one, or a learning game to reinforce one. Whatever form and format a positive psychology program takes, it uses some, if not all, of the techniques.

The Positive Psychology Teacher's Emotions Toolbox techniques include (1) meet and greet children, (2) begin with an emotions pledge, (3) conduct a meeting, (4) repair a mood, (5) study the brain, (6) play a game, (7) join a book or film club, (8) create a happiness project, (9) sing a song or bang a drum, and (10) spread the word. The teacher uses these techniques to teach different emotions and the pillars of emotional learning.

The emotion benchmark, and its associated indicators, ensures that children will better understand how they feel about their world and how to live in it pleasantly. The teacher uses the techniques to teach any one

Table 4.2. The Teacher's Toolbox: Pillars and Techniques of Emotional Learning

Awareness and Recognition	Assessment and Appraisal	Choice and Decision Making	Expression and Empowerment
Meet and Greet	Brain Study	Games	Sing a Song
Pledge and Creed	Book and Film Club	Repair Mood	Spread the Word
Class Meeting	Class Meeting	Happiness Project	Happiness Project

of the emotional pairs or indicators such as angry/caring or happy/sad. She can use a class meeting, book club, or a game to teach the benchmark of positive emotion and the pillars of emotional learning.

A meet and greet serves to make children more aware of their emotions and how they affect everyone's mood. A pledge helps them understand that positive emotion is a choice. Mood repair games teach them how to change it. The positive psychology teaching taxonomy of positive emotion uses these techniques to teach the learning pillars of positive emotion from awareness to empowerment. These are not discrete but expansive techniques. That is, any single technique can teach the pillars of emotional learning across the curriculum. The teacher is in the best position to decide what emotions to teach and what techniques work best so children can flourish in the elementary school classroom. In positive psychology classrooms, children leave school feeling braver because they read their poems out loud and everyone clapped, grateful because they were selected to lead the dragon parade, or hopeful that someday they may be real writers.

1. Meet and Greet Children

Using the language of positive psychology, the teacher meets the children at the door or greets them at the start of class with a sincere good morning. However, the positive psychology teacher begins the day in a deliberative way by opening the class with attention to specific feelings by commenting about emotions immediately at the start of the day. As children enter the room, she notices their facial expressions and reports the emotion observed back to them: "You look very relaxed this morning even though there is a thundering storm outside and a history test on the schedule." The intention is to make children aware of their emotional expressions and to help them connect the observed emotions to their thoughts. To one child, the teacher may say, "You look determined today. You must be thinking about becoming a spelling team captain." At the door, some older children offer the teacher an early morning emotional weather report: "I feel happy because I played baseball yesterday." "I feel grateful because Grandma read me a book last night." "I feel angry because I was embarrassed on the bus."

The teacher gives all the children a small whiteboard and they write down how they feel. Everyone holds up the board, and the teacher asks children questions about the feelings she sees on the board. Taking time to take the emotional temperature of the classroom gives everyone a general idea who may need to be reminded to increase their positive self-talk or who may need extra smiles.

Another way to greet the class is to wish everyone a good morning at the start of class and to play the Emotions Card game that the teacher uses to customize a class greeting. "Today will be a hopeful day as you learn new vocabulary words and a brave day because you are taking a tough test. Who feels brave enough to take the math test?"

One teacher greets children with a rap song about determination, and another begins the day by singing with the class a Disney song that inspires hopeful feelings. Some teachers meet at the door to greet while others open class with an emotions coloring page. A fun, interactive lesson about emotions is the best way to start the day or end the day. Every teacher customizes the way he or she processes emotional content when greeting the children.

The teacher may like to use some of the educational materials available to teach feelings at the meet and greet or throughout the day. Emotion Cards depict feelings pictorially to help young children focus on identification by naming emotions that help them master the language of feelings.[4] "That is a picture of happy." Older children respond to the Choose to Lose card game, which illustrates negative emotions and teaches them what not to do when feeling negative.[5] The card prompts, "If I feel selfish and choose to act selfish, then _____. The children shout out: "I lose friends." The teacher suggests, "Beware of anger today, if you choose it you will lose your temper and ruin the pleasant day ahead." Children consider the effects of positive and negative emotions. "If I choose grateful then . . . I enjoy what I have more."

The meet and greet aims to make the invisible self more visible even before the academic day begins. Whether the teacher meets and greets the children at the door or at an opening session each morning, the children understand that she cares as much about their feelings as whether they read well. Emotional awareness, the ability to recognize and identify feelings accurately, is the best way to begin emotional learning and the best way to start the day. The first and most important lesson of the day is always about emotional wellness because it reminds children that every day is a brand-new day with a brand-new start.

2. Begin with an Emotions Pledge

Kindergarten and first-grade children are standing in a circle and holding hands, ready to recite the class pledge selected by the teacher because it articulates the aims and language of positive psychology. Too often teachers choose a class pledge that is simply a recitation of rules: "I am in school to learn. I will follow directions." Another example of a pledge that misses the positive psychology mark: "We raise our hands to speak and sit quietly in our seats." Rule-oriented pledges tend to encourage passive acquiescence and are well intentioned but misguided because they do not help children to choose positive emotions for positive choices and active decision making.

A positive psychology pledge is different because it does not instruct children what to do—it tells them how to help. "Kind children wait their turn and take care not to disrupt others." A positive psychology pledge focuses children on their emotional life.

The Wings for Kids Creed is a good example of a positive psychology pledge that focuses on emotional growth.[6] The teacher says the pledge sentence by sentence and first-grade children repeat after her, taking a vow to be honest about their feelings and to listen for important emotional messages from others. Older children pledge to manage their emotions.

The creed teaches all children the if/then proposition of emotional learning: If children feel good, then they will do good. A positive psychology pledge is not only a promise but also a plan intended to remind children exactly what to do when they encounter a frustrating situation. The second-grade children may dance to the pledge; a third-grade class may sing it. Fourth-grade children could use a chart to record how high the class soars by honoring the pledge, and the fifth grade can help the kindergarten class to memorize it. The following is the Wing for Kids Pledge:

> I soar with WINGS. Let me tell you why. I learn skills that help me reach the sky. I love and accept who I am on the inside, and know my emotions are nothing to hide. If I can control myself I will have much better days. I understand the choices I make should be what are best for me to do and what happens is on me—and not any of you. I want to learn more about everyone I meet. I want to step into their shoes and see what they are going through. All of these things are why I fly.[7]

Children use this pledge to remind each other of the collective promise made using the words and aspirations of the pledge. "What you said to me surprised me, but I understand." "I don't have to hide that I am easily embarrassed." "I made a good choice today." Children learn that they cannot change their world but they can change the way they react to it. The pledge helps children better understand who they are and who they can become so that they are emotionally empowered to choose their actions and reactions rather than simply memorizing and reciting how others want them to behave. The pledge encourages them to go with the emotional flow.

The teacher also uses the language of the pledge to coach and correct. "If you control your anger you will have a better day." "If you are calm I can listen better." The teacher uses the language of the pledge to give strengths-based praise: "You controlled your anger very well today and acted calm despite your frustration."

3. Conduct a Meeting

Teachers can use classroom meetings to discuss various emotions and to teach all the pillars of emotional learning. This is why so many formal positive psychology programs and curricula use them.

A meeting is typically conceived and facilitated as a circle of friends and children have the opportunity to learn what they feel, why they feel that way, what they can do about it, and when they should change it to create a pleasant life. When primary-aged children gather in the morning circle, the teacher announces that today is an activities day and introduces exercises intended to help the class identify and describe their feelings.

First, the teacher passes around a jar that contains 101 little cards printed with feeling words that children randomly draw.[8] To play the Feelings in a Jar game, a child reads the feeling and then someone else volunteers to act it out. Other children guess the feeling, name it, describe it, and discuss it as either positive or negative and recall if they have ever experienced the emotion.

In the second activity, the My Favorite TV Show game, children describe a feeling they observed while watching a favorite show. They explain how they were able to recognize the feeling and the teacher guides the discussion about the feelings observed by using the language of positive psychology. "Yes, I agree that playing the tambourine makes Foofa and her listeners feel happy." The final exercise invites children to play the Kimochis game.[9] The tiny stuffed Japanese dolls turn inside out to reveal a feeling found inside of them and children express the feeling inside of them and whether it is the same or different. Older children begin the meeting by completing a sentence, "I feel…" The responses guide the group discussion. "Why did you feel that way? How frequently do you feel this way? What caused you to stop feeling this way? How do you change a negative emotion to a positive one or to keep a positive feeling going?"

At the end of the class meeting, the children sing a new song about emotions, "Let 'Em Out," with words that remind the class not to lose their cool and to let their good and bad feelings out in the best possible ways.[10] Class meetings teach the positive psychology benchmark of emotion and are an especially effective way to teach about emotion. In the process, the class meeting builds shared trust, responsibility, and decision-making skills. Meetings make children more aware of their feelings, actions, and aspirations, and they help them learn to enlarge their perspective by listening to others and reconstituting failure as success.

Three notable in-school comprehensive positive psychology programs are emotion-centric. The Caring School Community initiative,[11] the Six Seconds Self-Science program,[12] and The Tribes Learning Community[13] all have class meetings at the curricular core. The curriculum teaches the positive psychology benchmark of positive emotion by using structured class meetings as a central feature of the curriculum.

4. Repair a Mood

When emotions overwhelm, children exhibit all the earmarks of a bad mood. Telling children to stop having a bad mood is like telling a cloud not to rain. The teacher should move in a different direction and engage children in mood repair. She teaches young children to identify the feeling that put them in a bad mood and how to reverse it. Older children consider nuance and complexity of emotion, and they understand that irritability and annoyance are precursors to anger so they can take preventative actions to repair moods before they worsen. With this knowledge, all children can repair their moods by instigating positive emotions.

The Mood Barometer presented in Table 4.3 is a useful tool that helps children connect their moods to their emotions. The barometer takes a snapshot of the emotional state and requires each child to self-reflect and self-assess to become more conscious of his or her feelings.

Children use mood barometers to identify, assess, consider, and change or nurture a feeling. They identify how they currently feel, how

Table 4.3. Mood Barometer

Emotion Pair	Bad Mood	Good Mood	Great Mood	Super Mood
Kind/Angry	1	2	3	4
Grateful/Selfish	1	2	3	4
Brave/Afraid	1	2	3	4
Determined/Uncertain	1	2	3	4
Calm/Frustrated	1	2	3	4
Hopeful/Disappointed	1	2	3	4
Happy/Sad	1	2	3	4

they have felt in the past, and how they would like to feel in the future. In kindergarten, a simple sticker system tallies upsetting feelings, and children can put stickers on a desk log to count the times they get upset. Each of the seven basic emotions links to its polar opposite so that children assess 14 different emotions in relational context.

Students plot their daily moods, both positive and negative, along a continuum from worst to best mood. Children monitor different emotions at different times during the school day or week. First-grade children can choose one emotion to monitor daily, second graders can choose two emotions, third graders can choose three, fourth graders can choose four, and fifth graders can choose five. When children are aware of their emotional moods, they can choose to repair and change them as needed. Mood repair techniques teach children about the seven basic emotional pairs that children, and adults, frequently experience. Markus Drews created a graphic organizer of Plutchik's theory of emotions that offers another useful template for teachers to use in helping children identify the basic emotional pairs.[14] Emotion barometers, wheels, and other mood-assessment tools also help children think about their emotions.

A variation of the mood barometer is Plutchik's Emotions Wheel.[15] Adapting it, young children can color a basic two-dimensional Emotions Wheel in varying shades that represent different intensities of emotion. Older children use Plutchik's 3-D emotions cone to identify emotions as colors across a full spectrum of feelings from negative to positive. The Do2Learn website also offers an online Emotions Color Wheel that is interactive so that children can physically manipulate emotions based on color with dark colors representing dark emotions and light colors representing light ones.

When children use the mood barometer or a similar self-assessment approach, a teacher will find that children are better able to recognize their moods, understand them, and manage them with equanimity. When dark emotions overtake children, they learn how to actively repair their moods by using a variety of strategies to help lighten up.

Children learn to laugh at themselves and to consider events as funny rather than frustrating. "I forgot to put my name on my paper—again." They laugh at a mistake or the absurdity of the situation. Learning to laugh at their own miscalculations and mistakes—and learning to not take life too seriously—prevents children from becoming overly tense and upset.

When children are able to laugh at life's follies and predicaments, even when they initially might not seem very funny, the laughter changes their mood. Laughter requires children to breathe deeply, shift perspective, and go with the flow. Children acknowledge that not every circumstance is within a child's control no matter how much they wish it were so and laughter is the evidence that they know how to concede to life's demands. A humorous perspective requires a certain amount of detachment—you can laugh at the situation only if you are able to detach in a positive way. If children learn to laugh at themselves in gentle ways, they are able to use humor and laughter for mood repair.

One of the best antidotes for stress is learned laughter because it sets the mind free to flow. In the positive psychology classroom, the teacher directs children to laugh aloud for one full minute a day—until real laughter takes hold and the children are really laughing and having fun. If children can find the funny side of life, they can commandeer their feelings and repair their moods. Laughter is a staple in teaching positive psychology because a laugh a day keeps bad moods away.

5. Study the Brain

The capability for mood repair originates in the brain, as explained by researchers who have studied the neurobiology of emotion and personality. Almost 20 years ago, neuroscientists discovered the emotional circuitry of the brain and the evidence that emotion is a matter of unique affective styles and patterns. Neurobiology defines emotion as a pleasant or unpleasant state; fluctuation between the two states is based on the interaction of neurology with environmental, intrapersonal, and interpersonal factors. Emotion refers to an individual's idiosyncratic neurological mood sets or dispositions.[16] Positive psychology helps children identify and modify their unique, affective styles to increase positive emotion and decrease negative emotion.

> Carey and Amy are equally skilled and experienced musicians and today they will play in a piano recital at the school assembly. Both children play the piano with a high degree of technical precision. However, Carey and Amy do not come to the recital in the same mood. Before the assembly started, Amy was frustrated because she could not find her music and she was having an argument with her best friend. When the assembly begins, Amy bangs out the music while Carey plays her composition softly and gently.

When each child played the piano, the frontal cortex of her brain associated with musical talent lit up in similar ways. However, the audience heard very different performances because each one played the music very differently based on her individual emotional state. The numerous, deep connections between the emotional limbic system and the musical modules of the brain are highly reactive to emotional input. This is the reason one of the children played her piano piece playfully while the other played it angrily.

With positive psychology, children learn to neutralize negative emotion or transform it into positive emotion so Amy would have known how to calm herself down before she started banging on the piano keys. "Although heritable influences surely occur, environmental influences, particularly when they occur repetitively over time, can be powerful and produce lasting changes in the brain."[17] Positive emotional experience has the power to enhance performance, and negative emotional experience has the power to impair optimal function.

Whether playing the piano, spelling a word, or reading a book, performance is greatly affected, if not dictated, by emotion.[18] Because emotional neural circuits in the brain connect to cognitive neural circuits, emotions influence a child's attention, motivation, problem solving, decision making, and ability to extract positive meaning from experience. The biology of emotion affects the biology of cognition and vice versa. A basic understanding of the neurobiology of emotion is important if children are to learn to recognize, process, understand, and manage emotion. Every positive psychology classroom should include a learning center that teaches children about the brain in the classroom: the Brain Station.

At the Brain Station, children learn about the brain and how it affects their emotional states. They learn about the role that the biology of the brain plays in emotion so they understand their emotions as a part of their biology, just like the processes of walking and talking. The more children know about how their brains work the more they understand why they sweat and feel nervous when they give a speech, why they turn red and feel embarrassed when the teacher corrects them, and why their muscles tense when they argue with their best friend.

Props, such as neuron molds, models, soft toys, puzzles, minilabs, and games, are useful in teaching young children about the brain and are readily available for purchase. The station can also include books about the brain such as *How Does Your Brain Work? You Can't Use Your Brain If You Are a Jelly Fish*, *Young Genius: Brains*, and *Big Head!*[19] One of the newest books for young children is about brain plasticity, *My Fantastic Elastic Brain: Stretch It, Shape It."*[20] Working at the Brain Station, younger children use crayons, markers, and glitter to color in the *Human Brain Coloring Book* and they read the picture book *Think, Think, Think: Learning About Your Brain.*[21]

At the Neuroscience for Kids website, children can find interesting brain facts and enter a brain drawing contest.[22] On the Kid's Health website, they sing brain songs, take a brain quiz, and take a trip inside the feeling brain.[23] Older children put together anatomical models, complete a complex brain puzzle, use brain workbooks to learn facts, and play a board game about neurons and module regions.[24] On the Discovery Channel's Brain Anatomy website, they can investigate anatomy, function, and the origin of emotion.[25] On the Secret Life of the Brain website, they can review interesting brain scans and take a 3D tour of the brain; on the Nova website, they can watch a video about mirror neurons.[26]

Every Brain Station includes the Brain Wise Curriculum, K–5, which connects a knowledge of brain biology to emotional competence.[27] The curriculum teaches children 10 ways to recognize, understand, and appropriately manage their emotions in order to control impulsive reactions.

A unique project that guides children in consciously replacing negative emotions with positive emotions is the Brain Works Project.[28] The website offers an online program that teaches older children how to process negative emotion by using cognitive coping skills. They learn how the coping brain works and how negative emotions hinder learning. On-line exercises and games teach children how to manage loss, rejection, and humiliation.

As children explore their feelings from a neurobiology perspective, they learn that the biology of emotion can also explain animal feelings and that they really enjoy reading about them. The book *Do Animals Have Feelings, Too?* is a collection of stories about animal behavior and about the biology and psychology of emotion.[29] *The Secret Life of Animals* tells stories about how dogs help each other and how elephants weep.[30]

6. Play a Game

Emotional learning games are fun ways of teaching children to iden-tify, assess, understand, and manage their emotions. Positive psychology teaches the four pillars of positive emotional learning so every possible academic lesson includes emotional learning games and every non-aca-demic interaction promotes the positive psychology of emotional learn-ing. Emotional learning lessons, activities, and games teach children by having them answer important questions that make them more emo-tionally aware: What color is your feeling? If the crayon box could talk what would the color yellow say? How big is your happiness—the size of a whale or of a minnow? Will banging on a drum get the angry out? Is mad the flip side of the sad coin? How wide is your imagination and is there a better way? When is a whisper more than a shout?

To help identify feelings, once a week children play the Emotions Bingo game.[31] Younger children use bingo cards with faces depicting different emotions, and older children match synonyms to the emo-tion words called by the teacher. Young children can play the Clapping game, chanting and clapping in rhythm: "Today is a happy day because I made a new friend"; "Today is a grateful day because we learned a new dance." Older children work on a wall mural by completing and illustrating sentences: "Today is a beautiful day because I feel ____." "If I fail today I will ____." "My favorite thing is ____and makes me feel ____." "When I look in the mirror I feel ____." "I will change my heart today to feel more ____." Coloring games are an artful way to explore, express, and increase emotional awareness. When children finish their individual classwork, they take out emotion-themed coloring pages to complete. Two coloring books that appeal to young and older children, respectively, are *Colorful Garden: A Feelings Coloring Book* and the *Harry Potter Deluxe Coloring Book Series.*[32]

Emotional learning games that serve to help children assess their feelings are an important part of teaching the positive psychology teaching taxonomy. They can play the Tell the Good game. Working in small groups, they write a list of all the good that happened in the previous week and they clip articles from the newspaper to share good news from school, home, and the neighborhood. After this research, they list all the good they each did and how it made them feel. "I gave up my place in line and felt grateful to help another." "I loaned my friend a book and I felt caring toward him." "I raised my hand for every question and I felt brave." Using games, children inventory their feelings, appraise and process them, and make positive decisions.

The Kindness Project website is where Pass It Forward tokens are available for purchase and then distributed with acts of kindness so children can tally their acts of kindness.[33] Children can register their tokens online and assess kindness levels while learning geography as they follow a token's path on a map.

The ABC Plan game encourages children to brainstorm what will happen if Plan A does not work out and how to develop Plans B and C. Another game that requires children to shift focus is the Snap Out of It game. When children are feeling uncertain, they snap their fingers and tell themselves, and others, to snap out of it. They play the Next Best Step game to help each other figure out the next best step after a disappointment or discouraging news. In the positive psychology classroom, you often hear children say, "What's your plan for tomorrow?" "What is the next step?" "Snap out of it."

To use action to gain perspective on emotion, children can play the Step Back game. Standing in a tight circle, a child steps into the center and describes a frustrating incident recently encountered, and everyone in the group responds by saying, "step back" and everyone then takes a step back.

By taking a physical step backward, children can widen their perspective and remind themselves to disengage from a difficult situation. Children can play the Scavenger Hunt game in order to find others with the same emotional coping strategies. "I tell myself it could be worse." "I take deep breaths." "I imagine good news." "I talk to my friend." They find others who list the same strategies in their journals and discuss how they can decide to feel better.

Cognitive mediation of feelings bridges emotional awareness and management. Games that prompt children to think about their emotions in different ways are the precursor to self-regulation. Games that help shift children's perspectives and reframe their thinking about their feelings teach valuable emotional learning lessons.

To repair their mood and change or enhance an emotion, children play the Inside Out game and say those words when someone needs to turn a bad mood inside out to a good one. The Random Acts of Kindness Foundation website can teach children how to prevent anger by establishing a kindness zone in the classroom.[34] The Human Kindness Project website offers a monthly newsletter that older children can read to inspire their own class kindness newsletter and teaches children to turn angry inside out and be kind.[35]

A more exhaustive approach to using gaming to teach emotional learning across all the pillars is to create a Feelings Learning Center in the classroom. The learning center would feature one of the emotional pairs each month: one month it is the Happy/Sad Learning Center and the following month it is the Kind/Angry Learning Center. Children sign in and sign out at the center, set a timer to track their time, and select activities from a menu of emotions learning games. The teacher decorates the center with posters and banners about feelings, stocks it with a library of feeling-themed books, and provides quiet games that teach emotional learning. There is a cork wall where children pin art, a wall lined with paper to create a feelings graffiti wall, and art supplies to use. Ideally, there would be two mobile digital devices and a computer. There are also many card games about feelings: memory, thought prompting, and sentence-completion cards.[36] Board games for cooperative play include *Ungame*, *Life Stories*, *Peace Town*, *Wild Ride to the Heart*, and the *Stamp Game*.[37] There are feeling puzzles, journals, workbooks, activity books, coloring books, videos, stickers, graphic organizers, music, newsletters, magazines, activity books, software, and e-curricula, including digital emotion cards, exercises, games, mood journals, and more.

At every Feelings Learning Center, a children's book library is central to helping children learn to change a negative emotion or enhance a positive one. For example, a Kindness Center develops feeling lessons using dozens of children's books. The teacher selects books that are appropriate for each grade; such classics as *The Giving Tree*, *The Quilt Maker's Gift*, and *Shiloh* may be used.[38] These and other books are the basis for teacher-developed positive psychology lessons. For example, children can create their own paper quilts, decorating one side of a quilt square with a negative emotion and the other with a positive one.

When the learning center theme changes from kind to angry, the Angry Learning Center uses books about anger. There are approximately 100 children's books about anger for every age, grade, and reading level, such as *The Angry Octopus: A Relaxation Book* and *An Angry Drum Echoed*.[39] The website Get Your Angries Out is another resource to use in the Center.[40] The teacher might use the Feelings Learning Center as an alternative to a traditional, punitive time-out. The center can also function as a place to reshape and rehabilitate negative emotions and to reflect on the value and benefit of positive ones. Whether there is a single strengths game once a week or a learning center full of games, the positive psychology teaching taxonomy adopts an educational approach intent on teaching children to acknowledge, analyze, mediate, and manage their emotions in engaging, interactive ways.

7. Join a Book or Film Club

Reading books teaches four pillars of positive psychology. How do the characters use their emotions to make decisions? Did their emotions help or hurt them? Reading about how others express, understand, change, and manage their emotions has a powerful learning effect. For this reason, dozens of both formal and informal positive psychology curricula adopt a literature-based approach. Reading fiction and nonfiction is one of the best ways, if not the best way, to teach the positive emotion benchmark.

Carefully selected stories, biographies, fables, folktales, myths, and more teach emotional awareness, perspective, and mastery. Some books teach children about feelings. For example, in the book *My Many Colored Days* the characters wear different colored scarves to represent different feelings.[41] Other books teach children about particular feelings: *When Sophie Gets Angry . . . Really, Really Angry* and *Sometimes I'm Bombaloo*.[42] Young children learn to call a negative emotion "Bombaloo" and ask each other, "Do you feel Bombaloo?" Regardless of the particular emotion, reading, writing, and discussion help children to identify feelings, evaluate them, think about them in as many different ways as possible, and change them when needed.

Young children learn to reference the emotions of characters in books and refine their understanding of emotions by reading about them. The teacher uses stories to check whether children accurately perceive and interpret emotional content.

Here is an example: The primary teacher opens the book *The Lorax* by Dr. Seuss and the children begin to read along with the teacher. "Unless someone like you cares a whole awful lot. Nothing is going to get better. It's not." The children identify the positive feelings that motivated the Lorax to take environmental action. They list feelings that they have that have motivated them to positive action. They also discuss negative feelings that can cause inaction or harmful, hurtful actions. Using children's literature to increase emotional awareness and broaden the emotional perspective is important because children cannot change what they know about their emotions (cognitive learning) or how they think about their feelings or how they act on their feelings (conative learning) unless they learn to be aware of every shade of emotion. When they can assess the hue of an emotion, they can decide to make it brighter or dimmer.

The children's book *The Seven Habits of Happy Kids* teaches the habits of happiness or the ability to think about feelings and act on them in positive ways.[43] The happiness habits are listed as the following: get negative feelings in order, decide positive emotions are powerful, synergize emotions so positive ones diffuse negative ones, start out happy to end up happy, think win-win so every disadvantage is turned into an advantage, understand others' feelings so you understand yourself, and sharpen the saw so you are ready to work. Children also learn about the seven habits of happiness by visiting the land of Seven Oaks. They read seven entertaining stories about characters who live there and who learn how to be happier. They read about irritable Pokey the Porcupine, who learns to manage his prickly feelings, and shy Ernie the Snail, who learns to be braver. The stories prompt discussion about how to develop positive emotions. At the end of each story, there are discussion points and next steps to help children put happy habits into action. The book includes a Happiness Tree that illustrates how to grow tall and sturdy. A companion website offers children riddles, games, a virtual playhouse, and power words.[44]

The seven habits form the basis of a class pledge or can be topics at the weekly class meeting and are the basis for emotional learning. Children are very likely to imitate the positive emotional reactions and responses in books, and they learn to express emotions in balanced and helpful ways. This is why many of the best positive psychology programs are literature-based.

Columbia University's Project ExSEL teaches positive psychology through the language arts and social studies.[45] The program consists of

14 lesson plans that use exemplary children's literature to teach about feelings and the plans are available for download. Two of the books used—*My Dog Is Lost* and *Tops and Bottoms*—introduce characters who must cope with difficult experiences that cause them distress and arouse many negative feelings.[46] However, the characters are able to overcome adversity by replacing negative reactions with positive ones and, in doing so, positive feelings become emotional strengths. Children read the book selections, express their own emotions about the book, and then discuss the emotions in the book. The discussion focuses on how the negative emotions that spring from adversity can contribute to positive strengths. Eight enrichment videos and an online interactive game reinforce the lessons. There is a personality test to assess the color of personality and an online game to teach how the body responds to different emotions. A favorite is the Kid's Playground game where children manage their emotions within a virtual schoolyard.

The 4R's program also selects high-quality children's literature; the program was tested by the Morningside Center for Teaching Social Responsibility in partnership with New York City Public Schools.[47] Children participate in book discussions in order to deepen their understanding of the stories. The curriculum focuses on building the emotional skills that children need in their daily school lives to manage intercultural understanding and conflict resolution. Before moving from one book to the next, the children write reviews of the book in their journals. Empirical research proves that the curriculum can help children flourish in school; the bibliography of books is available for a teacher to access via the website.[48]

The 4R's curriculum identifies 43 grade-differentiated books for kindergarten through fifth grade that teach children how to make a difference in their own lives and the lives of others through emotional management. The kindergarten-level book, *Subway Sparrow*, tells the story of a sparrow that flies into a New York City subway car.[49] A young Asian girl solicits the help of a Spanish-speaking teen, a Polish-speaking woman, and another person to help her free the sparrow. The girl is very happy because so many different people come to the rescue.

In a small group, the children can consider how the young girl might have felt and reacted if the others had refused to help her and they consider how the little girl should have responded in that case. The children make a list of the feelings that made the characters respond helpfully and then they write about them. They also make a list of why the other people might not have felt like helping. The children role-play rival explanations and other outcomes.

The fifth-grade book, *The Keeping Quilt*, evokes strong emotions related to feelings of love and comfort.[50] For four generations, the quilt that Anna's mother made from a basket of old clothes was so much more than simply the sum of its parts, which were fragments of Anna's babushka, Uncle Vladimir's shirt, and Aunt Havalah's night dress. The quilt becomes a Sabbath tablecloth, a wedding canopy, and a blanket that warmly welcomes new babies to the world. The story of the family quilt inspires strong feelings in children, who can bring their own special family mementos into class to show and tell. They can also collect scraps of fabric to begin making their own quilts. In the process children consider what makes them feel loved and grateful in their own lives.

The 4R's positive psychology program has taught tens of thousands of children both cognitive reading skills and affective literacy by using the best children's literature. The opportunities to teach emotional lessons through classic literature—such as Greek mythology, Native American oral storytelling, African folktales, and American fables—are exciting. A teacher should place books about feelings into every nook, cranny, and corner of his or her classroom and into every lesson—every day. One of the best ways to become aware, understand, process, and manage feelings of all shapes and sizes is to teach the pillars of emotional learning through literature.

After reading a book, children work in pairs and choose books about opposite emotions. They discuss the books that represent different points of view in order to widen and deepen their emotional range. They write their own stories about the same emotions depicted, record each other reading the books aloud, write book reports focusing on the causes and consequences of the feelings expressed, and participate in acting out the stories. The teacher posts a weekly recommended reading list of books about feelings organized by reading level and features an Emotions Book of the Week. Children read it and complete a reading response form: What feelings did the characters possess? Were these strong feelings and how long did they last? Did the feelings help or hurt the characters in the story? Could they choose another feeling? Did they express their feelings in a balanced way?

Children especially benefit when they act out feelings in stories and poems. They can even perform an opera. In reading a play, children act out words. When acting, they express sadness, joy, anger, fear, courage, determination, and uncertainty based on the story at hand. Children throw things, screech, and stick out their tongues when displaying negative emotions. They speak softly, hug each other, and jump for joy when acting positive emotions. Acting out emotions is a great way to express them positively and negatively and to consider how changing them changes the story. They consider how deciding to change their own feelings will change how they act.

An opera is easy to act out because it is emotional poetry set to music. The So This Is Opera curriculum project invites children to sing emotions in a real aria: the hopefulness of Goldilocks, the anger of Puccini, and the humor of Mozart's "Ewwwww" in *The Magic Flute*.[51] Reading, writing, discussing, drawing, and acting all help children understand what triggers feelings of being angry or calm, brave or afraid, and hopeful or disappointed.

Another way children learn about feelings is by observing them in films. Children can relate to the feelings expressed in books, but by watching films, they actually feel the same emotions the characters feel. Third graders can watch an uptempo, award-winning music video from the Second Step Program—a global positive psychology program that teaches emotional awareness as the basis for emotional regulation.[52] After watching the video, *New Edition: Empathy*, the students each write a paragraph about the feelings exhibited and how the characters managed them. Fifth-grade children can use The Story of Movies project to study classic films and notice how music, lighting, and dialogue influence feelings, shift mood, and alter their perspective.[53]

Older children give examples of a television show or movie scene where the camera either zooms out so they see a larger panorama or zooms in for a close-up scene with a narrow view. They discuss how the angle of the camera changes perspective and emotional reaction; they conduct a formal character analysis that compares and contrasts the character's feelings to their own under similar circumstances.[54]

When children watch a video, film, play, or television show, they observe positive and negative emotions and actions and then consider their own best or worst reactions in a new light. No matter the age or grade, a favorite book or film helps children know their feelings better, think and rethink the utility of an emotion, and know how to change it or sustain it. When children balance, adjust, and express emotions with skill and at will, they are more even-tempered.

8. Create a Happiness Project

In her book *The Happiness Project*, Gretchen Rubin plans how to increase her emotional wellness and guides others in the process by suggesting that everyone create an annual happiness project.[55] A happiness
project is one of the simplest ways to prime the happiness pump. In the
elementary school classroom, the project takes the form of lists or col-
lages of personal activities that aim to increase children's happiness quotient without necessarily changing conditions or their circumstances.

The teacher helps children to construct the happiness project and
to ensure that children can think, "I am happy right now because I am
working toward accomplishing my happiness project goals." Rubin's
own happiness project established five goals that are useful for children
to consider as they develop their own happiness projects in accordance
with her guidelines. These first three guidelines are developmental in
nature and the final two focus on her implementation strategies: (1)
make the most of life as it exists and do not wish for what they do not
or cannot have, (2) use humor to get through difficult times, and (3)
practice gratitude and love in concrete ways by listing daily examples.
The final two suggestions address implementation: (4) ask for help when
needed and do not try to do everything alone, and (5) stop fixating on
results and enjoy the process.[56] Children keep these parameters in mind
as they fully describe and detail their happiness goals.

Children work on the projects in groups; they share their ideas, explain how the happiness project will make life more pleasant and fulfilling, and focus on positive emotion. Planning and executing a happiness
project is an effective way to identify and evaluate current emotional
states. Engaging in the project itself cognitively mediates mood and increases the positive affect associated with happiness. A happiness project
requires a change in understandings, outlooks, and actions.

The project is a written commitment to change feelings that is self-
imposed, self-directed, and self-monitored. A happiness project most
often takes the form of a journal, scrapbook, or portfolio that captures
the details of a personal happiness plan that the children add to over the
course of a year. Whether using a journal, a traditional parchment paper
scrapbook, a digital e-scrapbook, a colorful poster, or a simple list, the
happiness project is a promise to the self to make the changes needed to
live a more pleasant life as a happier person.

Younger children may simply develop a checklist of how they will
change in ways important to them. To begin their happiness project,

younger children gather three large pieces of poster paper, crayons, magazines, glue, glitter, and other art supplies. Working with a partner, they update and post a monthly happiness project. On one piece of paper the children draw and paste pictures of what possessions or occurrences will make them happy that they don't currently possess or haven't experienced: a new videogame, less math homework, a trip to Disneyland.

On the second piece of paper, the children draw and paste pictures of what they do currently possess, know, or do that makes them happy: a cozy home, dancing, or banana cream pie. They learn to focus on the list of what they possess, and they add to it and enrich it. Their happiness project serves to remind them every day that they are lucky and that they should enjoy the good and happy blessings they take for granted. The project also helps them to consider happiness opportunities that were neglected or overlooked.

On the third piece of paper, children list, draw, and paste what will make someone they love happy. Each week they list what they can do to give that person more happiness: sit on the couch with Dad and watch his favorite sports team play; help Grandma do the dishes; let my little sister choose the dolphin book that she loves best; help a friend build a tree house; watch the sunset with Mom instead of watching cartoons.

Finally, children collate a list of what will increase happiness in their everyday lives. From this list, an individual happiness project emerges. For example, Carey presents her project as a scrapbook that uses pictures that she drew and some that were cut out of magazines. Her project includes (1) smile at someone ten times a day, (2) take deep breaths when angry, (3) read one book to my little sister every week, (4) daydream about one favorite memory every day for five minutes, and (5) no matter what happens, remember it is not the end of the world.

Older children create a more detailed happiness project that include specific resolutions and that track their own progress with more precise metrics: I will read a new book a month, I will run a mile by year's end, I will give out three hugs a day, and I will tell my mother "thank-you" every night. As part of their project, they catalog jokes and cartoons they can use to cheer themselves up; collect words, quotes, and poems that motivate them; write happiness blogs to chronicle their happiness project; and fill treasure boxes with inspirational objects and talismans.

They envision and share their project by using the website Tel-A-Vision and developing a multimedia presentation of their happiness plan.[57] The video they create may include words, affirmations, poetry, quotes, photography, and music. They all include the following goal: act the way

I want to act the way I feel and feel the way I want to act. Their project lists the emotions they intend to feel and the actions that bring those feelings to life: I will feel more hopeful; when I am disappointed, I will tell myself and others that it does not matter whether or not you win, it matters more that you are proud to do your best.

There are many K–5 children's books written on the topic of happiness to read before developing their happiness project. Children read books such as *How Full Is Your Bucket?*, *The Happiness Tree: Celebrating the Gifts of the Trees We Treasure*, *Sachiko Means Happiness*, and *The Big Little Book of Happy Sadness*.[58] Books also lend themselves to follow-up lessons that supplement the happiness project and prompt children to think even more deeply about what makes them feel happy.

Children fill a bucket with their happiness goals, which are written on pieces of construction paper. They write the name of someone who makes them happy on a leaf, which they pin to the happiness tree. They earn pennies to give to each other to toss into the class wishing fountain, making wishes intended to bring happiness to the people they love. Barbara Fredrickson's happiness ratio suggests that children need to experience three positive emotions for every negative emotion in order to achieve the emotional balance that brings happiness.[59] This means that a happiness project must increase positive emotions and decrease negative ones, or both, to achieve a 3:1 positive-to-negative optimal happiness ratio. In other words, the happiness project must overflow with positive intentions, activities, and goals. If children deliberately consider what makes them happy, develop a concrete plan to pursue it, and commit to their happiness projects, it works.

At the end of each week, children review and chart the progress they are making on their happiness projects. When the review is complete, they play the Good Riddance game by listing all the negatives that intruded on their happiness on a piece of paper. They then tear the paper up, throw it away, and begin anew.

9. Sing a Song or Bang a Drum

Music is the melody of emotion, and children can use it to express feelings by whistling a happy tune or banging on a drum. They sing silly songs, tap rhythms, play kazoos, dance on tiptoes, or compose tunes to express their feelings. They listen to the strains of violins as background music while thinking quietly, reflecting on feelings, assessing emotions, and considering options. They remember the lullabies their mothers sang to summon positive memories and self-comfort. They listen to the lyrics of a song to mediate their thoughts, clarify a feeling, or encourage an action. They look forward to hearing the morning church bells or the night train whistle that is the measure of their days. All these sounds of music activate the recognition, strategic, and affective neural networks of the brain so that music burrows deep into thoughts and feelings.[60] The teacher can use music to teach the positive emotion benchmark.

A teacher in a positive psychology classroom picks a class theme song that expresses the emotion of the class members, and they sing it daily. Children nominate songs and often these will include movie theme songs, popular children's songs, Top 40 hits, and suggestions from the teacher, who can refer children to the Songdrops website for more options.[61] Children also invite parents to submit favorites songs with some interesting choices: "We the Cats Shall (Hep Ya)" by Joe Jackson, "Peter Pan You Can Fly" by Disney-Sing-a-Longs, "I Hope You Dance" by Lee Ann Womack, and "True Colors" by Cyndi Lauper. One grandmother suggested Doris Day's "Que Sera Sera."

One parent nominated the Beatles anthem "Yellow Submarine" as the happiest song she knows, advising children to sing along to it while they read the new *Yellow Submarine* book on their iPads.[62] Each day the children listen to the nominated songs and vote. When five top songs have been chosen, they discuss how each one makes them feel and they campaign for their favorite song, share lyrics, create campaign posters, and give speeches on behalf of the nominated songs. The final vote determines the song that the children will sing at the morning meeting or at the day's end.

Encouraging children to choose and learn new songs about feelings is an effective way to teach the lessons of emotional learning in ways that children remember. A children's songwriter, Jeremy, sings about feelings in three songs: *Use Your Words*, *Jump So High*, and *Happy Sad Silly Mad*.[63] The PBS Kids Music website plays songs from Steve Songs's album *Music Time*.[64] Steve writes songs for children about feelings themed around popular children's characters, such as the Lomax and the Hound of Music.

If making music is a way for children to express feelings, listening to it helps children assess their emotions. The teacher can play classical music selections from the Classics for Kids website, which offers many selections that appeal to children.[65] Children listen to the different sounds of the orchestra's instruments and then identify the emotions conveyed. They assess the emotional nature and intensity of the music and consider if it changes their feelings.

Once children understand how music communicates and mediates emotion, they learn to do the same by playing instruments to express feelings. Harmonicas, drums, flutes, and other simple instruments do just fine. One fifth-grade teacher shares positive emotion with ukuleles. Donors bought the instruments, and he taught the children to play old-timey 1930s songs: "Whenever I am upset the ukulele music fills my head and I feel better."[66]

Children play music to express feelings and to consider how the music changes their mood and prompts positive action. Many iTouch and iPad applications help children make music easily and transform a child into a virtual garage band, with guitars, ukuleles, xylophones, pianos, drums, and more. Never before has it been so easy for a teacher to use music to teach the four pillars of emotional learning. For example, the Singing Fingers virtual game connects the sound of musical notes to the lines and shapes that children draw on the screen of a mobile digital device; as children draw happy faces the music follows along.[67] E-curriculum enables children to find and memorize song lyrics that make them feel determined, listen to music that makes them feel motivated, or compose a melody that makes them feel calm.

Whether children make music or listen to it, they describe the emotions it evokes in them and what sounds and words contribute to those feelings. Children assess the musical message, think about how it affects them, and use it to help manage their emotions. At the end of the day, children become members of a marching parade with everyone playing musical instruments—or singing the class song—so children go home with music ringing in their minds. Whether singing, listening, playing, or marching, the discussion about the connection between emotions and music is important.

Older children enjoy researching the different music enjoyed during different periods of history and the types of musical instruments played. They investigate how music transformed political and social change movements—changing people's feelings and actions—on a large scale. From the marching songs of the American Revolution to the gospel songs of the American civil rights movement, music blends with emotion to change feelings, motivate decisions, and make a profound difference. The positive psychology teaching taxonomy uses music to teach the pillars of emotional learning so children find emotional harmony in learning and in life.

10. Spread the Word

Positive psychology spreads the word that positive emotions matter. Children learn about the power of feelings in stand-alone segments or infused in history, science, mathematics, and other academic subjects. Every academic subject becomes a chalkboard for teaching children how to self-examine and self-manage their feelings.

Academics in the hands of a skillful teacher can magnify the connection between feelings and thoughts—teaching not only emotional awareness but also emotional cognizance of the powerful mutual reciprocity between feeling and thought. In science class, kindergarten children can study different categories and types of flowers by comparing and contrasting them. First graders learn what flowers and children need to live and thrive, the climate zones where flowers grow best, and what they need to change and grow. Second-grade children learn addition by calculating the cost of sending virtual bouquets to their mothers, aunts, sisters, and grandmothers. Third-grade children measure the growth of the potted flowers that stand on the windowsill in the classroom. Positive psychology does not stop at teaching the science absent emotional learning because without emotionality, managed science is of little use.

Young children use their knowledge of flowers, gardening, and botany to assess and mediate their own feelings and thoughts in ways that positively affect their actions. Because botany is the academic subject, the teacher takes the language of science to express the pillars of emotional learning. The teacher reminds children that feelings are like pretty flowers in a garden and children must carefully tend to their feelings, too. The teacher depicts negative emotions as weeds growing in a garden and choking the flowers. While teaching the botany unit, the teacher uses biological science to teach psychological science by employing gardening analogies and metaphors to convey the language and practice of positive psychology.

To reinforce the lesson, younger children color whimsical pages of flowers using the *Colorful Garden: A Feelings Coloring Book* and they post them on the bulletin board that illustrates key content about botany and feelings.[68] Older children create detailed drawings of different indigenous flowers and plants, label them, and identify the feelings they evoke. The teacher can use almost any subject—botany, mathematics, physiology, or geography—as the medium to teach positive emotion.

Working in small groups, fourth-grade children measure physiological reactions to stress by graphing the results and reporting their findings with HeartMath software.[69] The assignments focus on measuring the biological effects of emotion. Fifth-grade children study geography by researching international celebrations of holidays and festivals, study economics by debating the economics of happiness, and study culture by comparing peaceful and more aggressive cultures. They distill the research in order to identify the choices and decisions that lead to happiness across the globe. All of the children then learn new words to express feelings in different languages: Spanish, French, Japanese, and American Sign Language.

Philosophy is another subject the teacher can use to teach positive psychology in the intermediate elementary classroom, because Greek philosophers bring clarity to children's questions about happiness. *Philosophy for Kids* presents the philosophies of happiness in simple and interesting ways so that children can easily discuss questions derived from various philosophies.[70] The book offers a child-friendly adaptation of the philosophers' ideas; after reading it, children respond to questions about their own lives and happiness.

Children ponder questions about the intricacy of emotion and use a philosopher's orientation, and specific premise, to learn more about emotions and how to manage them. "Should you let little things bother you?" "Will having fun make you happier than studying?" "Can another person understand your feelings?" "Are you the same person you were 5 years ago?" "Is it important to speak and write so you can be understood?" "Is it always easy to know what causes things to happen?"[71]

Studying Eastern philosophy, children practice writing Chinese symbols that represent Confucius's five virtues underlying his philosophy of happiness. They write fortunes for the fortune bag by putting a favorite Confucius saying into the bag and they draw one at the end of the day. One favorite quotation is "Our greatest glory is not in never failing but in getting up every time we do."[72]

The great Western and Eastern philosophies advance children's understandings of happiness. Even the contemporary philosophy found in J. K. Rowling's legendary Harry Potter book series can become a study guide for happiness. Children study the characters' emotional states, actions, and reactions. Harry Potter's definition of happiness is another touchstone that helps children understand and assess their feelings.

Children ponder what makes them feel light or dark, how those feelings affect their actions, and how they can modify those actions. As one quotation about happiness states, "We've all got both light and dark inside us. What matters is the part we choose to act on. . . . That's who we really are."[73] Positive psychology teaches children to encourage the light when they feel most dark, and in doing so, transcend their negative emotions to experience more happiness and joy. "Transcendence is when we choose to share caring moments without flinching from the fleeting frailness of life . . . to choose one's attitude . . . to choose one's own way."[74]

A number of research-based, self-contained, comprehensive positive psychology programs also teach children how to choose the benchmark of positive emotion. Yale University's RULER program distributes a language-based curriculum for K–5, and a literacy curriculum for K–12.[75] In grades K–8, the curriculum teaches children five emotional literacy skills: (1) recognize emotions in yourself and others, (2) label a full range of emotions using a rich vocabulary, (3) express emotions appropriately across different conditions, (4) understand the causes and consequences of emotions, and (5) regulate emotions to foster healthy relationships and goals.

Children learn to expand the amount of time between an emotional trigger and a response to the trigger, ensuring they have time to process a positive replacement emotion instead. They use a personal mood meter to help create this space. The teacher helps children identify individual feelings accurately by using multiple senses; children use this self-assessment data to develop a written blueprint that outlines a problem-solving approach to emotional management. In the process, they learn to evaluate their feelings on a two-dimensional axis: first, they rate a feeling as an unpleasant or pleasant emotion, and second, they rate it as a low-energy or high-energy emotion.

Teachers use meta-moments as "a-ha" teaching moments and these lessons deliberately teach children how to attend to the nature and intensity of the emotion, interpret it correctly, understand it fully, and manage it effectively. Another key feature of the RULER program is a class charter that is both a mission statement and a pledge to support the benchmark of positive emotion.

The Second Steps Program teaches children from preschool through middle school how to succeed emotionally, socially, and academically.[76] Each grade level curriculum kit includes a standardized assessment checklist, posters, color lesson photo cards, puppets, props, a DVD, a CD, a materials binder with cards and home links, a teacher guide, teacher unit cards, and enrichment activities. The program includes award-winning music videos and a CD created for every grade level. In this curriculum, music teaches emotion in the most upbeat and inspiring way. Early lessons teach children how to identify strong emotions while later lessons teach strengths to manage them, including conflict resolution and peacemaking.

Wellesley's Open Circle is a grade-differentiated positive psychology program that revolves around a 15-minute open circle meeting twice a week.[77] The K–5 standards-based curriculum includes 34 sequenced formal lessons and 38 enrichment activities such as role playing to facilitate dialogues and community-building exercises. The curriculum emphasizes the language of positive psychology and its interpersonal nature.

The HeartSmarts program is for children in third grade through fifth grade.[78] The program includes a leader's guide, slide show, activity books, posters, and assessment tools. The program explores emotions through the creation of emotional weather reports. The technology-based curriculum teaches how to self-regulate stressful feelings, strengthen friendships, improve learning readiness, and boost academic performance through heart-based education. Children synchronize positive emotions by reducing negative self-talk and learning to listen for others' emotions with their hearts. There are strengths-training activities, best-self exercises, and a module that translates feelings to accomplishment. The program is also available with software that older children use to monitor and practice self-regulation of emotions.

The after-school program, Wings for Kids Program, is a positive psychology program that encourages singing, dancing, movement, and games.[79] Teaching the life lessons that children need to be more positive and happy, the 15-hour-a-week curriculum establishes 30 goals related to self-awareness and self-management. Every Friday is "wild wings activity day," when children compete with each other on the playground in physical challenges that test emotional strength.

Children learn to choose happiness in both formal and informal programs and through the study of both traditional and less traditional subjects. Even the practice of simple exercises benefits children emotionally, promoting both self-awareness and self-control.

Yoga exercises the brain and the body by flooding the brain with oxygen and endorphins in order to create feelings of happiness. There is consensus that yoga improves mind and body performance by fostering the overall well-being that children need to flourish, and the practice of simple yoga builds emotional strengths such as grit, patience, and optimism. There is growing advocacy to teach yoga, as well as use yoga techniques, in the classroom.[80]

Yoga-4-Classrooms divides 67 activities into six categories. The categories are: let's breathe, at your desk, stand strong, loosen up, imagination vacation, and be well. Activity cards illustrate the lessons, provide instructions for teaching them, prompt discussion about feelings, and suggest enrichment activities to reinforce the emotional learning. In addition, the curriculum includes an additional 200 positive learning activities explicitly aligned with the academic curriculum and a companion website.[81]

At the Yoga Kids website, there are nine instructional videos that teach basic yoga movements, such as the tree pose, linking the pose to an instructional unit on trees.[82] The teacher's guide includes cards with photographs of the poses and tips for curriculum integration. Teaching yoga in a positive psychology program has the advantage of teaching calm and relaxed responses in lieu of angry and tense responses.

Whether reading books about feelings, listening to relaxing music, or learning simple yoga poses, both traditional and nontraditional subjects advance emotional awareness, understanding, and management when a teacher uses those subjects to teach the positive psychology teaching taxonomy benchmark of positive emotion. Emotional learning is the primary focus, and the teacher should examine every potential lesson through the positive psychology prism of "Is there an emotional lesson in this story?" "How can this lesson connect to the balance of emotions?" "How can I teach mathematical concepts and emotional appraisal simultaneously?"

Summary and Conclusion

The positive psychology teaching taxonomy benchmark of positive emotion does not manufacture extrinsic happiness or superficial emotion. The benchmark is teaching children how to generate an intrinsic and authentic happiness. Children's positive and negative emotions ebb and flow; sometimes they are strong and crashing and, at other times, soft and rippling. However, their feelings are always pushing them forward to learn more, and understand more, about themselves, others, and the world around them.

Teachers develop programs, curricula, units, lessons, activities, and games that teach children the four pillars of emotional learning: (1) keen emotional awareness and recognition, (2) careful emotional assessment and appraisal, (3) thoughtful emotional processing and decision making, and (4) balanced emotional expression and empowerment. The positive psychology teaching taxonomy defines specific content and identifies particular skills that are the gateway to the mastery of all subjects. The teacher weaves lessons into the curriculum both formally and informally by creating a mosaic of emotional lessons so that children master the emotional awareness, understanding, good decision-making, and cognitive processing needed to redirect strong emotions.

Positive psychology is unique in elementary education because it is both a discipline or subject and a set of learned skills. The benchmark of positive emotion makes academic learning across all disciplines more accessible to all children. Whether a teacher uses an in-depth positive psychology program that teaches anger management or a decorative poster about feelings hanging on the wall as a point of discussion, every effort to teach children to use positive emotion is important. Both integrated daily programs in the language arts, mathematics, social science, and more, and stand-alone full themed, interdisciplinary programs implemented once a week change the dynamics of learning in the classroom.

Most educators choose to infuse the benchmark of positive emotion into academic lessons. Others plan and implement interdisciplinary, project-based instructional units that add academic content to positive psychology lessons. The teacher identifies the positive psychology benchmark to teach and then connects the academic standard to it. For example, a lesson about emotional change also teaches science content and the concepts of equilibrium and homeostasis in nature as indications of well-being. The word *geistig*, meaning spirit, describes children's capacity for self-transcendence that is achieved when they learn to "choose to share caring moments with others."[83] Positive psychology is heart-to-heart teaching and it is transformative for all involved. In positive psychology programs, teaching the pillars of emotional learning creates emotional flow so children learn to listen for, and respond positively to, emotional content whether in a musical score or a friend's voice.

In the positive psychology classroom, children might imagine their favorite season, write about it, and discuss it so they are able to recognize the positive feelings engendered, analyze them, process them, and conjure them up as needed. In the process, they examine what truly makes them happy—and why—so they know how to find and enjoy the pleasant life. Happy children are welcome everywhere and contribute to the enjoyable lives of their teachers and friends. However, they also learn that a pleasant, happy life does not depend on others for happiness and so they learn to satisfy their own needs.

When children use positive emotions to help accomplish their goals, they work and play in more independent, autonomous, positive ways. They do not rely on others' applause, superficial praise, relentless cheerfulness, or transient pleasure. They know how to trust in their own ability to recognize emotions, appraise them, transform as needed, and empower themselves as cooperative, confident, joyful learners.

Case Study K–2: Teaching Positive Emotion

The second-grade children sit in a circle. In the morning meeting, the first question the teacher asks the children is, "How do you feel this morning?" John raises his hand. "I feel really scared and sad. My dog got lost last night." His voice is shaky and he is fighting back tears. "My dog is a beagle and I got him when I was little. I left the gate open and he went out it. We could not find him at all last night and I am afraid that he is cold and hungry and cannot find his way home." Other children offer sympathy and comfort. The children sitting beside him pat his hand and back gently. All of the children begin to share their own stories of lost and found pets of all varieties: hamsters, birds, pigs, dogs, cats, rabbits, and more. The teacher works to redirect comments to the emotions felt, the thoughts that ran through their heads, and the actions they took from hiding under the blankets, crying, or staring out the window. After the emotive analysis runs its course, they formulate a plan. "Can we make posters today for John to post in his neighborhood?" "Can we call the police to see if someone found him?" "When I go to Temple tonight I will pray you find Rascal or that another little boy finds him and gives him a good home." John leaves school that afternoon with 25 lost dog posters and a promise from animal services to look for Rascal.

Case Study 3–5: Teaching Positive Emotion

Eric is in the fifth grade and entering his third school this year. His parents lost their jobs twice that year and had relocated to find work. Eric is very gifted in mathematics, yet he is falling behind. He is feeling apprehensive about his first day at another new school. Wearing a pair of worn jeans—his only pair—his eyes are silent and lowered. Eric is ready to fight back if anyone trips him as he takes his seat. The first day at his last school, the teacher called him a gypsy student and, after that, all the other children called him the same. Today is different. When he walks into his new classroom, the Welcome Committee greets him. The Welcome Committee members wear nametags and give Eric one to wear, too. After introductions, they give Eric a decorated paper bag that contains coupons, school supplies, and welcome notes from all his new classmates. They interview Eric for the fifth-grade class paper. Eric lets his guard down and replaces his former fear with new anticipation. The committee invites him to help decorate the bulletin board that welcomes and introduces new children. They take his photograph and put it in the middle of the board. They work together to fill the bulletin board with pictures of Eric's favorite subjects, colors, foods, sports teams, television shows, songs, and more. Then all the children write a feeling word on a strip of paper to put on the board. Eric's new friends write "happy, caring, determined." Eric smiles and writes the word "grateful." Eric is grateful for the positive reception and all the positive feelings.

Guiding Question Exercise

Do you typically feel more positive or more negative? Are you aware of your emotional moods and can you identify the source of them? What helps you to regulate negative emotion and replace it with a positive one? Identify a positive emotion that you value or a negative emotion you had to tame. What negative emotions do you commonly encounter in the classroom? What positive ones? What pillars of emotional learning have the children in your class mastered? How would you teach the positive emotion benchmark? Do you already use some of the taxonomy techniques? Which ones work for you? What other ones could work for you? How would you help a child change a negative feeling or accent a positive one? Create a positive psychology lesson plan that teaches one or more of the indicators of positive emotion as well as a language arts standard adopting an interdisciplinary, project-based approach. Choose a book, poem, film, or song to include in the lesson.

Guiding Question Discussion

A teacher can use the Shel Silverstein poem "What Ifs" to teach emotions and academics. The poem presents a litany of common childhood fears:

"What if I'm dumb in school? What if they close the swimming pool? What if I flunk that test? What if I grow green hair on my chest?"[84] In small groups, children work together to memorize, analyze, and discuss four stanzas of the poem. They brainstorm ways to replace the different fears expressed with positive feelings, and they make a list of suggestions. They write their own positive "What If" poems: "What if I pass the test?" What if my score is best? Then I can sleep and rest." Children learn to change their reactions and use emotional skills to develop strengths to manage stressors, make friends, and assign meaning to all efforts and actions. The benchmark of positive emotion deconstructs the negative and reconstructs the positive.

Web Resources for Children

Art Zone for Kids Feelings, http://www.nga.gov/kids/zone/zone.htm/.
Arthur, http://www.pbs.org/parents/arthur/activities/development.html?cat=development
EmoSocial Developing People Skills, http://www.emosocial.com/.
Nick Jr. Rinto, http://www.nickjr.com/ni-hao-kai-lan/social-emotional-learning_ap.html
Teach Kids Feelings Drama Stuff, http://teachkidsdramastuff.com/top_50_list.html/.

Web Resources for Teachers

Action for Happiness, http://www.actionforhappiness.org/.
The Happiness Project, http://www.happiness-project.com/.
Nine Intense Experiences, http://www.intenseexperiences.com/.
Project Happiness, http://www.projecthappiness.org/category/activities/.
Responsive Classroom, http://www.responsiveclassroom.org/.

CHAPTER 5

Teaching Engagement and the Good Life: Strengths

Character is simply habit long continued.

—Plato

Positive psychology programs increase children's engagement in learning by teaching them to identify their virtues and strengths, and how to use those virtues and strength to succeed emotionally and academically. Children learn to live the good life by finding their individual virtues or strengths and using them to benefit themselves and others. They engage their inner abilities to fully involve themselves in a task; they put forward their best effort and summon their virtues and strengths for success in every situation. To engage with the learning task is to complete the task to the best of one's ability with heart, mind, and body invested in a positive outcome.

When virtue is defined in the traditional sense it describes a type of moral excellence or righteousness. However, as used in positive psychology, virtue is goodness or a particularly efficacious or beneficial quality that offers advantage and is an effective force of positive power. Virtue achieves good in children's lives when conceived as inner strength, and inner strength is defined as the virtue of acting strong or courageous and firm in commitment or conviction. Strength frequently refers to physical or mental stamina, steadiness, sturdiness, and substance.

Virtue and strength have been the subjects of contemplation and study by theologians, philosophers, and psychologists for centuries. From Plato's four cardinal virtues to Gardner's recent work on teaching truth, beauty, and goodness in education,[1] it is agreed that virtue and strength are essential for achieving the good life. If a teacher helps children develop their strength, gives them an opportunity to use it, and acknowledges it, children engage in the learning process and are more successful.

Based on a lifetime of longitudinal study, George Vaillant conceived of virtue as spiritual and healing strengths that are tests of personal adaptation and actualization.[2] Writing about the spiritual evolution of virtue, he defines spirituality as the "amalgam of positive emotions that bind us to other humans."[3] He lists love, hope, joy, forgiveness, compassion, faith, awe, and gratitude as intrapersonal virtues that build heart strength because they require engagement with others. From the interactive practice of virtue, seven healing strengths that are necessary for reconciliation and rejuvenation develop: identity, intimacy, generosity, generativity, integrity, ritual, and consolidation.

Vaillant's work also suggests that when protective defense mechanisms are misused to manage emotional pain there is a maladaptive response. Children who are not invited to a party feel hurt and may lash out, or withdraw, with an angry, automatic defensive reaction that is biological in nature: "I did not want to go to that party anyway. I don't like those kids." However, children learn emotional first aid and can figure out how to replace defensive feelings with emotionally positive feelings. In this way, they can help themselves soothe the hurt and not compound it. Positive psychology teaches children virtues such as humor and altruism that give them self-healing powers. Emotional and spiritual healing occurs when children learn to "regulate the blend of thought and feeling."[4] Many healing virtues are interactive in nature and cannot occur in isolation, so the elementary school classroom becomes a fertile ground for transforming inner virtues into outer strengths. The classroom is the perfect learning laboratory in which to develop those interpersonal strengths that are healing. Positive emotional and social interaction cultivates strength in children: Positive psychology facilitates those interactions.

The Virtues Project refines the idea of strength further and identifies five types of virtues that form the basis of strength: (1) core virtue, (2) guiding virtue, (3) strength virtue, (4) challenge virtue, and (5) sustaining virtue.[5] The core virtue is the strength needed in a particular circumstance and is situation-specific. The guiding virtue is the strength that informs decisions. The strength virtue is the emotional strength that children rely on effortlessly. The challenge virtue is the strength that children want to cultivate and it requires more focus, effort, and practice. The sustaining virtue is the one associated with endurance or flow—that children are able to exercise tirelessly and endlessly.

Another strengths-focused program, Do2Learn,[6] identifies positive psychology's signature strength as the child's home strength—the one they call upon to change life from frustrating and exhausting to easy and exhilarating. The home strength functions as the children's easy button—you push it and it makes life easier.

Christopher Peterson and Martin Seligman published *Character, Strengths, and Virtues: A Handbook and Classification* to scientifically categorize and classify human strengths by identifying 6 virtues and 24 associated strengths.[7] First, a comprehensive research analysis identified six core virtue categories: courage, justice, humanity, temperance, transcendence, and wisdom valued by moral philosophers and religious thinkers. Then the researchers listed the specific strengths associated with each category or the "psychological processes or mechanisms that define the virtues."[8] The strengths defined the virtues and are correlated with 10 ideal constructs that are intrinsically motivating and universally valued. The 24 universal strengths include both cognitive strengths, such as creativity, and affective strengths, such as optimism.

A review of the literature suggests a subset of these strengths that the elementary teacher most often targets and that positive educators most frequently investigate. There is some consensus that success in elementary school is associated with seven strengths: (1) empathy, (2) generosity, (3) courage, (4) grit, (5) patience, (6) optimism, and (7) good cheer. In most cases, children have a natural affinity for one of the strengths; and that strength is labeled as the child's signature strength, or what the child likes doing and does the best.[9]

The teacher capitalizes on children's signature strengths in learning because this will contribute to a fulfilling, good life. Imagine that a child's signature strength is empathy. The teacher enrolls the child in conflict-resolution training, and he becomes a peer mediator or class peacemaker. The practice and polish of the signature strength helps a child adapt to circumstances and actualize his inner assets in pursuit of the good life—a life that brings him and others cooperation, contentment, confidence, fortitude, serenity, inspiration, and joy.

In pursuit of the good life, a teacher should cultivate children's signature strengths as adaptive strengths taught and leveraged to advantage. The adaptive strength emerges from the resolution of emotional tensions and developmental crises so that children who conquer their feelings of pessimism and negativity emerge being more hopeful. These children might identify their signature strength as optimism. Renewed optimism fuels their motivation to succeed and the adaptive strength of trust emerges. The signature strength enables a child to trust her abilities and trust that others will support her—this adaptive strength or trust in self and others is fundamental to learning. The fully developed signature strength empowers self-governance and self-actualization.

When the signature strength is recognized, valued, and practiced, it is transgenic and becomes adaptive, transforming positive emotion into positive decisions and actions. The signature strength, or strength virtue, is especially important when threat or calamity, or a perceived threat or calamity, challenges children's emotional repertoire. Task demands easily overwhelm children who are not able to call upon their signature strengths. Children skilled at employing their signature strengths are more successful.

Neuroscience research reports that 10% of individuals know their signature strengths during a crisis and are able to act on them automatically, naturally, fluently, and fluidly. Another 10% are not cognizant of their strengths and the vast majority, or 80% of all individuals, recognize the strengths of others and will follow a strong leader but do not act on their own strengths.[10] Therefore, self-identification of children's signature strengths is an important survival skill that will serve them well whether they fail a test or get lost in the park.

Social science reports that natural leaders are highly self-aware of their own adaptive strengths. They automatically focus on their own strengths and the needs of others, and they know how to use their signature strengths strategically. If a teacher's goal is to create more leaders, then she should make more children self-aware of their strengths and comfortable with them. Leaders in the elementary classroom are children who know their strengths and know how to use them to help themselves and others.

If children know themselves and their strengths well, and how to use them to advantage, they are able to scaffold themselves to success. Practical application of the positive psychology teaching taxonomy benchmark of engagement through strength requires the teacher to understand the importance of the signature strength and the value of helping children to identify, use, and sustain it as a means to well-being.

The Importance of Engagement Through Strength Learning in Positive Psychology

Positive psychology catapults positive emotions to strength and strength to action. When positive emotions shape dedicated strength, children choose action over inaction, risk over hesitation, and potential success instead of failure. Well-managed emotions produce strengths that are the crux of the positive psychology teaching taxonomy; a central feature is the identification and assessment of strengths. A crucial first step is to help children identify their strengths. Before children can use their strengths in the classroom, they have to be able to identify them.

The teacher not only helps children to identify their strengths, but he also increases the likelihood that they will engage more fully in learning. When attention is concentrated almost exclusively on faults and insufficiencies, there is likely to be little or no engagement. The teacher remembers that children ". . . want to do more than just to correct their weaknesses. They want lives imbued with meaning, and not just to fidget until they die . . . the time has finally arrived for a science that seeks to understand positive emotion, build strength and virtue, and provide guideposts for finding what Aristotle called a good and balanced life."[11]

For example, a child determines that he feels hopeful most of the time and usually expects good outcomes even in times of difficulty. He decides that his persistent positive outlook is indicative of the signature strength of optimism. He describes how this strength helps him persist when he is tired and wants to give up: "I feel really tired and I don't feel like doing this work. However, I am an optimistic person so I know I can get it done quickly and it will be worth it when I am done. Because I am optimistic I can stay enthusiastic for longer."

Table 5.1. Signature Strength Benchmark and Indicators

Signature Strength Indicators	Demonstrate Friendship	Value Meaning	Accomplishment
Empathy	Forgiveness	Tolerance	Cooperation
Generosity	Gratitude	Helpfulness	Contentment
Courage	Honesty	Fairness	Confidence
Grit	Commitment	Resilience	Fortitude
Patience	Support	Peace	Serenity
Optimism	Enthusiasm	Anticipation	Inspiration
Good Cheer	Gladness	Enjoyment	Joy

Another child decides that she feels grateful most of the time and is inclined to share her blessings. She decides that this tendency to be unselfish is indicative of the signature strength of generosity. She describes how this strength makes it easy and satisfying for her to share with others: "Sometimes I want to just keep to myself and do the task alone. However, I am a generous person so I know that others like to work with me. Because I am a generous person, I am able to share my time with them to show my gratitude for their friendship and their desire to collaborate with me."

If children possess the signature strength of courage, it means they are more willing to take risks and try new approaches. If they possess the signature strength of grit, they are better able to delay gratification and pursue long-term goals. If their signature strength is empathy, they are forgiving and recover more quickly from rebukes or insults. If their signature strength is patience, they are not impulsive and so can offer reliable support. If their signature strength is good cheer, they offer others gladness and are enjoyable to be around. In the absence of a signature strength, children have fewer resources to use to make friends, offer service, and accomplish goals.

When each child can identify his signature strength, he is able to nurture it into a habit of excellence that flows through him intuitively, and he does not even hesitate to use it to contribute to the greater good. The teacher helps children build their own strengths and support others in building their strengths. Strength is the foundation of accomplished action.

Physical, outer strength is much admired and very visible to children. They can see the sweat drip off the tired 5K runner, they cheer the baseball player whose large arm muscles send the ball high into the stadium, and they are in awe of the Marine who can do a hundred push-ups. They understand the hours of practice, the grueling training, and the mistakes endured that it takes to build physical strength and accomplishment. They become aware that emotional inner strength takes just as much practice and hard training to build as physical strength does.

Courage is much heralded but it is difficult. Patience is the mother of success and yet it takes long practice. Grit is greatly prized but it takes many failures to perfect it. Emotional strength is invisible; however, it is as important to build through strengths training as physical strength. With emotional strength comes emotional endurance and stamina that children need to go the distance.

Children learn how to cultivate their inner strengths by emulating role models whether they are patient teachers, generous siblings, or brave firefighters. Role models make invisible strengths visible. The teacher, who is with the children every day, is one of the most influential strength models. A teacher who shows courage, generosity, and empathy demonstrates some of the most powerful lessons a child will learn. What the teacher does and says to children builds strengths by example. The teacher who does not give up on any child shows grit. The teacher who makes allowances for children shows empathy. The teacher who shares her time and talent shows generosity. The teacher who does not raise her voice shows patience. The teacher who reassures that tomorrow will be a better day shows optimism. The teacher who, especially on difficult days, teaches gracefully under pressure shows good cheer.

Children remember the positive psychology life lessons long after they forget the worksheet full of nouns and verbs. The words and actions modeled by teachers, friends, and family who are in direct contact with children imprint more permanently than words read in a book or actions watched on a screen. However, the main value of the positive role model, whether imprinting directly or indirectly, is that he or she offers immediate, tangible feedback to children about their strengths.

The real-time role model can offer input about the strengths that children possess with a voice of personal authority. If the teacher, who is a role model, also praises children's strengths it reinforces the strength doubly. For children to benefit, the teacher does not praise children for being smart, attractive, or athletic because these are attributes outside of their control; praising traits outside children's control may create anxiety.[12] If the teacher praises static traits, which children cannot really influence, it interferes with strengths training. Instead, the teacher gives precise praise to children about their specific strengths that are within their immediate control such as their determination, courage, or good cheer: "Using your time to help others is generous of you." "Every time you give a presentation you are animated, and cheerful, and include humor. I always look forward to your presentations because they are funny and enjoyable." "Even though you did not make the team, the fact that you stayed optimistic through all the tryouts is admirable." Likewise, negative comments or inattentiveness to strengths do not build them and are likely to thwart them. Strength correction is more likely to refocus children on building their strengths instead of tearing them down: "When you don't finish your history assignment it seems you are not using the grit I have seen in math class." "I was surprised when you ignored your friend and walked away. You are usually empathetic toward others and are careful not to hurt another's feelings."

The father of strengths psychology, Donald Clifton's work was the basis for a ground-breaking book, *Strengths Finder 2.0*, that details a common set of personal strengths.[13] He directed a team of researchers that developed the Clifton strength assessment tool, and the tool proved the connection between the focus on a strength and the degree of engagement with a task. Whenever a person is able to focus on strengths—and not on weaknesses—and do what they do well everyday, that person is "six times more likely to be engaged . . . and three times more likely to report they have an excellent quality of life in general."[14] The research also demonstrated that when someone else focuses on a person's strengths it has a dramatic impact on engagement. In contrast, if an authority figure focuses on a person's weaknesses, the individual is 27% more likely to disengage from the task. If an authority figure ignores a person, there is a 40% chance that person will disengage.

Engagement is a direct function of the teacher's focus on children's strengths. Not only does what others focus on build, or discourage, strengths, but how children self-assess their own strengths matters just as much, if not more. Research on self-narratives suggests that what children tell themselves affects self-efficacy and outcome.[15]

Children subscribe significant meaning to what they tell themselves about their strengths and weaknesses, and this self-talk is likely to dictate their actions and often decrees the results. When the self-evaluation is harsh and self-critical, children disengage. When the self-talk is positive and encouraging, children reengage. Children learn how to praise strengths when the teacher models it for them and offers them explicit self-talk instruction: "You are too hard on yourself. Learning to write well takes time. You are patient with others. Be patient with yourself, too."

Children learn how to incorporate strengths praise into self-talk: "I feel afraid I will never catch up in reading. I am so far behind and I feel so embarrassed. However, I know I have a lot of grit so I am just going to study an extra hour every day until the last day of school. I have caught up before and I will give it my all and do it again. It is hard but I am tough. My mom says, your ancestors survived the Irish potato famine so you can survive this because there is no doubt that you have grit in your genes."

The strengths-building process begins with a child's signature strength, just as physical training focuses on someone's best physical attribute. Everyone is good at a different sport or even a specific action within a particular sport. A sprinter needs a signature strength that is different from the strength a marathon runner needs. Nonetheless, athletes still cross-train to develop a new strength, such as endurance, and in this way a weakness emerges as strength. In the same way, children learn to cross-train to develop their emotional strengths.

The Virtues Project model teaches children how to classify and consider new virtues that they can cultivate, strengthen, or moderate.[16] The signature strength is the child's virtuoso strength or his natural emotional talent, and it lays the groundwork for the development of new strengths that do not come as easily or naturally. Once children identify and firmly establish their signature strengths, they can work to expand their range of strengths.

Each child can identify his or her core strength that does not flow as readily but is very important. The children may simply value the strength or decide that it is a survival virtue that they must cultivate, given certain circumstances in their lives. Either way, they decide to do the work needed to add the core strength to the signature strength.

Children also identify what is called a challenge strength, or a strength that they do not yet possess. During the process of identifying the signature strength that they do possess, they also identify one that they do not. While a child may be optimistic, she may also be impatient. She learns that her optimism can create patience. The teacher tells her, "Remind yourself it will turn out fine whether it gets done this minute or in 10 minutes." The teacher helps children to identify a challenge virtue and reminds them to practice it. She does not scold, threaten, or punish: "If you keep talking out loud, you will not go to recess." Instead, the teacher can encourage: "Your challenge virtue is patience because you are often impatient. If you practice waiting your turn today, it will build your challenge strength."

Positive psychology seeks, and speaks to, the strength and not the deficit. The child's responsibility is to practice and increase it. Cultivating a signature strength is relatively easy; building a challenge strength is a test in the sense that children must practice the challenge strength and also to evaluate their progress in acquiring it.

Children increase their signature strength, or they practice another strength by observing the ones that others exhibit: "He showed a lot of courage when he stood up to that bully. I think I can do it, too, next time." A boy may read a story about a local hero who rescued a lost, injured dog and is inspired to show more empathy to his own pets. Teaching children how to recognize signature strength in others is as important as helping them to recognize it in themselves. If they can recognize each other's strengths, they can compliment each other and can mimic the strengths.

Children are natural role models for each other. Positive psychology teaches them how to be positive leaders and it gives them the power of their potential for good as role models. The teacher supports a classroom effort to teach every child how to set the best possible example for each other. The positive psychology classroom is marked by how easily and how often children notice and appreciate each other's strengths because they have become experts at recognizing them.

When children are able to recognize and compliment the strengths of others, they remind themselves on their own as well: "You were generous to give your great seat to John at the assembly." They are able to renew their own strength goals: "If you can do it, I can do it." They are able to quickly recognize and label someone else's signature strength: "You always make me smile. Good cheer comes so easily to you." They are able to appreciate another's core strength: "I can always count on you to tell me the truth, and there is no doubt how much honesty means to you." They can encourage a challenge strength: "I remember when you did not care if you hurt someone else's feelings. You are such a different person now that you put yourself in their shoes and you show more empathy for others." Children act as mirrors for each other. When they recognize the strengths of others, it reflects back on them.

In the process of complimenting others, they also self-assess their own actions and they are better able to praise others if they are able to recognize, appreciate, and express their own strengths, set strength goals for themselves for others to emulate, and focus more deliberately on their own strengths. Children who have hidden strengths that go unrecognized and unused will lose these strengths as they eventually atrophy and go unused. If children use their strengths and deploy them whenever they encounter everyday academic and social obstacles, their strengths increase with practice. The teacher acts as a coach in the classroom by acknowledging, encouraging, and celebrating strengths.

Accomplishment is a process of identifying, building, extending, sharing, and using strengths. Positive emotional strength is the foundation for increased learning, more enduring and authentic friendship, and greater contribution. The teacher who values accomplishment teaches children to feel brave, demonstrate courage when afraid, offer honesty when it is uncomfortable, and to be fair in a difficult situation. Strengths function as protection against stress, they insulate children from misfortune, and they scaffold children to success.[17]

Children who feel caring toward others can be paired with struggling readers to tutor; such an experience increases their empathy for others, makes them more forgiving of themselves, teaches the value of tolerance of others who struggle, and trains them in the art of cooperation. The teacher aligns and realigns academic tasks and challenges commensurate with children's signature strengths by knowing that this is the key to well-being and success in school. The teacher who attends to children's strengths and who provides ample opportunities for them to use them every day increases engagement in learning, and engagement increases the likelihood of success.

The positive psychology teaching taxonomy benchmark of engagement—through strength—focuses on the strengths that are necessary to engage academically and feel satisfied with the effort and outcome. The pillars of strengths learning teach children to recover from any situation. The teacher who recognizes courage reminds children that what they most fear is probably not as bad as what they imagine. He teaches them to put their worries in the worry jar and to sing the rain away. He teaches them to fail with grace and understand that failure is the key to success. He teaches them to focus less on egocentric concerns and to concentrate on others' needs. He teaches them to identify, employ, extend, and share their strengths by building a reservoir of strength to use when the road is long and rocky. Strength lifts up burdens and children become experts at transforming positive emotional energy into strength.

The teacher who is not attuned to a strengths-building model of education and who focuses on correcting deficiencies will cause children to disengage from the learning process. The teacher who fails to recognize and appreciate children's strengths—or worse yet—ignores them causes children to withdraw from the learning process one way or another.

The Positive Psychology Teacher's Toolbox: Engagement Through Strength

Accomplished children recognize, build on, and use their strengths. The teacher develops this capacity in children by using the four general educational methods previously discussed: (1) language of emotions and strengths, (2) infused academics, (3) visual and performing arts, and (4) strengths training. The teacher combines these general educational methods with the techniques that the positive psychology teaching taxonomy recommends to teach the benchmark of positive strength along with the academic curriculum. Strength supports learning so the academic curriculum must incorporate it.

The teacher uses the methods and techniques of the taxonomy to teach the four pillars of strengths learning: (1) identify and recognize strengths in the self and others; (2) build a signature strength and increase other related or desirable strengths; (3) practice and use strengths to accomplish goals; and (4) encourage others to use their strengths.

The Positive Psychology Teacher's Strengths Toolbox provides specific techniques to use to teach strengths learning and integrate it into the traditional academic curriculum. The techniques help younger children become aware of their signature strengths, identify them correctly, express them easily, and connect them to their thinking and actions. Older children learn to acquire new strengths by practicing a wider range of strengths, encouraging strength development in others, sharing their strengths, refining them, and modeling them. Children learn to express their strengths in poised and well-composed ways.

The teacher may use the recommended techniques in the Strengths Toolbox as part of a larger program, within a comprehensive curriculum, as a themed unit, as stand-alone lessons, as enrichment activities, or as games that children play. Positive psychology programs may include a fully developed curriculum that teaches all the benchmarks, a themed unit that teaches one, a series of lessons to assess one, a weekly schedule of activities to process one, a daily exercise to practice one, or a game to reinforce one.

Whatever form and format a positive psychology program takes, it always uses some, if not all, of the Strengths Toolbox techniques. The techniques teach strengths learning best when the techniques are used within traditional academic subjects. The Positive Psychology Teacher's Strengths Toolbox techniques includes (1) conduct strengths assessment, (2) take strengths pledge, (3) study literature, (4) observe others' strengths, (5) envision positive strengths, (6) use self-talk, (7) meditate and move, and (8) participate in strengths training. Programs, curricula, units, lessons, activities, and other learning experiences teach children how to recognize, use, and report strengths. These also focus the teacher

Table 5.2. The Teacher's Toolbox: Pillars and Techniques of Strengths Learning

Identification and Recognition	Build and Increase	Practice and Use	Encourage Others
Conduct Strengths Assessment	Envision Positive Strengths	Strengths Training	Observe Others' Strengths
Take Strengths Pledge	Use Self-Talk	Strengths Training	Use Self-Talk
Study Literature	Meditate and Move	Strengths Training	Study Literature

on the strengths that children exhibit so that she can use them to engage children by providing opportunities to use them and encouraging them to do so.

The positive psychology teaching taxonomy benchmarks, and associated indicators, employ a strengths-based model to develop full-fledged strengths applied across the learning spectrum. The teacher uses assessments and pledges to teach children to recognize, identify, understand, and use their strengths. She can teach self-talk for self-reflection and self-understanding. Using envisioning, meditation, literature study, explicit strengths training, and more prepares children to use their strengths to doggedly persist, remain optimistic, and fully engage in the good life.

The positive psychology teaching taxonomy benchmark of strength uses the techniques to teach the strengths' learning pillars from controlling anger to staying hopeful. These are not discrete but expansive techniques. That is, any single technique can teach any one, or all, of the pillars of strengths learning across the curriculum.

The teacher is in the best position to decide what pillars of strengths learning to teach and what techniques work best so that children will flourish in the classroom. Children can cultivate the courage needed to make a mistake, the patience needed to take a turn, and the good cheer needed to work well with others. Through direct instruction, children formally develop the suite of expectations and skills associated with the increase of emotional strength.

Children fill out a strengths survey, participate in a strengths card pick, and draw pictures that depict themselves, and others, acting from a position of strength. They recite a pledge that articulates the positive psychology strengths that are shared. They envision alternative endings and what strengths might alter the end result. They learn to meditate to increase the flow of positive energy and to remove blockages that impede the use of it. They read books and watch films to increase their knowledge of strengths and how to use them by thinking and observing and discussing the strengths the characters possessed, or lacked, and how this affected the outcome.

The teacher typically focuses and comments on academic strength: "You are strong in geometry and learn it very easily. You would make a good architect." The positive psychology teacher adds, "You are strong in empathy. You would make a good diplomat." "You are strong in good cheer. You would make a good tour guide."

1. Conduct Strengths Assessment

Formal assessment uses various standardized measurement tools, including tests, surveys, checklists, reflections, and more. Informal assessment may take the form of an observation or game. What the teacher should remember is that the purpose of strengths assessment is to help children identify their strengths, whatever the approach.

The *Values in Action Inventory of Strengths* (VIA- IS) is derived from the "Character Strengths and Virtues Handbook."[18] The VIA-IS is a 240-item measure of 24 character strengths with 10 items per strength that assesses strengths and generates an individual profile. The *Values in Action Inventory of Strengths Survey for Youth* (VIA-Youth) is an assessment tool with 198 questions for children 10 to 17 years old. The survey takes about 40–45 minutes to administer and yields a detailed personal strengths profile that is the starting point for lessons that aim to maximize those strengths as learning assets.[19] This evaluation tool resembles the Gallop Organization's Strengths Finder and measures strengths as traits that are stable over time but are always in flux and influenced by environment.[20] The metric is a cross-cultural study to classify and measure strengths. There is also a Strengths Explorer for Kids used to identify the strengths of young people aged 10 to 14 years.[21]

The University of Pennsylvania's Center for Positive Psychology (CPP) publishes many other surveys that also assess strengths such as gratitude, optimism, courage, and empathy. The elementary school teacher can adapt many of these instruments for informal use with children and can modify the surveys to accommodate age, grade, reading, and cognitive levels.

Many strengths-based positive psychology programs include formal pre- and post-measures to evaluate strengths gain. The teacher administers the assessment and connects the process to content learning. A mathematics lesson might invite children to score the assessment, collate the results, report the findings, and graph them. Strengths assessment data enable children to establish an initial baseline of virtue and strength.

Almost all positive psychology programs use some means of formal or informal quantitative and/or qualitative measurement. The Second Step program is a strengths-based positive psychology program that uses the Devereux Student Strengths Assessment (DESSA) as the pre- and post-test measures of program impact.[22] Another valuable informal strengths assessment resource is *40 Fun Tests for Children*.[23] This book consists of two volumes with a total of 80 fun and informal tests that assess emotions and strengths.

The self-assessments identify both emotions and strengths and help children understand how these personal characteristics affect them. The teacher can also use informal activities and games that include qualitative self-reflection as a component of the lesson or activity. There are many games that give children the chance to self-evaluate their strengths and develop a blueprint for developing them. Self-assessment exercises organize and structure self-study and self-advancement of positive strengths.

The Virtues Pick game is a good example of an informal assessment that doubles as a learning activity. The Virtues Project website offers 52 full-color virtue reflection cards for educators featuring photographs of natural beauty.[24] Each card includes a definition of the strength, six suggestions for practicing it, a quotation, and an affirmation. Younger children use the cards to identify their signature strengths and older children identify their core or challenge strengths. The teacher may use sample cards as inspiration and then children make their own.

Using the Virtues Project for Educators curricular framework, the teacher can help younger children identify a signature strength needed for a specific task: "If you are going to get this work finished, how can you use your signature strength to do it?" The teacher helps older children identify their signature strengths and the challenge strengths that they need to increase: "Calmness comes naturally to you, and you should use that strength to help others calm down. However, you seem to get disappointed and gloomy easily so you need to work on building your challenge strength of optimism." The teacher uses the educator's guide and other resources to enact the Virtues Project, including a virtue wall mural, wallet-sized reflection cards, a virtue songbook, and posters. Children play the project's Virtue Game, which assesses strength by determining if children can be trusted with a pet fish or what five strengths they have in common with a friend.[25] The goal is to earn virtues by completing strength tasks on the cards they draw.

An award-winning, global, grassroots initiative, the Virtues Project advocates the practice of virtues in everyday life. Educators in more than 95 countries use the project to create "safe, caring, high performing learning communities teaching children to commit acts of generosity and to heal violence with virtues."[26]

The 52 Virtues Project uses the 52 virtues collated in the Virtues Project for Educators and offers additional resources specifically intended for the teacher who is implementing a Virtues Project in the classroom.[27] The 52 Virtues Project explores 52 universal virtues for children in a child-friendly way—one for every week of the year—through the art and writing of children from around the world.

Children visit the Virtues Project virtual art gallery on the website to view the artwork of children from various cultures. The artwork posted offers inspiration and helps others identify, define, and illustrate their own signature strengths through art. Children discuss one of the strengths illustrated and then assess the degree to which they personally possess it and use it, identify who in the class possesses it to the greatest degree, list friends and family that they know possess it, and talk about what famous people might possess it. Children connect strengths learning to history, current events, or language arts by researching the artist's country of origin.

Strength Cards for Kids are ideal for younger children to use to consider and identify their strengths by featuring cute monkeys engaged in strength behaviors.[28] There are 40 laminated full-color cards and a 24-page booklet packed full of great ideas for using the cards to identify and recognize strengths in the classroom. Older children respond to the advanced set of Strength Cards for Kids, which is a set of 40 cards or stickers with practical, positive, affirming statements and fun-loving cartoon-style graphics.[29] The 24-page teacher's guide encourages children to solve their problems using strengths they know they possess.

The cards also bring attention to what children already do well, and they serve as reminders of what they do well. Strength cards can identify inner strengths and begin the discussion about how to use them to make friends and a contribution. Children participate in the Signature

Strength of the Week activity and they pick a card for each person in class that identifies the signature strength of that child. On wall posters, they place strengths stickers next to their names every time they practice the strength. The cards help children to become more mindful of their strengths and help them develop a strengths vocabulary. They learn to reframe a problem in terms of the strength needed to solve it: "If I give to others, what do I get back?" "If I show grit, what can happen?" "What would I do if I was not afraid?" All strength card games ground children in strengths identification, recognition, and use theory. Playing with cards, purchased or created by children, nurtures new ways of thinking about strengths, and there are many learning resources available to teach about strengths. There are cards, stickers, posters, and books available to use to get children talking and learning about the importance of using their strengths.

Using the web-based graphic organizer, Inspiration or Kidspiration software, children develop a strengths map listing three academic tasks they find hard to do or do not enjoy.[30] They add three reasons for why they find the task difficult and they describe the signature strength that they possess that can help them accomplish the task. This project connects challenging tasks to signature strengths so that the impact of one on the other is clear.

In the Superpower game, young children imagine a strength is a superpower and write a story about it. Older children play the Favorite Character game. They choose a favorite book, film, or cartoon character and make a list of the character's strengths that they also possess. Strength is children's greatest asset, and the positive psychology teaching taxonomy strength benchmark teaches children how to identify, recognize, assess, and appreciate it.

2. Take Strengths Pledge

Strengths pledges, promises, creeds, and agreements teach the four pillars of strengths learning by highlighting the virtues and strengths cherished by all in the classroom. When teaching about strengths, pledges are useful in helping children and the teacher to focus on, acknowledge, build on, and use strengths. A strengths pledge invites children to dedicate themselves to the good life and it codifies the positive traits associated with excellence that children intend to use for the benefit of the self and others.

Most often, the pledge is a public commitment to exercise the strengths of the mind as well as the strengths of the body. It is the daily articulation of intention and works best when it is simple and concrete. The much beloved 4-H rural education programs were early adopters of positive psychology principles, and the programs include a time-tested strengths pledge: "My head to clearer thinking, my heart to greater loyalty, my hands to larger service, my health for better living."[31] There is also a detailed and time-honored 4-H creed that reads, "I believe in work…for the opportunity it will give me to become a useful citizen. I believe in the training of my head for the power it will give me to think, plan, and to reason. I believe in the training of my heart for the nobleness it will give me to be kind, sympathetic, and true. I believe in the training of my hands for the ability it will give me to be helpful, skillful, and useful. I believe in the training of my health for the strength it will give me to enjoy life, to resist disease, and to work efficiently. I believe in my country, my state, and my community and in my responsibility for their development. In all these things, I believe, and am willing to dedicate my efforts to their fulfillment."[32]

The Educational Pledge Partnership (TEPP) is a private venture founded to advance educational opportunities for youth by helping them find the key to positive self-development.[33] The TEPP pledge is as follows: "I pledge to paint a positive picture of where I plan to be tomorrow and to not allow obstacles to stop the growth of my plans. The hard work today will serve as my strong tree tomorrow."[34] The philosophy espoused is it is "never too late to make a U-turn in life, life is a game, setbacks are tools that educate you and teach you how to play the game . . . build strengths through education and planning."[35] TEPP solicits contributions from businesses to send the strengths pledge packet to urban classrooms. In funded classrooms, each child receives a pledge wall poster, tote bag, hat, pen, fliers, T-shirt, and magnet. The packet also includes a personal growth board that outlines a plan to implement the pledge. Assembly speakers, event support, and two books about strengths and the concept of second chances are also available.

The teacher may use an inspiring poem, an affirmation, or a quotation that speaks to a specific strength as the pledge. Sometimes the teacher finds the perfect poem such as the "Don't Quit" poem that cheers children to strength: "So stick to the fight when you're hardest hit—It's when things seem worst that you must not quit."[36] Kipling's "If" poem is also suitable: "If you can keep your head when all about you men are losing theirs . . ."[37]

For additional inspiration, children can visit the Favorite Poem Project website.[38] The project is dedicated to encouraging, documenting, and celebrating poetry in Americans' lives and is a source for poetry that speaks to the strength of individuals and the nation. Robert Pinsky, the 39th Poet Laureate of the United States, founded the project in 1997.[39] In that year, 18,000 Americans aged 5 to 97 from every state, and from diverse backgrounds, volunteered their favorite poems.

From the recommendations, the project culled several enduring collections. The project now offers books, videos, community readings, and lesson plans online. There are numerous educator resources, including a summer institute that they can attend. Using the project resources, the teacher guides children to favorite poems about strengths: empathy, generosity, courage, grit, patience, optimism, good cheer, and more. Some classrooms write their own poems about strengths to use as their pledge. They can use the Scholastic website poem generator and choose one to use as the class pledge.[40] One child wrote a simple one: "We try our best and don't give up helping ourselves and others win the golden cup."

Whether with narrative or poetry, children can post the class strengths pledge and recite it daily. Using the Animoto multimedia website, children can make a music video using the pledge.[41] Children might share their work through a YouTube video or illustrate it with a PowerPoint presentation. A class strengths pledge substitutes for traditional rules and guides children's actions in more transformative and less rigid ways. Children commit and re-commit to the strengths of positive psychology by reciting a positive psychology pledge or creed. For example, children in a Tribes Learning Community program read the agreement aloud each day, post it in the classroom, and print it on bookmarks and posters they make or can buy.[42]

The positive psychology class pledge or creed articulates the common good and the universal value of emotional strength. The teacher should not confuse a recitation of acceptable behaviors for a positive psychology pledge because articulation of strengths distinguishes the positive psychology pledge: "I promise to be strong by acting brave when I am afraid. I promise to be strong by acting patient with myself, and others, when I am frustrated. I promise to be strong by acting hopeful when I am discouraged." The pledge is an agreement to use strengths in a way that makes a difference in academic achievement and personal accomplishment.

Whether using a strengths pledge, creed, or an agreement, children publicly proclaim that they will bring their strengths to the classroom—

they will bring their best game. Research confirms if children 8 to 16 years old promise to tell the truth, they are 8 times more likely to tell the truth. There is also evidence that a group discussion of honesty, and giving children a second chance to tell the truth, predicted whether they were likely to be more honest the next time.[43]

For this reason, many positive psychology programs adopt a pledge, whether narrative, poem, or song, as a means to help children identify, recognize, assess, and use their strengths. They commit to be honest and to give themselves, and others, a second chance. A strengths pledge keeps children engaged in learning by focusing on strengths and not on compliance. They promise to be strong.

Engagement is the metric of children's dedication to learning and is the result of recognition and encouragement of strengths, and it provides the chance to apply those strengths every day. Acting on strength is the key to greater engagement and greater engagement predicts greater achievement. As self-awareness of strengths grows, children find their "strengths of being" by using them to contribute to overall well-being.[44]

3. Study Literature

To teach the positive psychology teaching taxonomy benchmark of engagement through strength, the teacher can use every kind of literature available: fiction, nonfiction, magazines, comics, textbooks, and more. The stories of characters, and especially heroes, are the essence of a strengths-based curriculum. Hero study especially captures heroes' signature strengths. Children enjoy learning about every kind of hero: artistic, cartoon, entrepreneurial, historical, humanitarian, military, mythical, political, scientific, and athletic. They also enjoy learning about local heroes and sharing stories about their personal heroes—such as a grandpa. Historical biography is an ideal way to teach strengths with an interdisciplinary approach. Connecting history and strengths learning, children can research a historical figure, write a paper, and give a presentation while assuming the perspective of the historical person, emphasizing the strengths behind his or her decisions and actions. They simultaneously study history, geography, politics, economics, science, literature, and more.

The online My Hero Project website is a good place for older children to begin their research by using the world's largest database of heroes and a catalogue of their strengths.[45] The not-for-profit project uses multimedia and technology to share heroic stories and invites children to submit their own stories, films, or artworks about known or unknown heroes. The teacher will find a booklet, lesson plans, resources, and multiple videos about the project itself and the heroes that it honors. The site even provides a unique interactive calendar that lists the birthdates of 365 heroes from Paul Revere to Sir Isaac Newton. The teacher can plan a Hero of the Day lesson with this calendar. There is also an interactive journal where children post online tributes to their personal heroes, as well as an annual children's hero film festival.

Younger children enjoy participating in a similar project, the Teach Giraffe Heroes Project, which is an age-differentiated literacy curriculum to help children identify their own strengths and the strengths of others.[46] The curriculum has three parts: hear the story, tell the story, and be the story. Children read the "Voices of Hope" stories that describe real people who took heroic actions and were honored by the project. The online stories prompt a conversation about how to turn strengths into action and service.

Stories about individual heroism are easy to find and are the centerpiece of themed curricula, learning units, and individual lessons that share the stories of heroic strength. One particular heroine who has a profound effect on children is Irena Sendler. Irena rescued 2,500 children from the Warsaw Ghetto during the Nazi occupation. The Hallmark Hall of Fame produced a video named *The Courageous Heart of Irena Sendler*, which is inspirational. There is also a teacher's guide available for teachers to use to plan an instructional unit for children ages 9 to 12.[47] Children can also read her story themselves in a new book for children, *Irena Sendler and the Children of the Warsaw Ghetto*.[48]

Numerous websites introduce the eighth-grade history students who had found out about Irena while working on a history fair project. The play the children wrote and performed as part of their project brought Irena's courage to light so that the world could honor her, and thank her, before she died. Children can learn more about the students and their remarkable research at the website Life in a Jar: The Irena Sendler Project.[49]

Other curricula also use the drama of history to teach strengths offered by museums, such as the National Holocaust Museum, and by using Holocaust teaching projects such as the University of South Florida Holocaust Teaching Guide.[50] When older children see how true courage happens, inner strength becomes a precious ideal.

Groups of children can plan and execute a bulletin board that highlights a hero of their choice. Children add their own strength cards to the board as well as personal hero cards they create with the names and photos of heroes in their own lives. Each month a different team researches and creates the bulletin board for the class. Reading, writing, and talking about heroes while trying to be an everyday hero will teach children how to live a good life.

One group of children chose books about Jackie Robinson and Helen Keller, whom they had voted to study. Older children read *Helen Keller: A Light for the Blind* and *Jackie's Gift*.[51] Younger children read the *Helen Keller Picture Book* and *A Picture Book of Jackie Robinson*.[52] All are excited about adding the strengths that these heroes exhibited to the bulletin board.

Children in the second grade are featuring heroes from fairy tales and third-grade students create a bulletin board theme around folktales and legends. The fourth grade's bulletin board tells the stories of mythological heroes. The fifth-grade children adopt a superhero theme for the board and include a recommended reading list about fictional superheroes, including a list of the superheroes' strengths. From the list of favorite chapter books about superheroes, the class will vote to pick a recommended reading. When they are finished they work with the kindergarten to help them put up a bulletin board based on two superhero books, *Super Sam* and *Zero the Hero*.[53] Other storybook characters are also popular picks. Two award-winning books about courage are recommended to the children: *Li Lun, Lad of Courage* for younger children and *Red Badge of Courage* for older children form the basis of strengths study, with reading, writing, and arithmetic on the side because they can even calculate mathematics problems based on the story.[54]

There is a ready supply of books about heroes as children read and learn about environmental and conservation heroes, space heroes, American heroes, animal heroes, and all manner of other heroes who teach the power of strength to the classroom while training reading skills such as vocabulary and comprehension or writing skills such as topic sentences. Reading books about heroes helps children learn to identify their own strengths, recognize others' strengths, consider how strengths develop, and conceptualize a standard of heroism to emulate. Children can readily recognize their own signature strengths by comparing and contrasting them to any number of real and imaginary characters. Analyzing character strengths is an important part of strengths learning. Many positive psychology comprehensive curricular programs also use character studies to teach the taxonomy benchmark of engagement through strength.

For example, the Learning for Life program teaches children how to use their strengths in lessons that fully integrate with core academic subjects including language arts, social sciences, and health education.[55] The curriculum is grade-differentiated by using small group activities to teach core strengths including trust, honesty, caring, fairness, courage, self-regulation, and citizenship. The teacher selects from 61 lessons organized and filtered with an online tool by age, grade, academic subject, or strength. For example, a fourth-grade activity, connected to language arts and social studies standards, focuses on developing trust, fairness, and honesty. In the first activity, children work in small groups and tell each other a true story about honesty, fairness, or trustworthiness. The second activity uses a sentence completion task, and children respond to sentence stems: "I treated my friend fairly when ____." "My friend trusts me because ____." "The most honest person I know is ____." In the third activity, the children read a case study about honesty and act it out for the class.

The teacher can use enrichment activities to complement the formal curriculum. She might ask children to vote for the most honest child in the class and then have the top five candidates give a speech about honesty. All children rank themselves on a one-to-three point scale on their strengths of honesty, fairness, and trust as a signature strength and give examples of using it. The teacher should ensure that she does not overlook anyone and that she acknowledges those children who practice a quiet honesty that might otherwise go unnoticed.

Another formal strengths-based program is Project ExSEL.[56] This positive psychology program teaches strength through language arts and social studies. Fourteen lesson plans using 14 exemplary children's books teach strength through literacy. Children read the curriculum's carefully selected books and discuss the strengths demonstrated in the stories. The stories are all success narratives about characters using their strengths to live good lives. The curriculum helps children identify, recognize, and appreciate strengths by considering how to use those strengths best. The entire curriculum, including eight enrichment videos, is available free for download.

Another literature-based program from the Heartwood Institute is a literature-based program differentiated by grade.[58] The curriculum organizes around seven universal positive virtues also referred to as ethical attributes or core strengths: courage, loyalty, justice, respect, hope, honesty, and love. The lessons are based on award-winning children's literature categorized by grade level and strength. Elementary curriculum kits include a teacher's guide, lesson cards, and a world map to pinpoint the universality of the attribute. The list of books used in the curriculum is available for download.

The book list is a culturally rich reading list that includes excellent books for grades K–6. *The Honest to Goodness Truth* and *The King's Fountain* teach about honesty; *The Gardener* and *Brave Irene* teach about courage; and *Amelia's Road* and *The Cherry Tree* teach about hope.[59] Both the primary and intermediate books cross-reference to strengths and a new book of the month is available online to keep the reading list current. The current recommended book is the Caldecott Award winner *Mirette on the High Wire*.[60] Children acquire self-knowledge by reading, thinking, discussing, and writing about literature; they also increase personal strength while improving reading skills.

The third-grade lesson cards teach hope by using social studies, language arts, mathematics, and art. Children can read the story of a young, blind Navaho boy in *Knots on a Counting Rope*.[61] They follow up with a discussion and interactive activities like the Map Pin game. They pinpoint where the boy, Boy-Strength-of-Blue-Horses, traveled. Children learn the Navaho word for *hope* and write a sequel to the story. They complete sentence stems such as "I hope ____." "My hopes for the world are ____." Children play the Hope Pot game and make a list of reasons to be optimistic. They put their lists in a pot in the corner of the room. These are just a few examples of many lessons and book-based activities that are free to download.

To enrich the teaching of strengths, the program also offers the teacher large-event planning materials and gives the teacher the necessary tools to organize a whole-school heroes' assembly. Children invite local heroes to tell their stories while the school community listens with rapt attention. The best way for children to learn about strengths is directly from the people who have cultivated them and have demonstrated them through direct action.

Books easily build a themed strengths curriculum. Even reading a children's book once a week about a character with strength prompts good feelings, thoughts, and actions based on the events they learn about in the stories. A search of books finds strengths-based stories for all ages.

Books such as *The Good in Me from A–Z* and *Dottie and Me Celebrate What Makes Us Great* teach strengths to younger children. Early reading books that emphasize persistence, such as *Try Try Again, Humpty Dumpty After the Fall, Little by Little, Hurrah for Diffendoofer Day,* and *The Boy Who Harnessed the Wind,* teach resiliency. Older children relate easily to chapter books about grit such as *No Castles Here and Little by Little.*[62] Children know their strengths by reading, writing, and discussing the strengths of the characters in books that teach them the most important lessons of all.

4. Observe Others' Strengths

Observational learning teaches strengths learning by having children simply watch role models. Role-plays, drama activities, and film study all engage the power of imitation. Children who watch others engage with strength are inspired to do the same.

Role-playing and other dramatic activities make children aware that keen observation and imitation are learning tools. Children can participate in an improvisational theater activity to identify strengths, and the learning activity can be as simple as telling a fairy tale in 3 minutes or developing a story to play-act. Young children act out a fairytale in 3 minutes by emphasizing the strengths of the characters and the audience identifies the strengths they observe. In small groups, older children write their own play to act out based on a particular strength. Children's ideas for a play about strengths come from their reading and personal experiences.

Not only does playwriting and acting give children the opportunity to study these strengths, discuss them, process them, observe them in action, and imitate them, but this activity also teaches them about geography, history, language arts, and cultural studies. Scripts inspired by folktales, fairy tales, and legends from Asian, African, Middle Eastern, and Native American cultures are readily available to the teacher and lend themselves to classroom adaptation.

Even simple drama games promote imitative and observational learning. The Storm game is one such popular activity. Children sit in a large circle and act out the mounting fury of a story with movement and sound effects. After the storm peaks, children slowly phase out the stormy weather by returning to a pleasant state, ending with a gentle breeze. They identify the strengths needed to prepare for a storm, weather it, and recover from it. This drama game introduces a discussion about the power of the storm and survival strengths as the children also consider the storm as a metaphor for their own inner feelings and how to calm them by using their strengths while studying meteorology.

Film is a first cousin to stage drama and an equally effective tool in teaching strengths by observation and imitation. A wealth of feature films, short films, and documentaries with plots that celebrate strengths are readily available for download. Hallmark Hall of Fame movies, Disney films, and others are available with teacher guides to help implement follow-up lessons.

The Teach With Movies Project website is a contributor to the U.S. Department of Education's Gateway to Educational Materials project, which provides a central clearinghouse for the best web-based lesson plans and teacher resources.[63] The project focuses on films that teach positive psychology lessons, especially those that teach positive emotions, virtues, and strength. The library of film and associated lesson plans teaches strength across the curriculum by also targeting English, social studies, and science standards.

There are now more than 350 films catalogued with teacher guides and lesson plans organized by age, 3 to 15 years. Children who are 7 to 9 can watch *The Adventures of Huckleberry Finn* and children who are 9 to 12 can watch the film *1776*. The films teach emotionally powerful lessons.

Another valuable resource for teachers is the recent book *Positive Psychology at the Movies*, which identifies 100 of the best movies to use to teach the strengths of positive psychology.[64] The authors use the 6 virtues and 24 strengths listed in *Character, Strengths, and Virtues* as the criteria to select and cross-reference all the movies.[65] According to the authors, the most common positive psychology strengths portrayed in films are creativity, bravery, persistence, hope, love, kindness, and spirituality/meaning.

Livewire publishes a film curriculum, Film Clips for Character Education, for K–12 children.[66] Children watch an eight-part video series featuring 12 film clips in which characters replicate strengths such as honesty, empathy, courage, and determination. A teaching guide is included with each video and contains discussion questions, writing assignments, and follow-up activities to support the lessons in both English and Spanish. Film study is a natural way to build a whole curriculum to teach strengths through observation, imitation, visualization, and inspiration.

As the authors of *Positive Psychology at the Movies* have stated, "Strengths are often connected with the individual's sense of self . . . and character strengths abound in cinema . . . it is relatively easy to find films that embody strengths."[67] Dramatic arts and film lessons offer opportunities to teach the positive psychology taxonomy benchmark of strength through observation. Children replicate the strengths in film and video by exhibiting what they learned in puppet shows or skits. They can write their own stories or they can act out books about strengths. Whatever action they take, students watch and read, watch and discuss, watch and write, and watch and do. Whether the teacher encourages them to try out improvisation, puppet shows, narrative pantomime, drama games, or fully staged Shakespearean plays, children can generate, imitate, identify, observe strengths, and pretend practice strengths.

Simple games can also reinforce other strengths learning. Young children play the Pink Cloud game to learn how to decide to apply strengths to change outcomes. The teacher passes around a black cloth cloud that the children hold over their heads while identifying their disappointments and difficulties. Then the teacher passes around a pink cloth cloud and each child then exchanges the black cloud for the pink one, telling the class the signature strength that he or she will use to turn the black cloud into pink. The following week, each child reports how the plan worked; the class keeps track of how many black clouds turned pink each week. This helps the students to consider how their strengths change outcomes.

The Fortunately Story game has someone begin to tell a story with a negative event occurring, and children add sentences that change the negative circumstance by invoking a positive strength. For example: "Unfortunately, the boy could not finish his work. Fortunately, his generous friend offered to help him. Unfortunately, he thought it would take him so long he would miss recess. Fortunately, he used his grit to keep working and not watch the clock and so he finished on time." Children consider both sides of a situation.

The teacher implements simple strengths games throughout the day that flow easily into the students' learning to teach them the four pillars of emotional strengths learning as they simultaneously build social strengths. Practiced strength comes through observation, imitation, exploration, and inspiration as children learn to go with the flow of strength.

5. Envision Positive Strengths

Children employ visualization for the purpose of building strengths to overcome obstacles and attain goals.[68] Children use the power of their imaginations to mentally envision their strengths and rehearse the practice of them. They learn to use visualization techniques to alter a limiting mind-set and create a growth mind-set—the belief that they can learn, improve, fail, try again, and, in time, succeed if they build and apply their strengths.[69]

Children learn the four pillars of strengths through conscious visualization. The classic children's story *The Little Engine That Could* changes children's mind-sets from "This is too hard and I don't think I can do it" to "I think I can." Whether visualizing themselves as little trains chugging up a big hill or learning 10 new spelling words, if they think they have the strength to do it, they will do it or will at least try harder.

Visualization creates mental self-efficacy or the belief that a signature strength can bring success and create the preconditions for that success by freeing the mind of past failure and lingering doubt, activating brain action pathways, and using strength energy to bounce back more quickly.[70] Children have a virtual, wireless world inside their brains that can produce positive imagery about their signature, and other, strengths. They visualize themselves using their strengths to build a platform for success, no matter what particular challenge, roadblock, or setback is in the way. Children imagine and mentally practice the strengths that are needed to succeed.

Before he shoots the ball, the basketball player visualizes the basket in his mind, imagines lifting the ball over his head, and sees the ball flying through the air into the basket with a swoosh. Visualization is a strengths-based movie with a happy ending and children play it on demand in their heads. The ability to visualize is an important predictor of success, and it enables children to dream a life of strengths ahead. To visualize is to daydream with a purpose.

Some children spend too much time visualizing their worries and stresses, so images of impending gloom and doom dance in their heads. As Shel Silverstein writes in his poem "What If," "What if I'm dumb in school . . . what if they closed the swimming pool?" Positive psychology teaches children to visualize their strengths instead. They change the voice in their head to say, "What if I know the answer? What if I win the race?" The power of children's imagination and tendency for natural optimism can increase their strengths—empathy, grit, optimism, and more.

Visualization details a strengths map for success and imagines the happy destination: the happy smile of someone who was generously helped or the sigh of empathic understanding after finishing a favorite book. Children learn to visualize with a positive end in mind. They imagine using their courage and reading calmly and fluently when the teacher calls on them to read aloud. They imagine themselves calling their friends to report their success with good cheer or turning cartwheels after they patiently complete their homework. They imagine feeling elated emotions when they act on signature strengths. In their mind's eye, they feel it, think it, and do it with good outcomes. Charlotte Reznick's book *The Power of Your Child's Imagination* offers instructions that she calls the "nine foundation tools" needed to take children through a number of guided visualizations including discovering your special place, meeting a wise animal friend, and receiving gifts from inner guides.[71]

In a research study, participants who were advised that they could do a problem, or who were directed to visualize previous successful experience, strategies, and strengths they had used in the past, were able to solve complex mathematical problems with more accuracy.[72] The teacher prepares children mentally for academic success—the spelling test and the new vocabulary words—by using guided visualization to help them envision and act on their strengths. She takes them through a guided visualization exercise with their eyes closed and the room quiet. The children follow her voice as they imagine jumping higher, writing faster, or enjoying the science lesson. If children want to achieve something positive tomorrow, they should picture themselves using their strengths to do it today. When children think more about their strengths and not their weaknesses, they experience less stress and anxiety.[73] Creative visualization was described by one child as a "force field that makes everything easier." Another visualization approach adopts a third-person perspective and children visualize themselves as others see them. "Would the teacher approve of what I am doing?" How does this look to my friend Sam?" "Would I like someone to record what I am saying or take a photo of what I am doing?" A positive third-party point of view broadens children's perceptions and frees them to use their strengths or set a new course.

Surprisingly, visualization of a worst-case scenario is also an effective tool. Defensive, adaptive, or anticipatory pessimism, or the power of negative thinking, is the basis for adversity training.[74] Mentally practicing how to manage a negative outcome by imagining how to deploy strengths to handle it decreases the fear of it. Imagined limitations do not entangle children because they invent a strengths-based alternative.

Children visualize what might go wrong in a situation, imagine the details of the possible negative outcome, and shift their attention to facts rather than random worrisome speculations. They visualize a contingency plan.

The teacher might also increase the positive effect of visualization by using some of the most recent findings in brain research or the elephant-in-the-room theorem. When the teacher tells children not to think about something—such as chocolate—they can't help thinking about it so they also eat more of it.[75] The teacher can trigger focus by telling children not to think about something. If she tells them not to laugh, they are more likely to laugh. The teacher tells them not to think about writing a great paragraph.

The teacher enriches children's natural ability to generate positive strength imagery that they can call upon as needed. Whether recollecting the strengths of a role model, remembering positive scenes in a film, or recalling a character's strengths in a story, imagining a positive outcome and envisioning strengths are the basis for success.

6. Strengths Self-Talk

The language of positive psychology that articulates positive emotion and signature strengths is one of the general educational methods always used to teach the taxonomy, no matter the technique. In strengths-training lessons, it is especially important.

When teaching about the four pillars of strengths learning, a specific technique of self-talk coaches is private speech. Private speech is "typically defined, in contrast to social speech, as speech addressed to self, not to others, for the purpose of self-regulation rather than communication."[76]

Children use private speech to manage overwhelming feelings, direct attention, self-motivate, process demands, and activate strength. Private speech is the cognitive bridge between affective thought and action. Jean Piaget and Lev Vygotsky originated the concept of private speech, and both of these early developmental psychologists were interested in children's use of self-talk as a window into their cognitive development.[77]

While Piaget considered private speech as a bridge to social speech, Vygotsky considered it to be a cognitive-linguistic function for self-management. He believed that as children grow older, private speech, or self-directed speech, is transformed into the individual's inner voice.

Inner speech "is the silent dialogue that we carry with ourselves."[78] Children invoke private speech when they face a daunting task and it externalizes their feelings and thoughts to help control them through strengths training.

Speech can be either interpersonal or intrapersonal and often these interweave so that dialogue between one child and another converts into a dialogue between the child and self. What children hear others say about them, they repeat to themselves. How many adults still hear the voices of their mothers in their heads? Children's inner speech surfaces as self-talk and gives silent thought voice. Some part of that voice emanates from social discourse. What children hear matters because they repeat it verbatim both out loud and inside their own heads.

If children hear the language of positive psychology, their self-talk is about their strengths and not their deficits. How others talk to children and how children talk to themselves, whether criticizing, shaming, demeaning, encouraging, forgiving, or comforting, matters a great deal relative to their ability to capitalize on their strengths. How children learn to talk to themselves and how the voices in their heads get them there can disable or enable strengths. Children repeat to themselves what others tell them and how they interpret those voices changes self-efficacy or belief about self.

Parents, teachers, and other adults are the ones who teach the voices in children's heads to talk. For this reason, the teacher must understand the power of words as one of the most important, although often overlooked, positive psychology teaching methods and self-talk is one of the most important techniques.

The teacher's words, phrasing, pacing, and tone can encourage children to move toward self-control, increase their sense of affiliation, and provide scripts for their own self-talk. In this way, the language of positive psychology creates a strong personal narrative. The way we relate to self—kindly or critically—has a major influence on well-being, contentment, and ability to deploy strengths to cope with setbacks. "Developing compassion for self and others may be key to emotional well-being."[79] A teacher's words can lift students to their highest potential or tear them down.[80] A harsh critique crushes: "I don't know why you even bothered!" A kind suggestion uplifts: "This is a good start. Keep going." In this way, children learn to use positive self-talk to manage emotions and use strengths. Children decode the strengths language directed to them and they repeat it with self-talk. The language of positive psychology is not praise of positive behavior or performance. The language aims to stimulate strength.

Given that behavioral training is dominant in many teacher-training programs, many teachers learn to offer praise for performance by focusing on behavioral outcomes expected rather than praise for the process of strength acquisition and application. The teacher is more likely to praise children for passing the test than for the grit it took to prepare for the test. She is more likely to praise them for the correct answer to a question than for the courage it took to answer the question. She is more likely to praise them for raising their hands rather than for their patience in waiting their turn. The teacher needs to shift her or his focus from behavior to action; even more important, a teacher has to understand the emotional strength that was behind the action—or needed for the action. The language of positive psychology values form over function and formative process over summative result.

What children do is not as important as how they do it and what they think while doing it. The teacher addresses the signature strength needed to produce a positive outcome rather than applauding the outcome only. The language of positive psychology is precise and complex, specifically identifying the emotion and the strength. The Responsive Classroom is an educational resource group composed of educators who are long-time advocates of positive language in the classroom. They offer many resources that train the teacher to focus his or her language on strengths so children will hear messages about empathy, determination, patience, appreciation, gladness, and optimism and can repeat what they hear to themselves.

The teacher uses the language of positive psychology in a way that teaches children to praise themselves for their efforts, concentration, and strategies and not only for their feats or results. A child can learn to praise herself for helping the math team stay determined rather than because she feels she is the smartest one on the team. As a result, she is less likely to be anxious about whether or not she can meet future expectations. Performance anxiety is diminished because myopic self-talk about performance does not engender fear of future disappointments. The taxonomy teaches children healthy self-talk that identifies strengths of self and others, encourages those strengths, builds those strengths, and uses those strengths. Self-talk changes expectations.

Carolyn Dwek's theory of mind-sets explains how children have idiosyncratic understandings of their strengths.[81] Children's mind-sets are expansive and not cramped, and when they conceive their strengths as within their personal control, they flourish. This type of mind-set is a growth mind-set because a child will approach problems with an open, wide-angle perspective that engages the problem so he or she can brainstorm strengths-based solutions.

A growth mind-set is open to the self-talk that builds opportunities for change. Children with growth mind-sets show the strengths of grit, optimism, and good cheer. Others with more constricted, closed mind-sets tell themselves it is too hard, and they pretend to try but quit outright or never even begin to try. They act to either avoid failure or accept it because a closed mind-set convinces with negative self-talk that no effort really matters and nothing will ever change. The good news is that fixed mind-sets are relatively easy to change with strengths praise that acknowledges effort over performance, Telling success stories to the self and consistent social support also changes fixed thinking to open-minded thinking.[82] The teacher is in an ideal position to open up children's minds with positive self-talk by using the language of positive psychology.

The Who Moved My Cheese? program helps children understand the concept of a fixed mind-set so that they can change their minds by focusing on strengths and by using strengths self-talk.[83] The book and accompanying cartoon tell the story of two mice faced with a crisis, and each mouse reacts differently to the crisis—one has a fixed mind-set and the other has a growth mind-set. Eventually the mice change their mind-sets, tell themselves they can control their destinies, and identify and use their strengths to change the outcome. The curriculum kit also includes plush toys, handwriting-on-wall posters and cards, a stress cheese wedge, reminder cards, and post-it notes. There is also an edition of the book for children under the age of 8 years.[84]

Focused journal writing is another technique that helps children change their mind-sets by using self-talk. Children have the opportunity to record, explore, and modify their mind-sets. Journal writing transfers self-talk to paper. They write journal notes and letters to themselves that echo what they hear from others, and then they modify or upgrade it. "I was able to finish that job quickly and I can do it again." "I was more patient today than yesterday and I know I can be even more patient tomorrow."

The Tribes Learning Community program and many other positive psychology programs use daily journal writing as a technique to focus on children's strengths as a means of engagement. Children use ready-made-journals to structure positive self-talk as self-reflection. In their journals, they write about their strengths and consider how they demonstrated them yesterday and how they will use them today.

How self-talk sculpts personal narrative, and the power of it, is the subject of much discussion in the neuroscience community. Scientists report that the brain is hardwired to tell life stories and that resilience depends on the nature of the stories children tell themselves. Children find it is easier to remember facts embedded in a story than presented in a list.[85] When children tell themselves a story using strengths self-talk, they expect change, are ready for it, and actually enjoy it. However, the self-talk that tells the story must provide enough mental space to broaden perspective and gain strengths insight.[86]

The positive psychology teaching taxonomy benchmark of strength teaches children how to create self-narrated stories with a bias toward a good outcome. "If I hadn't failed that test I would never have met my study buddy who is now my best friend." Children learn to tell themselves optimistic stories because their explanatory style matters. As Martin Seligman has stated, "Your habitual way of explaining bad events, your explanatory style, are not just the words you mouth when you fail ... [Words determine] whether you think you are valuable and deserving or worthless and hopeless."[87] A child's explanatory style determines how a negative or traumatic event is explained and influences cognitive expectations regarding future events. Self-talk can be used to forecast good outcomes over bad, playing an important role in building the strength of optimism over pessimism.

Children's brains are like closets that hold all their beliefs about themselves that they have heard and internalized. Some closets are tidy, organized, and free of negative clutter and others are not. However, all children can use self-talk to clean out and rearrange these beliefs. One way the teacher can help them clean out their emotional closets is by teaching them the complex language of positive psychology so that they can tell their stories while using strengths-based self-talk and affirmations.

Each child learns to take a deep breath, look in a mirror, and recite an affirmation—a pronouncement about self that asserts a positive outlook, builds a positive strength, expects a positive outcome, and makes a positive prediction. Each week a child chooses an affirmation to repeat out loud because this enables it to be absorbed as part of self-talk. The teacher chooses the affirmations that teach the positive psychology teaching taxonomy strengths: empathy, generosity, courage, grit, patience, optimism, and good cheer. Children collect the affirmations and make laminated flip cards to use whenever they need to change their self-talk. The teacher can also purchase a number of affirmation cards developed for children.

Instead of handing out referral notices, the positive psychology teacher distributes strengths cards. There are three different types of Louise Hay affirmation cards that older children use. They include positive thought cards, forgiveness cards, and wisdom cards. A sample card reads, "Everything I do, I do by choice."[88] Affirmation cards designed especially for younger children—Kids Time—shows a colorful picture of a kite with the affirming words, "I am aware of the power of my words . . . may all be spoken with truth and kindness."[89] The affirmation cards remind children that thoughts create the self-talk that decides the action.

There are also many delightful affirmations within the pages of Louise Hay's children's book *I Think, I Am!* Reading the book, children learn the definition of affirmation: "words that you think or say, and believe to be true."[90] The book espouses the philosophy that children's thoughts and self-talk create their life stories. Another children's affirmation book, *On My Way to a Happy Life*, teaches seven simple lessons and brings simple affirmations to life: "With the gift that you have been given you can create anything whether great or small."[91] Both of these books have applications on mobile digital devices for multimedia access to affirmations.

In the children's book *The Affirmation Web*, children go on an adventure that requires them to choose, affirm, and visualize outcomes to succeed in the quest.[92] The book, a charming tale of sea life, describes a dolphin searching for confidence. Children relate easily to this story about turning self-doubt into self-belief with self-talk. The book weaves together affirmations and delightful storytelling.

Whether using wisdom cards or stories about dolphins, children change their world by changing their self-talk. Using affirmations, children learn to talk to themselves in helpful, healthy, strengths-focused ways. Affirmations help them balance their perspectives and moderate their self-talk, and they enjoin emotion-focused self-talk with strengths-focused self-talk.

Children learn not to expect too little, or too much, from themselves and learn balanced responses. They learn not to be too hard on themselves, knowing that they are doing the best that they can do under the circumstances. They learn to stop self-blaming and to encourage themselves by focusing self-talk on their strengths and not their faults. They eliminate negative emotions in response to stress and balance their thinking about the stressful incident with a positive strengths focus: "It will all work out for the best." Emotion-focused self-talk is "directed at regulating emotional responses to problems" while problem-focused or strengths self-talk reappraises and reinterprets the situation.[93]

Children learn to combine positive emotional reactions with positive strength actions: "I am upset I got the answer wrong and I just want to yell but that will only make the problem worse, so I will just practice my optimism because I know I can do better next time." Self-talk cannot just rant and rave. Emotional venting only discharges the distress while strengths talk modulates it.[94] Self-talk must work to calm and quiet the mind.

Strengths-focused self-talk helps children learn how to have positive, adaptive, and emotionally fulfilling conversations with themselves. Self-talk helps children "to understand the positive, the adaptive, the creative, and the emotionally fulfilling elements of human behavior."[95] Absent positive self-talk, children may become more easily discouraged and disconnected and therefore more comfortable avoiding or accepting failure: "Oh, it doesn't really matter if I do this or not."[96] Children use myriad distractions to take their minds off their problems rather than using self-talk to rouse strengths to solve any issues. When they use positive self-talk, there is less disengagement that causes feelings of helplessness and fear that, in turn, cause children to abandon the attempt altogether.

Using positive self-talk brings emotional release and self-guiding suggestions as to how to proceed by installing their strengths. For example, self-talk about feelings of sadness caused by an embarrassing incident brings relief from overwhelming emotion.[97] Self-talk about how to use the strengths of optimism and courage to jump-start a new confidence despite the embarrassing event brings a new start. Self-talk is a simple coping strategy that helps children to devise a plan to use their strengths.

According to Fredrickson's broaden-and-build model,[98] self-talk serves to activate children's thought-to-action mechanisms so that they consider more options, so learning is increased. The more they self-talk themselves into new options and perspectives, the more emotional and intellectual strength resources they create for future use. Self-talk persuades children to reduce their emotional intensity and replace it with their signature strength of good cheer or empathy. Children who talk themselves into a strengths-based approach reduce tension.

Humorous self-talk may be the best kind of self-talk. Humor is the capacity to perceive life as comedy instead of tragedy and, in so doing, forestall bitterness and cynicism. Learning to use humor to offset life's turmoil can increase children's internal ability to adapt.[99] Children are well-served by a good sense of humor that shifts their perspective and lightens their mood. A sense of humor can create a remarkable feeling of control and strength. A third grader said, "I keep all these school jokes in my head and when something goes wrong I just tell myself a little joke. Only I hear it and it works for me: 'Teacher: could you please pay a little attention? Student: I am paying as little attention as I can.'" The little boy confided that he also clips cartoons from the newspaper about school and tapes them to his desk to cheer himself up. Laughter every day keeps the doctor away, promoting both physical and mental health.

Children learn to mentally summon their signature strengths when most needed to cope with stress. The program Happiness Is Up To You teaches children to accept themselves unconditionally and to talk up their strengths when negative experiences overwhelm them.[100] The curriculum explicitly targets four resiliency outcomes, including positive self-talk as a means to give praise, live a balanced lifestyle, and recharge emotional resources. In a journal, children monitor self-criticism and work to decrease it. If children feel self-critical, they stop, take a few breaths, slow down, and remind themselves of the strengths they possess. The curriculum trains them to tell themselves that they have the strength needed to do the job and solve the problem. Like an actor preparing for a part, children's strengths grow to meet the need.

Self-talk is self-teaching that creates a sense of self-efficacy and possibility. The Efficacy Institute toolkit and instructional guide[101] teaches children to build confidence by using workbooks that teach them a growth mind-set: Smart is something you get by changing how you think and what you say to yourself and others. Working through a problem internally has great benefit even if the final decision is to seek external support so children can hear others repeat or challenge their own thoughts.[102] Children can test their self-talk on others to get a reality check: "So what do you think?" "So what is your plan for tomorrow?" "What do you envision for yourself next year?"

The traditional teacher who writes names on the board when children behave badly or who calls them out for their infractions focuses on their deficits and so automatically disenfranchises them from the learning enterprise. The teacher who gives children strength cards to remind them to use their strength reengages them. The golden rule of positive psychology is to acknowledge strengths not deficits and to encourage children to use those strengths.

7. Meditate and Move

The teacher does not overlook the mind-body connection because the foundation for mental strengths is physical strength. Teaching the four pillars of strengths learning includes the exercise of both mind and body by introducing physical learning into the classroom.[103] Children benefit from as little as 15 minutes of exercise a day, and they benefit the most from 60 minutes of whole body movement, so it is important to get children moving throughout the school day, not just during recess or after school. There are many means of introducing 60 minutes of movement into the classroom, including yoga, fitness exercises, and dance.

Previous chapters discussed the benefit of yoga relative to emotional learning as it promotes emotional strengths to increase overall well-being. Other types of movement get similar results. Routine fitness exercises also bring strength through movement to learning. There are numerous guides published that suggest movement activities adapted for elementary classroom use. For example, the teacher chooses a daily action word and whenever the teacher says it, the class does 5 push-ups, 10 jumping jacks, or 12 touch toes while spelling the word. In mathematics, children act out number problems by using gross motor skills. Four jumping children plus one stretching equals five children. The teacher asks children to spell words or recite multiplication tables while exercising. He can turn any academic assignment into a movement exercise like math basketball or spelling jump rope.[104]

Action songs and other simple indoor games get children moving and are effective as transition activities that provide movement throughout the day. The Silly Move game is a favorite with children of all ages. A team works together to create a silly move each week and teaches it to the class. Whenever the teacher rings a bell, everyone makes the silly move until the bell rings again, and then they stop. The teacher connects the game to making silly decisions based on emotional impulses. In the Walk and Talk game, children discuss a book or a current events topic related to emotional strength as they walk around outside in pairs.

Old stand-by games like Simon Says improve auditory processing, directionality, and observational learning skills, and the teacher notes that if you are too emotionally impulsive you lose the game. In some classrooms, children wear a pedometer and walk in place every hour; they can measure and graph their progress, recording the physical indicators of stress and well-being. The Let's Move in School website describes hundreds of in-class movement activities.[105] There are brain breaks, energy balance 101, just a minute, and play works programs.

These movement ideas turn a sit-down classroom into a stand-up-and-move classroom that uses physical strength as a metaphor for emotional strength. The teacher connects movement to emotional strength: "I am determined to do 10 push-ups."

Dance is artistic movement and is a universal behavior unique to humans, although researchers have recently observed birds, and possibly elephants, dancing.[106] Dance, the rhythmic movement of the body to an internal or external beat or music, is an aesthetic, artistic, cultural, and social form of nonverbal communication. For this reason, dance is able to convey emotions and tap into physical and emotional strengths. There is a value-added advantage to using dancing as a classroom movement activity because it releases emotions and expresses strengths. Dance is the epitome of a mind-body connection, whether someone is actually dancing or watching a dance. There is evidence that synchronized dancing, like flash mob dancing, increases group solidarity and all dance is also associated with increased optimism and good cheer.[107]

From the gratitude dance in Papua, New Guinea, to Nintendo's Just Dance for Kids I & II game, dance increases the flow of emotions and strengths. The Nintendo Wii video dance game has 40 dances created by choreographers for children, and within the game children are the instructors. The Activity TV Dance Moves website also teaches children simple dance steps from the cha cha to the chainé turn with both video and print instructions.[108]

The opportunity to dance is everywhere, is accessible to children, and is associated with both physical and mental fitness and strength. Dance serves to broaden children's outlook when they watch classic films or dancers from all over the world on YouTube. The World Cultural Dance website teaches children dances from around the world and help them learn more about geography and culture.[109]

Dance serves to discharge, stabilize, and recalibrate children's emotions and build their strengths. Children love to move and the teacher brings movement to class as a part of, or as adjunct to, academic instruction. Movement increases engagement and flow of strength.

Similar to the burgeoning interest in movement in the classroom, there is increasing interest in teaching children meditation as a technique to cultivate positive psychology strengths as evidenced by dozens of meditation books for children. Meditation is a discourse that guides self-contemplation for the purpose of finding strength and using it for the greater good. Meditation can be as simple as a brief affirmation or a 5-minute breathing exercise.

Animal characters in books have taught kindergarten and first-grade children to meditate: *Peaceful Piggy Meditation*, *Moody Cow Meditates*, *Mindful Monkey*, and *A Boy and a Bear*.[110] Second- and third-grade children can read the book *Indigo Ocean Dreams* while listening to the 60-minute audio CD that teaches them four stress-management techniques: affirmation, diaphragmatic breathing, progressive muscle relaxation, and visualization.[111] Children use these techniques to concentrate on their strengths.

Older children can read books that teach both meditation and practical wisdom. *A Pebble for Your Pocket* uses metaphors to introduce the teachings of Buddha and the joy of living fully in the moment.[112] *Three Questions*, based on the work of Tolstoy, asks three questions that help children decide the best course of strengths-based action: "What is the best time to do things? What is the most important thing to do? What is the right thing to do?"[113]

Children confront negative experience they cannot control. However, exercise, dance, and meditation can help them to focus on the strengths needed to cope. When children are most discouraged or disappointed, movement and meditation cultivate the strengths of physical and emotional resilience.

If the teacher wants children to run a triathlon, he can train them to do it but does not expect them to just start running. Yet every day in the classroom teachers ask children to run a mental and emotional triathlon with little preparation or practice. Teaching the positive psychology teaching taxonomy benchmark of strength corrects that oversight.

8. Strengths-Training Curriculum

The most direct and deliberate way to teach the four pillars of strengths learning is to develop and deliver a strengths-training curriculum. The positive psychology teacher builds children's emotional strengths by incrementally teaching children to take small steps to begin and to keep walking until ready to run, and then soar. Emotional strength training—like physical strengths training—is a regime of exercises that build on the capacity to use emotions and strengths efficiently, persistently, and without tiring.

Children recognize, build, and use their strengths to bring out the best in themselves and others. They learn to help children build empathy, generosity, courage, grit, patience, optimism, and good cheer. A primary commitment of the positive psychology teacher is to connect children to their signature strengths by using strengths-based programs, curricula, themed units, lessons, activities, and games.

Children learn that their feelings of caring and kindness translate into empathy for others, and this strength is rooted in positive emotion. If children feel caring, they act caring. They learn that having grit means they are able to be resilient in the face of adversity and this strength emerges from their feeling of determination and it ensures that they stay committed to friends, service, and goals. An understanding of resilience theory traces directly to hope theory and it suggests that optimists are better able to establish goals, forge pathways, and apply willpower or grit to life's greatest challenges.[114]

Teaching resilience helps children overcome the contemporary stressors of life in a busy household or the academic pressure at school. It also benefits children who live in poverty, move frequently, experience violence, or suffer loss. If stress overwhelms their coping mechanisms, children must be able to either decrease it or increase the ability to cope with it. Children learn an effective set of strengths-based responses to adversity that include accurate emotional appraisals and the ability to mediate emotional reactions with strengths that engage effective problem-solving mechanisms. Cognitive reprocessing of experiences, thoughts, emotions, and memories occurs when children can summon a signature strength that helps to activate their resiliency. The most important predictor of resiliency is the degree of cognitive-affective-conative fluency or flow children can muster.[115] Children learn to think, feel, and act with positive resilience.

For this reason, many positive psychology programs focus on teaching resiliency, which is defined as resolve, strength of character, and single-minded and strong-minded tenacity in the face of hardship or misfortune. The teacher can choose to use a research-based strengths curriculum such as MindUP, which features 15 lessons for children in third through fifth grade by using the latest neuroscience information to focus attention, reprocess negative emotion, improve self-regulation skills, build resilience to stress, and develop a positive mind-set.[116] The curriculum includes a very large, colorful teaching poster with fascinating facts about the brain to post in the classroom; the lessons fit easily into any schedule and require minimal preparation.

Another program teaches children to value resilience and practice grit because if they are stout-hearted, they can turn defeat to personal triumph, happiness, and success. The Resiliency Self Acceptance Skills Model curriculum teaches happiness by helping children to think objectively, thoughtfully, and kindly about their challenges.[117] Children learn to stop thinking in self-defeating damaging ways, and to think instead in self-nurturing ways.

The curriculum teaches 10 protective strength skills to use when confronted with overwhelming feelings or demands—all of the lessons teach self-acceptance of emotions and strengths. Self-acceptance counterbalances negative experiences to build resilience. Self-acceptance predicates the ability to reinterpret all experience as positive rather than perpetuating a negative and pessimistic outlook that impedes resilience. Children find a grade of D on a history quiz easier to accept if they offset the disappointment by reminding themselves that mathematics is their strong subject and so they should allocate more homework time to history.

A strengths-training curriculum that adopts the neurocognitive approach is the Providing Alternative Thinking Strategies (PATHS) curriculum.[118] The PATHS curriculum teaches the positive psychology teaching taxonomy benchmark by using precision teaching. The PATHS curriculum facilitates development of self-control, emotional awareness, and interpersonal problem-solving skills by using signature strengths. There is an intentional and intensive focus on helping children verbally identify and label feelings in order to manage them using their strengths. The curriculum logic aims to help children to become less emotionally impulsive, more mindful, and better able to use their strengths. An instructional manual, six volumes of lessons, photographs, a research book, and other materials are included.

Research proves that there are significant improvements in both inhibitory control and verbal fluency as a result of participating in the PATHS curriculum so children can stop, think, and change their reactions. Therefore, they express their feelings positively and use their strengths strategically.[119] "These findings provide empirical support for the neuroscience theory of action that underlies the PATHS curriculum model. That is, child neurocognitive functioning plays a key role in children's social and emotional adaptation and changes . . . and directly relate(s) to reductions in behavioral problems."[120]

Work in neuroanatomy is beginning to identify the precise brain regions and structures involved in strengths-based emotional regulation, which depends on the intercession of the executive brain functions. Work in epigenetics is also beginning to identify mechanisms involved in the overlap of biological development and environmental effect. The blend of neuroscience and positive psychology validates the PATHS curriculum that promotes emotional and strength environmental awareness as a means to cognitive and conative moderation.

The PATHS curriculum accelerates this process by using a neuroeducational model with an emphasis on vertical control of emotion: "Vertical control refers to the process of higher-order cognitive processes exerting control over lower-level limbic impulses via frontal cognitive control."[121] A strengths-processing poster hangs in the classroom to remind children how to use patience, grit, and optimism to systematically solve problems. The teacher guides children to control actions and reactions by using emotions reprocessed as strengths. Affect, language-based thought, and strengths-based action combine to exert vertical control over children's actions to help them flourish emotionally and academically. They must learn to express emotion through strength, and the PATHS curriculum serves this purpose.

Another well-researched program that teaches the positive psychology taxonomy strengths benchmark is the Core Virtues Program.[122] This program is a K–6 literature-based curriculum that cultivates strengths such as compassion, perseverance, courage, and patience. There are grade-specific goals and reproducible definitions of the virtues by grade level. All lessons connect to an academic core knowledge sequence and include an exhaustive literature guide organized by virtue and grade with 600 entries.

Cars-R-Us adopts a different method and explores feelings and strengths-based responses by using a goal-setting approach. It contains 52 car fleet cartoon cards in the kit.[123] These cards include 16 know-your-vehicle cars, 10 thinking bubbles, one trip planner, and a car owner's manual. Cars-R-Us poses questions to children about the strengths they use to drive their cars, where they want them to go with a tank full of strengths fuel, and how to tune up their strengths engines. The children check their strength tires and get a map for the trip ahead. The first lesson card asks a child to choose the car that best represents him. The fleet of cars with human faces represents a range of emotions and strengths that reflect children's basic temperaments. The children pick strengths to fill up their tanks and tune their engines. They choose strengths they will use on their journey and plot them on a map that has many vicissitudes. The cars answer questions like: "What are you thinking? What are you feeling? What is your car doing? In what direction do you want to go? What did you learn from that wrong turn? Is what you are doing working for you?"

Livewire's Auto-B-Good is also a video-based, car-themed curriculum.[124] The Auto-B-Good curriculum is an award-winning animated series that includes CDs, printable activity cards, posters, and storybooks. The stories takes place in Auto City, a metropolis where all the inhabitants are cars of all ages, makes, and models, who teach valuable life lessons about how to develop strength of character. This extensive video collection includes 63 short stories in 21 volumes so there is a video for every week of the school year. Each volume in the series contains three 10-minute episodes and a teacher's guide with discussion questions, student interactions, and activities that support the lesson.

Livewire produces a number of other video-based strengths-training programs that teach the positive psychology teaching taxonomy benchmark of strength. Character Counts is a multimedia-based approach that presents the Popcorn Park: Six Pillars of Character curriculum for children K–5.[125] The videos explore six character virtues, and children enjoy watching the Popcorn Park puppets become entangled in problems that require them to sort out their feelings and use positive strengths to succeed. Each video is approximately 25 minutes in length and is paired with a facilitator's guide that contains discussion questions, writing assignments, and follow-up activities. Supplemental materials include classroom posters, banners, and a companion storybook. Inspiring songs and delightful humor engage children in thinking, talking, and writing about strengths.

The Character Way video series teaches the strengths of honesty, fairness, and altruism. Using video dramas, fables, documentaries, and games, children identify strengths and figure out how to use them effectively.[126] The video and book titles include *Groark's Birthday Surprise*, about honesty, and *Angry*, about empathy.[127]

Lastly, the Livewire Character Chronicles curriculum uses a digital approach to offer strengths training to older children. Six middle-school children host the videos and act as role models, facilitators, and bloggers.[128] The series contains many elements such as inspiring documentaries, humorous vignettes, and insightful teen commentaries helping intermediate elementary-aged children figure out how to meet contemporary challenges with strength.

The Comic Book Project website hosted by Columbia University's Teacher's College invites children to write a comic book about strengths. The project launches activities that stimulate creativity and teamwork. A small group works together to write two- and four-panel mini-comic books based on superheroes and current events.[129]

After a brainstorming session to adopt a theme, children plot, sketch, and draft their comic books by using the online manuscript starter that is a template for generating the story. The template provides blank comic-book panels to use to produce the final document—they draw characters, write dialogue, color backgrounds, and finalize the cover. The template is especially helpful for visual learners, struggling writers, and English-language learners who rely on the pictorial aspect of comic books to make the connection between what they draw and write. All comic books that are uploaded are then posted on a worldwide, web-based comic-book art gallery about strengths. The children have fun sharing their comic books and reading others from around the world.

Another web-based digital resource that teaches comic book writing is the MakeBeliefsComix website where children can write comic books in seven different languages, including Latin. As the founder writes, "After all, there is no greater force in life than the power of the imagination to free us from our immediate problems and to spur our energies [and strength] to find solutions to our befuddlements."[130]

While working on the comic-book lesson, children read the series *Amelia Rules* about an extremely likable but flawed comic-book character whose life is not always easy.[131] Some of the titles include *What Makes You Happy?*, *When the Past Is a Present*, *Superheroes*, and *The Meaning of Life*. Other literary comics from *Hercules* to *The Count of Monte Cristo* teach strengths lessons.[132] The graphic-novel format motivates children to read the classics and to write comic-book stories about strengths. Creating comic-book characters and reading about them, with their flaws and strengths, broaden and build children's own strengths. Books, whether comic books or traditional books, lend themselves to teaching the positive psychology teaching strengths taxonomy by using stand-alone lessons. "Reading is an adventure, full of discoveries: new lands, new words, and new emotions."[133]

Kindergarten and first-grade children read the book *Tiger, Tiger, Is It True?*[134] This is a story about a little tiger who is worried that his world is falling apart. A wise owl asks him four simple questions and the tiger realizes his thoughts cause his worries. He learns that suffering is a choice, that asking a different question changes everything, and that he can choose how he feels. After reading the story, all the children make a tiger button to wear. The buttons remind them to be strong tigers when life goes wrong. Whenever a child is worried, the teacher or other children ask, "Tiger, tiger, is it true?"

In the third and fourth grades, children read *Mistakes That Worked*.[135] The book reaches out to children who give up easily or are afraid to make mistakes. They learn about inventions stumbled upon accidentally that did not work out until years later. The list includes patented inventions like Silly Putty, Popsicles, and Coca-Cola, as well as generic discoveries like bricks, donut holes, and cheese. The loony watercolor sketches and all the extras in the book—fun facts, recipes, and anecdotes—are perfect for creating a lesson about determination, grit, and unintentional discovery. After the children read the book, they prepare a presentation about one of the inventions and the inventor.

Fifth-grade children read books about dog heroes, horse heroes, animal-shelter heroes, war heroes who are animals, whale heroes, and wild animal heroes. The book *Animal Heroes: True Rescues* tells stories about heroic animals rescuing humans, including the guide dog who saved her blind owner on 9/11 by leading him down 77 flights of stairs in the World Trade Center before the building collapsed.[136] There are stories about a dolphin, a gorilla, a small dog, and many more, who used their instinct, intelligence, and courage to perform heroic deeds. Children research and present an animal hero story to the class.

If the well-being of children matters, then strengths training matters. If the teacher cannot commit to a full strengths-training program or curriculum, he or she can develop individual daily or weekly activities and games to build signature strengths within the positive teaching taxonomy. The teacher can plan an art activity, such as making strengths sentence completion and concentration card games, language arts activities such as writing appreciation or empathy letters, and history activities such as the Guess the Hero game.

Some activities and games are prepackaged such as the *Boat Full of Animals* activity book in which there are multiple activities and games that teach young children 30 different character strengths.[137] They creep toward the finish line like a determined turtle and, acting as the King of the Jungle, they decide what moods they wish to keep or send away. When children play games, their feelings come alive and they fashion new strengths.

A book series Harry and the Bucket Full of Dinosaurs is complemented by videos that present real-life situations about how Harry solves his problems and reduces his frustrations by using the dinosaurs that come to life in his imagination to help him.[138] Some of the strengths Harry builds are empathy, gladness, courage, and perseverance. Children play the same dinosaur game as Harry, and they use their dinosaurs' strengths when frustrated.

Another learning game that easily connects to science and strengths is the Core Samples game.[139] Core samples are fascinating columns of rock and mineral cut from deep below the Earth's surface with a drill. This geology game explains how core samples serve as a record of history and the composition of a particular piece of land. Children can study samples such as marble with shades of color and light and they can identify their own core strengths using the core samples as metaphors. They make lists of their own personal core strengths and those of friends and family. Gemstones can represent core strengths, too. Children can research and collect photos of both core samples and gemstones; children discuss the similarities and differences exemplified by the core strength or gemstone samples.

Children's brains seek new and novel stimulation so the interest in the new toy will fade and have a short-term effect unless it makes a positive memory. For example, playing games alone, or with others, has long-term benefits, and the best kind of play concurrently forges a good memory and teaches strengths. Through play, children learn to use their strengths to win graciously, lose gracefully, and play again. Play puts children in the zone of strengths-based positivity.

Empathy—To harness the power of the mirror neurons to build empathy, children play the Role Model game. A name is randomly drawn and that child acts as the Role Model of the Day. The child wears a role model button and acts out his or her signature strength all day, and others imitate the role model's actions. The teacher wears the role model button on special days.

Generosity—To practice sharing the good life, children play the Favorite Day game. Children write a paragraph to describe an ideal day they would share with their favorite person. They read the paragraph aloud to other children and discuss why sharing the day with someone makes it more special and benefits all.

Courage—To elevate feeling brave to acting courageously, children play the I Was Brave When game. Children write a story, real or imagined, about a time when they were brave, recalling the strengths that helped them gain courage.

Grit—To understand the power of determination, children play the Pigs Fly game. They offer silly ideas to complete the sentence starting with "I will not quit until": "I will not quit until . . . I get a pet monkey." "I will not quit until . . . I land on the moon." "I will not quit until . . . pigs fly."

Patience—To learn how to stay calm, relaxed, patient, and go with the flow, children play the Don't Lose Your Head game. At the morning meeting, children list some of the stressors they may encounter in the coming day. After the list is complete, they stand up, grab their heads, and shout, "Don't lose your head," diffusing the tension by dissolving into laughter. They remind each other, "Don't lose your head!"

Optimism—To practice changing negative expectations into positive ones, children play the Microphone Check game. Throughout the day, the teacher cues the class with the words "microphone check" and the children stop to repeat the affirmation she reads: "I express my needs and feelings positively." "Life is joy filled with delightful surprises." "I will be strong and allow wonderful things to flow into my life."

Good Cheer—To act out gladness, children play the One Fun Thing game.[140] The children write down the one fun thing they would like to do as a class—fly a kite, find a Jell-O recipe, doodle, sell lemonade, have a silly-string fight, plant a flower, watch a movie, and more. They write it on a piece of paper and put it in the "one fun thing" box. Each week the teacher picks one fun thing randomly from the box, discusses if the class can do it, and then the whole class decides if doing the one fun thing will build any strengths. Then, they do it.

What is most important is that the teacher decide to teach the positive psychology teaching taxonomy strengths benchmark in a systematic, purposeful, and committed way—and not as an afterthought. He or she uses whatever resources are available to infuse strengths training into the traditional curriculum; it is regularly scheduled and carefully orchestrated based on class needs, challenges, and current levels of strengths' development. The goal is to teach the pillars of strengths learning so children demonstrate more empathy, gratitude, courage, grit, patience, optimism, and good cheer so that they can live the good life.

Summary and Conclusion

The positive psychology teaching taxonomy benchmark of strength teaches the four pillars of strengths learning: (1) identify and recognize strengths in self and others, (2) build a signature strength, core strength, and challenge strength, (3) practice and use strengths to accomplish goals, and (4) encourage others to use strengths to accomplish their goals. Teachers use the methods and techniques of positive psychology to ensure that children can moderate emotions with their strengths. Children identify, build, extend, and apply empathy, generosity, courage, grit, patience, optimism, and good cheer. They learn to use their signature strengths as a framework for all learning and living. In the positive psychology classroom, children learn to read, dance, meditate, self-soothe, and play games in order to increase the strengths that bring accomplishment.

Children learn that they do not always get what they want or want what they get. They understand life is not always easy and it can be messy, hurtful, and discouraging. Moreover, they learn to use their signature strengths to make the best of it and to look toward a better day tomorrow. Children learn that they will stumble and fall, and they learn to pick themselves up and begin again with a deep breath, a quick tap dance, or an encouraging self-talk. When they fall, they quickly forgive themselves, reappraise the situation, decide their best is always good enough, and reconsider their options. The pursuit of perfection does not paralyze them.

Children learn to show empathy toward those who hurt them by saying, "I understand"; they show generosity toward those who help them by saying, "thank you." They show courage when befriending children different from them and they remain determined to do their best. They are optimistic that they can pass a difficult test if they study; they learn to use their grit to try, to fail, and to try again. They use patient research to seek out new books to read and new puzzles to solve.

Children may need good grades to accomplish their goals; however, they need more than academic achievement for success. They also need to be highly accomplished in the art and science of emotional strength. One cannot substitute for the other and children must pursue them in equal measure. To succeed children need to develop "clear-eyed energy and motivation, and clearly understood strengths."[141]

Children remind themselves that their lives are full of good and that most of the time they are sufficiently engaged that they lose track of time so the day flies by. "I can't believe how fast the day went and how much I learned." No matter what children do, or how they act, the teacher only uses the language of strength and never fails to suggest or correct actions related to the strength. He or she never criticizes or chastises the students. Instead, the teacher waves a magic wand to cue them to use their strength. Positive psychology significantly advances the efforts to promote emotional strength as essential to well-being. Close your eyes—shut the negative classroom door. Open them—walk through the positive psychology classroom door.

Case Study K–2: Teaching Strengths Learning

Robert was terrified of taking tests and knew that one test was so important that, if he failed it, he could fail second grade. His hands were sweating. He felt afraid all his friends would go to third grade without him. He took a deep breath and composed himself. He thought about his best strength—hard work. He would work hard to pass the test except this test was the kind that you cannot really study to do well. His head hurt and he felt panic. He remembered what Mr. Lewis had told him: "You do not only work hard—you think hard. So don't think too much about the test and don't try too hard." Robert also remembered that he had told him he was an optimist and to expect the best—not the worst. "You can handle anything. Do not let worry defeat you. Before you begin, put your worries in the worry jar and look at the birds and trees outside. The trees will still be there when you are done. Look at the birds flying high across the field. They do not have to think to fly. They just fly."

Before the test started, Robert imagined himself as a free bird with wide wings. In his mind, he watched the bird glide out of a tall tree toward the sky. He sat quietly for a minute, imagining flying higher and higher into the bright blue sky and fluffy white clouds he saw outside the classroom window. He felt himself relax. He picked up his pencil and soared away. He was not sure if he would pass the test. He did know he would keep flying as high as he could fly.

Case Study 3–5: Teaching Strengths Learning

Edward was one of the smartest students in class. He scored so high on a national fifth-grade test that he earned a Presidential award. The first-grade teacher asked him to tutor a boy in her class. Edward was happy to do so, and he loved tutoring Jacob in reading and math. Edward worked hard to think of fun ways to teach Jacob and even spent his allowance to buy him stickers although he was from a poor family and did not have much spare money. Edward tutored him all year and Jacob was doing much better. At the end of the year, Edward was excited that the tutors were going on a special field trip together. Edward had never been to an amusement park and he was looking forward to going with Jacob. About three days before the field trip, the doctor hospitalized Edward's father, and in the rush at home, he left his homework on the kitchen counter. His teacher, Mr. McManus, told him that he could no longer tutor Jacob because of the rule that if you don't turn in your own homework—even one time—you can no longer be a tutor. Edward felt so embarrassed because Mr. McManus announced to everyone that he was no longer a tutor and could not go on the field trip. The first-grade teacher took Edward aside and told him what a wonderful tutor he had been and was very sorry this unfortunate incident had happened. She told him, "Thank you for helping Jacob improve. You were an empathetic friend to him." Edward was still very sad and wanted to cry. He could hardly get home before the tears spilled out. The next day he was so angry that he wanted to scream and throw a tantrum. He came very close. But, instead, he calmed himself and reminded himself how much he enjoyed tutoring and how much he had helped Jacob. He knew Jacob would do so much better now and not be embarrassed anymore about his grades. He decided to focus on his empathy for Jacob instead of the field trip. He knew he had shared his time, talent, kindness, and generosity without fail for the good of another. He decided to stay optimistic that someday he would get to that amusement park. He decided to show courage when the others left on the field trip. "Maybe I will be a teacher someday," he said to himself. "I will never do what Mr. McManus did so this was a valuable lesson." Edward did eventually become a teacher—a teacher who teaches with strength.

Guiding Question Exercise

Imagine receiving medals for your strengths. What strength would earn you a gold medal? A silver medal? A bronze medal? Think of a difficult task that you were able to accomplish. What strength did you use to accomplish the task and how did you use it? Think of a difficult task that you did *not* accomplish. Did you deploy the same strength? Would you deploy different strengths now? What is your signature strength? Is there a challenge strength that you need to develop? What strength do you use most often in the classroom and model for children? Do you notice children's strengths? What strengths do the children in your classroom possess? Do you use praise? Have you ever tried using strengths-based praise? Have you ever conducted a strengths assessment? Do you teach any of the positive psychology strength benchmarks in your classroom? Which one do you teach? Which one would you like to try to use? Can you connect strengths training to academic standards that you teach? Choose one technique to use with children to teach strengths and develop a lesson plan for it.

Guiding Question Discussion

The teacher helps children identify strengths through formal and informal assessment and to recognize the strengths of self and others. He or she pays special attention to finding the signature strength or the one that comes most easily and naturally, and that is relied on most often. The teacher also pays attention to developing the challenge strength needed. Children seek feedback about their strengths and what others tell them. What they tell themselves also matters. They consider how to increase their signature strengths, how to build on the ones they possess, and how to develop new ones. They practice using their own strengths and emulate each other's strengths for the betterment of all. Their accomplishments are the direct result of their habitual and expert practice of strength for the pursuit of a good life and excellence. The teacher acknowledges that a strengths focus engages children in learning.

Web Resources for Children

Adding Assets, http://www.freespirit.com/book-series/.
Ben Franklin 13 Virtues T-Shirts, http://www.cafepress.com/+ben_
franklins/.

Imagery for Kids, http://www.imageryforkids.com/.
Myths and Legends, http://myths.e2bn.org/index.php/.
Paul Revere House, http://www.paulreverehouse.org/.

Web Resources for Teachers

The Empathy Symbol, http://www.empathysymbol.com.
Good Character.com, http://goodcharacter.com/.
Strengths Literature Finder, http://www.teachingvalues.com/childrensbooks.html.
Strengths Quest, http://www.strengthsquest.com/content/141365/resources.aspx/.
The Twelve Best Comic Books for Education, http://www.openeducation.net/2008/01/27.

CHAPTER 6

TEACHING RELATIONSHIPS AND THE CONNECTED LIFE: FRIENDSHIP

Good actions give strength to us and inspire good actions in others.
—Plato

Positive psychology empowers children to forge deep and lasting friendships by managing their emotions and directing their strengths toward initiating, maintaining, and improving their relationships. With the practice of positive psychology and the training of social emotional skills, teachers help children to build positive connections between, and among, each other by teaching them to trust each other, understand each other, and rely on each other for support. They learn to transfer their positive emotions and signature strengths to their friendships so that they are forgiving, generous, loyal, committed, and supportive in all of their interpersonal interactions.

Friendship is an interpersonal relationship that creates positive emotions and cultivates positive strengths that promote intrapersonal growth: the teacher is the key to the connected life in the elementary classroom. Positive psychology teachers recognize that friendship is a pillar of school success and that it is essential in order to teach the positive psychology taxonomy of relationships. These relationships can predict children's overall well-being and the research is clear that children without friends, or with few friends, are at risk for academic failure, emotional stress, and psychological disorders. In school, children learn to use their emotions and strengths to meet the mutually reciprocal expectations of friendship. They build rapport and relationships in the classroom and connect to each other, their schools, and their communities through work and play. Children learn the give and take of friendship, and the teacher opens the door of friendship to all.

Whether or not children have friends reliably predicts whether or not they report that they are happy and whether or not they enjoy going to school.[1] Maslow proposed that, immediately after children fulfill basic physical needs for water, food, and shelter, they seek affiliation and a sense of belonging, because friendship serves a critical bioadaptive function.[2] The affection, goodwill, and assistance provided by friends play an important role in both physical and personal adjustment. Teachers tell you that children without friends do not fare well in the classroom. They suffer more reported physical complaints and do not possess the same emotional poise that children with a strong network of friends typically possess. School connectedness predicts every facet of physical, mental, emotional, and academic health.[3] The teacher must understand more about relationships and friendships in order to increase school connectedness by using the positive psychology teaching taxonomy of relationships.

Aristotle, the happiness philosopher, wrote at length about friendship and was the first to distinguish between types of friendships. He described friendships for mutual utility and friendships for mutual goodwill, and he claimed that the hallmark of true friendship is reciprocal altruism.[4] Contemporary psychology identifies four different types of friendship defined primarily by the function of the relationships.[5]

As they grow and learn, children make four different kinds of friends: (1) acquaintance friendships, (2) casual friendships, (3) agentic friendships, and (4) deep or true friendships.[6] Every child has different types of friends throughout elementary school and each type of friendship serves an important and unique purpose. Engaging in all types of friendships creates well-rounded and emotionally engaged children; however, true friendship is a staple in the lives of children who flourish. True friendship is the gold standard and creates mental and emotional well-being.

Acquaintances are children in frequent contact with each other such as text friends, Facebook friends, or playground friends. However, this group does not know each other very well, and so they interact in superficial ways. They do not share the emotional content of their lives and they may even hide their true emotional selves from acquaintances.

All children in a classroom are—by definition—acquaintances and the positive psychology teacher's job is to turn acquaintances into friends.

Casual friends share some thoughts and feelings in very careful and cautious ways. They interact within closely held boundaries and rarely reveal their emotions or discuss their strengths. They tend to self-edit and do not discuss sensitive or difficult topics. Children enjoy the company of their casual friends who are an important part of their social circle and who are quite compatible. However, they rarely share their innermost thoughts or feelings and are not emotionally close. They work well on the group history project and play kickball together on the playground. Because they like each other, they are easily motivated to get to know each other better.

Agentic friendships are pragmatic friendships and typically share a common task, goal, or passion.[7] This type of friendship is utilitarian in nature and children have many agentic friends in school. By definition, classmates, club members, and teammates are all agentic friends who learn to cooperate and collaborate for the good of all. Agentic friends often develop strong bonds quickly because when children share a common goal the relationship deepens quickly. Children feel an immediate sense of affiliation because these friends share common interests, beliefs, and goals. Given a supportive environment, an agentic friendship is likely to mature into true friendship and children who enjoy true friendships are much more likely to thrive and flourish in the classroom.

True friends express authentic emotions, and in a true friendship, there is trust, honesty, empathy, and an exchange of material and social gifts. True friends show trust, forgiveness, gratitude, honesty, commitment, support, enthusiasm, and gladness toward their friends without expectation of gain. They share their emotional lives and use their signature strengths, offer to help each other, and form committed relationships based on unconditional support. Children who are true friends act in generous and supportive ways and understand that friends must be able to trust each other when they are most vulnerable.[8] The mark of true friendship is mutual aid, regard, and concern.

Teachers are in an advantageous position to facilitate all types of friendships and especially to teach the practice of true friendship. They can create the climate, the culture, and the circumstance for true friendships to blossom; to leave the development of friendship to chance alone is a survival-of-the-fittest approach. Instead, positive psychology teaches children the art and science of relationships. Without true friends—relying only on acquaintances, casual friends, and agentic friends—children never really connect to anyone in school and are more likely to feel isolated and alienated. Without a strong sense of affiliation, children do not connect emotionally, socially, or academically to school. True friends take good care of each other's hearts and minds.

The Importance of Friendship Learning in Positive Psychology

The journey from the first tentative meeting to a lasting friendship is often a winding road. Along the way, children deal with conflicting loyalties, heart-breaking rejections, sad breakups, and happy make-ups. Children use their signature strengths, and other complementary strengths, to make and keep friends. Meeting the challenges of friendship requires emotional awareness and applied strengths. Friendship is a highly complex and emotionally demanding transaction.

Strengths give friendship its footing as children show forgiveness with friends who do harm, gratitude with friends who help, honesty with friends who are protective, grit with friends who commit, patience with friends who are supportive, optimism with friends who enthuse, and gladness with all friends. The positive psychology teaching taxonomy benchmark of friendship, and its associated indicators, teaches children to apply emotional strengths to the task of friendship.

Children who are not honest with themselves or others, who act in egocentric or unreliable ways, and who are gloomy and doomy, have a difficult time making friends. Those who do not learn to forgive and who are selfish or impatient cannot keep friends. The strengths that children possess are the building blocks of relationships, and friendship comes naturally to children who know their strengths and how to apply them to initiate and maintain friendships.

Emotional strength is a precondition for social strength. Children who are able to manage their emotions and engage with others can use their strengths and make best friends. Positive psychology helps children to channel their emotional strengths into social competency.

The teacher focuses on the five pillars of friendship: (1) encouragement of friendship, (2) maintenance of friendship, (3) reliance on friendship, (4) repair of friendship, and (5) value of friendship. To make and keep friends, children must learn to read others' emotions, honor

Table 6.1. Friendship Benchmark and Indicators

Friendship Indicators	Value Meaning	Accomplishment
Empathy	Tolerance	Cooperation
Generosity	Helpfulness	Contentment
Courage	Fairness	Confidence
Grit	Resilience	Fortitude
Patience	Peace	Serenity
Optimism	Anticipation	Inspiration
Good Cheer	Enjoyment	Joy

others' wishes, meet others' needs, and support others' intentions and accomplishments.

Given all of the requirements, demands, and nuances of friendship, it is not surprising that many children do not make friends, especially true friends, easily. The teacher's challenge is to show all children how to build positive relationships. The aim of the positive psychology teaching taxonomy benchmark of friendship is to teach children how to make friends by teaching them how to look and listen for others' feelings and strengths, communicate their own feelings to friends, share their strengths with friends, resolve conflicts in a friendly way, and address unfriendly behavior.

Children learn how to connect in ways that develop new friendships, teach them to get along to sustain existing friendships, enable them to support each other to repair fraying friendships, and encourage them to celebrate friendships. For many children, the most difficult part of relationship building is making a friend. To make a friend, children must risk rejection and use their strengths to manage the friendship-seeking process. To do this, children first identify friendship feelings and enlist their strength: "I feel brave enough to talk to her and determined to make a friend." "I feel hopeful that he will like me and glad he seems to like sports, too."

A child learns to capitalize on his or her signature strength, offering to share it, to accomplish a friendship goal: "I noticed you lost your pencil. I have one you can borrow." "You seem a little quiet today: Is everything okay?" Friendship begins with social awareness, attention, and interest. Children who are socially adept seek and approach potential friends more mindfully.

Social awareness is the ability to take the cognitive, social, and emotional perspective of others and to appreciate individual and group differences.[9] Children work and play well with others when they have sharp social awareness of each other's needs, intentions, and desires. Children establish and sustain considerate, cooperative, and caring relationships that strengthen connections. They meet their potential friends in the classroom, and every encounter presents a chance to make a new friend. Therefore, the teacher is in the very best position to help children develop the social competencies that are important to the successful pursuit and development of new friendships.

The teacher helps determine whether children ostracize new class members, whether they look beyond their cliques for new friends, whether shy children are included, and much more. Essentially the teacher designs the class sociogram and uses his or her influence to facilitate positive relationships and social dynamics. Positive psychology proponents understand that the classroom must become a friendship laboratory.

Initial superficial attraction may occur around pleasing characteristics or personal gain. A first grader tells the teacher, "My friend likes to wear pretty dresses and eat cupcakes, too. Sometimes, she brings me a cupcake. I really like her." The teacher can extend this view with some simple questions: "What strength does she have that you also like? What strength do you have that you can share with her?"

Casual attraction occurs around mutual interests or common goals. A third grader says, "My friend and I love baseball so we are trying out for the same team together." The teacher adds, "That will give you a chance to get to know each other better. Do you know how he will feel if he doesn't make the team?" Children practice how to use empathy to make a friend: "I understand how you feel." They practice gratitude: "That was thoughtful of you, thank you."

Initial mature attraction occurs around common beliefs and shared values. A fifth grader tells the teacher, "My friend and I both love animals and are sad when we read stories about people who hurt them. She gave me a book all about animal emotions. I just knew dogs had feelings. We are going to pool our allowances to buy dog and cat food for the local humane society." The teacher smiles and says, "That is a wonderful and deep connection. Because you both feel so caring toward animals and are so empathetic, I know this friendship will just strengthen and grow. You are lucky to find such a friend."

The positive psychology teacher's job is to mature and deepen superficial and casual attractions into deeper and more meaningful friendships. With the friendship benchmark, children learn to look beyond immediate gain and to value the long-term benefit associated with having a true friend.

For example, a teacher can assign every child a learning partner based on common talents or interests. She then suggests that children approach another by inquiring about a similar hobby or pastime. She directs and accelerates the process with a social scavenger hunt that structures interpersonal interactions so children can easily find another who shares the same favorite color, pet, team, or music video. She can help them role-play how to approach a child whom they do not know and teach them how to start a conversation by establishing common ground: "You look just like a friend of mine in Florida. Have you ever been to the beach?"

The positive psychology teacher instructs them how to notice details that communicate their attentiveness and openness to friendship: "You use your left hand to write? Me, too. Sometimes it was hard for me. Now I like being a lefty. How about you?" The teacher helps them to overcome their fears and to show courage by using strength skills in the face of possible rebuffs. Children learn that making friends is worth taking a risk.

Sometimes a particular child is just not a good friendship match. Children learn to tell themselves that it was worth a try anyway or that a friendship that did not work out was just not the right one. A teacher can help them overcome discouragement that comes if they have not been able to make friends in the past and help them use their natural optimism to remind themselves that their past experience does not mean they cannot learn to make friends. They understand that past difficulty in making friends does not mean there is not a new friend out there and they keep initiating. With support, it gets easier to sustain the effort to find and make a friend because children learn not to internalize setbacks as failures.

Children talk themselves into and out of friendships by using a positive explanatory style to write their friendship stories. They believe that there is a friend for them just around the corner—but only if they keep trying. They tell themselves that the last friendship they initiated did not work out because they did not have much in common. If children use their emotional strengths, eventually they will make friends.

As self and social awareness evolve, teachers notice that children's ability to reach out to make a friend improves. "We have no choice but . . . to learn how our children become socially wise, to provide opportunities for them to do so, and to try to understand through both 'educational' and 'naturalistic' research how . . . [to turn] interpersonal wisdom into best practice."[10]

Friendship is a comforting transaction because it brings us a friend to rely on when most needed. When children have colds, their friends can share tissues. When someone is cut from the team, a friend promises to help him practice for next year's tryout. When someone has to move away, her friend promises to stay in touch. A trouble divided by two is a burden that is easier to carry. If emotions are out-of-kilter and strength fails, friends share their balanced response and substitute their strengths. In short, friends offer each other emotional support and balance each other.

Children help each other in times of need and success because, with friends in tow, daily lows are not as low and the highs are higher. The truest friends clap the loudest when their friends win the award. They revel in their success, celebrate their achievements, and praise their accomplishments. Sharing success intensifies the experience of it. Throughout the world, children celebrate life markers, significant moments, important transitions, tragic sorrow, and boundless joy with friends. The teacher brings apple cider champagne and plastic champagne glasses so children can toast their friends.

With friends, children feel happy and glad to come to school; they act more cheerful, and they earn better grades.[11] If children go to school every day because they look forward to seeing their friends, they go with anticipation rather than apprehension, with optimism rather than pessimism, and with assurance rather than unease. Children arrive at school feeling happy, expressing their good cheer, and sharing their gladness. They go to school better able to manage their emotions and utilize their strengths because, with a true friend, the path is less lonely and the road is less frightening. Even a single friend whom a child can count on when optimism and courage fails, makes all the difference. A true friend is worth all the effort it takes to make one.

Making a friend, especially a best friend, is not the end of the quest for positive lifelong relationships. The real challenge is to keep a friend. Friendship demands a substantial investment of time, positive emotion, and emotional strength. Sooner or later a friendship will fray around the edges or rip apart completely. When that happens, children need to know how to repair it. They must learn how to painstakingly stitch it back together or patch it up. When severe conflict has ruptured the relationship, they may have to invest heavily in its restoration. This can be a daunting task for children, and so they simply walk away. However, this approach teaches children nothing about how to repair broken relationships.

Children learn that the best way to avoid a damaged friendship is preventative. The teacher helps them to understand what they must do, and how they must act, to nourish a forever friendship. The teacher invests time and effort into teaching friendship so children learn to give a friend time and attention, show caring feelings, and share emotional strengths to nurture the friendship over the long term. To maintain a friendship, they learn to negotiate their boundaries and know when to give and to forgive.

Children learn ways to develop interpersonal accord, find common ground, and make peace with each other. If they self-regulate their emotions using their strengths—so they don't call names when feeling angry or refuse a favor when feeling selfish—they do not lose friends. Children learn to be mindful of how they want to feel in the relationship—happy, calm, and determined to keep their friends. More important, they are mindful of how they want to make their friends feel in relationships: grateful, kindly, and hopeful. Friends take care of friends.

Even when children tend to their friendships with positive emotion and emotional strength, conflict and discord are inevitable. Children fight with their friends, and these disputes are normal and expected. Actually, this friendship friction serves an important purpose because only the failure of a friendship can teach someone how to repair it. Social conflict requires children to reflect on how effectively they are able to self-regulate their emotions and how easily they apply strengths to make up and make peace.

Children's ability to keep their friends is the litmus test of positive psychology. "I am smarter. No, I am. No, I am. Well, I am better at soccer. No, you are not. I hate you. I hate you, too." From this point forward, it only escalates and, sometimes, it is contagious as children line up their allies. Some children feel sheepish after a fight, others feel dejected, and still others feel angrier depending on their emotional strengths inventory.

Conflict means to collide or disagree and it creates at least some small degree, and often a large degree, of emotional tension. Conflict can be a short-term fight or a long-term battle and it always interferes with rational thought, effective action, and consensus. Children in conflict with one another, or the larger group, usually contest and oppose some group idea or action and cannot find any accord or common ground.

Children learn to navigate around intense feelings and unregulated emotions. They also learn to use positive emotion to keep their negative emotions in check so that their own poorly managed emotions do not exacerbate the situation. They never fail to bring their strengths to the table and use them to reconsider their position, negotiate differences, compromise, and act in conciliatory ways. They learn to use non-confrontational strategies to diffuse negative emotion and infuse positive strengths. These abilities do not always occur naturally and so teachers educate children to be peacemakers. "I am willing to talk to you because I feel hopeful that we can solve the problem and because I have caring feelings for you. However, I will need to be patient, and you will need to be supportive, so this friendship is less volatile and more serene." Relationship dialogues and friendship reconstruction are so important to academic achievement, and all other accomplishments, that they should be taught in every grade as a subject or course. All other academic subjects can also be taught under the auspices of friendship so children can study conflict resolution by using their reading, writing, and mathematics skills. If children learn how to avoid conflict, manage it, and surmount it, conflict does not end in combat.

True friendship helps children resist negative social pressure and kindly rely on positive relationships to soften the irritation of differences and the sting of disputes. When a new friend betrays a child, the child is able to nullify the negative experience by remembering the loyalty of an old friend or experiencing the faithfulness of another friend—and turns silver into gold.

Children with friends look forward to coming to school, remain more engaged while in school, and reach out to each other after school to do homework and ride bikes. The path to a pleasant, good, and connected life is through a friend's gate. As Winnie the Pooh says, "It is more fun to talk with someone who doesn't use long, difficult words but rather short, easy words like 'What about lunch?'"

The Positive Psychology Teacher's Toolbox: Connected Learning

The teacher does not underestimate the importance and benefit of social relationships to improve academic performance. She understands that children's daily emotional and academic health depends on the quality of their relationships. The teacher always uses the general educational methods previously discussed: (1) the language of emotions and strengths, (2) infused academics, and (3) visual and performing arts, and (4) strengths training. The teacher fuses these with the techniques recommended to teach the positive psychology taxonomy benchmark of friendship along with the academic curriculum. Friendship supports learning so the academic curriculum must incorporate it.

To teach friendship, the teacher plans effective ways to teach the five pillars of friendship: (1) encouragement of friendship, (2) maintenance of friendship, (3) reliance on friendship, (4) repair of friendship, and (5) value of friendship. All of these create the relational insight needed for children to make and keep friends. The teacher focuses on teaching these by using Positive Psychology Teacher's Friendship Toolbox techniques so children learn to start a friendship, strengthen it, rely on it, renew it, and celebrate it.

The Friendship Toolbox provides specific techniques the teacher uses to teach friendship and integrate it into the traditional academic curriculum. The techniques help those who are younger to reach out to make new friends. Older children learn to expand and deepen their social networks.

Children use enthusiasm and gladness to make friends; support and commitment to keep friends; honesty and gratitude to reassure friends; and forgiveness to reconcile with them. The teacher may use the recommended techniques in the Friendship Toolbox as part of a larger program, within a comprehensive curriculum, as a themed unit, as stand-alone lessons, as enrichment activities, or as games that children play. Positive psychology programs may include a fully developed curriculum that teaches all the benchmarks, a themed unit that teaches one, a series of lessons to assess one, a weekly schedule of activities to process one, a daily exercise that practices one, or a game to reinforce one. Whatever form and format a positive psychology program takes, it always uses some, if not all, of the techniques. The Positive Psychology Teacher's Friendship Toolbox techniques include (1) build social awareness, (2) conduct a friendship meeting, (3) start a friendship center or club, (4) host a festival, (5) practice friendship training, and (6) use conflict resolution training. The teacher uses these techniques to teach about relationships and the pillars of friendship. The positive psychology teaching taxonomy of positive friendship uses these techniques to teach the pillars of friendship learning from two friends' first "hello" to their 30-year school reunion. These are not discrete but expansive techniques.

Table 6.2. The Teacher's Toolbox: Pillars and Techniques of Friendship Learning

Develop Friendship	Maintain Friendship	Rely on Friendship	Repair Friendship	Celebrate Friendship
Social Awareness	Friendship Meeting	Friendship Club	Friendship Meeting	Build Social Awareness
Friendship Meeting	Friendship Club	Friendship Training	Friendship Training	Friendship Meeting
Friendship Club	Friendship Training	Friendship Training	Conflict Resolution Training	Host a Festival

That is, any single technique can teach multiple aspects of friendship across the curriculum. The teacher is in the best position to decide what pillars of friendship to teach and what techniques work best so children flourish in the elementary school classroom. Children learn how to start a conversation with a child they do not know, learn to better understand the feelings and strengths of children they do know, and appreciate their personal contribution to the friendship. Ask children how it feels to have a true friend and they invariably respond with "happy."

1. Build Social Awareness

Children need to know what they should bring to the friendship. To begin, teachers help children understand and accept a different point of view, to see other children with a more open perspective, and to help them understand other children's sentiments. The first step in teaching social awareness is to spend time helping children to get to know each other on a deeper, more intimate, and less superficial level. They learn to take a walk in another child's shoes.

Social awareness engenders social empathy. The pursuit of true friendship begins with less egocentrism and ends with more social empathy. The Livewire DVD program, *What Does It Mean to Be a Good Friend?*[12] features real kid-on-the-street interviews, entertaining animation, and typical scenarios about friendship dilemmas. Worksheets, lesson plans, and a teacher's guide promote classroom discussion and encourage children, in third through fifth grades, to think about what it means to be a good friend. Watching, writing a response, and discussing the purpose and challenge of friendship develop social awareness and social empathy.

Another Livewire DVD program, *You Can Choose*, is a warm, humorous approach to teaching children, K–5, how to make good decisions that help them get along better with others.[13] Using comedy, drama, music, peer education, and role modeling, dramatic skits depict a problem situation that the children must resolve.

The facilitator's guide contains discussion questions, writing assignments, and follow-up activities that support the lesson. If children decide to forgive others instead of punishing others, offer to share with others instead of taking from others, and learn to support others instead of rejecting others, they make and keep true friends.

The *Life Skills Training—Elementary* program teaches children in third through fifth grade general social skills such as overcoming shyness, using strengths to clearly communicate emotions to others, building relationships, and avoiding violence.[14] One of the lesson plans asks children to identify the various qualities they believe are important in a friend. The lesson explores how some children think the most important thing about a friend is that they will keep a secret and how other children think a friend should always be fun to be around.

Teacher-developed lessons that focus on generating increased social awareness can be equally effective. Any lesson that requires children to consider whether their feelings, thoughts, and actions are conducive to making and keeping friends is useful. Any lesson that connects the strengths of children to friendship so that they come to understand how true friends are forgiving, generous, loyal, committed, supportive, excited, and enjoyable is encouraged in the positive psychology teaching taxonomy of friendship. In any lesson, pairing children to work as partners is an excellent means of increasing social awareness. Children who are assigned to work together on academic or positive psychology tasks must learn to accommodate each other, to rely on each other's strengths, to yield to each other's preferences, and to modify their own actions accordingly.

The teacher should not undervalue the power of the pair in the elementary school classroom. At the start of the semester or month, the teacher plays the Starburst game. Children choose three Starburst candies that represent favorite colors and then pair up with other children who exactly match or come close to matching each other—for example, a yellow and an orange are matched. The Starburst pair works together for the rest of the month on every academic and positive psychology task. In the process, there is the opportunity to get to know each other better and to become true friends. The teacher can use any number of pairing games such as matching children by astrological sign, favorite television show, or signature strength. The primary purpose of the learning partner is to help each other and work together on all classroom lessons and activities. The partners exchange phone numbers and let each other know when they will be absent, collect missed handouts for each other, eat lunch together, help each other with homework, and study together for tests.

When children have the time and opportunity to get to know each other well, they develop greater understanding and tolerance for each other. Teachers can also help children embrace tolerance by formally teaching it. On the time-honored and highly respected Teaching Tolerance website teachers post ideas for teaching tolerance in the classroom.[15] There is also a monthly magazine with articles and suggestions about teaching tolerance to children of all ages, information on how to become a mix-it-up school, and a teaching kit for the early grades. A teaching kit, Starting Small, uses a video to tell stories of tolerance from around the country so children learn to care about another child's feelings, beliefs, and welfare so that there are fewer "hurt feelings, sad faces, and lonely outsiders in schools."[16] Children reflect on how to reach out to others with an open, tolerant mind-set that encourages reflection. This activity, and others like it, teaches generosity of spirit, commitment to tolerance, and empathetic action.

Empathy is defined as a level of understanding and intimacy such that one child readily comprehends the feelings, thoughts, and motives of another. Empathy is at the core of the positive psychology teaching taxonomy benchmark of friendship. Promoting empathy is a major undertaking in any classroom.

Many of the activities on the website examine the importance of attachment and trust in friendship. Children use Braille, research fashion style messages, write global pen pals, create tolerance flags, and construct a global holiday calendar to increase understanding and empathy for others. In the Happy Face game, young children give out happy face cards to anyone who seems to need cheering up.

Schools can participate in National Mix-It-Up Lunch Day. K–12 teachers develop inclusive communities by requiring children to eat lunch with other children they do not know and who do not look like them. The project offers activities to prepare children to organize and participate in the event. Diverse groups might rate food likes and dislikes; Skype with other participating schools in other states and nations; post Twitter or Facebook comments about the event before, during, and after; and research what different names mean. Schools can also apply to become a model mix-it-up school.

Whether using the standardized kits, shared activities, or planning a national mix-it-up day, the website is a source of rich ideas to teach social awareness by insisting that children assume a different perspective, embrace diversity, and adopt a broader, friendlier worldview. Positive psychology teaches that empathy is a bridge that all children must cross moving toward each other in an interactive process of discovery that seeks tolerance.

The positive psychology teaching taxonomy friendship benchmark teaches children what strengths to use so others will want to get to know them better. If another child seems discouraged, they offer their optimism. If another child seems afraid, they share their courage. If another child seems sad, they share their good cheer. Friends fill in the blanks and finish sentences. They know when the other needs quiet or noise. Positive psychology teaches that there is friendship in strength and there is strength in friendship.

2. Conduct a Friendship Meeting

The teacher constructs meetings for children to get to know each other better. The children consider how they feel about each other and how they rely on each other. They identify each other's strengths, appreciate each other's concerns, and announce each other's accomplishments. Many teachers refer to the class friendship meeting as a friendship circle. The teacher often uses it to increase social awareness so children will better understand who wants to be their friend and how to make it happen. Social awareness is necessary for children to know how to successfully approach a potential new friend or interact with an old one.

In the elementary classroom, the friendship meeting is a daily circle meeting focused on fostering new friendships and deepening existing relationships. The classroom friendship meeting is a very versatile technique that the teacher can use to arrange, explore, boost, reconfigure, mend, and commend friendships. At the friendship meeting, the teacher may ask children about friendship, about how they think friends feel, and how they use their strengths to help friends. They may be asked to share good news about friends, complete open-ended sentences about friends, describe how a friend is generous, or compliment a friend. They write down recommendations to put in the friendship suggestion box, play a game with a friend, or brainstorm ways to enjoy their friends more. Each month children work on a different friendship project or discuss a different friendship topic during the meeting. The goal of all activities and games is to help every child know what strengths to use to initiate a friendship. If another child seems discouraged, they know they can offer their optimism. If another child seems afraid, they can share their courage. As children master strengths learning, they use their signature strengths to invite others to get to know them better. Each month they learn a song about friendship to sing together or listen to a popular song about friendship of their choosing.

Children discuss what the songs teach about friendship. In coming months at the meeting, the children make friendship bracelets for children they do not know well and interview children they want to get to know better. They make a friendship chain from construction paper and put an action word about friendship inside each circle in the chain.

A favorite game played during the friendship circle meeting is the Buy a Present game, which teaches children how to rely on others to know what they need and provide it. Children each draw a name of one of their classmates from a hat. They all get an imaginary budget of $1,000 to shop for the friend. They browse catalogs to select the gifts. As a less commercial alternative, children make gift certificates or coupons that give gifts of help and assistance such as help with a book report. They can also make special event tickets to give away such as a lunch date.

The class friendship meeting teaches children how to prevent fights and how to use conflict resolution skills to repair friendships. Circle time may teach conflict resolution lessons, recognize the most improved peacemakers or peace leaders in the classroom, or chart how many disputes were resolved in the prior week as well as record the nature of those disputes. Children also discuss solutions to individual or class conflicts working toward common solutions, acting as a democratic forum that encourages debate, addresses problematic issues, and proposes corrective actions. Class officers organize and facilitate the friendship meeting as a problem-solving meeting.

Class meetings, by their nature, can build and broaden positive relationships or disrupt and narrow positive interactions. The Caring Schools Community developed a comprehensive unit on class meetings that outlines a detailed plan of action for the conduct of weekly themed classroom meetings differentiated by age and grade level.[17] The teacher uses the unit to conduct class meetings that give children a more meaningful voice in the classroom and build class unity through friendship.

The goal is to build collective strength and give students more meaningful options in the classroom. The unit structures meetings that help children establish common class values, create action plans, and solve real-life class problems. The meetings emphasize greater understanding and empathy for others. In the meeting, children ask each other questions to extend thinking and open up new ways of considering the issue. They agree and disagree with each other, contribute ideas, and make observations and comments based on the questions they ask and answer. Peer-to-peer, open-ended questions probe divergent solutions through meaningful conversations.

There is a lesson plan for a start-up meeting during which children introduce themselves and participate in get-to-know-each-other exercises. There is also a lesson plan for a final meeting during which children plan their transition to the next grade. Closing activities include sharing good-byes and signing autograph books. In between the start and end of the school year, there are lesson plans for a weekly friendship meeting.

The friendship meeting lessons teach children how to be playground friends, be helpful to classmates, share supplies, welcome new children, listen actively, share ideas, and argue positively. All the friendship meetings help students get to know one another better, understand class values, and apply positive social strengths to their interactions.

At the meetings, children play the Think, Pair, and Share game: They think about an issue, share ideas with a partner, and use chart paper to record meeting notes and present their ideas. One of the meeting lessons presents how to welcome a new child to class. Another lesson for children in second through sixth grade discusses the challenges that occur on the playground. Children generate ideas, recommend actions, and report their results. In the class meeting kit, there are 30 detailed friendship lesson plans for K–1, and 35 lesson plans for children in grades 2–6, a teacher's calendar, an implementation guide, and supplemental videos. The unit also includes an initial survey that assesses to what degree children believe their class is: (1) a community whose members are supportive, (2) a place where everyone is concerned about others, and (3) a space where all have the opportunity to exert influence. The survey also determines to what degree children perceive that each has the opportunity to participate in classroom planning and making positive and balanced decisions.

Children identify problems encountered, they categorize the problems, and they brainstorm solutions. In particular, they consider how the qualities of true friendship can serve to alleviate conflict on the playground. The teacher uses a friendship meeting to teach the five pillars of friendship because children learn to share what they know to give.

Children need a friend who forgives them when they are wrong and they need a friend to hug them when the day is cold and long. They need an honest friend who does not lie to them and they need a friend to help them laugh, learn, love, and live with them—happy, strong, connected, and confident.

3. Start a Friendship Center or Club

When children plan and build a project together, they become true friends who have proved they know how to work together in personally satisfying ways for the collective good. There is no better project for children of all ages to build that rapport than a friendship center. The children are assigned to teams that will plan and develop various aspects of the class friendship center: wall posters and other center décor, children's literature, learning games and materials, a menu of activities, and a schedule of special events.

The children create a shopping list and plan to sell friendship bracelets they make in their spare time to generate funds to support the center. They plan to trace handprints for every child in the class and line the center with the construction paper hands.

They also plan to use a large bulletin board to recognize their friends' accomplishments. Another team of children conducts research and creates a list of recommended children's books to order for the center. Limiting the list to only 25 books is difficult because there are so many to choose from for every age and grade level. The team has decided to choose all that they find interesting and they then vote on the finalists.

Younger children really like the book *Argus*, which urges children to accept differences, understand through listening, think about the feelings of others, and accomplish tasks through cooperation.[18] Older children choose the book *Crossing Bok Chitto: A Choctaw Tale of Friendship and Freedom.*[19] Strong characters in this story implore readers to listen to, and empathize with, others. Children draw on wall murals depicting similarities and differences of friends; they also learn to play simple flute and drum songs to bring the Choctaw tale to life.

The children select a variety of learning materials that help them explore friendships by connecting them to their feelings and strengths and their friends' feelings and strengths. To practice using positive emotion to sustain friendship, they play games and take actions that are incompatible with anger. They add silly games to the menu: laugh like a hyena, speak gibberish, and drink a laughter milkshake. The teacher adds: a book about hyenas to read, a stack of gibberish language cards to use, a milkshake tumbler to pretend, and bubbles to blow to the list of friendship materials. They listen to William Jay Smith's poem "Laughing Time" and watch the Gazillion Bubble Show video together.[20] Children play the Friendship in a Jar game: They pick the name of a classmate out of a jar, read a book or visit a website to learn how to make that friend a bracelet, share a quote from the quote jar with their friend, and create a certificate acknowledging their friend's signature strength.[21] They also advertise all friendship activities in the monthly friendship blog.

The center also includes a friendship stamp set to make appreciation cards and friendship stickers, and pins to collect.[22] There is a friendship magnet that they can borrow to put on their desks to remind them of strengths they need to use to be a friend magnet.[23] There are friendship songs on CDs and as MP3s as well as card and board games to play with each other.[24] There are friendship card games: Go Fish, Good Friend, and Know the Code.[25] These games identify positive friend traits and best ways to communicate with a friend. Favorite board games are available for children, in first through fourth grade, to play in small groups. The *Friendship Island* board game teaches social skills needed for positive peer relations.[26] The social strengths skills training includes making friends, being a good friend, and resolving disagreements in a win-win way. The game allows players to cooperate and help each other as well as to answer questions about friendship to win points for themselves.

The *Ungame* board game works as a great icebreaker, and children play it to get to know each other better.[27] Players progress along the playing board by answering questions like "What are the four most important things in your life?" and "What do you think life will be like in 100 years?" The questions also serve as writing prompts. Younger girls play interactive My Little Ponies and the Magic of Friendship video games online with other children on the Hub Network website.[28] Younger boys watch the *Thomas the Train and Railway Friends* videos and make a construction paper train with the name and signature strength—forgiveness, generosity, loyalty, or support—of a classmate on each car.[29] The children depict the train as chugging uphill because friends help overcome challenges. The center's activity menu varies and includes teacher updates monthly with input from the class. The center provides a place and space for friendship lessons.

When the children have finished sharing their popcorn, interviewing their friends, trading friendship bracelets, writing friendship poems, and singing friendship songs in the friendship center, they are ready to join a friendship club. The club is a way to make new friends, play with old ones, commit to each other, prevent disputes, and celebrate relationships.

The teacher noticed the fourth-grade girl sitting alone at lunch every day for a week. The girl was very smart and shy and she seemed lonely and sad. At lunch one day, the teacher sat down at the lunch table with a group of lively girls who were leaders in the class and asked if they could have an important conversation. "Let's talk about an opportunity for you to be generous and kind. Do any of you know what it is like to feel alone and afraid?" Stories about not knowing anyone at camp or a party ensued. One girl talked about moving to a new neighborhood. All could relate to feelings of loneliness, fear, and rejection at some level. "I think that is how Amelia might feel. She seems very lonely," the teacher said. The children protested. "No, I think she just doesn't like us. She didn't talk to us last year either." One added, "Or maybe she is afraid that we don't like her." The teacher responded, "Yes, that sounds right. Amelia is probably afraid."

The teacher suggested that the children form a friendship club, and she promised to sponsor the inaugural friendship party. She asked them to send Amelia the first invitation to join. From that point forward, the club grew quickly. The girls planned meetings, elected officers, and organized fund-raisers. They had a motto, a color (purple), a secret handshake, and even a secret code.

They sponsored recess activities from flash mob dances to jump-rope contests. Amelia never ate alone again and, through the club, made a best friend, Kelly, who lived near her house.

They became true friends and remained friends for a long time. At the monthly friendship club party, everyone danced to a playlist full of friendship songs that the club members had created.

A club connects children to others in the class so they develop a greater affinity for collaborative learning through the club. When children join a class club, they get a ready-made group of friends. A class club can advance academic skills, but more important, it breaks barriers and builds bridges to friendship. A most welcome invitation to friendship begins with the words, "Do you want to join my club?" A most welcome response ends with the words, "I had such a great time with my friends, and I learned so much in my math club today."

To promote friendship, teachers sponsor in-class clubs around common interests: chess, dinosaurs, Legos, stamp collecting, coin collecting, rock collecting, ecology, eco-literacy, bugs, space, exercise, sports, weather, programming, drama, film, Animoto, magic, 4-H, penguins, the stock market, travel, global studies, art, books, yoga, meditation, and Harry Potter. In some cases, the club serves to teach the characteristics of true friendship and, in all cases, it requires the practice of friendship for the club to function. In the clubs, friendships and learning come alive around mutual interests and benefits. The perfect cooperative learning group is a club.

4. Host a Class Festival

Festivals create a sense of belonging and community, stimulating generosity and enthusiasm among participants. A festival connects children to friends in a creative way and is visual evidence that a class celebrates as a community of learners.

The class community hosts the festival that energizes children of every age, whether it is a small, simple festival or a large, grand event. No matter the size and scope of the festival, organizing it requires children to work together with enthusiasm by supporting each other to accomplish the goal. Festival planning compels children to establish working friendships quickly connected by a common goal and eventually connected by the festival experience.

Festivals are celebrations of family, friends, community, and culture. There are endless ideas for festivals; basic classifications include (1) harvest or season festivals, (2) festivals of art, (3) cultural, holiday, and religious festivals, and (4) life festivals. Children connect to numerous online festivals, including popular festivals celebrating Shakespeare, art, music, and film. World culture and legacy festivals broaden perceptions by widening children's worldview and they connect children to their wishes, hopes, and dreams for themselves, their friends, their communities, and their world. Many festivals create positive change through music and art.

The Playing for Change website hosts an online worldwide music festival that occurs on the same stage on the same day.[30] This is a multimedia movement working to inspire, connect, and bring peace to the world through music. Online audiences enjoy listening to musicians who traveled thousands of miles from their homes from all over the world to perform on one stage. The idea for the festival emerged from a common belief that music is a message that has the power to break down barriers between people and places because music is a common language. A mobile recording studio, equipped with all the same equipment used in the best studios, travels to the music site. In this way, the festival supports brilliant street musicians from all over the world who are playing, literally and figuratively, for change.

Listening to musicians playing for a few coins and the sheer joy of the music they create is a transcendent experience. Children watch the online videos of these musicians broadcast from Barcelona to Cape Town to Kathmandu. Reading the blogs about the musicians, their music, and their lives, children learn about the annual global day of musical action.[31]

On this day, musicians perform on stages, in cafés, in city squares, on street corners, in boardrooms, and in schoolrooms all over the world. They play for themselves, they play to connect with others, and they play to raise money to build music and art schools.

Online audiences see and hear the musicians, who traveled thousands of miles from their homes to perform. The festival connects children to the world through music and to the people in it who make music. Children plan their own music festival to coincide with this worldwide festival as a means of deepening their own friendships.

In a small, rural school, the fourth grade has assembled all the instruments they begged, borrowed, or bought at yard sales. The instruments scrounged up include an old fiddle missing some strings, a drum, an older brother's keyboard on loan, and more than enough harmonicas. Dan positions himself at the front of the fourth-grade group, Backyard Band, playing on the street corner just outside of the school. There is a big jar in front of them with a couple of dollars in it. Joe puts up a sign about the fund-raising project and the band plays "For He's a Jolly Good Fellow" about 100 times. They play it for all the other classes, invited parents, and passing pedestrians, and the jar quickly fills with coins. After they are finished, the band watches and listens to the video of the online music festival.

The teacher can connect children to music and film festivals in order to enhance relationships. As videos get simpler and easier to produce, children's film festivals are becoming increasingly available even to young children. Kid's First is the world's largest film festival for children.[32]

This festival gives children a true voice as curators, audience members, film critics, volunteer staff members, and filmmakers who can show their own work. The New York International Film Festival is the nation's largest festival for children and teens.[33] The festival presents four weekends of groundbreaking and thought-provoking new film for ages 3–18. Children can attend screenings for 100 new films, opening and closing galas, six short-film programs, filmmaker question-and-answer sessions, filmmaking workshops, and other special events. Children can take classes that teach them how to make their own films. Films about friendship teach the lessons of friendship and the exercise of filmmaking also becomes a means for children to become better friends. Children make their own videos of their friends in class and write review of the films they create.

Cultural festivals such as Chinese moon festivals, African harvest festivals, U.S. pumpkin festivals, and other seasonally related festivals can excite children to research and explore. The Emerson Waldorf school is one of the few educational models that embraces festivals as central to the academic curriculum.[34] This model values a creative, supportive learning environment designed to bring interdisciplinary and multisensory learning in response to the needs of the child with a rich blend of academics and the arts rooted in teaching truth, beauty, and goodness.

At Waldorf schools, children typically celebrate seasonal festivals throughout the academic year: Michaelmas, Martinamas Lantern Walk, Dia de Los Muertos, St Martin's Day, Thanksgiving, Winter Light Faire, Christmas, Three Kings Day, Easter, Candlemas, Spiral of Light, Santa Lucia, Shepard's Play, and May Day. Festivals are a central part of the curriculum and incorporate all the basic elements of a festival—light, food, song, and story—into the classroom every day. Celebrations, ceremonies, and rituals lighten and enhance seasonal moods rooted in ancient histories and cultures.

Different ways of celebrating both religious and secular holidays invite children to work together toward a common goal and learn more about their common humanity. Many festivals and celebrations also incorporate nature awareness and study that blends with science-based ecology and environmental lessons as well as geography, linguistics, history, and cultural studies. An interdisciplinary curriculum encourages and promotes independent thinking and social responsibility in consonance with academic and artistic excellence.

Most important, children's definition of friendship expands globally as children celebrate culture, values, traditions, and friendship. Festivals and celebrations make it easy to deepen friendship by working and playing together. However, it does not matter what festivals are celebrated; it matters that there are festivals to celebrate. Teachers can choose a representative sampling of different ethnic, religious, and cultural festivals, both ancient and contemporary. The book *Children Just Like Me: Celebrations* introduces children from around the world, through interviews and photographs, as they celebrate 25 of their favorite holidays and traditions.[35] The young reader meets the children, learn the significance of the celebrations, and chooses one of the holidays or traditions to replicate in the classroom. Another book that children enjoy reading, and that sparks ideas for class celebrations, is *Kids Around the World Celebrate: The Best Feasts and Festivals from Many Lands.*[36]

Whether celebrating the Chinese New Year by reading about how to make dumplings or tasting date-nut cookies (*amoul*), children play and learn together in meaningful ways. They make elaborate Venetian masks to wear at a masquerade ball in Venice during Carnival and bang out a festive rhythm on Igbo drums during the Nigerian Iriji Festival. The book *Windows on the World* can also assist teachers in planning festivals that help children celebrate cultural differences.[37]

Older children read about the complex, international aspects of friendship. The book *Children Around the World* introduces children from every continent and more than 140 countries.[38] Each page of the book includes the child's name, photo, and nationality. A second page shares the child's food, eating utensils, housing, favorite games, school, friends, family, and hopes for the future. Children discuss what emotions the stories describe and what strengths would make them good friends in their communities. No matter where children live, they are curious to understand children who live in other parts of the world so they can find the common denominator in human relations.

Children who participate in team competitions for children—poetry, mathematics, spelling, art, essays, history, science, physical education, and other contests or fairs—bond with each other, rely on each other, and pursue a common goal by participating in competitions. They might compete in the Olympics of the Mind or the Math Olympiads by working together. They rally at their collective success and comfort each other in collective failure.[39] To compete they must also cooperate in "coopetition"—the concepts of cooperation and competition combined.[40] Children working in teams take more learning risks because they win or lose together as friends.

Success shared is success magnified, and failure shared is failure managed. The true value of the team is in the value of the relationships and the potential of the friendships. Children who participate in meetings, join clubs, host festivals, and enter group competitions make new friends, work with old ones, rely on each other, avoid disputes, appreciate others' strengths, and accomplish a common goal. Children with friends feel safer, are more comfortable, and are more accepted, engaged, and connected to learning.

5. Practice Friendship Training

Children with emotional literacy and strength skills are better equipped to use those abilities to ensure that they have the benefit of true friendship. True friendship is central to children's overall wellness. For this reason, there are many programs, curricula, units, lessons, activities, exercises, and games available to teach the positive psychology teaching taxonomy of friendship through relationship training. Literature-based programs, in particular, teach the positive psychology teaching taxonomy friendship benchmark, and children's books deliver friendship-themed lessons.

Children's books about friendship easily lend themselves to classroom lessons that teach the pillars of friendship. For young children, the teacher chooses books about making and losing friends: *How to Be a Friend* and *How to Lose All Your Friends*.[41] Follow-up activities supplement the lessons. After reading the books, the children make a large poster to share their own ideas about how to be a good friend and another large poster with warnings about how to lose friends. After reading the books and making the posters, a second-grade child remarked, "Wow. Now I know what I was doing wrong. No wonder they didn't like me."

As they continue to explore the parameters of friendship, children read the book *Friendship Rules*.[42] To follow up on the reading, children create pocket cards to carry with them that list the top three friendship rules they want to remember to practice. Other books easily shape friendship lessons and the children next read *Friendship Wish* and *Friendship Tree*.[43] Follow-up activities invite children to write good wishes for friends on index cards, and they drop the cards into the class wishing well. The teacher and children read the wishes once a week. They also plant a friendship tree and write strengths their friends possess on stones to put around the tree, creating their own strength rocks.

Books about animal friendships also teach children the pillars of friendship in memorable ways. The teacher develops a friendship-themed unit by using three touchstone stories of animal friendships. Using these stories, the teacher can easily build an interdisciplinary themed unit about friendship in the animal world while also teaching academic subjects. First, children are introduced to a stranded baby hippopotamus and a 130-year-old turtle by reading the book *Owen and Myzee: The True Story of a Remarkable Friendship* and by visiting the Owen and Myzee website.[44] When children read about this special pair, they discover that they are best friends. They write a report about them and compare their relationship to their own friendships.

Suryia and Roscoe are another unusual pair of friends. Suryia is an orangutan and Roscoe is a Blue Tick hound dog. They are best friends and the book about them, *Suryia and Roscoe: The True Story of an Unusual Friendship,* tells their incredible story.[45] Children learn even more about this pair of friends and keep track of them on the Suryia and Roscoe website.[46] The two animals originally became friends when their paths crossed at a South Carolina preserve for endangered animals: They are now constant companions. They swim together and play together, and Suryia even takes the dog for his walks. This is a very special friendship because dogs are usually afraid of primates.

Another bittersweet friendship story is told in the book *Tarra and Bella: The Elephant and Dog Who Became Best Friends*.[47] The story of this lifelong friendship between Tarra, an elephant, and Bella teaches how they showed generosity, commitment, and support to each other.

Children visit the Elephant Sanctuary website to learn more about them and their friendship.[48] Sadly, children will discover that Bella, the dog, died recently.

The sanctuary reported Bella's death by noting how the two put aside their immense differences to be friends. Bella trusted Tarra so completely that she let her stroke her belly with her trunk. Indications are that Tarra was the first to learn of Bella's demise, and the elephant picked up Bella's body in the woods and carried it to a place where they had spent happy times together, where it was found by sanctuary staff. The story provokes deep feelings and generates important conversations about loyalty and loss of friends. Children learn how friendship survives even the most difficult situations. They learn that friendship is about the feelings children have toward each other, the strengths they share with each other, and the trust and gladness they show each other.

Because literature is a rich source of content about friendship, many formal, comprehensive programs teach the positive psychology teaching taxonomy benchmark of friendship by using a literature-based pedagogy. One example of a fully infused language-arts program is the Voices Instructional Plan.[49] Six relevant learning themes organize the curriculum: identity, self-awareness, perspective taking, social awareness, love and friendship, freedom and democracy, and conflict resolution. The lessons present a guiding question for children to answer, followed by engaging activities that require children to read, express, and practice learning the social skills associated with positive relationships and a better quality of life.

The children connect to the story in personal ways with pre-reading activities. They then read the book, discuss in a whole-class group the ideas presented in the book, and express their understandings related to the guiding questions by using a variety of writing genres, including literature responses and journal entries. The teaching guide includes writing prompts for narrative, persuasive, expository, and descriptive oral and written responses. The final activity is participation in a service-learning project that connects friendship to the community.

The reading list is the foundation of the curriculum and includes books for children, PreK–8, that focus on the importance of building relationships and gives examples of how various, diverse characters make this happen at home, in school, and in the community. The book list includes such wonderful reads as *Jamaica's Find*, which is a story for grades K–2 about losing a puppy and finding a friend.[50] *Crow Boy* is a story for third- and fourth-grade children about a Japanese boy excluded by his peers who perseveres until his classmates learn to appreciate his special talents.[51] Older children read the book *The Heart of a Chief*, which tells older children the story of the Penacook Native American tribe who lived and worked alongside their New England neighbors, owning homes and stores, working in mills, and farming with them.[52]

Open Circle is another high-value literature-based program that teaches the positive psychology teaching taxonomy benchmark of friendship; it is research-based and consistent with academic language-arts standards.[53] The program is a comprehensive, whole-school, grade-differentiated social-emotional learning curriculum for grades K–5. Teachers use it to foster the development of relationships that support safe, caring, and respectful learning communities of children and adults.

Two 15-minute weekly open circle meetings are a key feature integrating research findings in child development and best positive psychology teaching practices. At the meetings, children move their chairs into an open circle, and they always leave one chair empty as a symbol that there is always room for another person. The meeting emphasizes the program's strong commitment to positive relationships and focus on friendships: "Positive relationships are essential for highly effective teaching and learning."[54] Relationships create the opportunity for personal risk taking, interpersonal connection, community building, and social change: "Strong connected relationships strengths create social and emotional health and wellness."[55]

Videos are an adjunct to literature programs that teach the same friendship themes. One award-winning friendship video includes a facilitator's guide, discussion questions, writing assignments, and follow-up activities to use after the lesson. The video, *Being Friends,* teaches children about the value of having friends, the benefit of having diverse friends, and how friendship works.[56] Live Wire's *Popcorn Park: Getting Along With Groark* video is a 28-minute funny video about friends for grades K–8.[57] The video covers the topics of anger, disagreement, listening, bullying, and prejudice. Puppetry, music, real child actors, entertaining stories, and fanciful visual elements capture attention and spark ideas. The four pillars of friendship learning are embedded in the videos so children learn them systematically.

The Stop, Think, and Do program is an age-differentiated program for elementary children.[58] A traffic light—stop/red . . . think/yellow . . . do/green—helps children self-monitor their interactions. The curriculum consists of 20 lessons that teach children the social skills needed to make friends, improve group interactions, increase active participation with in-group learning, and practice cooperation. The curriculum also uses role-playing to practice the skills of friendship, art activities to document the nature of friendship, and group games to practice the skill of friendship. Children put miniature stoplights on their desks so that they can "stop, think, do."

Another friendship-focused program is the time-honored Self-Science, which advocates for high-quality interpersonal relationships essential for emotional literacy and social strengths.[59] The goal is to shift the learning environment toward collaboration, inclusion, and compassion, creating a more respectful, responsible, and resilient whole-school community. The lessons flow in such a way that a teacher can adapt them to current topics and academic subject matter. Teachers present the lessons as a stand-alone class or fold them into the dominant curriculum by using positive psychology teaching taxonomy techniques such as class meetings or community service.

Even the simplest interventions, such as playing friendship games, advance children's progress toward mastering the learning pillars of friendship. Playing friendship games serves the dual purpose of teaching the positive psychology taxonomy benchmark of friendship while providing for the practice of it. The act of playing a game builds relationships and improves social skills while at the same time the games themselves teach about the strengths that are needed.

Getting to Know Each Other (Honesty)—In the News Reporter game, some of the children play the role of journalists. To get to know each other better, they interview a classmate and write articles about him or her to publish in a monthly class newsletter and blog.

Keeping Each Other Happy (Generosity)—Children play the Secret Pal game. They draw the name of another child. Acting as the secret pal, they spend a month showing that friend generosity, support, and gladness. The children befriend their secret pals, play with them, pick them for teams, eat lunch with them, and think of special surprises for them. All children maintain a list of all the positive, friendly actions that they took on behalf of their secret pal. At the end of the month, children reveal the identity of their secret pals at a class party.

Relying on Each Other (Support)—Children play the How Are You Today? game. Children ask their friends and classmates every day, "How are you feeling today? What are your plans for tomorrow?" They practice showing support and these questions convey the message that what happens to their friends matters to them.

Repairing Rifts (Commitment)—Children play the Telephone Tree game. They transmit apologies, compliments, or other positive messages from child to child. Young children whisper a compliment about another child in the ear of the child sitting next to them, creating a message chain or telephone tree. Older children whisper a sentence that tells something good about a friend and a message is sent along the chain. The last child repeats the word or sentence heard. The children discuss the intended message, how it changed, when it changed, and why it is important to send the correct message to a friend. They also consider how positive messages undo negative ones.

Celebrate Friendship (Enthusiasm)—Children play the Let's Cheer game. The teacher randomly selects a child's name. Every hour on the hour, the class does a cheer for that student. At the end of the day, they sing, "For Charlie's a jolly good friend." When others cheer for them, they feel appreciated and a sense of belonging. Cheering children use their own good cheer to make another feel valued by friends.

In all friendship lessons, activities, exercises, and games, teachers apply a cognitive template that teaches the positive psychology teaching taxonomy benchmark of friendship. Children learn to stop and observe their friends, think about their own feelings toward their friends and their friends' feelings towards them, consider the best reactions and actions toward their friends, and make the right decision to keep, help, and support their friends. Children learn to walk the walk—and talk the talk—of friendship. They learn how to act with forgiveness, generosity, honesty, commitment, support, enthusiasm, and gladness whenever they work or play with a friend.

To assess children's relationship skills and progress toward meeting the taxonomy benchmark of friendship, the teacher can use Self-Science's Social Emotional Inventory–Youth Version (SEI–YV).[60] This inventory measures five essential social barometers such as emotional awareness in relationships and eight core emotional quotient (EQ) competencies such as optimism in relationships. The assessment assesses children ages 7 to 18 and generates an individualized self-report to use to customize friendship education based on a strengths profile.

6. Use Conflict Resolution Training

Children who can play together stay together because they know how to avoid or resolve conflict. The positive psychology teaching taxonomy benchmark of friendship teaches children to reduce conflict and increase peacefulness. Verbal abuse, mean-spirited assaults, angry insults, and cold disdain are the weapons of childhood: At the least, they sting and, at the worst, they may do lasting emotional harm. Children's brains store the memories of rejection, humiliation, and sadness so a preventative approach to conflict resolution is important so children can replace those negative experiences and emotions with positive ones.

Children use their strengths to put a Band-Aid on emotional hurt. They learn to use empathy to reflect another child's feelings back to him, use humor to divert anger with good cheer, and protect themselves with honesty, "What you said to me made me feel like I wanted to cry. I know you are not an unkind person so I wanted you to know how much it hurt me." Children also learn to extend their strengths and use complex strategies to resolve conflict. They learn to prevent ordinary quarrels with active listening, deescalate tension with the language of negotiation, intervene to help others with compassion, and rehabilitate relationships with peacemaking dialogue.

Many conflict resolution programs improve the quality of relationships by increasing children's ability to reduce the tension and distress associated with disagreements and to depersonalize it. The curriculum in these programs taps children's emotional strengths and motivation to salvage the friendship. The Resolving Conflict Creatively Program (RCCP) is a well-established and highly regarded relationship and conflict resolution program that is available for children in kindergarten through fifth grade.[61]

The mission of the programs is to teach self-management, cooperation, and problem-solving skills that promote interpersonal effectiveness and intercultural understanding by establishing peer mediation programs. The curriculum builds student leadership in conflict resolution and intergroup relationship skills; lessons teach children how to communicate, negotiate, mediate, and cooperate with their friends and peers. Younger children request an older peacemaker to intervene in a quarrel before it escalates, and the peacemaker works to help children with disputes, identify feelings, issues, and solutions. Fourth- and fifth-grade children train as peacemakers and work with younger children to resolve everyday conflicts so they are available to prevent conflict before it begins and to solve it after it develops.

The Connected and Respected (C&R) program is an extension of the Resolving Conflict Creatively Program (RCCP) that differentiates learning activities by age.[62] The Alike and Different lesson encourages kindergarten children to compare each other's similarities and differences. First-grade children actively defend and support differences in the Help Others Stand-Up lesson. In the Active Listening lesson, second-grade children practice paraphrasing friends' statements and they clarify communications by using strategic questions. The Win-Win lesson builds on prior learning as third-grade children solve problems in a mutually acceptable way and reconcile their differences peacefully. Fourth-grade children participate in lessons that develop empathy to use to build mutual understanding agreements. Fifth-grade children combine these strengths to calm the situation and become experts in crisis intervention. The program provider kit includes all the activities, and materials, needed to implement the program, including such hard-to-find items as buddy-ropes.

The C&R Parent Connection Kit includes a family at-home component with 12 peacemaking activity sheets to help parents promote the peacemaking themes learned at school. There are also two comprehensive reading indexes: *Book by Book: An Annotated Guide to Young People's Literature with Peace-Making and Conflict Resolution Themes"* and *Links to Literature: Teaching Tools to Enhance Literacy, Character and Social Skills.*[63] These identify relevant literature.

Conflict resolution training is a critical component of the positive psychology teaching taxonomy of friendship because it requires sophisticated transactions. That is the reason why so many relationship and friendship programs emphasize conflict resolution and peacemaking as subjects. PeaceBuilders is a research-validated curriculum that teaches a common language to children, PreK–12, to discuss, model, and practice six principles: (1) praise people, (2) give up put-downs, (3) be wise people, (4) notice hurts, (5) right wrongs, and (6) help others.[64]

There are activities such as 184 one-minute recipes for peace, first-aid activities for anger, peace referrals, wise people agreements, and a book list. Children use the specially designed graphic organizers to write stories about peacebuilding. There is also a PeaceBuilders pledge, flag, t-shirt, poster, praise/apology notepad, pencil, pen, bookmark, tags, buttons, lanyards, and stickers.

Connecting With Others is another research-based program for K–5 children. The curriculum teaches the positive psychology teaching taxonomy of relationships by helping children to effectively connect with others using their emotional and social competencies. The preventative curriculum for kindergarten children reduces conflict by teaching them sensitivity to differences, tolerance, and acceptance of others, and how to resolve conflicts without anger or abuse.

In the primary and intermediate curriculum, there are 30 grade-dif-ferentiated lessons that divide into five skill areas: (1) concept of self and others, (2) socialization, (3) problem solving, (4) conflict resolution, and (5) communication, sharing, empathy, and caring. Instructional strate-gies include storytelling, relaxation activities, teacher and peer model-ing, direct coaching, rehearsal of effective actions, reinforcement, and acknowledgment when there are positive emotions and strengths, cre-ative expressions of disputes and solutions, self-instruction, and more. In one of the friendship lessons, children create an acrostic and discuss common idioms such as "A friend in need is a friend indeed" and "You need to be your own best friend."

The Peace Education Foundation is another leader in the field of child conflict resolution curricula, and it trains children in all elemen-tary school grades. They conceive of conflict as a natural, unavoidable phenomenon that offers an opportunity to practice emotional regula-tion and signature strengths. The mission is to educate children in the dynamics of conflict and to promote the skills of peacemaking in the home, school, community, the nation, and the world. The philosophy is to teach peace education, within a strengths training framework, in every classroom as a subject. The methodology includes modeling peacemaking skills, explicitly teaching the skills, coaching students in practice of the skills, encouraging children to use the skills, and urging them to export them to others. They publish a wide range of grade-spe-cific materials that teach strength training, mediation instruction, and conflict diffusion. A favorite lesson for grades 4–8 is the Fighting Fair for Kids: Dr. Martin Luther King Jr.'s lesson about peaceful protest.[65]

There are two after-school programs of note: the Peace from A–Z After-School Program (PAZ), and After School: Adventures in Peace-making.[66] Both of these elementary programs teach conflict resolution. The PAZ program provides instruction in conflict resolution, coopera-tive games, sports, and homework assistance. Children learn to identify and express feelings, manage anger, handle conflicts nonviolently, coop-erate with peers, respect differences, and stand up to bias and stand up for social justice.

In the Adventures program, the teacher's guide describes more than 150 activities that promote positive relationships using the positive psychology teaching taxonomy benchmark of friendship. Activities include music, games, team challenges, stories, reading, arts and crafts, drama, puppet play, cooking, feeling cards, and more. Whether in school or after-school, children engage strengths to resolve conflict so that they are better able to increase positive emotions and decrease the negative emotions that incite it.

The education field does not lack programs, curricula, lessons, activities, or games, both formal and informal, to teach the positive psychology teaching taxonomy of friendship.[67] What it does lack is a clear commitment to the importance of friendship related to school success and to teach children how to make and keep friends so they feel more connected to school, benefit from knowing that others accept them, and understand that they truly belong.

True friends offer each other forgiveness when they do not feel forgiving, act generous when they do not feel like giving, are honest in the face of rejection, commit when it is hard, support friends when others do not, show enthusiasm when others are indifferent, and share their gladness with friends. No one likes to travel the road to school alone, and the positive psychology teacher should ensure that every child makes, at least, one true friend. Children with friends are more accomplished children who do better in school.

Summary and Conclusion

The positive psychology teaching taxonomy benchmark of friendship teaches the five pillars of friendship so children form deeper relationships that are more meaningful and lasting. They understand the traits of friendship: (1) encouragement of friendship, (2) maintenance of friendship, (3) reliance on friendship, (4) repair of friendship, and (5) value of friendship. Children translate emotional needs to friendship opportunities by using their signature strengths.

The power and importance of connection in the lives of children is not lost on the teacher. She knows that to succeed children must feel that they belong in their classroom, that other children care about and accept them, and that they are useful and appreciated contributors to the classroom. Children must feel that the classroom climate is warm and friendly and that the classroom culture is generous, forgiving, and tolerant.

School affiliation or connectedness is defined as school engagement, attachment, and bonding, and it predicts school success across every variable. A confluence of research has found that there are seven factors associated with school connectedness: (1) feeling a part of school, (2) liking school, (3) perceiving teachers as supportive and caring, (4) having good friends at school, (5) having an interest in subject matter, (6) knowing consequences imposed are fair and gentle, and (7) participating in extracurricular activities.[68]

Teachers are in the best position to activate these affiliations at the macro school level and at the micro class level. At the class level, the positive psychology teaching taxonomy benchmark of friendship promotes social, personal, teacher, peer, academic, safety, extracurricular, cocurricular, and after-school connectedness. Affiliation is the antidote to feelings of loneliness and isolation that overwhelm coping mechanisms and derail academic success. With friends, children experience a pleasant, good, and connected classroom experience.

Children may be afraid to sing alone, but they do not hesitate to sing in the chorus. They may be afraid to show their drawings alone but are not afraid to display their artwork in a group exhibit. No one hears the mistake of a child who stumbles reading an unfamiliar word out loud if she is reading aloud with a partner. There is strength in partnership as children learn to support each other and stand up for each other in victory and defeat.

Case Study K–2: Teaching Friendship

The first-grade children are planning a talent show. First, children draw names randomly and pair up to work with their partners to identify a common strength. Based on that common strength, they choose to write and perform a skit or puppet show, learn and sing a song, or read and tell an interactive story. The strengths identified vary and the acts planned are entertaining. One group of children creates the stage by measuring, cutting, and pasting the backdrops and hanging the curtains.

The day of the big show finally arrives and the fifth grade invites the first grade to the show. The teacher is videorecording it to post on the class website so family and friends can also enjoy it. The announcer begins in a big voice: "This is Friendship Idol." The juggling act takes to the stage and invites audience participation. They emphasize that friendship, like juggling, requires balance and patience to learn. The second act is lip-syncing and dancing with much enthusiasm to a classic Beatles song about friendship.

The third act is a puppet show with giant child-size puppets clearly inspired by the Muppets. The two characters include Sour Sue dressed as a lemon and Gilbert Grape, who is very sweet and generous to everyone. Gilbert is trying to teach Sour Sue how to make friends because she does not have any. He gives Sour Sue grapes to share with the audience. The teacher is laughing as she records the performances; however, she knows that the children are clearly able to identify and explain friendship strengths through performance art. The audience applauds wildly and everyone votes for their favorite act. They admit it is very hard to choose a favorite because they enjoyed all of the performances. Most important, it is clear that children understand the basic requirements of friendship and the social skills needed to live a connected life.

Case Study 3–5: Teaching Friendship

Two fifth-grade boys were about to leave the classroom on a Friday afternoon. The teacher had stepped out of the room and the teaching assistant worked busily with another student at the other end of the room. As the two boys were packing their book bags at the end of a long week, one of them became visibly upset with the other. Joe noticed that Kyle had drawn a heart with his initials and the initials of a girl in the class on his desk. Joe was angry and feeling embarrassed. One of the class peer mediators noticed the commotion and stepped forward. "Is there a problem? Can I help?" he asked. Andy wanted to try to stop the situation from escalating.

Joe said loudly, "I have to catch my bus or I am going to miss it but Kyle is going to pay for this one." Kyle just laughed and replied, "Yeah, right!" Andy said, "Joe, I know you must be embarrassed and don't want anyone else to see this so I understand completely. Kyle, how would you feel if Joe did something that embarrassed you? Do not worry, Joe. You go and catch your bus. Kyle and I will get some paper towels and get this cleaned off your desk right away. No one will see it. I promise. You can trust me." Joe looked hesitant, nodded, and left to catch his bus. "Okay, Kyle," Andrew said. "Get scrubbing and then we will go play some ball until the next bus comes. If I were you, I would write a sorry note and leave it on Joe's desk so he will find it on Monday. You guys are friends and should be able to trust each other." Andrew helped Kyle clean up

Joe's desk until the telltale heart was completely gone. He also coached Kyle into writing an apology letter to Joe and leaving it for him on his desk. Andrew's peacemaking skills avoided further conflict and solved the real problem of Joe's feelings of embarrassment. He helped both Joe and Kyle use their strengths to solve the problem. Kyle understood what he thought was funny was not funny to Joe, and the experience left him more empathetic. Andrew was proud that his mediation skills had worked well. Joe accepted Kyle's apology.

Guiding Question Exercise

Think about the friendships that you had in school. Did you have a large circle of acquaintances or one close friend? Did your friends change over time? Did you find it easy or difficult to make new friends? Do you still have a friend from elementary school? Why do you think the friendship endured? What types of friends do you have now? Do you have a best friend today? What are the strengths your best friend brings to the relationship? What strengths do you bring to the relationship? Is there any conflict in the relationship? What is the primary source of the conflict? How do you resolve conflict in the relationship? Do you teach friendship in your classroom?

What positive psychology teaching taxonomy benchmark of friendship technique would you use to teach friendship? Give an example of why you think it is important to teach friendship. Develop a friendship activity or lesson that uses at least one of the techniques to teach at least one of the pillars of friendship. The lesson should be interdisciplinary in nature and project-based with the purpose of developing the emotional awareness and strengths needed to develop positive relationships in the classroom.

Guiding Question Discussion

Friendship is a complex interpersonal transaction that involves emotional maturity and mutually reciprocal exchange of strengths. As children become knowledgeable about the types and nature of friendship, they learn how to strengthen it. They are able to change a casual friendship into a true friendship. They learn to act in forgiving, generous, loyal, committed, supportive, excited, and enjoyable ways with their friends. To initiate and sustain friendship, children must learn to manage their feelings and to use strengths in the interest of the friendship. Friends are an important developmental asset and children who know how to make them and keep them fare better. Human relationships are the foundation of lifelong connectedness that predicts success. Children who feel connected to teachers and peers perform better across every metric of accomplishment. There is a friendship workshop conducted daily in the positive psychology classroom.

Web Resources for Children

Being Friends Video, http://www.goodcharacter.com/YCC/Being Friends.html.

International Kids Club, http://www.planetpals.com/IKC/.

PBS Its My Life Digital Games, http://pbskids.org/itsmylife/friends/index.html/.

Peace Corps Challenge Game, http://www.peacecorps.gov/kids/.

Peace First, http://www.peacefirst.org/site/.

Web Resources for Teachers

Building Community Initiative, http://www.cliftontaulbert.com/products.html.

Peaceful Solutions Lesson Plans, http://www.peacefulsolution.org/.

Peace Read, http://www.peaceread.org/non-violent-video-games.html.

Project Achieve, http://www.projectachieve.info/stop-think/social-skills-program.html/.

Social and Emotional Learning Resources, http://www.teachervision.fen.com/.

CHAPTER 7

TEACHING MEANING AND THE PURPOSEFUL LIFE: CONTRIBUTIONS

Man is a being in search of meaning.

—Plato

Meaningful positive psychology lessons serve a real purpose and make an important contribution to the class, school, and community. Children learn to extract meaning by connecting their learning to what they know about themselves and about others. To the degree that children relate to academic content in personal and emotional ways, they are more likely to understand it, remember it, and use it to build strengths. Strengths, in turn, fortify relationship bonds that vest learning with purpose and meaning. Meaningful learning connects to children's emotions, strengths, and relationships, motivating them to contribute to the greater good. Children find meaning in school when they are able to express their best feelings, use their best strengths, and enjoy being with their best friends.

As intentional human beings, children choose feelings, strengths, friends, and legacies to construct personal meaning in learning and life. Children learn to value whatever they are doing no matter how grand or simple and imbue it with meaning. "I want to make my family proud of me." "I want to do my best no matter what the task." "The job does not seem important to others but how well I do it is important to me." Meaning emanates from connection to others and to the greater good inherent in all effort, from contribution to others and the greater need, and from a choice to pursue excellence and inner strength no matter the circumstances. Children learn to find meaning by connecting to others, by contributing to the larger community, and by choosing to be mindful of the past and future legacy. They also learn to imbue whatever they are doing with meaning by taking a wider perspective and using their imaginations.

Victor Frankl proposes three courses of action toward a meaningful and transcendent life: (1) demonstrating personal values through deeds and actions, (2) finding personal values through the media of literature, art, music, religion, and nature; and (3) finding personal value through the exercise of choice in every situation, no matter how painful.[1] The positive psychology teaching taxonomy benchmark of meaning encourages purposeful deeds and actions that express personal emotions, connect to personal values, reflect good choices, and make important contributions.

When children perceive learning as personally meaningful to them, they define it in many different ways. First, they define meaningful learning as relevant, practical, and useful to their own lives. In this regard, the teacher might ask children to write their own word problems in mathematics. She gives them general parameters to follow so that a problem has to include multiple operations including addition, subtraction, multiplication, division, and percentages. A fourth-grade boy writes, "A family went to buy a car. They really need a car so the dad can get to work and the car they have now does not work at all. The sales guy gives them two different figures. One price is higher and one price is lower. There are different interest rates, too. The child must help the dad figure out the better deal. The two prices are . . ."

Second, meaningful learning is a lesson that enables them to work together, share knowledge, exchange ideas, solve problems and complete projects as a team, and collaborate to accomplish an authentic goal. They engage more fully in the task when others share their perspectives and solutions and when they know that they are working for collective success to help all succeed. When they work in a small cooperative learning group and know how to recognize and use each other's strengths, they are more likely to succeed. Children who can find their place in a group can more easily find their place in the world.

Third, meaningful learning has a larger influence and makes a contribution that extends beyond their immediate reach. The lesson promotes big-picture thinking and offers service to another person or teaches children more about someone who lives in a faraway place or practices a different religion. When children learn new and novel information that is not familiar, they must find a personal way to connect to it so it becomes meaningful. New information that connects them to a larger community of learners creates interested and invested learners who can find meaning in whatever they do.

Fourth, meaningful learning is legacy learning. Children connect learning to those who came before them and those who will come after them. Positive psychology teaches history as a lively, emotional drama that affects each child's own story in a personal way.

Lastly, meaningful learning is what children choose as important to them for whatever reason, including the practice of their strengths in the pursuit of excellence. What is meaningful is motivating so the teacher offers children structured choices so they can choose a task perceived, constructed, or reconstructed as important to them. "This is important to me because _____." Positive psychology teaches children how to fill in the blank. Affording children the opportunity to make meaningful decisions and act on them teaches not only the skill of learning to read and write but also the will of learning or the desire to read and write with an intent and purpose in mind. As the book whisperer writes, "I no longer spend my time crafting these glorious novel units. Instead I focus my efforts on designing a classroom environment that engages my students."[2] The opportunity to exercise personal judgment and choice teaches practical wisdom and motivates children to read because the story imparts knowledge of value to them. Knowing how to connect to what is important makes learning meaningful. Knowing what is meaningful motivates accomplishment and makes life worth living.

Meaningful learning that engages children is ultimately emotional learning. Children are hard-wired to remember emotional content, and when emotion activates, they engage. "How can I help my father pick the most affordable car?" "What strengths can I use to make my team more successful?" "Where do children in Uganda go to school?" "Why did my grandfather volunteer to fight in World War II?"

Children learn almost effortlessly when they decide that they need and want to know how to play and work with others, help others, value differences, respond fairly, encourage others by their own resilient example, anticipate and enjoy the task at hand, and find peace in the effort no matter the outcome for themselves. In this way, children learn to share the best of themselves with others and, in the process, create meaning in their own lives. Children learn that not all gifts are wrapped up in pretty paper and bright bows. They learn that tolerating others' idiosyncrasies when it is tiring, helping others when it is inconvenient, deciding fairly when it is difficult, staying resilient when tired for the sake of the team, making peace when upset, anticipating the good when weary, or sharing enjoyment when bored is a more important gift than anything else they can give to another.

The Importance of Meaningful Learning in Positive Psychology

Practical wisdom is the "will and skill" to do well and the ability to extract meaning from experience in order to act with purpose.[3] Practical wisdom is the basis for positive momentum and balanced decisions in all situations and contexts because it contemplates the importance of each task to act accordingly in a meaningful way. Absent practical wisdom, standardized rules and consequences alone are insufficient to accomplish the difficult task of education in a contemporary classroom. Children who exercise practical wisdom are able to interpret the inherent meaning in each situation and assess each on its own merit.

Children learn to respond appropriately with positive emotion, balanced strength, social skill, and meaningful judgment to accomplish the purpose. If children do not consider the purpose of the experience, and comply by rote without choice, they gain no practical wisdom, an important education outcome.[4]

The Forum for Education and Democracy is a national education action tank that spearheads a movement to promote the democratic role of public education. In their view, the primary goal of democratic education is to graduate thoughtful, helpful, honest, tolerant, and active citizens. The forum shares a vision of the common school committed to the restoration of meaningful learning and choice in the democratic classroom as essential to the care and custody of a democracy. The forum enunciates five core values that bring meaning to learning in a child-centered classroom and that emphasize community, connection, and contribution.[5]

1. Public education is foremost in enabling all young people to develop their strengths, use their minds well, and become connected to their communities.

2. Public education is intellectually challenging, connected to the skills needed for real-world success, and personalized so teachers know their children well.
3. Public education is fundamental to a democratic, civil, and prosperous society and critical to breaking the cycle of poverty and redressing social inequities.
4. Public education is dependent on engagement, community support, and adequate and equitable resources, and parent and community involvement.

The magazine published by Rethinking Schools adopts the same philosophy publishing work about equity in education and discussing it as central in a humane, caring, multiracial, and meaningful democracy.[6]

The Democratic school movement strives to transform schools into places of hope and purpose, encouraging all children to use positive emotions, signature strengths, and their friend networks to contribute to the greater good by their own choice. "Schools do not exist to only produce efficient workers or future winners of the Nobel Prize. Schools are places where children from a variety of backgrounds come together to learn, talk, play, and work together in meaningful ways deliberately constructed so they make authentic contributions."[7]

The positive psychology teaching taxonomy benchmark of meaning teaches the four pillars of meaningful learning that increase academic achievement and scholarly accomplishment: (1) authentic and pragmatic learning, (2) social and service learning, (3) intuitive and contextual learning, and (4) legacy and global learning.

Children connect to the value of all authentic effort: "This conservation lesson will really help me because at home our electricity bill is too high." Children connect to the needs of others: "Now I can read to my little brother." Children connect to the big picture: "This may not seem very interesting to me now. However, if I want to be a dolphin trainer I am going to have to do well in all science." Children connect to their past and their future: "If my ancestors could endure so much hardship, I can sit here and pay attention a little longer. If I want my future to be safe and peaceful, I need to learn as much about the world as I can."

The pillars of meaningful learning teach the ecology of learning or that personal decisions and actions have far-reaching consequences for others in both children's immediate sphere of influence and globally. Children are interested in topics of emotional use and value to them and in finding ways to be obliging and helpful to others. Their natural instinct seeks a connection to others past and present, the world around them, and how they fit into it. They intuitively understand purpose and seek a rationale for their activity within a larger context.

Children are naturally motivated to build new biological and conceptual connections between experiences assimilating new ideas with old ones always accommodating learning flow—the very definition of attentive learning. They understand that they have the power to help or hurt in their classroom, across the hall, down the street, or around the globe. They understand that choices have consequential implications and they build confidence that they can make the correct one. The pillars of meaningful learning also link the past and the future to create a continuity of understanding. Children comprehend that the past contributions of others bind them to make future contributions so that they do not break the intergenerational contract to strive to live cooperatively, contentedly, confidently, and serenely with fortitude, inspiration, and joy.

Authentic learning delivers academic content connected to real-life problems and projects, excites anticipation, and promotes enjoyment in learning. Learning in ways that arouse emotional connection intrinsically motivates children to engage their strengths more fully in the learning process. Meaningful, relevant, individualized work, not based on worksheets or found in textbooks, ensures purposeful learning. Children will intuitively choose options meaningful to them and pursue excellence at their own pace. Lessons that teach tolerance, helpfulness, fairness, resilience, peace, anticipation, and enjoyment give them a reason to personally invest in the learning process.

Children learn to make good decisions that are compatible with their emotional interests and learning strengths by identifying what book they want to read in language arts, what project they want to complete in mathematics, and what medium they prefer to use to acquire and demonstrate what they know and can do. External requirements wholly imposed by others do not teach the self-will and self-skill of practical wisdom. When children engage in activities meaningful to them, the self-regulation of flow ensues and self-motivation endures.

Children choose to pursue activities that they enjoy and the experience causes positive brain chemistry changes—dopamine increases and cortisol decreases—and they learn self-control naturally. Research suggests that the opportunity to make learning choices, derived from choice theory, trains the self-control mechanisms correlated to almost every measure of future success from standardized test scores to college admissions.[8]

Social contribution involves helping others by raising money, volunteering time, or applying their signature strengths to help others solve a problem or accomplish a goal. Using their strengths and abilities gives children a chance to show competence, assume responsibility for accomplishing a goal, and influence their world in a positive way. Children involved in social and service learning share a goal with friends, work confidently toward it, and enjoy the camaraderie of a cooperative community.

When children give without any expectation of receiving, when giving is not a quid pro quo exchange, they experience a natural contentment.[9] The roots of satisfaction may be found in the pleasure center of the brain because when there is giving, there is increased activity in the nucleus accumbens and increased stimulation of the limbic system's pleasure pathways.[10]

Children's neurology rewards them when they give to others in the same ways they feel pleasure when they eat a piece of candy or ride a roller coaster at the fair. Stephen Post refers to this affective-cognitive-conative feedback loop as self-giving love, defined as "a warm unselfish love that is not held hostage to reciprocal calculations."[11] He explains that self-giving love stimulates the brain's feel-good chemicals like dopamine and serotonin. Helpfulness is the means to the end: children's meaningful happiness. Children experience recompense. That is, they learn that earned happiness or effort to help others ends up helping them. In this sense, happiness is hard work as well as self-perpetuating.

Every kind of play also creates meaningful learning because it is the act of occupying oneself voluntarily, alone or with others, for a particular purpose, whether pretending to cook a meal or practicing a new dance step. The great paradox of education is that play is the universal path to learning, and yet in contemporary education, play and learning diverge instead of converge. Play connects children to the big picture and contextualizes learning so it is inherently more meaningful task engagement.

Meaningful learning gives children a stronger sense of identity and place in the world by connecting them to their personal history and the global community. A sense of identity grounds them and is a source of strength and social capital. Social capital is the degree to which children feel part of a larger community and have access to a supportive social network.[12] Positive psychology interventions increase the social capital that children have to spend.[13]

Research suggests social capital predicts health and well-being of children. "Social capital is the raw material of a civil society. It originates with people forming social connections and networks based on principles of trust, minimal reciprocity, and norms of action."[14] Children who earn social capital in the classroom can spend it to increase the likelihood of success in every developmental area.

Another powerful catalyst for meaningful learning is legacy learning. Children who feel connected in their classroom are more cognizant of their role in the larger community and mindful of their heritage. Children with meaningful connections to their families, both past and present, are better equipped to move into the future with more confidence and certainty. Research finds that recalling memories about ancestors activates the emotional learning center of the brain and stimulates positive feelings such as hopefulness and invigorating strengths such as optimistic outlook.

One particular study found that, before a test, when individuals thought about previous generations who acted bravely, they performed better on the test.[15] The authors of the study hypothesized that simply thinking about ancestors who endured troubles converts optimism to resilience in others, and it convinces them that they can overcome hurdles, too. Children use imaginative play to project into the future and to look back to historical legacy to connect to the past.

Children study fundamentally meaningful subjects such as philosophy and nature to learn more about themselves and their world. Philosophy teaches them to be introspective, and nature study teaches them to be investigative as they discover new ideas and connect them to advance inquiry and gain insight. They learn the quotes of philosophers and names of common plants and animals as well as the characteristics of the sand beneath their feet and stars overhead. From dandelions to toads to star constellations, nature study immerses them in the natural world. From truth to beauty to justice, philosophical study immerses them in the epistemological world.

Children find meaning at the intersection of what they think, feel, and experience. The aggregate of positive emotions, strengths, and relationships expressed through connection and contributions helps generate meaning in all endeavors.

The Positive Psychology Teacher's Toolbox: Meaningful Learning

A meaningful life depends on the quantity and quality of the connections children make to learning and the contributions they make to the greater good. Using the positive psychology teaching taxonomy of meaning, children learn how to channel their positive emotions and use their strengths to derive meaning from the curriculum and offer service to others. The teacher always uses the general educational methods previously discussed as the blueprint to teach the taxonomy: (1) the language of emotions and strengths, (2) infused academics, (3) visual and performing arts, and (4) strengths training.

The teacher fuses these with the techniques recommended to teach the positive psychology taxonomy benchmark of meaning within the academic curriculum. Meaning enriches learning so the academic curriculum must incorporate it. To teach meaning, the teacher plans effective ways to teach the four pillars of meaning: (1) authentic and pragmatic learning, (2) social and service learning, (3) contextual learning, and (4) legacy and global learning. All of these create the educational purpose needed for children to form meaningful understandings. The teacher focuses on teaching these by using the Positive Psychology Teacher's Meaning Toolbox techniques so that children attach emotional meaning to academic learning.

The Meaning Toolbox provides specific techniques that the teacher can use to create meaning and integrate it into the traditional academic curriculum. The techniques help younger children learn in authentic ways and see the big picture. Older children learn the value of legacy and global learning. Meaningful learning inspires all learners to be tolerant, helpful, fair, resilient, and peaceful. They learn to anticipate the joy of learning by inspiring themselves and others to do what they decide is important to do. The teacher may use the recommended techniques in the Meaning Toolbox as part of a larger program, within a comprehensive curriculum, as a themed unit, as stand-alone lessons, as enrichment activities, or in learning games that children play. Positive psychology programs may include a fully developed curriculum that teaches all the benchmarks, a themed unit that teaches one, a series of lessons to assess one, a weekly schedule of activities to process one, a daily exercise that practices one, or a learning game to reinforce one. Whatever form and format a positive psychology program takes, it always uses some,

Table 7.1. The Teacher's Toolbox: Pillars and Techniques of Meaningful Learning

Authentic Learning	Contextual Learning	Social & Service Learning	Legacy and Global Learning
Play and Storytelling	Philosophy	Volunteerism	Legacy Learning
Volunteerism	Social Justice	Service Learning	Global Lessons
Natural World	Natural World	Restorative Justice	Natural World

if not all, of the Meaning Toolbox techniques. The Positive Psychology Teacher's Meaning Toolbox techniques include: (1) engage in play and storytelling, (2) giving, volunteering, and service learning, (3) legacy learning and global study, (4) the natural world, and (5) philosophy and social justice.

The positive psychology teaching taxonomy benchmark of meaning uses these techniques to teach the pillars of meaningful learning from the satisfaction of helping others in exploring family roots. These are not discrete but expansive techniques. That is, any single technique can teach multiple aspects of meaning across the curriculum.

The teacher is in the best position to decide what pillars of meaning to teach and what techniques work best so that children can flourish in the elementary school classroom. Children learn how to tell each other a story that has a meaningful message, identify endangered species in North America, share their perspective on what defines beauty, raise funds for a good cause, or research their family tree. Ask children how they feel after they finish a service-learning project and they typically answer, "satisfied."

Meaningful learning is satisfied learning that not only teaches the skill of learning but also the will of it. "I want to make a difference." "I want to learn more about my country." "I want to know the names of all the oceans because my dream is to someday swim in all of them." The teacher designs and delivers programs, curricula, themed units, lessons, activities, and games that teach children to find meaning in learning, to identify the purpose of the lesson, and to make positive contributions to self and others. When children subscribe meaning to what they are doing, they are better able to self-motivate and self-propel to accomplish the goal.

1. Engage in Play and Storytelling

Play is real-world practice and is authentic, pragmatic learning that children imbue with an idiosyncratic meaning and purpose. In play, children focus and self-regulate with little conscious effort because they fully immerse themselves in the activity, and the flow of the play enjoins their affective, cognitive, and conative learning processes. Children's imagination transports them into the future and pretend play engages the mind and heart in skill development. The positive psychology teacher creates a flow class period. During this daily learning session, children can play in any way they choose alone or with others with the intention of making children aware of flow as a learning asset. They can read a book, play a card game, put together a puzzle, or listen to music and memorize lyrics.

The only expectation is that children must alternate between solitary and group activity each week. The flow class period, whether daily or weekly, inspires children to construct their own learning as play and play as learning. An essential component is the element of choice introduced into all learning so that learning mimics play. The greatest advantage of playful learning is that it trains attention and develops brain circuitry that increases the flow and focus of learning.

The National Institute of Play (NIP) lists six different types of play: (1) fantasy play, (2) object play, (3) social play, (4) body play, (5) attuned play, and (6) narrative play.[16]

In fantasy play, children simply pretend. They dress up as Harry Potter and act out his joyful reunion with Sirius Black. From a fantasy colony on Mars to wigwams in the woods, children pretend to live in different types of shelter and environments. They imagine themselves as an explorer traveling the Amazon, a firefighter in New York City, or a hurricane tracker in Oklahoma.

Pretending to be a hurricane tracker, a student learns the concept of wind velocity and the skill of measuring and tracking storm movement. Teachers conceive of fantasy play as a means to teach almost any subject using a project-based, e-learning, interdisciplinary approach. The teacher identifies the concepts children must learn and the skills they must acquire, and he or she constructs fantasy play around those learning goals.

Object play is play with toys and other manipulative learning tools. Playing cards, dominoes, puzzles, and board games are examples of object play, and there are endless opportunities to use objects that teach concepts and skills directly or incidentally in learning. Young children play with blocks to learn counting, geometry, and spatial relations through formal instruction or informal exploration.

Older children enjoy a series of books about energy, physics, chemistry, matter, and solids, liquids, and gases. A teacher plans how to integrate a rich assortment of hands-on learning materials and resources that, in effect, serve as teaching toys. There are archaeology kits, electronic kits, rock tumblers, soil-quality kits, acid-rain kits, chemistry kits, creature habitats, molecular model sets, bean-bag numbers, clocks, recorders, magnets, inflatable globes, a classroom election kit, a language detective board game, a big box of word chunks, and a phonics fishing game.

Social play is interactive and can be either associative or cooperative play.[17] When children are engaged in associative play with each other, their communication and activity centers on a common, unstructured activity. When playing as associates rather than partners, children share toys, give each other directions, and follow each other around. However, they do not assign roles, divide labor, enforce rules, or acquiesce to the common consensus. Cooperative play is more formal than associative play and requires children to follow group rules and defer to the majority.

In cooperative play, children organize the play and direct it toward a communal goal that has a specific group purpose: make some product, complete some activity, or achieve some goal. Cooperative play serves to advance all areas of development and teaches children to relate to each other in meaningful, democratic ways.[18] To play well socially, children must adhere to the "meta-rules" of play that include (1) input and choice in rule making, (2) tolerance for individual variation, (3) respectful interactions, and (4) the freedom to leave the play at any time.[19] In other words, the best player is the player who values and exhibits tolerance, helpfulness, fairness, and resilience, and who keeps the peace in the pursuit of play so that all children anticipate and enjoy it.

Play is inherently rewarding and meaningful so children want to participate, and it requires the cooperation of the group or the play collectively fails. As a result, almost all children will work hard not to lose the opportunity to play with each other because play is a brain-based desire that naturally satiates novelty and curiosity. "Children cannot acquire democratic values through activities run autocratically by adults. They can and do, however, experience and acquire such values in free play with other children."[20] Because children genuinely like to play with each other, and are biologically driven to play, they work hard at play.

The most energizing type of play is body play because it is both emotionally and cognitively invigorating. Salsa dancing improves mood, tango dancing reduces stress, and ballroom dancing creates mindfulness.[21] Any athletic activity offers more or less the same advantages, whether it is walking a country mile, playing third base in softball, or running a 5K. Children need to take their bodies and minds out to play, climb trees, glide down tall slides, run the bases in kickball, and ride their bicycles in the park. Recess may not only be their favorite subject, but it may also be their most important subject. The positive psychology teacher ensures that body play occurs every day.

Recognizing and understanding the nuance of events and interactions is attuned play and is the kind of play that builds keen attention and observation skills. Attunement is the ability to connect with the world around you and the people in it in meaningful ways. Attunement play trains children to notice what is important and acclimates them to the meaning of the play, and this aligns efforts with purpose. For example, children engrossed in a videogame exhibit mind-body attunement. Video and online games attune the brain to respond quickly and automatically to visual and auditory stimulation.

Children who play the piano listen for the sweet and sour notes produced, and children who sing in choir blend their voices in attuned harmony. Children who bond with their friends while picking up trash attune to each other, and children who grow a garden attune to nature. Meditation and yoga create mental attunement and doing 100 push-ups creates attunement with self. However, the best kind of attuned play is play that results in emotional attunement. Emotionally attuned children respond appropriately to cues so they can meet each other's needs and expectations so that they are able to play together without fault or friction. During attuned play, the teacher notices and asks children, "Are you attuned to what Michael wants to do?"

Lastly, in narrative play, children tell stories or narrate the action observed like a sportscaster or weather forecaster. "Humans are not ideally set up to understand logic."[22] Some claim all learners prefer to hear and tell stories because listeners enjoy storytelling, and because stories provide a script for reflection about old learning and a script for new learning. Narrative play is the best way for children to tell their own stories and to explore potential storylines. Young children create plots and dialogue for their puppets, speak through their dolls, and talk as their trucks and trains. In so doing, they express their feelings, thoughts, and dreams through out-loud narration of their play that dramatizes their self-talk. In older children, narrative play matures into commentary.

Children discover stories that speak to their own lives, emotions, strengths, and friendships in meaningful ways. They read those stories, note the lessons learned, and share those stories with others, bringing a deeper and more personal meaning to learning. Using storytelling in the curriculum to explore emotions, strengths, and relationships begins by creating a listening doll. ArtsEdge offers many interesting art lessons organized by academic topic that complement positive psychology lessons.[23]

One of those activities is the listening doll activity based on the storytelling traditions of the Pueblo people. The Pueblo Indians are especially good at creating small figures of people or animals. In the Native American tradition, the children select a story to tell and fashion a clay storyteller doll.[24] Children sculpt the doll to represent the signature virtue of the main character.

If the children are already well versed in the culture of language, dress, tools, art, and housing of the early Native Americans, storytelling adds to that knowledge base and personalizes the learning by emphasizing shared values, spiritual beliefs, folklore, and history. To prepare for the storytelling, children read the story, develop an outline for it, collect props, create visuals, and prepare questions for the audience. Excited to hear another story, the class gathers in the storytelling circle. After the story, the group discusses the men's courage when they took women and children to safety only to return to fight to save their land, even though they were likely to die. One fifth-grade boy says, "They loved their land. The bank took our home away a little while ago so I know how they felt about losing their home." The discussion then turns to whether the women and children felt abandoned or protected. One child quietly poses a question that they all ponder in silence: "What's worth dying for?" Each week children tell the stories of the Pueblo, Navaho, Cherokee, and Sioux. With the quiet rhythm of drums in the background, they tell the stories of Wounded Knee, Michigan Creek, and the Trail of Tears.

The learning is lasting and meaningful. The teacher chooses any content or interest area to find literature that lends itself to storytelling. Children search the Internet for feel-good stories to tell. The Feel Good Stories website features stories about sports.[25] One of the stories is about teddy bears that rained down at a hockey game and another is about two Americans running 4,300 miles across the Sahara to raise awareness about Africa's water crisis.

The world is full of stories that share feelings, recognize strengths, and cherish friendship, and that touch children emotionally in meaningful and poignant ways.[26] When children play with other children, tell stories to each other, comment about the world around them in speeches or on the editorial page in the class newspaper, learning is meaningful and joyful. When children share positive emotions and strengths with their friends, they all happily anticipate purposeful, meaningful, and enjoyable learning.

2. Giving, Volunteering, and Service Learning

Children learn to be tolerant, helpful, and resilient by volunteering their time or committing their talent to service learning. When altruism is a part of the curriculum, children benefit from meaningful learning that engages their sensibilities. Individual or class work meets the positive psychology teaching taxonomy benchmark of meaning in four ways: (1) gift giving, (2) volunteer activity, (3) fund-raising, and (4) service learning. The Buddha word for the practice of giving is *dana*; in the Qu'ran it is called *zakat*; in the Jewish tradition it is *tzedakah*; and it is the Christian's *tithing*. The practiced strength of a grateful heart cultivates a generosity of spirit that brings confidence, contentment, and joy. Children do good to feel good and learn to feel grateful and show appreciation for what is good in their life. Throughout time and across religious traditions, the act of giving is valued as the essence of humanity and spirituality. The art and act of giving is an ideal way to bring meaning to learning by putting children on the path to giving.

You are what you do—not how much you give but what you give with a humble, open heart. Children learn the Buddhist concept of one-half. That is, one-half of whatever children have they can choose at times to give to others whether it is one-half of a cookie or one-half of the extra recess time earned. The teacher smiled one day when she saw a kindergarten girl break her favorite crayons in half and give them to a girl who had none. A fifth-grade teacher laughed when two boys in the class exchanged one-half of their shoes and started a mismatched shoe trend. Tangible gifts carefully selected or lovingly crafted with the wishes, desires, and dreams of the receiver in mind are meaningful in their own right. Sometimes the most meaningful tangible gifts convey an even more meaningful, intangible message. The intangible message is often the true gift. Intangible gifts create emotions, positive memories, and meaning for the giver and receiver.

Young children make a list of intangible gifts they can give to another. Older children write daily in a gratitude journal about everyday gifts that bring confidence, contentment, serenity, inspiration, and joy. They write about the daily gifts found in the sunshine and shadow of life: daffodils blooming in February, a distant train whistle at the same time every night, homemade soup, rain on a roof during a thunderstorm, the smell of freshly baked bread, sunshine on the windowsill, tea with honey, and a new friend.

Children learn selective attention and how to focus on the wonderful world found outside their own disappointments and sorrows. The teacher asks the third-grade class to make a list of three intangible gifts that they could give to someone that would be meaningful to that person. "My mother would like peace and quiet and to go to the bathroom alone." "My friend wants me to play ball with him even if he can't catch at all." "My friend wants me to show him how to do the math homework." "My sister is sick and wants me to shave my head, too." The responses are a litany of purposeful positive psychology responses emblematic of meaningful giving.

The book *29 Gifts* inspired the 29-day gift-giving project.[27] The author tells how giving one gift each day for 29 days changed her life. She made an entry into her giving diary every day to describe her acts of giving, and as it turns out, how she received gifts in return. Many of the giving actions entered into her diary were simple, random acts of kindness toward her friends, family, and strangers: a phone call to a friend, spare change to a stranger, or a Kleenex for her sister. Children can read examples of giving acts on the 29 Gifts website.[28]

A teacher can begin a class 29 Gifts project by creating a starter gift bag for each child, seeking funds to purchase a gift bags that includes the book, a journal, 29 gift tags, and a 29 days bookmark. The teacher can also create her own gift bags for children in the class. The bags can include excerpts from grade-leveled books about generosity such as *The Giving Tree* or *Stone Soup*.[29] She or he might also include an illustrated quote about giving. Children make the bookmarks and gift tags for each other to put in the class gift bags. Children use the gift tags to record the intangible gifts they give away and put them in the classroom gift box. At the end of the 29 days, the teacher gives each child a gift at a giving party. At the party, the children read all of the gift tags aloud and post them on the 29 Gifts bulletin board.

The teacher can download a free giving journal that older children use to record the gifts that they give in addition to filling out gift tags.

The teacher may find it a relatively easy task to find a benefactor to support the 29 Gifts project in the classroom. Teachers themselves can seek gifts for their classrooms through three websites: Adopt a Classroom, Donors Choose, and Teacher's Wish List.[30] Funds might purchase gift bags or library books to launch the 29 Gifts project. *The Giving Box*, written by Fred Rogers, also teaches children the lessons of a generous community and brings authentic meaning to the classroom and the neighborhood.[31] Fables from around the world inspire gift giving as a meaningful endeavor.

The class makes a pretty gift box to collect spare coins all year to donate to a class cause. A similar approach is to play the Gift Box game. The children decorate a big box as the gift box and children donate to it on a regular basis. The gift can be as simple as a found penny, a shiny pebble found on the way to school, a drawing made with paper and crayons, an extra pencil, a toy rarely used, a sweater that was outgrown, or an extra blanket bought at Goodwill. The gift itself is not as important as the action of giving it. The 29 Gifts project and the Gift Box game teach children the art of giving.

Intangible gifts like a shared lunch or a favorite flavor of ice cream are more valuable for the memory. These intangible gifts do not just collect dust and are especially meaningful, whether offering help with chores or sharing a long talk. In giving gifts and doing good deeds, children learn to pay it forward.

Children make "pay it forward" bracelets, or colorful rubber wristbands, to wear. When they find someone in need, and do a good deed, they pass the bracelet to the recipient to pass it on again. Some teachers support the activity daily while others plan a pay-it-forward day once a month. Whenever they give away a bracelet, younger children draw a picture about it, and older children write a story about it to capture the good deed or favor done. At the end of the year, children publish their stories and drawings in a yearbook that passes their good deeds forward as they move to the next grade.

Paying it forward is a simple concept to implement with children, and it encourages meaningful gestures. Organizing a Kids Care Club forms a cadre of helpers who can pay it forward by doing good work together or encouraging good work in each other.[32] The club's website posts sample activities and meaningful hands-on volunteer projects, locally, nationally, and globally adapted for the elementary classroom.[33] The club builds a team of volunteers who coordinate service.

Children download a Kids Club "Start-Up Handbook" and they can receive monthly e-newsletters.[34] Fact sheets for kids, suggested meeting activities, information on possible service partners, and other resources are available. The club is also eligible for in-kind product donations and mini-grants. A pony at a birthday party does not have lasting impact because children acclimate quickly to novelty. Although it is a positive and memorable experience, it is not necessarily a meaningful one. A research study reveals that, over the long term, increasing the frequency of small, positive actions has a longer after-life.[35] Playing cards every day with friends for a half-hour or growing a potted plant together is more meaningful. Regular exercise, quick affirmations, and daily good deeds that are short, frequent, routine, or shared are more meaningful over time.

Many books motivate young children with stories of helpfulness and gratitude of service such as *Thanks and Giving, The Secret of Saying Thanks*, and various *Care Bears* and *Berenstein Bears* books.[36] These sharing and caring books teach giving and philanthropy. The manual *The Giving Book: Open the Door to a Lifetime of Giving* teaches children, 6–11 years, how to give back to the world.[37] The manual is a unique, interactive book that combines colorful illustrations with an entertaining narrative featuring fun learning activities about giving and the power of generosity and service. There is a movement afoot to teach children philanthropy as a school subject to channel individual giving into a larger, coordinated effort. The premise is that in the process of planning charitable events and fund-raising projects, children improve reading, writing, arithmetic, leadership, tolerance, fairness, and resilience.

The doctors diagnosed Alexandra "Alex" Scott with neuroblastoma, a type of childhood cancer, shortly before her first birthday. The day after her fourth birthday, she received a stem cell transplant. On that same day, Alex said to her mother, "When I get out of the hospital I want to have a lemonade stand. I want to give the money to doctors to allow them to help other kids, like they helped me." True to her word, the young philanthropist held her first lemonade sale later that year. With the help of her older brother, her lemonade stand raised an amazing $2,000 for her hospital. While bravely battling her own cancer, Alex and her family sold lemonade at their front-yard stand every year. News spread of the remarkable sick child dedicated to helping other sick children. People from all over the world sold lemonade at their own stands to raise money for her cause. In August 2004, when she was 8, Alex died, knowing that, with the help of others, she had raised more than $1 million to help find a cure for the disease that took her life. Alex's family, including her three brothers and community supporters around the world, continue her legacy through the Alex's Lemonade Stand Foundation.[38]

Children themselves have founded any number of successful not-for-profit associations. In 1999, 7-year old Ryan Hreljac built his first well in a Ugandan village. Today, the Ryan's Well Foundation has grown into a family of people committed to delivering access to safe water as an essential way to improve the lives of people in the developing world.

Even if children do not start the project, every child can make a difference. Rachel Beckwith also left behind a one-million-dollar legacy for the Charity Water Foundation.[39] She intended to raise $300 by her ninth birthday to supply clean water to African villagers. She had raised about $220 when her life ended suddenly in a car accident. However, friends, church members, and total strangers from around the world picked up where she had left off. Donations in her memory quickly hit the million-dollar mark as tens of thousands of people—most of them strangers—donated to her cause.

Children also raise money for local charities in their own communities. They brainstorm ways to help a local family who lost their home to a fire or to help the lost pet rescued on the highway. They use the handbook *How to Be an Everyday Philanthropist* to build the will and the skill for philanthropic practice.[40] The book offers 330 concrete ideas to use to embed small, meaningful acts of philanthropy into everyday life. The book trains children to think about giving in a new and inventive way and teaches children to be helpful by using their (1) belongings, (2) bodies, (3) families, (4) time and talent, and (5) computers.

An old blanket keeps an abandoned animal warm, legs run for a cause, eyes watch for frogs, and hands stuff comfort bags for homeless children in a shelter.[41] Children become citizen scientists and log bird sightings or the first buds of spring.[42] Do children have an old pair of sneakers lying unused around the house? Nike's Reuse-a-Shoe program will recycle them into safe playground surfaces.[43] Is a parent getting rid of an old cell phone? ReCellular tells you where to donate an old cell phone to soldiers or poor families.[44] Children can start a petition, sign a petition, or send an e-mail to recruit others to sign a petition at Care2.com.[45]

The book lists more than 600 charitable organizations and suggestions on how to integrate the work of those organizations into the traditional academic curriculum so that charity and service work complements academic learning. In science, the comparison of American forests to South American rain forests uses lessons from American Forests and Kids Saving the Rainforest websites.[46] Many of the not-for-profit associations develop programs and projects that align with traditional academic standards so the teacher can combine a traditional curriculum, e-curriculum, and service learning based on the advocacy or charity of the organization. The teacher can use the resources of a wide range of not-for-profit associations to connect academic subjects to philanthropy, volunteerism, and service learning.

The American Institute for Philanthropy ranks organizations to help teachers identify the national and international associations that have an educational component and offer the teacher learning resources such as lesson plans.[47] Some examples include but are not limited to Africare, Blanket America, Dian Fossey Gorilla Fund, International Gorillas, Give2the Troops, Guide Dog Foundation, Heifer Foundation, Helen Keller International, Hunger Project, Keep American Beautiful, Rainforest Alliance, Save the Children, Share Our Strengths, and the Wildlife Conservation Society.[48] A few national programs connect children to meaningful service learning in their own neighborhoods, and the teacher can easily find many local charities to adopt that connect to the academic and positive psychology curriculum. The teacher finds many opportunities to turn a traditional field trip into a day of service learning at the local kennel or zoo.

The National Service Learning Clearinghouse website offers service learning ideas, inspiration, tools, and materials to implement meaningful service learning from whole projects to one-time activities.[49] A guide helps teachers connect service learning at the local, state, and national level to academic, social, and emotional learning.

From simple to elaborate service learning projects, children are the architects of their own learning and can choose what is meaningful and important to do. Children apply their knowledge and strengths to contribute and solve problems in their classroom, school, neighborhood, community, nation, or around the world. The best service learning appeals to children's sensibilities, enriches academic learning, and offers lessons and teacher guides for implementation.

Service learning distinguishes itself from general volunteer service by the requirement that it connect to the traditional academic subject in explicit ways. Service learning is a more formal, structured type of giving that engages in meaningful work that applies their practical wisdom—their knowledge, skill, and will. The teacher identifies the standards, core concepts, and targeted skills to teach and then matches her instructional intentions with a philanthropic cause that enriches the curriculum with experiential learning.

When children collect trash in a stream, they are providing a valued volunteer service. When children collect trash from an urban stream, analyze their findings to find possible sources of pollution, and share the results with neighbors, they are engaging in service learning. Ideally, children choose service learning based on class interests and to enhance the academic curriculum, and it becomes their mission to succeed. Service learning is the action of helping others by sharing signature emotional and academic strengths in meaningful ways. With careful planning, teachers build a comprehensive curriculum using service learning projects so that children learn to not only give to others, but also learn from the process of giving. By making brochures, they improve writing skills. By collecting and counting pennies, they practice mathematic skills. By reading books on the subject, they improve reading skills.

To prepare for service learning, children in second through fifth grade can read a service learning guidebook written for them such as *The Kid's Guide to Service Projects: Over 500 Service Ideas for Young People Who Want to Make a Difference*, which can help them brainstorm and plan action.[50] Learn and Serve America is another federal program that supports service learning and provides resources and funding for individual children, classes, and whole schools.[51] To date, this program has connected more than a million children to their community in meaningful ways and every year it facilitates the involvement of hundreds of thousands of K–12 children in academically oriented service learning.

Elementary-level service learning is a transformative experience offering multiple ways to introduce authentic, pragmatic, project-based, and meaningful learning. A class-level program that researches recycling options, a school-level tutoring clinic where client progress is measured and charted, and a community-based wildlife project that culminates in a report sent to the city council are all examples of service learning.

Service learning is the practical application of academic content knowledge, positive emotion, signature strengths, and relationship skills. Service learning extends the reach of the educational curriculum to the field. Giving to others is important for physical, emotional, and mental wellness, and it imparts meaning in life. Studies show that providing social support for others is more beneficial than receiving it; also, doing good deeds helps build resilience to endure difficulties and persevere on tasks.[52] The reason there is benefit in the act of giving is that it gives children a good reason to perfect will and skill for the sake of others and to experience the serenity, peace, and joy of self-transcendence. The poet Ralph Waldo Emerson concurs: "It is one of the most beautiful compensations of this life that no man can sincerely try to help another without helping himself."[53] This is the law of compensation: The good you do will come back to you.

3. Legacy Learning and Global Study

A legacy is a gift passed from one generation to the next and it often refers to a tangible bequeathal of money or property. It may be a tangible or intangible gift bequeathed to a child and can take the form of a monetary inheritance, a national forest, a family tradition, a scrapbook of happy memories, a favorite uncle's banjo, a love for music, or a shared travel experience to a far-away place. A legacy spends social capital on emotional connections, shared strengths, and lasting memories.

Children are curious to know more about their extended family and family roots. Through legacy exploration, children learn about the strengths of their families and achieve a deeper sense of belonging to their family's past, present, and future. Programs, curricula, units, lessons, activities, exercises, and games that teach children about their place in the family can help to make reading, writing, and mathematics interesting and significant.

Children eagerly consume these lessons because they are meaningful to them and they enjoy learning about their families and family history, especially in the context of historical eras and events. They learn about inherited traits such as eye color, hair color, nose size, aspects of personality, and more. They also learn that customs, traditions, and names pass through the generations. The book *Who Do You Think You Are?—Be a Family Tree Detective* provides the tools children need to begin to investigate, discover, and preserve family treasures.[54]

Guided activities include bringing in family photos, letters, and heirlooms to share with the class and using these to prompt additional research: creating a family keepsake treasure book, making a family crest, creating a time capsule, completing a family tree poster, and conducting family interviews. The *Kids Family Tree Book* is another excellent resource to use to help develop meaningful, legacy lessons for children of all ages. Young children are naturally curious and always bursting with questions about their ancestors, their nationality, the jobs they held, the places they lived, and more. This book provides instructions to preserve such as family stories, photographs, or recipes by assembling it in a crayon-Batik family tree or a homemade diary.

A legacy project, activities, and games can combine to form a unit of study—young children interview older family members, or friends, and then generate a family tree. The teacher commissions children as family detectives helping them to understand their personal history and lineage. For younger children, the Family Tree Kids website offers a series of legacy lessons to implement in the classroom.[55] The lessons, activities, and games change weekly: One week there are instructions on how to make a family tree magnet, and the next week there are links to child-friendly genealogy forms and charts. The next week there are simulated games like the Scavenger Hunt in Grandmother's Closet game, and children really enjoy searching online for uncommon historical objects found in Grandmother's virtual closet.

Older children are encouraged to write a family newsletter or plan an online Skype family reunion. They play the Oldest Family Member game and identify the oldest living member of the family, take a photo of that person, interview that person, and write a letter to him or her. Another game is the Family Reunion game. Children plan all the details for a family reunion down to the invitations and menus.

In the Family Vacation game, children can plan a vacation that visits all the places an ancestor lived and they write a travel diary describing what they expect to see and do. For inspiration, children read books based on true, historical stories that may have affected their own relatives in some way. They read books about legacies that beloved family members left behind when they died—their songs, stories, diaries, dolls, baskets, gourds, hope chests, and dream catchers. They discuss the fond memories and lingering examples of their signature strengths also left behind and connect it to their own families. There are numerous children's books about grandmothers and grandfathers, from every culture, that tell the story of the tangible and intangible gifts they leave behind for their grandchildren.

Younger children read *My Grandfather's Journey*, a deeply personal story about a love of two countries and a boy's journey from one to the other.[56] This award-winning book begins a unit of lessons on family history and immigration. There are many books about arrivals at Ellis

Island and other immigration stories from every land for every age. A meaningful learning lesson instructs the children to plan the same journey: What could they take and what would they have to leave behind?

Beetles and Angels tells older children the story of Mawi's remarkable journey from a civil war in east Africa, through a refugee camp in Sudan, to a childhood on welfare in wealthy suburban America, and, eventually, to a full-tuition scholarship at Harvard University.[57]

At every step—whether learning a new language, overcoming racial discrimination, or succeeding despite personal tragedy—Mawi forges ahead with unshakable optimism and devotion to his family. Legacy learning involves an understanding of the roots of family origin that connects children to their past so they are more aware of their future.

A story with a similar theme, *The Feather Bed Journey*, tells the story of a grandmother's torn feather pillow and her childhood in Poland during the Nazi occupation.[58] The children, in first through fourth grade, follow up the reading with their own stories about special and meaningful objects: favorite pillows, stuffed animals, dolls, quilts, and other comfort treasures. The class decorates a special class feather pillow with their names and strength words on it. Through research, reading, and writing, children come to know the strengths of their relatives. To lighten the mood, the children sing along to the John Denver "Grandma's Feather Bed" song.

Older children write in personal and meaningful ways about family history, experience, and lineage. Writing to discuss feelings, appreciate strengths, and communicate with others is meaningful learning, and children learn to write well what they come to know well. As a guide, they use the genealogy book *Climbing Your Family Tree*.[59]

This is a comprehensive, kid-friendly genealogical primer for the 21st century. Children research important family documents, including ships' manifests, naturalization papers, and birth, marriage, and death certificates. They create oral histories, make scrapbooks of photos and sayings and legends, and compile a family tree. To follow up on the lessons in the book, the children research the meanings of first names and discuss family names that have been passed down. They draw their ancestors' coats-of-arms, guess places of origin with geography clues, listen to songs of the era, and identify unfamiliar language usage such as "ragamuffin" and "scallywag." They use real census data in mathematics lessons and maps in geography lessons that are connected to the immigrants' stories.

Emotional learning connects easily to academic learning using legacy learning. There is a companion website with record-keeping pages and supplemental e-resources. When children personally connect to history lessons learning through stories that relate to their own lives, those lessons activate curiosity, capitalize on novelty, and engage them emotionally. This kind of emotional commitment to learning is the high water mark of the positive psychology teaching taxonomy benchmark of meaning. The study of family is a meaningful endeavor that children can undertake in the classroom. They learn that there is dignity and value in whatever circumstances occur and in whatever their families learned to do to survive, whether farming hard ground or working off a boat passage while scrubbing the decks. The key to happiness is choosing to make whatever you do meaningful and finding the contribution to current or future generations in the effort.

The Colonial House, an interactive adventure, uses web-based games to explore a common past and find the common denominator in a shared history so it comes alive in meaningful ways.[60] Children embark on the journey by listening to video diaries and deciding if they could survive the hardships. Understanding how families endure hardships, manage changes, maintain traditions, celebrate milestones, transmit touchstones, enact rituals, and share accumulated practical wisdom from harvesting corn to playing the fiddle forges a sense of belonging and membership. Most important, it builds resilience for children who know that persistence and stamina are legacy obligations.

The intangible inheritance is most meaningful and resonates with children—a treasured object, favorite story, joyful memory, a tree planted together, a principle to uphold, a thought to ponder, or strength to build. A familial value is transformative when children learn to articulate and embrace it. What children do with or for those that they love is lasting.

The Arbor Day Foundation reforestation initiative uses every dollar donated to plant a tree in celebration of a special life event or in memory of a loved one.[61] This initiative enables even urban children to plant a lasting legacy within the nation's forests. Legacy learning, whether finding the address of a long-lost relative or planting a tree in her memory, is meaningful because it teaches children to see the bigger picture and to stay mindful of the long-term goal. Legacy learning focuses children on what came before and what will come after.

In *Fahrenheit 451* Ray Bradbury writes, "Everyone must leave something behind when he dies, my grandfather said. A child, or a book, or a painting, or a house, or a wall built, or a pair of shoes made. Or a garden planted. . . . Something your hand touched [so] when people look at that tree or that flower you planted, you're there."[62] In that spirit, the *Honoring Our Ancestors* book teaches a lesson about kinship and universal connections.[63] All the artists honor the strength of the spiritual ancestors who most shaped their lives.

The book presents the work of 14 outstanding and diverse artists who honor their ancestors. They pay playful tribute to the influential and loving people who came before them through their art. Some of the honored relatives include Caryl Henry's grandmother, Madame C. J. Walker, America's first black female millionaire. Nancy Hom honors her father, who possessed the strength of a mighty warrior, evident even when working in a Chinese restaurant. George Crespo honors both his Puerto Rican grandfather and his own Taino ancestry. Mira Reisberg honors her Jewish grandparents who were killed in the Holocaust.

The stories of strengths are compelling and the art is inspiring. Through stories, art, and photographs, the artists share a legacy book that inspires children to think about what relative has most influenced them. In doing so, they seek pride and strength in their own past and ask themselves, "Whom do I honor?"

The Legacy Project is a fully developed curriculum for children of all ages that teaches children how to build a legacy by using strength, connecting to others across generations, and changing the world in small and large ways.[64] The Legacy Project banner programs are literature-based and developed for children in kindergarten through fifth grade. Each program addresses one of the three levels of legacy learning and growth: personal, interpersonal, and community legacy. Natural and social science research inform the program's lessons that use problem-solving activities and project-based lessons. The project distributes three award-winning legacy programs: Life Dreams, Across Generations, and For Our World. The Life Dreams program focuses on what is important in children's lives and their aspirational hopes and dreams for themselves and for their world.[65] The project crosses academic boundaries and arbitrary subject-area distinctions, specializations, grades, ages, politics, and trends requiring inductive reasoning.

The Life Dreams curriculum includes a book about dreams and 75 online dream activities, including activities for the start and end of school. Writing in a dream journal is one of the language arts lessons. Children ask themselves, "What is my dream for my future?" "If I could do anything, go anywhere, learn anything, what would I choose?" The project sponsors a dream essay contest, a traveling dream exhibit, and an electronic newsletter. There is a companion website with record-keeping pages and supplemental e-resources.

The teacher's guide explains how to teach literacy by reading, writing, and discussing students' hopes, aspirations, and dreams. Supplemental learning tools include a traveling dream exhibit that comprises children's art, a replica of the book's hope chest, a set of enrichment activities, and teaching tips. Throughout the year, children write down their hopes and dreams and put them in a class hope chest: they can describe places they want to travel to, service they want to offer, or books they want to read. Children consider how what they do today is important for tomorrow.

The Across Generations curriculum teaches interviewing techniques so children are skilled at conducting life interviews with family, friends, and neighbors.[66] The curriculum includes a book that tells the true story about a grandmother who leaves her granddaughter an intangible gift that she cherishes. The curriculum helps children to consider where they came from, where they are now, and where they are going. In addition to the companion book, there are online activities, and a teacher's guide with special reports, articles, and suggestions.

The project also sponsors an online library that archives the audio life mission statements that children record and post to share with others in this permanent archive. Children also use the audio library to listen to others' life statements. A life statement is an ethical will that passes intangible values or strengths instead of tangible valuables to others. A life statement is a record of emotions, strengths, and contributions preserved for posterity. Life statements are a gift given to others to celebrate a birth, to celebrate an accomplishment, or to honor a memory, and these are intended to create a sense of continuity across the generations.

From connecting across generations to connecting with the larger world, the For Our World curriculum teaches children about the seven billion people living on seven continents in 194 different countries.[67] Children consider how they can think more globally and act locally, how to build more sustainable communities, and how to connect with others who live a continent away. There are more than 450 activity ideas, attention-getters, experiments, projects, puzzles, games, and stories covering all areas of science so children study the world through an environmental filter. The goal is to teach children that there is meaning in everything, from picking up trash to contemplating shapes of clouds.

Even if the teacher does not adopt a full-scale legacy or global curriculum to teach the positive psychology teaching taxonomy of meaning, he can develop many of his own activities for global study.

Children relate easily to a perspective of having a global family. They learn to consider their own families in a larger global context, and lessons facilitate the study of family systems, structures, and customs around the world. They discover surprising facts that can change their worldview completely. Some facts that they learn surprise children and they exclaim over the fact that in some cultures the whole family sleeps in one room and sometimes in the same bed. The nature of family housing and the nurture of generations living in the same neighborhoods or villages fascinate them. How families live, work, play, and learn in countries around the world shifts children's perspectives and gives them a broader understanding of their own family attributes.

When children imagine themselves living with other families, they discover new meaning and value in their own family. They play the Blessing in Disguise game in which they list what aspects of their family lives are most meaningful to them and what aspects they overlook or take for granted. Children play the Meant to Be game by listing aspects of family life meant to be in any particular family. They randomly draw a locale and research what is the common experience for children in an Aboriginal tribe in Australia, for a nomadic child in Egypt, or for an urban child in New York City. These lessons teach the importance of accepting self and others.

Young children delight in the 17 babies from 17 cultures in the book *Global Babies*.[68] The photographs depict diverse traditions and costumes and the reader identifies how the babies are alike and how they are different. The book *Carry Me: Babies Everywhere* shows how families around the world transport their babies.[69] Whether babies are tucked in a blanket, peeking out of a basket, riding in a backpack, sleeping in an elaborate pram, or wrapped in a parent's arms, babies worldwide are carried in various ways. The study of global neighbors broadens emotional perspective, changes worldview, and teaches tolerance. The lessons emphasize the value of the global community and human relations learning.

Older children also enjoy the book *Families*, which uses real photographs of families from the United Kingdom, the United States, Ethiopia, Canada, Vietnam, South Korea, Brazil, Saudi Arabia, Russia, Japan, and India. An index of photographs identifies each family group and nationality, and a map pinpoints where each family lives so children can learn more about the locations.

They use the book *Children Just Like Me* to research daily living factors that affect children around the world. An earlier book from the same series focused on celebrations. For this book, the authors spent two years meeting and photographing youngsters from every continent and more than 140 countries. The book organizes the material by chapter, and each begins with photos of children, their names, and their nationalities. Each page features pictures of each child's food, eating utensils, housing, school, friends, and family. The text gives the young people featured in the book an opportunity to comment on their favorite games, friends, and hopes for the future.

The book is factual, respectful, insightful, and used as a starting point so that children can research the different lives that children live and learn what is important and meaningful to them. As a capstone lesson, the class watches how multigenerational families care for children in the feature-length film *Babies*.[70] The meaning of children's place in the global family is a natural extension of legacy learning.

An understanding of self, family, and culture in meaningful ways inevitably invokes children's place in the global family, because so much of the emotional learning curriculum is global in focus. For example, the Society for Safe and Caring Schools and Communities[71] offers an elementary curriculum that combines three projects differentiated by grade and subject, including mathematics, language arts, physical education, health, or art: the Global Education Project, the Aboriginal Students Project, and the Interfaith Project.[72]

The Global Education Project's curriculum is highly interactive. Children take Earth quizzes, plot data on a large wall map, and review professional PowerPoint presentations to understand global challenges and study the ecological health of Earth. They use real-life and real-time data to solve real-world problems and complete real-world projects. Using a data-driven, graphics-based methodology, children study meaningful international issues related to ecology, energy supply, human living conditions, fishing and aquaculture, food and soil, fresh water, toxic pollution, weapons, wealth, development, and debt. They also participate in current event scavenger hunts, study geometric art common across all cultures, and research details about villages. Using the e-curriculum, they can shadow other children through a day-in-the-life to get a close-up view of how other children around the globe live so they feel more connected.

The Heifer International program offers classroom activities and games that inform about world hunger and poverty while also teaching academic subjects.[73] Supplemental resources include videos, success stories, and a library of publications for the teacher to use in the classroom. The program also sponsors a unique fund-raising project: Read to Feed.[74] Children read books to raise money to buy chickens for eggs and goats for milk to feed hungry children.

During this project, the teacher hears someone say, "Well, I helped buy a goat by reading three books. We named the goat Mambi, because he lives in Mambi Village in Tanzania. She makes milk for the children there. I have never tasted goat milk and I hope it tastes good." There is nothing like buying chickens for a village to get reading and meaning flowing in the classroom. All of the Read to Feed instructional materials are available online and include lesson plans that are based on national educational standards for the PreK–8 levels.

Another global program is the Global SchoolNet.[75] Its mission is to support 21st-century learning and to improve academic performance and emotional connection.

Children are involved in collaborative, meaningful, worldwide, e-learning projects to create multicultural understanding. Children fully participate as productive and compassionate world citizens by using three highly innovative elementary global learning programs: Global Expeditions, the GeoGame, and the Newsday Project.

On the Global Expeditions page, children participate in travel groups with other children from around the world by going on virtual expeditions to faraway places. They may find themselves exploring a polar ice cap, camel riding in Australia, or flying a small plane around the Fiji Islands. They are tasked with bringing back as much information as possible from the expedition, organizing it into categories of knowledge, presenting it to their class, and sharing it on the Internet. While on the expedition, they share stories, photographs, maps, postcards, letters, travel diaries, and travel tips. Technology enables children from all over the world to travel and study climatology, geography, political science, cultural study, and more. In the process, children use their academic knowledge, emotional strengths, human relation skills, and sense of purpose.

GeoGame is a virtual learning game that teaches elementary children how to read and interpret world maps, learn key geography vocabulary, and identify cultural issues. Children join the online world competitions four times a year as class teams and they choose the game to play in each competition. There are game files, competition problems, and practice problems posted on the site, and children share clues with each other online just as they often share videogame advice, clues, and codes. There are non-competitive games also available to play as individuals, or as a class, throughout the year. Children can use prior competition problems and resources available online to play in teams in their classrooms on their own schedule and at their own pace.

Has your class ever created a class newspaper? Children write articles for the Newsday Project about current issues and events that affect them locally, nationally, and globally. The writing is posted on the site for the world to read. Students can then read and choose articles from other schools to download and include in their own electronic newspaper that is shared digitally or printed for distribution.

One World Classrooms also builds cross-cultural understanding by using the connective power of technology in K–12 schools.[76] There is an emphasis on the arts with an international online art exchange, on the environment with an Amazon rain-forest project, and on geography with travel lessons. Using this digital curriculum, children take photo-poetry tours, embark on an animal poetry safari, and visit historic and modern China; all the while, they can note the sights and sounds enjoyed in their travel e-journal.

A narrow focus on a discrete standard or a disconnected task does not encourage mindful, meaningful engagement in learning. Children cannot find the meaning if vision is constrained or learning compartmentalized, so legacy and global learning matter. Legacy learning and global lessons require inductive reasoning and children have to stitch together the affective, cognitive, and conative quilt of learning piece by piece. Using legacy and global learning, the teacher gives children the whole puzzle to take apart or deconstruct before putting it back together. Divergent thinking takes fixed ideas apart and puts them back together with a better understanding of how it all fits together. Legacy and global learning is meaningful to children because it enlarges their perceptions and extends the definition and boundaries of friendship.

In legacy learning, children find meaning through chronesthesia, or mental time travel. Students can project into the past or the future and move back and forth in time and space, easily imagining themselves living as early pioneers in Oklahoma or in a futuristic house. In global lessons, children's imaginations are their passport to understanding the global community, fairness, tolerance, and peace. As Albert Einstein wrote, "I am enough of an artist to draw freely upon my imagination. Imagination is more important than knowledge. Knowledge is limited. Imagination encircles the world."[77]

There is meaningful learning all around children. There is meaning in giving, in connecting to the past, and in projecting into the future. There is meaning in a found object that tells a story about family and meaning in the stories of families. There is meaning in corresponding with a pen pal who lives 5,000 miles away who tends his father's sheep or survived a tsunami. The positive psychology teaching taxonomy benchmark of meaning develops and delivers lessons that have a purpose, and it simultaneously helps children to find the point of all lessons for themselves. Children find meaning in an understanding of the big picture. For this reason, the first, most persistent, and most important question children ask, and the most important question the teacher answers, is "Why?"

4. The Natural World

Few legacy or global learning programs, projects, or curricula do not include a lesson, an activity, or a game to teach nature study. The environmental health and the well-being of the Earth is a global concern that is a meaningful subject. Nature learning is the awareness of, appreciation for, and engagement with nature. The study of nature encompasses the study of all living things such as milkweed, fish, flowers, house mice, muskrats, and red foxes. Nature study is also the study of non-living things such as rocks, clouds, and volcanoes. In nature study, children ask questions that perplex them: Where do you find a cricket's ears? Why does a lightning bug light up? What is wind? For centuries, philosophers, writers, artists, and children have been trying to understand the natural world.

A highly recommended 800-page book that guides elementary teachers in nature study is Charlotte Mason's classic work *The Handbook of Nature Study*.[78] While the photographs are not in color, this book is the foundation for any nature study curriculum and teachers can easily supplement with colorful photographs, web pages, and e-resources.

There are two other colorful supplements the teacher can use for nature study to focus children on a mindfulness of the environment around them so that they learn to make the most of every minute, whether digging in dirt or collecting leaves: *I Love Dirt! 52 Activities to Help You and Your Kids Discover the Wonders of Nature* and *It's a Jungle Out There: 52 Nature Adventures for City Kids.*[79] All of the activities help children understand nature so they can connect it in meaningful ways to their own lives.

E-resources complement nature handbooks so children benefit from outdoor experiential nature learning as well as indoor virtual nature learning. The PBS Nature Channel website offers a video library that organizes by topic, animal, and grade level with some teacher guides available.[80] Children watch and ponder urban raccoons scurrying to feed their raccoon babies, killer whales hunting for herring, a tiger with a broken tail making his last journey, and salmon swimming upstream. The *Loneliest Animals* video has a guide to teach the concept of extinction and protection of endangered species. Every video teaches science facts and a positive psychology lesson. Older children watch the videos on National Geographic's website about various animal and environmental topics focusing on survival and balance in nature. The teacher focuses and connects children to the benchmark of meaning through the topics of energy, freshwater, global warning, habitats, national disasters, and the oceans.

The website inventories the "Nature Untamed" series that includes information and videos for more than 350 different animals from the aardvark to the zebra. Each video teaches about animal houses and animal conservation, and children begin the process of researching, reading, and writing on the topics and discovering what these topics mean to them, connecting them to their emotional development, suggesting ways to contribute, and reminding themselves that they have a choice to positively or negatively affect the environment.

Younger children use the National Geographic children's website about animals that features children's videos about popular animals like penguins and pets like dogs. Using the online Creature Feature lessons, children learn about the Mallard duck's layers of waterproof feathers, the length of the average African elephant's trunk, and how the Atlantic puffin flies through the water.

There is also a colorful magazine for children, *National Geographic Kids*,[81] that supplements the website information and videos. National Geographic also sponsors the Animal Jam website for children, which is a safe, online virtual playground for children who love animals and the outdoors. The interactive games inspire children to explore and protect the world outside their doors whether woods, seashores, or gardens. Through all these works, children find emotional meaning in the moment and the effort.

Natural history museums are some of the best sources of online nature learning and offer a rich inventory of exhibits about the Earth and its creatures with teacher guides and lesson plans.[82] Using the museums' websites, children play the Nature Photography game. They find a favorite nature photograph online or in a magazine that is meaningful to them, and they print it out and enter it into the weekly classroom photography contest. The children post their photographs in the classroom and, at the end of each week, they vote for the best photograph and the winner discusses what meaning it has, or brings, to his or her life.

At the end of the school year, children enter photographs of nature that they take themselves. Photography is a meaningful medium that connects children to nature study. An artwork can be as simple as a coloring book page; there is a wide range of nature coloring books for younger children on almost every topic. Name any natural science topic and you will find a corresponding coloring book to teach it. A small sampling of the many coloring books available includes *A Walk in the Woods Coloring Book*, *Language of Flowers Coloring Book*, *Wild Animals Coloring Book*, *State Birds and Flowers Coloring Book*, *Constellations of the Night Coloring Book*, *African Plains Coloring Book*, *Butterflies Coloring Book*, and *Snakes Coloring Book*.

The meaning of the flowers or snakes in the larger scheme of life is a meaningful lesson. How can I be more mindful of the world around me whether I take a walk in the woods or around my neighborhood attuned to the sights, sounds, and smells? How does understanding the nightfall enrich my life? How can I use the language of flowers to convey my feelings? How do I fit into the overall ecology?

While younger children are coloring, older children are writing. They write Earth gratitude letters to various audiences in order to identify the blessings the Earth bestows. Some of the children can write letters to the newspaper supporting a conservation initiative with data collected; some write letters to community officials sharing the same data; and some write letters to environmental groups using their data. The letters emphasize their appreciation for nature, the reasons that they want to preserve it, the data that concerns them, and how they will work to protect nature in meaningful ways. Teaching children about nature is important so that they can enjoy it, connect to it, and find consolation. "If the sun is shining and the sky is blue, how bad can it be?" "If I take a short walk and pay attention to the birds singing, my troubles seem less so."

Children learn the 3R's of environmental science—reuse, reduce, and recycle—and that healthy green space is important for healthy emotional development.[83] Research finds that a 20-minute walk in a park increases children's concentration and sense of calm when compared to children who walked in a town or city. This effect may be as strong as, if not stronger, than medication. The findings are consistent with prior research that demonstrated that direct experience of any green environment facilitates calmness and attention. Research also suggests that the more biodiversity there is in the green space, the greater the benefit to all.[84] The benefit of nature study and experiences is apparent and there is no substitute for authentic nature experiences to bring meaningful learning to class.

Spending time outdoors reading in circles, collecting leaves for a collage, participating in nature scavenger hunts, and observing wildlife teaches academic content in an emotionally fulfilling and meaningful way. Joseph Cornell, an educator and the author of the *Sharing Nature* book series, created one of the best examples of an outdoor nature curriculum.[85] His concept of "flow learning" introduces nature study in playful ways to stir meaning that "awaken children's curiosity and enthusiasm so learning becomes fun, immediate, and dynamic, instead of static and secondhand."[86] The curriculum suggests four methods: (1) awaken enthusiasm, (2) focus attention, (3) experience directly, and (4) share inspiration.

First, children explore nature with their senses. Second, they focus their attention on particular parts of nature such as the sounds of the birds or the types of bark on trees. Third, they immerse in an experience such as planting a tree or photographing squirrels. As a culminating activity that encourages synthesis of learning, children share what they learned with others by writing, discussing, drawing, or singing. Meaningful activities that increase children's understandings of nature teach the positive psychology taxonomy.

"Flow learning" includes both process and product lessons that are authentic and unique.[87] The Making a Rainbow game is a natural process game. Children discuss the natural phenomenon of a rainbow and then act out their understandings. The Sound Map game is another natural process game and directs children to listen to natural sounds and record them on a map. They cup their hands around their ears and make fox or rabbit ears to improve their hearing. In the Bird Call game, children learn the calls that bring birds closer for observation. These are just a few examples of a curriculum full of wonderful ideas for nature study. In the flow process, immersed in the awe of nature, children learn how their actions can change the world and how the world can change them.

The National Audubon Society website offers instructions for teachers to create a nature discovery center in the classroom by creating a wall collage about a wild place in the local area.[88] The nature wall collage brings outdoor nature experiences inside and teaches children important natural science lessons. Children adopt a multimedia approach and the collage fills a large space in the hallway outside the classroom. They glue and label pinecones, bird feathers, seeds, leaves, stones, and more onto the mural.

They learn that an act as seemingly harmless as dropping a candy wrapper on the ground affects every part of the ecosystem. As children become more cognizant of the meaning and value of the gifts of the Earth, they are encouraged to record their nature observations in a field journal as a naturalist would do by using *The Nature Log: A Kid's Journal to Record Their Nature Experiences*.[89] Writing nature observations and making notes about the environment makes children more mindful of the nature they encounter every day that might otherwise go unnoticed and overlooked. They share their awareness with others by making and sending Earth Day e-cards to save paper.[90] They discover that their work to preserve the environment, whether studying the garbage in the ocean or the national park, leads to personal preservation, too.

The environmental activist Rachel Carson wrote, "Those who contemplate the beauty of the Earth find reserves of strength that endure as long as life lasts." A flower garden or a vegetable garden is a metaphor for how children must tend their inner gardens to thrive, whether they grow a single potted plant or a vegetable garden on school grounds. The Kid's Gardening website teaches children the basics of gardening and they can use the information to research climate zones, temperature, type of soil needed, intensity of sunlight, and water requirements.[91] Younger children prepare to plant and tend a garden by using simple steps on the My First Garden website.[92]

All children enjoy giving away vegetables that they grow or giving bouquets they pick for families and friends. If a garden is not feasible, children research how a particular flower or specific vegetable is grown. They draw a picture of it and share the gardening instructions with their family and friends. Absent a real garden, children can send virtual bouquets to friends and family and include gardening instructions for those flowers selected. Whether they grow a real plant or send a virtual bloom, children learn the language of flowers and research the emotional meaning of various flowers: "I didn't know that daisies are a symbol of gentleness." The teacher brings daisies, or another flower, to distribute to children who share the message of the flower. When she sees children acting gently, they get a flower.

The positive psychology teaching taxonomy benchmark of meaning uses nature to teach children the importance of, and reverence for, nature in their lives and to understand themselves. Children respond emotionally to nature learning and learn to balance their own emotions as nature balances itself. The concept of homeostasis in nature study teaches children the concept of self-regulation in the positive psychology teaching taxonomy of meaning. They learn what it means to restore their own equilibrium as nature does. They use their signature strengths to leave a natural legacy that requires them to use their signature strengths to be good friends of the Earth.

Positive psychology teaches the resilience of nature to motivate children to use their own resilience and other emotional strengths. Whenever possible, nature is the teacher. Nature study is mindful and meaningful learning. Children learn to go to the mountains to remember that their problems are small, listen to the geese overhead to find their way home, and sit in a garden for comfort. The study of nature is the study of flow, balance, and meaning.

5. Philosophy and Social Justice

The study of philosophy is literally the study of meaning and the fundamental problems of existence and life. Philosophy attempts to answer vital questions such as what is justice or what is love? Philosophers are seekers of knowledge and wisdom. Philosophy is gaining popularity as a subject in the elementary classroom because it blends cognitive and affective learning with the positive psychology teaching taxonomy of meaning. If knowledge and wisdom are the expected outcome of schooling, it makes sense to teach children outside the narrowly defined academic subjects of the 20th and embrace the new disciplines of the 21st century such as geography, family and cultural studies, nature study, and philosophy taught in transgenic and transformative ways.

The book *Big Ideas for Little Kids* has a companion website that guides the conduct of philosophical discussions with children.[93] The website presents book modules that identify the philosophical question raised in each book, and it rates the level of difficulty of the book and the philosophy concept. For example, books that consider aesthetics include, but are not limited to, *Lily Brown's Paintings* and *Shrek*. Examples of books that are a catalyst for a discussion on ethics include *Where the Wild Things Are* and *The Gold Coin*. Books that consider the philosophy of the mind include *Harry and the Purple Crayon* and *The Little Prince*. Contrary to what some teachers may think, even little children can come up with answers to the big questions of life.

The Kids Philosophy Slam website promotes an annual competition designed to make philosophy fun and accessible to children in grades K–12 and to promote critical thinking skills through meaningful dialogue.[94] The Philosophy Slam asks schoolchildren to answer a philosophical question such as "What is the meaning of life?"

Depending on their age, children express themselves in words, artwork, poetry, or songs, and each grade level has its own national winner. Answering the question "What is the right thing to do?" a third-grade winner wrote, "This is a difficult question because there are a lot of different answers and there is no one right answer. Sometimes the ends justify the means and sometimes they do not. Is there a situation when the means to the end are not justified? I do not think the means are justified when the goal is not noble, or good, or honest. However, who is to decide? An example is the story about the Little Red Hen because depending on the point of view the little hen did the right thing and depending on another point of view, she did not." The Slam posts resources to help teachers bring philosophy to the elementary classroom.

The Philosophy for Kids website also identifies common children's books, such as *Stone Soup* and *Miss Rumphius* and the underlying philosophical questions presented in the stories.[95] This website also provides original stories that young children finish by resolving a philosophical dilemma and, in the process, changing the ending. Older children enjoy the philosophy lessons on the Northwest Center for Philosophy for Children website.[96] On that website, there are four ethical puzzles to solve and discussion questions for Plato's Ring of Gyges: "What would you do if you had a ring that made you invisible?" and "Do you think Plato is right that people only choose not to do something bad because they are afraid they will get caught?"

Educators debate whether children are cognitively and affectively able to discuss the abstract ideas of philosophy, and anecdotal indicators in favor are persuasive.[97] For example, "Tim, who is six years old, was busily engaged in licking a pot when he asked, 'Papa, how can we be sure that everything is not a dream?' "[98] When teachers ask children questions that have no obvious answers, their ideas flow fluently: "How much do you love me?" "Is there life in the universe?" "How many grains of sand are on a beach?" "Can you go back or forward in time?" "Where do dreams come from?" Teachers of every age have many of their own examples that leave them wondering if educators tend to underestimate children's receptive cognition as they often underestimate their receptive language abilities.

When Dr. Seuss wrote the book *Horton Hears a Who*[99] he did not shrink from introducing epistemology to young children by asking a variation of the famous philosophical question, "If a tree falls in the forest and no one hears it, did it really fall?" The story raises questions about the nature of human knowledge and what is necessary to justify a claim to having knowledge. Children ask questions to find meaning. A teacher can ask children, "Do you believe everything that you hear? What are examples of something you heard that you do not believe? How do you test the truth of it?"

Older children espouse their philosophy in six-word sentences. They use only six words to respond to a philosophical question such as "What is love?" Children's responses are surprising. "Sharing my sandwich when I'm hungry." "Walking the dog for my mom." "A pretty Valentine card for little sister." "My dad calls me every single day." "My mom mows. My dad dusts." "Crayon marks. Bad on good walls." Sometimes complex philosophy sums up in a few words.

The highly respected Teaching Tolerance program enlists children in the cause of social equity and justice.[100] Children find meaning by acting with fairness and tolerance toward others, especially others who are vulnerable or hurting. Children learn to understand each other in meaningful ways, respect diversity, and solve problems peacefully.

The theme of the curriculum is common humanity and fellowship, and it offers varied resources that connect children to each other in emotional and personal ways. The website offers a comprehensive inventory of curricula, units, lessons, and activities, including ideas teachers post to share. There is also a monthly print magazine with articles about teaching tolerance to children of all ages, information on how to become a mix-it-up school, and a teaching kit for the early grades.

Many of the lessons and activities encourage introspective and philosophical thinking. One activity directs children to write about a place that is special and meaningful to them and to explain why. All children have a special place in their lives that has special meaning for them and that connects them to their emotions, strengths, families, or friends in some way. Differences in special places also reveal emotional differences between them. In the lesson, children write about boats, forts in the woods, fishing holes, and under the bed. They write about cozy living rooms with a fireplace, a church bench under a stained glass window, a sunny beach along the shore, and under the covers with their puppy on a cold night. Kerry wrote about the weeping willow tree in his backyard where he and his sister eat picnic lunches. His sister is his best friend, and he wrote poignantly that it is "where we tell secrets and sometimes we don't talk at all but we can still hear each other. The tree is like a curtain that keeps its secrets inside." The website catalogs dozens of creative elementary teaching activities by grade level and subject. For example, the discussion activity Allies teaches children how to become allies and stand up for each other by using their signature strengths.[101] The K–12 lessons coach children toward a philosophy of fairness, equity, and social justice. Children study the philosophy of law, or jurisprudence, to understand the interpretation of law in society. One of the key social justice philosophies compatible with the positive psychology taxonomy of meaning is the idea of restorative or reparative justice.

The Center for Restorative Justice and Peacemaking describes it as the "development of community-based responses . . . that strengthen social harmony and individual healing through dialogue, repair of harm, and peace-building."[102] In the elementary classroom, restorative justice programs emphasize healing of harm done, reparation after transgression, and restoration of damage done. The process of emotional repair brings a deeper understanding of relationships by changing negative experiences to positive, meaningful learning experiences.

Children use their signature strengths to undo the harm they did to themselves and to negate the harm done to others. Putting significant emphasis on helping others, restorative justice teaches children to restore balance using resilience, fairness, and tolerance in meaningful ways. If a child spoke angrily to others, she repairs the damage of hurtful words with a calm apology. If a child broke the rules of the game, he repairs the damage by volunteering to act as the referee in the next game. Children commit to specific strengths-based actions to demonstrate their good intentions to right the wrong. Sincere expressions of regret, written apologies, and formal rehabilitative contracts are the currency of restorative justice—because you did this, you will have to do that to make it right. If you drop trash on the floor, pick up trash on the playground for a week. If you make fun of a slow reader, tutor him in reading for two weeks. If you have a meltdown, learn five yoga poses. If you are unkind to someone, give her ten compliments. If you argue or fight with another child, work on a project with him.

> Two fifth graders who do not get along have a fight in the cafeteria. Craig and Jarrod come from very different backgrounds, and their feud is not abating with typical interventions. The teacher assigns both boys to a restorative justice study hall. In the study hall, the teachers direct them to choose a topic of mutual interest to work together to research each day for a week under the direction of the restorative justice facilitator.
>
> At the end of the week, they have also written each other an apology, listed their own strengths, and listed what they do like about the other. They are getting along much better now. They are expected to submit a joint, comprehensive report on the topic by the end of the semester and are given time in class each day to work on the report together. In the process, they discover they both love all-terrain vehicles, develop their research project around that topic, and bond as friends.

Restorative justice expects children to choose what to do in a particular situation to make it right and to make the wronged person whole. The corrective action must always be a sincere expression of regret and should be meaningful to both parties. The practice of restorative justice is the amplification of practical wisdom. By engaging in compensatory actions that have meaning to them and others, children relieve their own shame, guilt, and regret. If children learn how to restore balance in their lives by making a contribution that benefits all in a meaningful way, they learn how to flourish in the best and worst of times. Children learn to create powerful change one meaningful step at a time.

One of the best ways to do this is to adopt a restorative justice curriculum for elementary schoolchildren. The Society for Safe and Caring Schools and Communities developed one of the most comprehensive restorative justice elementary-school programs.[103] The K–6 curriculum,

Restorative Justice for the Classroom, teaches the philosophy and actions of restorative justice so children learn to repair and redress interpersonal damage.[104] The curriculum proposes that children learn non-violent responses in systematic ways in emotionally safe and caring classrooms. The objective of the program is to develop knowledge and skills using a prescribed curriculum that teaches eight lessons: (1) respect, (2) empathy, (3) anger, (4) staying on track, (5) practice makes perfect, (6) the healing wheel, (7) healing values, and (8) helping the community.

The lessons are literacy based and taught concurrently with traditional academic subjects and aligned with expected learning outcomes in language arts, science, social studies, physical education, mathematics, health, music, and drama. Each of the lessons includes dozens of learning activities and hundreds of resources. A key aspect of the curriculum is the concept of healing values or strengths identified as forgiveness, compassion, concern, tolerance, consideration, justice, and generosity. Children use the healing wheel to change negative interactions into positive outcomes and as a tool to assess the harm done to others when they violate healing values. They keep the healing wheel at their desk to help identify transgressions.

If one child excludes another child from the lunch table, the healing wheel finds a violation of tolerance. If one child calls another child a name in anger, the healing wheel pinpoints a violation of compassion. If a child refuses to talk to another child after an argument, the wheel helps the child identify the virtue of forgiveness as lacking. The healing wheel also aligns with suggested restorative actions and suggests the remedy necessary to restore the balance and cure the harm. The children learn about the value violated, the strength needed to rectify it, and the particular practice that will make it right and cure the harm.

The ostracized child receives an invitation to lunch and shares a special treat, the name-calling child offers an apology and gives a compliment to the same child daily for a week, and the ignored child is given an apology card. The curriculum teaches children how to use their strengths to give back to both themselves and others. Sometimes restorative justice takes the form of an Alabama wildflower garden planted by an 11-year-old who lost his mom in the Pentagon attack on 9/11, and subsequently lost his way. He found meaning again in her hometown where he planted a flower garden near the place that she grew up. Later, this young man showed emotional strength when, 10 years after his terrible loss, he commented to a reporter, "You can't go around being mad forever. It does not make sense."[105] The positive psychology teaching taxonomy benchmark of meaning teaches children the wonder of the meaningful moment and to celebrate today—that is the power of the meaningful moment to heal.

If the teacher cannot commit to a full restorative justice curriculum, there are many enrichment activities and games that help children understand the concept of restorative justice and help them use it on a daily basis. The Good Remains game asks children to describe a good deed done to make up a harm and what good came from it. Children describe what the other child did and why it was meaningful to them. They also play the Grudge of the Moment game and discuss a grudge that they held and how they let go of it. Moreover, they play the Missed Opportunity game that asks children to write about an opportunity that they missed to make things right with someone and what they would do differently the next time. Restorative justice does not teach the reward-consequence model and it does not define justice as punishment. The restorative model gives practice to meaningful learning that is proactive and rehabilitative.

Some teachers introduce a peer review panel or a circle of justice that encourages children to discuss a harm done. The panel or circle determines the form that restorative justice will take and what the offending child must do to make amends. As members of a peer review panel or justice circle, children learn to regulate both themselves and help others to do the same. Children become accountable not to the teacher but to each other and that results in more meaningful solutions that are based on increasing positive emotions, strengths, and relationships. Restorative justice is a strengths-based approach to teaching social justice and equity, requiring children to use their strengths to correct their course. Children learn how to find meaning in their lives, create it for themselves, or assign it in their lives.

A child can find meaning in the fact that his grandfather was a war hero and they have the same name. Another child may create meaning because she values her job caring for the class plants. Students have a new philosophy for life: "Find meaning in every day."

Summary and Conclusion

The positive psychology teaching taxonomy benchmark of meaning teaches the four pillars of meaningful learning. The four pillars of meaningful learning are (1) authentic and pragmatic learning, (2) social and service learning, (3) intuitive and contextual learning, and (4) legacy and global learning. Teaching the four pillars using the positive psychology taxonomy techniques helps children to connect learning to their personal experiences, service to others, the big picture, and legacy. The positive psychology teaching taxonomy benchmark of meaning is the circular good: the good feelings children express, the good strengths they express, the good relationships they build, and the good contributions in which they find meaning even in mundane daily tasks.

Children learn to stay mindful of the moment and to imbue everything they do with meaning. They learn to give simple gifts not expecting anything in return, contribute their time and strengths to others, work toward a legacy, take care of nature, and ponder the important questions. They understand that connection, contribution, and choice are the essence of meaning, and they learn to connect to others in meaningful ways, contribute to the good, and choose to repay a kindness or make restitution for a mistake.

When children read history, learn geography, write about the natural sciences, measure dimensions, play music, create geometrical art, plot latitude and longitudinal coordinates, and discuss philosophy, they are also learning about feelings, strengths, relationships, and meaning. Children learn to derive meaning no matter what the teacher expects them to do and they tell themselves: "This is important because the others are relying on me to get it done." "My uncle is a very fair man and I want to be like him." "I am not going to litter because taking good care of nature is important to me." Children learn tolerance of everyone who lives in the global village and how to help others succeed, treat others fairly, pick themselves up when they fall down so they can keep giving, offer each other peace, anticipate the good, and enjoy the moment. Children find meaning in every task they undertake, every book they read, and every dream they dream. Meaning is everywhere and the positive psychology teacher helps children find it.

Case Study K–2: Teaching Meaning

Ellen, a second grader, loved her little brother more than anything in the world and took care of him all the time since their mom died. She knew he was a sweet and caring little boy in kindergarten. She also knew that he had stolen another child's crayons in class that day. When she asked him where he got them, he said a classmate had let him borrow them and he "forgot" to give them back. Ellen knew her father had just lost his job and the family had little money for extras like crayons even though Sammy loved to draw. Ellen understood her father would be very angry and would likely punish Sammy and she knew the principal could suspend him because he, too, was very strict. She thought about the justice circles in her classroom. The teacher had selected her as a member of the justice circle this month and she was learning how to make amends for mistakes, take actions to fix the error, repay the debt, and do better the next time. Ellen said to him, "Sammy, you did wrong. Those crayons do not belong to you and your friend will feel sad when she cannot find them. She was kind to let you use her crayons and you cannot repay a kindness with dishonesty. That is just not fair to her. How would you feel if someone took your superman figure? I know it is hard to not have your own crayons. You just have to be brave and wait until it gets better—it will—I promise. However, you cannot just steal from a friend to get them." Sammy looked chagrined and said, "I am sorry. What should I do now?" Ellen helped him write a note apologizing. "Give the note and the crayons back to her tomorrow." After school the next day, Sammy ran to find Ellen. "Guess what? Guess what?" he asked. "I have a new box of crayons. Sarah said I was so honest that she wanted to give me a reward. She said she has an extra box of crayons at home that she will give to me. We are friends now."

Case Study 3–5: Teaching Meaning

Eric is big for the fifth grade and he is a rough-and-tumble boy on the playground. The other children look up to him because he is great at sports and a natural leader. He is quiet and does not have much to say in class. Eric is definitely the strong and silent type. He lingered behind when the class went to lunch the other day. Shyly, he asked the teacher, "Guess what?" She smiled and he continued. "My great-grandfather was in World War II and I didn't even know it. When I visit him at the nursing home I never know what I should say to him and neither does he. Most of the time, we just sit there and make small talk. I ask him about the weather and he asks me if I do my homework. He seems lonely and I always wish I knew what to say to him. Yesterday was different. I told him I was studying World War II at school and I wanted to interview him about it. He looked at me funny and started talking like he never talked until yesterday. He did not stop talking the whole hour until my dad came to pick me up. I am going back to see him again next Sunday and cannot wait to hear more of his stories. I didn't even know he was in the war." The teacher had hoped one of the students would make a connection to a relative and share what they were learning about World War II. Eric pulled a very worn and yellowed photograph out of his pocket. A young uniformed man, about 18 years old with Eric's smile and coal black hair, was standing in a field. Eric looked up and said, "Thank you. Thanks for giving me something to tell my grandpa and him to tell me. It means a lot to me."

Guiding Question Exercise

What matters to you? Can you make a list of the three most important things in your life? What makes these aspects of your life so meaningful to you? Have you made any contributions that make you proud? What motivated this effort? Is it a grand effort or a simple effort with profound meaning to you? What do you think matters to the children in your classroom? What do you think is meaningful to them? Has there ever been an especially meaningful event or interaction in your classroom? What made it meaningful or memorable? Do you help children figure out how what they are doing is meaningful outside of tests, grades, and performance metrics? Do you try to make lessons meaningful to learning? Do you connect prior emotional learning rather than academic learning to a lesson? How do you make lessons meaningful to children? What positive psychology teaching technique could you use to infuse meaning into the classroom? Use the six-word story or memoir technique to answer the question "What means the most to you in your life?" Think about tangible and intangible gifts you have given and received. Think about positive emotions, signature strengths, and important relationships as these impart meaning in your life. Use the technique to write about what matters most to you and about how you feel in this very moment. Use it to write about something you do not want to do and about meaning that you can find in what you want to do and do not want to do. Read some six-word stories and memoirs online for inspiration.[106]

Guiding Question Discussion

Meaning empowers us to do what we like to do, and what we do not like to do, better.

What do you like to do? What do not you like to do? What matters to you? These are sometimes difficult questions to answer because the answers require reflection and clarity. They require emotional precision and laser-like introspection. One way to practice is to write six-word stories or memoirs.

Ernest Hemingway's challenge to tell a story in six words is an excellent exercise to use to focus on mindfulness and meaning. The exercise focuses thoughts and feelings on what is most important to us, what has inherent meaning, and how every word, thought, feeling, connection, contribution, and choice matters. Six-word stories and memoirs inspire us to sort through the distractions and attend to core meanings. Finding meaning requires emotional transparency, keen insight, and the flow of self-disclosure. Six-word stories demand meaningful discipline of thought, word, and affect. Some wonderful examples of six-word stories found on the website include "Am artist. Lost arms. Still artist." "Moved to mountains. Mountains moved me." "Always nice people in garden aisles." "Transfer to public school. World discovered." "Through mud. Under bullets. Found freedom."[107]

Web Resources for Children

Earth Calendar, http://www.earthcalendar.net/index.php.
ePals Global Learning, http://www.epals.com/.
Generation On, http://www.generationon.org/kids.
Kaplan Learning Company, http://www.kaplanco.com/.
Learning to Give, http://learningtogive.org/.
Yes Kidz Can, http://www.yeskidzcan.com/.

Web Resources for Teachers

Greater Good Science Center, http://greatergood.berkeley.edu/.
National Council for Social Studies, http://www.ncss.org/.
Pay It Forward Day, http://payitforwardday.com/.
Restoring Meaning to Teaching, http://www.sedl.org/pubs/tl01/.
TisBest Charity Gift Cards, http://tisbest.org/.

CHAPTER **8**

TEACHING ACHIEVEMENT AND SUCCESS: THE ACCOMPLISHED LIFE

Excellence is not a gift but a skill that takes practice.
—Plato

Children spend approximately 1,602 hours in a classroom each year. In one study, they rank their desire to go to school slightly above going to the dentist and well below going to a theme park.[1] In a theme park, the sights and sounds stimulate the senses and arouse emotion. Heightened sensory demand fully engages children in the experience of a tilt-a-whirl or a roller coaster. However, the thrill of the theme park is short-lived. The promise of the positive psychology teaching taxonomy of accomplishment is that it teaches positive emotions, strengths, relationships, and meaning that thrill children in ways that are enduring and satisfying in the long run.

Ask a parent what he or she most wants for a child and most will answer, "I want my child to be happy." Others will respond "success." Ideally, every elementary-school child learns how to be both happy and successful because these are mutually reciprocal. A teacher's challenge is to define the success that makes children happy and to help them appreciate the kind of happiness that is the purview of the accomplished child.

What is success in elementary school? Is success compliance in a quiet classroom or a noisy debate? Is it meeting an externally imposed standard or understanding an internally meaningful concept? Is it completing the prescribed curriculum or pursuing guided inquiry and discovery with enthusiasm? Is it attending to a regimented lesson or creative investigation? Is success meeting a standardized metric or individual growth? Is success earning a good test score or grasping the content and command of a subject? Is it mastery of the discipline or mastery of emotion, strengths, relationships, and purposeful endeavors? The benchmark for the positive psychology teaching taxonomy of success is accomplishment. Success is not only what children know, but it is also the nature, scope, power, and meaning of what they choose, overcome, and accomplish. Children's belief that they are capable of success predicts that success. Success is a mind-set.

Accomplishment is the pursuit and practice of academic, social, and emotional intentions and excellence at home, at work, at school, and at play, by meeting personal goals and deriving satisfaction from the attempt of the goal. Success is accomplished satisfaction of best efforts, such that discontent and doubt do not overshadow diligence. Successful children work toward cooperation, contentment, confidence, fortitude, peace, inspiration, and joy in learning and life without fail. They are excited to learn and listen to others, do not give up easily, and spend less time in the principal's office and more time solving problems. Emotional proficiency predicts children's academic accomplishment.

An accomplished child is the leader in the friendship club, plays the piano because he loves music, and reads a book because he is curious about a subject. She studies for a test because she wants to do well; she writes a letter because she misses her aunt; she draws a picture because it calms her; she acts brave because others are counting on her; and she teaches tolerance because she empathizes with the sting of unfair treatment.

Accomplishment is the inventory of what children have done well in the past and what they aspire to do well in the future for personal satisfaction and lasting fulfillment. The positive psychology teaching taxonomy of success is associated with better grades and higher test scores. However, that is a secondary benefit of accomplishment. The true benefit is that children will grow into adults who enjoy physical, mental, and emotional well-being and who flourish.

The Importance of Successful Learning in Positive Psychology

The positive psychology teaching taxonomy benchmark of success is the culmination of accomplishments that mark the well regulated, balanced, supported, and defined life. The positive psychology teacher enjoins a curriculum that activates emotion, strength, friendship, and meaning as the means to accomplishment and academic achievement. The most important academic lessons in positive psychology are life lessons.

Children use academic subjects to learn about feelings, strengths, friendships, meaning, and pride in accomplishments. Stories that children read not only teach about vocabulary and grammar, but also teach about generosity and optimism. As one little girl asked the teacher after reading a book about caterpillars, "Do caterpillars have grit?" The positive psychology teaching taxonomy benchmark of success focuses on the means to the end—and not only on the end result. The teacher does not teach to the standard: He or she teaches to the child and meeting the standard is a by-product of that successful endeavor.

Academic achievement standards are a set of standardized curricular content requirements that identify the concepts a child should understand and the skills a child should acquire at a particular grade level. More often than not, the standards imposed are relatively global in nature and incorporate a scope and sequence component articulated as benchmarks. For example, the Florida language arts standard in third grade, LA. 3.3.5.1–3, requires children to "write a product for the intended audience prepared in a format appropriate to the audience and purpose, add graphics where appropriate, and share the writing with the intended audience."

While there is endless discussion about the standards, the standard itself is less important than the taxonomy, and associated techniques, that the teacher adopts to teach it.

Using a conventional textbook approach, the teacher can require that third-grade children memorize the format and the parts of a proper letter. Students then fill out a worksheet to test their knowledge of the format and parts of a letter. The teacher assigns homework: write a generic letter using the conventions of English.

The positive psychology teacher takes a different approach. Adopting the benchmarks of friendship and meaning, the teacher assigns children pen pals in Vietnam. They then write to their friends and share their plans for a water puppet festival. They illustrate their letters with detailed drawings of water puppets. As they write, they help each other write the letters and correct each other. They are proud to use their writing strengths in an authentic and meaningful way to accomplish a personal and academic goal. There is an even greater sense of satisfaction when children share their strengths and accomplishments with others.

In the positive psychology classroom, the academic content standard is secondary to children meeting and making new global friends, getting to know them in meaningful ways, sharing an exciting learning lesson with friends, gaining a sense of confidence in their skills, encouraging cooperative endeavors, sharing the purpose of written communication, and ensuring the joy of learning. When they finish this lesson, the children feel accomplished. However, even when they are only filling out a worksheet, they find it satisfying to do it well. Academic achievement is a by-product of emotional well-being, and every positive psychology lesson prioritizes the positive psychology teaching taxonomy. When children engage their hearts, their minds will follow. Typically, the teacher cultivates cognitive strengths of the mind, such as creativity and analysis, to increase academic performance. However, the positive psychology teacher also cultivates affective strengths of the heart.

The emotional strengths of the heart, such as gratitude and forgiveness, are more predictive of subjective happiness and are a prerequisite for academic achievement and personal accomplishment. The best lessons help children sort out emotions when they are confused, engage strength when they are discouraged, make friends when they are lonely, summon courage when they are called to do so, contribute in meaningful ways when they are uncertain, and enjoy authentic accomplishment as the fruit of their labor.

The positive psychology teaching taxonomy of success balances the cognitive brain and the emotional brain. It balances content learning and social emotional learning, balances reason and emotion, and balances the heart and the mind. Success in school is the ability to accomplish goals that enable children to flourish in ways that make life worth living.

Children learn to leverage their emotional skills to accomplish their personal and academic goals. The goal of positive psychology is to systematically teach children about their emotionality, their strengths, the requirements of friendships, the meaning of life, and how to take pride in their efforts and accomplishments. Success is facilitated by using the positive psychology teaching taxonomy benchmarks: create positive emotion instead of negative, engage strengths instead of faults, make true friends instead of acquaintances, offer contributions instead of criticism, and accomplish more and not less.

The positive psychology teaching taxonomy benchmark of success abandons the deficiency model, and attention shifts from what is wrong in education to what is right and how what is right can be replicated. Positive psychology teaches to success by increasing children's strengths. The teacher stops focusing on what children are doing wrong and how to fix them and instead starts focusing on what children are doing right. A teacher develops the hardiness of children, which trumps the hardness of learning.

The positive psychology teaching taxonomy benchmark of strength builds resiliency, commitment, and persistence in learning even when the task is daunting or the barrier is high so children anticipate the challenge and enjoy the effort. The accomplishment that begets success requires deferred gratification, self-efficacy, and tenacity that empower determination and motivation despite adversity. The measure of the positive psychology teaching taxonomy of success is the degree to which children can establish personal goals, direct effort toward those goals, and accomplish them or edit them with equanimity.

An educational irony is that the positive psychology teaching taxonomy benchmark of success does not overly emphasize the academic lesson plan other than as a means to teach its taxonomy. In the positive psychology taxonomy of success, the positive psychology of children is the most important factor.

The *New York Times* recently profiled one of the highly ranked teachers in the New York City public school system, determined in large part by her class's test scores.[2] Ms. Alison Epstein describes a lesson that is consistent with the positive psychology teaching taxonomy benchmarks. In the interview, she states that her work and efforts focus on the individual needs and skills of each student. In the process, it is clear that she also engages children's emotions, requires them to reflect on their strengths, teaches friendship learning, and uses global study. Understanding the concepts of comparison and contrast is the standard and the skill is to be able to compare and contrast ideas.

To do so, her students read about a Pakistani girl's daily life, compared and contrasted her life to their own lives, and wrote an essay about their discoveries and conclusions.[3] How are they the same and different? How are your families different? How is your dress different? How is your schooling different? How is your religion different? What strengths does she possess? How are your strengths different? Are the hardships that she encounters similar to or different from your own? Could you be her friend? The lesson not only meets the standard, but is a resonant lesson that also lends itself to the comparison and contrast of emotional strengths. The lesson teaches friendship in the global community and is authentic and meaningful in engaging children for success.

The Positive Psychology Teacher's Toolbox: Successful Learning

Accomplishment is the pillar of successful learning and the positive psychology teaching taxonomy success benchmarks facilitate that accomplishment. Accomplished children achieve success because they are cooperative, content, and confident, and they know how to bring serenity, inspiration, and joy to their learning. Successful learning requires fortitude to sustain the effort and accomplish the goal.

The teacher always uses the general educational methods previously discussed as the blueprint to teach the taxonomy: (1) the language of emotions and strengths, (2) infused academics, (3) visual and performing arts, and (4) strengths training. The teacher fuses these with the techniques recommended to teach the positive psychology taxonomy benchmark of success along with the academic curriculum. Accomplishment is the by-product of successful learning so the academic curriculum must teach it. Children able to successfully pursue and accomplish goals are also more likely to improve academic performance and generate a sense of closure, satisfaction, and fulfillment.

To teach accomplishment, the teacher plans effective ways to teach the four pillars of success: (1) well-regulated actions, (2) well-balanced actions, (3) well-supported actions, and (4) well-defined actions. All of these contribute to the educational success that depends on accomplishment. The teacher focuses on teaching these by using the Positive Psychology Teacher's Success Toolbox techniques so children accomplish more in the classroom.

The Success Toolbox provides specific techniques the teacher uses to teach accomplishment and integrate it into the traditional academic curriculum. The techniques help younger children establish goals, discover their assets, and get comfortable with individualized e-learning. Older children learn how to achieve goals, use their assets, and maximize the power of the e-curriculum to ensure accomplishment. The teacher may use the recommended techniques in the Success Toolbox as part of a larger program, within a comprehensive curriculum, as a themed unit, as stand-alone lessons, as enrichment activities, or in learning games children play.

Positive psychology programs may include a fully developed curriculum that teaches all the benchmarks, a themed unit that teaches one, a series of lessons to assess one, a weekly schedule of activities to process one, a daily exercise that practices one, or a learning game to reinforce one. Whatever form and format a positive psychology program takes, it always uses some, if not all, of the Success Toolbox techniques. The Positive Psychology Teacher's Success Toolbox techniques include (1) goal setting, (2) asset development and exploitation, and (3) e-curriculum and democratic education. The teacher uses these techniques to teach children how to accomplish their goals and achieve emotional, social, and academic success. Children practice how to express feelings, rally strengths, acknowledge relationships, and articulate their potentialities and commitments.

The positive psychology teaching taxonomy benchmark of accomplishment uses these techniques to teach the pillars of successful learning by teaching students to establish goals, develop an action plan, monitor goals, assess progress, and reengineer plans as needed. The taxonomy of success teaches them to identify the personal and community assets available to them and leverage them for success. The taxonomy of success teaches them to exploit e-learning to customize and democratize their learning based on interests, comfortable pace of learning, and an individualized learning experience. The e-curriculum engages multiple senses, stimulates natural curiosity, develops inductive reasoning, captures emotion, directs strengths, and brings authentic meaning to the process. The techniques are multidimensional, and each targets one of the indicators of success.

The teacher is in the best position to decide what pillars of success to teach and what techniques work best so children flourish in the elementary-school classroom. Children choose the goals they want to accomplish by working toward them confidently. They decide what assets

Table 8.1. The Teacher's Toolbox: Pillars and Techniques of Successful Learning

Well-Regulated Actions	Well-Balanced Actions	Well-Supported Actions	Well-Defined Actions
Goal Setting	Goal Setting	Goal Setting	Goal Setting
Asset Development	Asset Development	Asset Development	Asset Development
E-Curriculum	E-Curriculum	E-Curriculum	E-Curriculum

are available and how to enlarge them. They learn how to take advantage of technology to augment learning assets. They use the strengths of emotional fluency, social flexibility, and purposeful inquiry that preface accomplishment.

The positive psychology teaching taxonomy of accomplishment teaches self-interest, not self-sacrifice. Can children summon a positive emotion, engage a strength, solicit a friend, or find new enlightenment to build success? What contribution do they make that compensates all involved, including themselves? Are they able to do a humble task with the same level of engagement as a grander one? Are they able to find meaning when most bereft? Emotional strength is its own reward and the earned currency of success. The promise of positive psychology in the classroom is that it is not a tournament model where some win and some lose—instead, everyone wins.

1. Goal Setting

The positive psychology teaching taxonomy benchmark of success helps children to define their goals. The teacher does not impose goals. Instead, he or she gives children a voice in setting them and teaches a process for pursuing them. When children believe they have control over outcomes, and that their feelings, strengths, relationships, and purposes matter, they are more likely to feel satisfied with their efforts and results. Children who exhibit an external locus of control—or the conviction that outside influences are not controlling—are more likely to accomplish their goals.

The positive psychology teaching taxonomy shifts the focus from building self-esteem to building self-efficacy. When children learn to establish clear personal academic, social, and emotional goals, and then complete them, there is an expected accomplishment that is self-directed and not teacher-imposed. Goal setting involves high-level, deductive critical-thinking skills as children define their goals, imagine different paths to the goals, plan their actions, execute those actions, assess the success of their actions, decide to continue or discontinue their actions, record their actions, review performances, report accomplishments, and reformulate the goals or the process to accomplish the goals as needed. Goal setting helps to ensure a well-defined life necessary for success.

Goal setting requires children to define the goal in operational and measurable terms, and they learn to communicate it in concrete ways.

"I want to be an astronaut" becomes "I am interested in the NASA Mars mission. I will research Mars and write a five-page report because astronauts need to know as much as possible about the planets."

Children learn to list as many ways to accomplish a goal as they can generate, and this component of goal setting requires emotionally creative, flexible, fluent, and original thinking. They learn to consider a goal in a flexible way from multiple perspectives and find more than one path to accomplish a goal. They learn to consider the goal in a fluid way by connecting it to other goals and recognizing how multiple accomplishments are connected. They learn to substitute one goal for another as they use original thinking.

If children approach a goal in this way, they choose from multiple options if the first attempt fails. The first step to success is deciding on the goal and establishing it. The second step is choosing the best path to the goal and then committing to it. The third step is listing the action steps and flowing with it. Lastly, as children progress toward their goal, they assess their progress toward it and make adjustments and course corrections as needed. Their action plan has checkpoints, so children monitor their own progress toward the goal. For children to accomplish any goal, the plan must be developed, monitored, assessed, implemented, reported, and reformulated as needed. Children are action-oriented in a well-planned and purposeful way.

Journal writing is a precursor to goal setting for all children. Children use journals to list their goals, detail their action plans to accomplish them, report success or not, and describe reformulated plans. The act of writing goals clarifies their plans, makes them more concrete, and increases the expectation that the goals are achievable. There are a number of goal-setting and planning books to use. Younger children use the book *Star of the Sea* to help them begin their goal work.[4] This inspiring story informs children about the important role of a small but fascinating sea creature with a hope. The *Reaching Your Goals* book is another excellent resource for children 10–12 years old.[5] The book begins, "I want to be the fastest runner on the track team." From that point forward, children develop an action plan to move closer to that goal. The Goalforit website complements the ideas presented in the book and offers goal-setting tutorials, videos, behavior charts, chore charts, to-do list templates, and more.[6]

Young children just beginning to learn about goals enjoy the Magic Wand game. Children sit in a circle and take turns making a wish. The teacher waves the magic wand and says, "For me and you —wishes come true." Then she asks the children how likely it is the wish will come true and guides them in a discussion about the differences between wishes and goals. The class picks one wish each and develops an action plan to make the wish come true. They also play the How Long Will It Take? game. The teacher describes an accomplishment and the children discuss how long it will take to achieve it. Another game for young children is the I Want to Be game. Children discuss what they want to be when they grow up and consider what they will have to do to become a ballerina or a firefighter.

Children develop near- or far-term academic and career exploration goals that direct their attention to long-term plans. In an ever-changing world, career accomplishment is an important variable in life success, and discussing career goals cultivates a sense of accomplishment and, eventually, results in a planned, informed career pursuit. Young children explore career goals and older children research them.

The Learning for Life program is a grade-differentiated integrated academic and character development program for K–12, with a career education focus.[7] The curriculum teaches eight core character traits: respect, responsibility, honesty/trust, caring/fairness, perseverance, self-discipline, courage, and citizenship through career exploration.

The curriculum consists of 61 lesson plans at each level (K–2, 3–4, 5–6) that teach empathy, critical thinking, conflict resolution, responsibility, perseverance, courage, interpersonal skills, and ethical decision making with career planning. A formative assessment is available to monitor student progress, and sample lessons are available in both English and Spanish.

Helping children to explore the affective requirements of any career teaches the positive psychology taxonomy benchmark of success. What strengths do pilots need? What feelings are good for a nurse to possess? Why do construction workers need friends? Do you think working as a zoologist is meaningful? The KidsGov website is an interactive experience that exposes children to every career option available from A to Z (accountant to zoologist).[8] Children decide what emotions, strengths, and relationships certain jobs require and what the contribution of that job to helping self and others would be.

Goal setting and goal pursuit make children more likely to believe that they can accomplish a goal and know how to do it. If they can imagine it, and write it down, they can do it. The positive psychology teaching taxonomy benchmark of success helps children understand a goal as a concept and teaches them skills to accomplish a goal. The positive psychology teacher links goal development and strength-based actions. Goal: To be kind to everyone I meet this week. Strength: Giving at least three verbal compliments a day.

A child's goal is not to "be smarter." Rather, she learns to set a goal to be more determined or to be more forgiving. Accomplished children know what they want to do, when to do it, where to do it, why to do it, and how to do it well. They have goals and plans.

2. Asset Development and Exploitation

Emotional assets are the key to a well-regulated and well-balanced life. Recent research on asset development identifies "what kids need to succeed."[9] Based on surveys of more than three million children in more than 60 countries, the research identified 40 specific developmental assets as predictive of children's success. The research proved a direct link between developmental assets and academic achievement.[10] The more developmental assets available to children, the greater the likelihood of success as measured across all variables.

Elementary-aged children need 40 specific developmental assets to succeed.[11] The particular assets vary somewhat by age, differentiating assets for children in grades K–3 and grades 4–8. However, both lists include internal and external assets organized into the same two categories: (1) internal commitment to learning, positive values, social competencies, and positive identity, and (2) external support, empowerment, boundaries and expectations, and use of time. For all children aged 5–12, the internal assets parallel the positive psychology teaching taxonomy benchmark of accomplishment.

For example, children need positive identity assets such as caring, honesty, and social justice. They need social competencies such as conflict-resolution skills, interpersonal skills, and planning abilities. They need a sense of belonging at school, engagement in learning, and pleasure from reading. These assets help children balance their emotions with strengths.

The Search Institute offers resources for teachers to use to develop the assets that easily transplant into a positive psychology program. There is an asset checklist to use with children for self-assessment purposes. An activity generator suggests activities that build assets: encourage children to write letters to the editor of the local newspaper about an issue of concern. A conversation generator suggests conversations that build assets: What is your biggest dream? What is the first step you can take toward achieving it? There are e-cards, bookmarks, posters, newsletters, podcasts, and a library of publications offering ideas to develop assets by age.

The Search Institute publishes *Building Assets Is Elementary: Group Activities for Helping Kids 8–12 Succeed*, which offers 60 activities to build 40 assets. Activity sheets such as "What a Kid Needs and What a Kids Wants," "Care Package," and "That Reminds Me" all cultivate one of the 40 assets. The Friendship Sandwich game directs children to write down suggestions for anyone who sees another child eating lunch alone. The activity sheets put the positive psychology taxonomy to work.

For younger children, there is an eight-book series, the Adding Assets Series for Kids.[12] A favorite title, *Doing and Being Your Best*, teaches children to act in accomplished ways by showing cooperation, confidence, and fortitude as correlates of success. Accomplished children compile a portfolio of assets that uses positive emotions, strengths, relationships, and contributions to attain their goals. Positive psychology teaches emotional equations that add up to the assets needed for success and these support good actions and outcomes. Accomplishment is the peak achievement of positive psychology.

The positive psychology teaching taxonomy creates the framework for asset development and provides a teaching manual for turning those assets into accomplishments. Many children do not accomplish their goals because the positive psychology teaching taxonomy is often absent in the curriculum.

Martin Haberman encapsulates this same concern in his article "The Pedagogy of Poverty."[13] He cites a wide range of effective teaching functions such as peer tutoring or cooperative learning; however, he laments that none has emerged as a basic style or technique. Instead, he lists 14 teacher actions commonly produced and labeled as teaching functions: some examples are giving information, asking questions, giving tests, reviewing assignments, marking papers, and punishing noncompliant behavior. He also makes note of ancillary tasks such as record keeping and parent meetings. He claims that urban teachers function primarily using this basic menu approach at all levels and subjects and argues that these "traditional, basic, orderly" teacher functions do not work.[14] Instead, these functions are emblematic of how schools typically do business, and define a pedagogy of poverty.[15] This pedagogy of poverty appeals to educators with less compassion, who substitute conventional wisdom for thoughtful analysis, exercise soft bigotry, and who are not conversant with a full range of more effective options.

Haberman goes on to describe what *does* work, based on his extensive and impeccable body of research. Education works when children are engaged in lessons that address vital concerns, consider human differences, discuss important ideas, promote choice, apply ideals such as fairness and equity, design active learning, group diverse peers, shift perspective, review and revise work and decisions, use technology, and require reflection. "Whenever students are involved with explanations of human differences [including strengths,] good teaching is going on."[16] His conclusions as to what constitutes effective teaching reads like a litany of positive psychology. The positive psychology taxonomy benchmarks, and associated indicators, define a new pedagogy of success in the elementary classroom. When schools adopt a pedagogy of success, all children will have the opportunity to achieve their potential. "A positive psychology perspective . . . challenges us to think critically about the degree to which schools and school processes support children's optimum adjustment. We believe schools . . . contribute to a student's positive adjustment when schools function as psychologically healthy environments."[17]

The positive psychology teaching taxonomy benchmark of success teaches the interpersonal and intrapersonal assets of positive psychology. Success is not assessed based on how children measure up but on what they try to do and what they accomplish. Asset identification and use ensures a well-regulated, well-balanced, and accomplished life.

3. Democratic Learning and E-Curriculum

A well-supported life is the premise of democratic education. Children have choices and make decisions in a supportive environment as a matter of civic engagement. There is a resurgence in the democratic learning movement, tagging schools as essential to the preservation of democracy and promoting democratic practices in the classroom as a means of teaching children participatory democracy.

From the Free School Movement, where all decision making rests with children, to the League of Professional Schools, which emphasizes a democratic learning community, there are more guided choices for children and more opportunities for contribution to the larger community.[18] The Forum for Education and Democracy adds to the list by suggesting the importance of habits of good judgment that nurture the democratic life, a common knowledge base for understanding the self and others, and personalization of education.[19] The former director of the Forum, Sam Chaltain, writes, "My passion is helping people create democratic work environments where everyone is learning and empowered and supportive of each other, and where it's always a good idea to ask tough questions, challenge assumptions, and experiment with new ideas and ways of unleashing human potential."[20] Democratic education is well-supported education.

The Institute for Democratic Education in America defines democratic education "as learning that equips every human being to participate fully in a healthy democracy and empowers young people to be autonomous, responsible members of their community and the larger world." To accomplish this end, children help shape their own learning as citizens of the classroom. Factory schools and assembly-line education is rejected, and unique emotional strengths are celebrated. The positive psychology teaching taxonomy benchmark of success provides an overarching schematic for democratic education. A flourishing democracy is dependent on citizens who understand it and can fully participate in it. To fully participate in a democracy, children must learn the pedagogy of success.

Support for individual advancement, tolerance for diversity of thought and ideas, active participation in learning and decision making, and sensory immersion in the democratic process are the corollaries of democratic education and positive psychology benchmarks. Positive psychology marries democratic education with an understanding of neuroscience.

E-learning is a positive psychology technique that democratizes education and supports children in their learning to scaffold them to strengths-based success at their own pace and in their own way. E-learning supports individual gain and the collective good. In the 21st century, an e-curriculum is a near-perfect platform for teaching the benchmark of success. An e-curriculum is high-quality, online, and digital. Self-directed, self-guided e-learning teaches emotional regulation and engages signature strengths. The interactive nature invites children to play together and to choose content, forms, and formats meaningful for them. The learning is accessible, widely available, and underutilized.

The more exposure to e-learning a child has, the more accomplished he or she becomes. Students can visit the world without leaving their desks. They listen to symphonies at Carnegie Hall, travel into space with NASA, join an African safari with National Geographic, and listen to librarians read them a book. There are museum, encyclopedia, newspaper, tourism, and special-interest websites to teach children whatever captivates their imagination and enlightens perspectives in personal and motivating ways that engage their emotional strength, assign meaning to what they are doing, and share their learning with friends in class and around the world.

The best e-curriculum requires children to produce authentic work products and to solve challenging problems with balanced emotions and strengths while working in teams. For example, in science, children design and test online roller coasters and explore how their bodies work.[21] There are approximately 6,000 educational applications for mobile digital devices with the catalog always growing and expanding. These applications are engaging children with technological wizardry from interactive e-books that invite children to read along to simulated chemistry experiments done in the palm of the hand. There are hundreds of interactive educational websites and applications that deliver e-curricula in every subject and that teach every academic standard.

The Stock Market Game requires reading, research, and problem solving in mathematics, history, and economics, as well as the skills of data tracking, data analysis, and data valuing. At the same time, fifth-grade children work cooperatively with others by using their emotional strength to make informed decisions and decide on investment goals to establish and pursue.

E-chess also teaches the positive psychology teaching taxonomy of success and children can play chess online with each other or with children from all over the world on the ChessKid website.[22] The teacher can have children play each other on chess day, sponsor in-class chess clubs, and register them for tournaments. The website offers free online tutorials and games.

Chess engages the executive functions of the brain and matures cognitive, affective, and conative skills. On a cognitive level, children who play chess must focus intently, analyze concrete sequences of events, and think abstractly. On an affective level, they must self-regulate emotions, relax and understand their opponents, use strengths of visualization and shifting perspectives, anticipate outcomes, and plan their next moves. On the conative level, to accomplish the tasks and succeed in the game, they execute the best action based on balanced emotion and reasoned thought. When children play a chess game, whether they win or not, they use their entire repertoire of positive psychology abilities—strengthening affective, cognitive, and conative learning. Playing chess is emotionally transformative and creates the positive psychology of flow that generates satisfaction and fulfillment whether children win or lose. The process of chess, not the product or result, creates chess success.

Another e-curriculum option is the e-civic lesson. The iCivics website is an outstanding website that prepares children to become knowledgeable, engaged 21st-century citizens by creating online materials.[23] In 2009, former Supreme Court Justice Sandra Day O'Connor founded iCivics to reverse Americans' declining civic knowledge and participation in their democracy. She believed that it was critical to teach the next generation to understand and connect to the democratic system of governance. iCivics is committed to passing along the legacy of democracy to children and produces online educational videogames and curriculum materials.

The iCivics curriculum is organized into 14 units: Boys and Girls Clubs, budgeting, citizenship and participation, civil rights, foundations of government, international affairs, media and influence, persuasive writing, politics and public policy, state and local government, the Constitution, the executive branch, the legislative branch, and the judicial branch of the United States government.

There are 16 high-quality interactive games, and each is playable within one class session. Children play the games on computers individually or in a group using a smartboard. The games are self-contained and suitable for elementary students in grades 1–5; they do not require any prior knowledge. The games provide a detailed printed progress for assessment purposes. Quick, interactive webquests enrich the games and teach specific civic topics in more detail. They include reading and questions with links to specific web resources that help older children understand how the topic relates to the real world. Teachers deliver web quests by a projector, smartboard, or individual computers.

Each unit includes many lessons differentiated by grade level; each includes everything the teacher needs. The teacher simply prints the materials and follows the step-by-step instructions to teach the lesson. The lessons are practical and engaging, individual activities are easy to manage and self-contained, and there is always an authentic work product to collect at the end of the lesson. The lessons use a problem-solving approach that is relevant to children's own lives, visually appealing, written in a conversational tone, and important.

Teaching positive psychology benefits not only individual children, but also the larger community. Children are academically competent and they are prepared to take their place in a complex, dynamic democratic system. They learn to manage their emotions in the town square, to use their strengths to preserve self-governance, to work cooperatively, and to build consensus with fellow citizens from diverse backgrounds. They learn to accommodate different points of view; tolerate political, ethnic, and religious differences; and contribute to the greater good through meaningful engagement. An e-curriculum uses civics education to teach the positive psychology teaching taxonomy benchmark of success so children flourish.

On another website, children take the U.S. Citizenship Quiz online—the same test that immigrants take to become naturalized citizens.[24] The quiz is a catalyst for discussion of immigration issues and teaches children that if they truly support their country, they must learn as much as possible about it. After they learn about it, they practice acting on their new learning. The PBS Kids Democracy Project is a presidential election website that sponsors a sticker race.[25] The children research profiles of candidates and their positions on the issues, and then they participate in a mock election in order to vote and learn how government affects them.

The Khan Academy is e-tutoring with 15-minute micro lessons in mathematics, science, finance, history, and more that are focused, personal, accessible, visual, self-paced, and self-engaging.[26] The e-tutoring approach provides customized, self-directed traditional academic instruction and complements the positive psychology teaching taxonomy benchmark of accomplishment. Free of the limitation of direct content instruction, the teacher can focus on emotional and strengths learning as the children work on the problems. She can enrich morning e-lessons with afternoon class journals, service learning, and clubs that enrich both the academic and emotional curricula.

An e-curriculum engages cognitive, emotional, and conative learning so that children achieve academic objectives and accomplish important positive psychology benchmarks using technology. Children explore academic subjects that are meaningful to them by using their individual strengths, both alone and in groups, using the e-curriculum to develop divergent thinking so they can reflect meaningfully on themselves, their strengths, friends, intentions, contributions, goals, accomplishments, and overall well-being. Coupled with the new social media, an e-curriculum is also an outlet for the practice of positive psychology, whether writing in a private online journal, assessing strengths using online surveys, sharing thoughts and feelings with friends on social media, or signing online petitions about important issues.

Self-published books that tell the stories of their family heroes, a random kindness class wiki, a pass-it-forward tweet, or a blog about friendship offer opportunities to share emotions, learning engagement, and meaningful actions with friends and others. There are many e-curriculum production tools to use to spread the promise of positive psychology and to create a well-supported life of success.

Summary and Conclusion

The accomplished child is a successful child. If children truly know their emotions, identify their strengths, build grit, connect with others, find meaning no matter the task, and become accomplished citizens, they will achieve more academically. The positive psychology teaching taxonomy benchmark of success emphasizes accomplishment. Accomplished children express and regulate emotions, activate signature strengths, develop positive relationships, and assign meaning to their work. Children are accomplished and successful when they know how to apply the principles and practices of positive psychology.

Children can move beyond traditional academic constraints so they learn to know themselves, others, their convictions, and their potential: Increased academic achievement is the by-product. Teachers infuse academic knowledge into the positive psychology teaching taxonomy of success in a systematic and dedicated way every day by meeting the benchmarks and demonstrating the indicators while teaching subjects such as history and academic skills such as reading.

The nations attending the first International Summit on Education agreed that the key indicator of quality education is how well teachers develop the whole child.[27] Many nations are ahead of the United States in the area of positive psychology education. For example, the Global Chinese Positive Psychology Association is now one of the most authoritative psychology organizations in China. Its mission is scientific research and application of positive psychology to improve well-being.[28]

As the positive psychology teaching taxonomy spreads across the Chinese countryside, there is the potential to touch 300 million elementary-aged schoolchildren. As it spreads around the world, its influence will be remarkable. As teachers in the United States practice and perfect it, they will find themselves at the forefront of an educational renaissance, sharing the positive psychology taxonomy of success.

In his book, Yong Zhao makes the case that it is imperative that children are encouraged to travel diverse, flexible paths toward meaningful learning.[29] He writes about how China decided to change its "test orientation" education system to an "innovation-orientation" system because high test scores do not guarantee the number of Nobel Laureates, original patents, and scientific discoveries that the United States produced in the 20th century—more than anywhere else in the world.

The Chinese attributed this to the open, creative, individualized, U.S. public education system in place before the reform movement copied China's abandoned test-oriented and standardized model. Grounded in the neuroscience and social science of learning, positive psychology changes children by teaching them to change themselves in healthy and adaptive ways. Every day in the classroom, children manage difficult emotions, conflicting virtues, problematic relationships, unclear purposes, and varying degrees of competency across a multitude of academic subjects.

Accomplished children work more cooperatively, feel greater contentment, exude more confidence, show more fortitude, embrace more peace, seek more inspiration, and find more joy in learning. They honor pledges to stay positive and finish projects, make friends using signature strengths, find meaning in every experience, and seek to accomplish their goals. They look forward to coming to school in the morning and leave feeling satisfied in the afternoon.

The pinnacle of accomplishment in positive psychology is the harnessing of positive emotions, engagement, relationships, meaning, and success to achieve academic, emotional, and social well-being. Rather than learning compliant behavior for an external reward, children learn autonomous behavior for internal benefit. Instructional strategies such as service learning, conflict resolution, resiliency training, flow play periods, journals, and much more explicitly teach the correlates of well-being.

Children learn new and better ways to live, love, work, play, and learn. Positive psychology teaches children the art and science of self-assessment, self-discovery, self-calming, and self-actualization by using positive emotions, strengths, relationships, purpose, and satisfaction of accomplishment across the academic curriculum. Positive psychology takes children up the down staircase to find happiness, strength, friends, and purpose.

This is not only the promise of positive psychology—it is the gift of positive psychology to education. It is a gift that, when a teacher gives it to children, she or he also gives it to herself or himself, the community, and the future. The teacher sends children into a future where he or she will not go. Students will go alone, and no teacher can foresee which one will be sent to war, lose a child, go back to night school, compete in the Ivy League, survive a tornado, invent a gadget, become a leader, make a fortune, or lose their health.

Despite their knowledge and teaching tools, teachers do not have crystal balls. The very best that they can do for the children sitting in front of them—for one short year—is send them into their futures with positive emotion, strength, friendship, purpose, and a few accomplishments tucked into their backpacks. If this is a teacher's legacy, it will be lasting and such a teacher is always fondly remembered.

The Positive Psychology Teaching Taxonomy: Guiding Propositions

Positive psychology teaches children the emotional strengths needed to self-regulate and generate positive emotion, build and broaden signature strengths, create and maintain relationships, find and invoke meaning, and accomplish their dreams. Five propositions synthesize the positive psychology standards, clarify essential understandings, and guide teachers in the implementation of the taxonomy. The guiding propositions compose the fundamental values of positive psychology and help teachers understand them in a simple and pragmatic way.

There are five guiding positive psychology propositions that cultivate emotional strength: (1) create positive emotion by learning to tell a positive **emotional story** about feelings, (2) cultivate engagement by developing **emotional buoyancy** as a signature strength, (3) share **emotional strengths** with others to foster intimacy, (4) find meaning in failure by developing a growth **mind-set**, and (5) envision accomplishments by using emotional **imagination.**

1. **Positive Emotional Story** (http://www.redemptiveself.northwestern.edu/). Self-narrative aggregates what children hear and learn to tell themselves. Children who tell themselves a hopeful story, convince themselves there will be a positive outcome, and persuade themselves they can manage their feelings do better

in school. Children learn to self-promote and to self-talk themselves into success. Teach children happily ever after and to find the golden self.

2. **Emotional Buoyancy** (http://theoptimismbias.com/). Emotional buoyancy enables children to pick themselves up after falling down, brush themselves off, and get back to work. Children exhibit a resiliency that is courageous enough to bend but not break. They know that success is bold, to take chances, and to not falter. They succeed and fail with equal grace, knowing that failure is the first step on the ladder of success. Teach children grit.

3. **Positive Emotional Strength** (https://www.strengths-explorer.com/). Emotional strength empowers children to mediate their feelings so they take balanced action. Children learn to act from a position of strength toward self and others. They know engagement occurs when they and others acknowledge strengths and provide opportunities to demonstrate them. Teach children that strength is power and to find the golden mean.

4. **Positive Mind-set** (http://mindsetonline.com/). Children understand that failure is a natural part of the developmental process. They learn to avoid a fixed mind-set that expects success every time and to develop a growth mind-set that associates accomplishment with persistent effort and an open mind. Teach children to overcome.

5. **Emotional Imagination** (http://www.positivityratio.com/). Children imagine positive potentialities and possibilities to explore and envision positive efforts and outcomes. They deploy inventive thinking that suggests new approaches and strategies, and they conjure up, and capture, positive feelings to replace negative ones. Teach children positivity.

Case Study K–2: Teaching Accomplishment

Amanda arrived at school at mid-year and could not read or write. She had missed the first semester of first grade due to her family's financial struggles and relocation. Every day she worked with the reading coach before and after school for 4 hours each day. She earned an F on her spelling tests weekly. She knew how to spell the words but could not write them down fast enough. She was not in a reading group because she was too far behind and she had few friends. Other children laughed at her. Yet she was kind to them and smiled through every day. She was determined not to give up. Every day, she tried hard although it seemed that she would never catch up. By the end of year, she was reading at grade level. At the end of eighth grade, she went to college, and she graduated before she turned 18. When you ask her what she learned, she says, "I learned to never give up and to be strong no matter what. I will tell you learning that lesson was just as important as learning to read—maybe even more important."

Case Study 3–5: Teaching Accomplishment

Chris had been at his new school for a week. He had made a few acquaintances but was still feeling uncomfortable. His family had moved five times in the past 4 years and being the new kid again was hard on him. He was a smart boy with a very kind heart. However, he was shy and did not feel safe enough to reveal his feelings. On the playground, he walked around, pretty much keeping to himself, when he noticed a group of boys from his class picking on a classmate. Gabe tried to run away but they ran after him and threw rocks at him. Chris sprang into action, going to Gabe's defense. Surprised, the boys backed off but one pushed him and he pushed back. He did not know he was in a shoving match with the principal's son. The principal ordered them both into his office. Chris figured he was now the one in trouble because he was the new kid. After all, no one knew him and, if that was not bad enough, this kid's dad had all the power. He was scared the principal would punish him for trying to do the right thing. It would not be the first time. The others would lie and no one would believe him because he was the new kid that no one knew. Gabe would be too afraid to tell the truth. The rumors would start—that new kid is a troublemaker. Chris was almost crying thinking he would never fit in anywhere . . . he would never have any friends. Then an amazing thing happened. The boy who shoved him told the truth. The principal told Chris he was brave to stick up for Gabe and welcomed him to school. He told his son to write a letter of apology to both of them and that he and the other boys involved would spend a week of recess on the kindergarten playground playing with the little ones and picking up all the rocks on the playground. The boys shook hands and were told to eat lunch together. The principal's son invited Chris over on Saturday to play video games. He was sure that this was the happiest day of his life. He was going to like it here.

Guiding Question Exercise

What is your definition of success? What three accomplishments make you most proud of yourself: How do these accomplishments make you feel? What signature strength did you use in pursuing these accomplishments? Are the accomplishments the results of goals that you established or a by-product of other effort? Are your accomplishments the result of your own efforts or did others help you? What makes these accomplishments meaningful to you? What is your hallmark accomplishment? Do you have a hallmark goal for the future? How do you define success for the children that you teach? What have the children in your class accomplished? How do you think accomplishment is different than achievement? What positive psychology teaching taxonomy technique do you currently use to ensure accomplished children and scaffold their success? What positive psychology teaching taxonomy technique would you like to begin using? Do you think this technique can change accomplishment in your classroom? If so, how?

Guiding Question Discussion

Teachers distinguish between accomplishment and achievement with one constructed as intrapersonal and the other as interpersonal success. One is a gain score and one is a normed score. Accomplishments are meaningful when connected to our emotional lives and our signature strengths. Accomplishment flows from what we are naturally good at thinking, feeling, and doing—and what we choose, decide, and desire to do. When we regulate our emotions and engage by not only using but by bringing attention to our strengths, we become accomplished in the area of endeavor. Accomplishment may be individual or dependent on the support of others. When we identify exactly what we want to accomplish, it is easier to identify the emotions and strengths we need to succeed. To accomplish our goals, we must fall down, learn to get up, learn to begin again, learn to retell the story, and imagine a new and better ending.

Web Resources for Children

Enchanted Learning, http://www.enchantedlearning.com/Home.html.
Goal Setting Activities for Kids, http://goalsettingactivities4kids.com/.

The Happiness Club, http://www.thehappinessclub.com/.
KidsKnowIt, http://www.kidsknowit.com/.
Time Magazine Election 2012, http://www.timeforkids.com/
minisite/election-2012.

Web Resources for Teachers

Center for Civic Education Lesson Plans, http://new.civiced.org/
resources/.
Chess Academy for Teachers, http://www.thechessacademy.org/
lessons.html.
Well-Being Finder, http://www.wbfinder.com/home.aspx.
William Glasser Institute, http://www.wglasser.com/.
Zhao Learning, http://zhaolearning.com/.

POSITIVE PSYCHOLOGY TEACHING TAXONOMY: BENCHMARKS AND INDICATORS

Positive Emotion	Engagement Strength	Relationships Friendship	Meaning Contribution	Accomplish Success
Feeling Indicators	Strength Indicators	Friendship Indicators	Contribution Indicators	Teach Success Indicators
Feel Caring/ Kindly Not Angry	Demonstrate Empathy	Offer Forgiveness	Value Tolerance	Embrace Cooperation
Feel Grateful Not Selfish	Demonstrate Generosity	Offer Gratitude	Value Helpfulness	Embrace Contentment
Feel Brave Not Afraid	Demonstrate Courage	Offer Honesty	Value Fairness	Embrace Confidence
Feel Determined Not Unsure	Demonstrate Grit	Offer Commitment	Value Resilience	Embrace Fortitude
Feel Calm/ Relaxed Not Frustrated	Demonstrate Patience	Offer Support	Value Peace	Embrace Serenity
Feel Hopeful Not Discouraged	Demonstrate Optimism	Offer Enthusiasm	Value Anticipation	Embrace Inspiration
Feel Happy Not Sad	Demonstrate Good Cheer	Offer Gladness	Value Enjoyment	Embrace Joy

POSITIVE PSYCHOLOGY PLANNING TEMPLATE: TAXONOMY OF TECHNIQUES

Method	Positive Emotion	Engagement and Strengths	Relationship	Meaning	Accomplishment
Class Greetings					
Journaling					
Class Meetings					
Pledges and Creeds					
Art, Music, Dance, and Drama					
Stress Reduction					
Precision Language					
Learning Centers					
Teams and Clubs					
Positive Psych Exercises					
Infused Academics					
E-Learning					

Notes

_____

_____

_____

_____

_____

_____

_____

_____

POSITIVE PSYCHOLOGY PLANNING TEMPLATE: CLASS MEETINGS

Meetings	Feelings	Engagement	Friendships	Service	Mastery
Class Meeting					
Sharing Circles					
Curriculum Focused					
Literature Circles					
Brainstorming					
Problem Solving					
Interview and Exchange					
Good News					
Celebrating					
Recognition					
Appreciation					
Exercises and Games					
Suggestion Box					
Goal Setting					

Notes

_____
_____
_____
_____
_____
_____
_____

POSITIVE PSYCHOLOGY PLANNING TEMPLATE: EMOTIONS LITERATURE CIRCLE

	Empathy	Courage	Gratitude	Grit	Optimism
Kindergarten Book(s)					
First-Grade Book(s)					
Second-Grade Book(s)					
Third-Grade Book(s)					
Fourth-Grade Book(s)					
Fifth-Grade Book(s)					
E-Learning					

Notes

POSITIVE PSYCHOLOGY TEACHING TAXONOMY: GRAPHIC ORGANIZERS

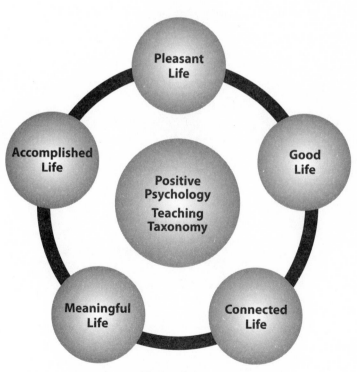

Figure A.1.

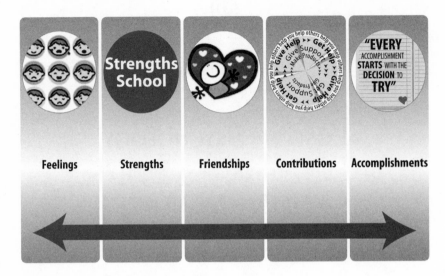

Figure A.2. Positive Psychology Teaching Taxonomy Continuum

Positive Psychology According to Winnie the Pooh

Positive psychology teaches children the emotional strengths needed to self-regulate and generate positive emotion, build and broaden signature strengths, create and maintain relationships, find and invoke meaning, and accomplish their dreams. The guiding propositions summarize the core standards, clarify the essential understandings, and guide teachers in the implementation of the positive psychology teaching taxonomy.

Teach Children Positivity (http://www.positivityratio.com/)

> *Nobody can be uncheered with a balloon.*
> —Winnie the Pooh

Teach children to recognize, express, and moderate feelings and strategies to replace negative emotions with positive ones. Teach children to stretch their emotional imagination so they are able to visualize positive potentialities and possibilities by enlisting their natural curiosity to explore and envision a successful effort and positive outcome. Children learn to deploy inventive and innovative thinking that suggests new positive approaches and strategies. They conjure up positive feelings to replace negative ones. They recall a positive feeling and capture it at will.

Teach Children the Golden Mean (https://www.strengths-explorer
.com/)

> *It is hard to be brave when you are only a Very Small Animal.*
> —Winnie the Pooh

Teach children to identify their emotional strengths: they need to know what they like to do and what they are good at doing whether it is courage or patience. Teach children to use their emotional strength to mediate and moderate their feelings to they can choose balanced actions. Children learn to act from a position of strength. They know engagement occurs when they acknowledge strengths in themselves, and others, and when there are opportunities to demonstrate it. They empower themselves using their strengths.

Teach Children the Golden Self (http://www.redemptiveself.north
western.edu/).

> *Did you ever stop to think, and forget to start again?*
> —Winnie the Pooh

Teach children to tell themselves a hopeful story and convince themselves there will be a positive outcome. Teach children to aggregate what they tell themselves, and what others tell them, into a positive explanatory style that enlightens them. Children learn to self-promote and to self-talk themselves into success. They learn to create a self-narrative that encourages success and manages disappointment with equanimity, and they use private speech to navigate both calm and troubled waters. They tell themselves a happily ever after story and find the golden self.

Teach Children to Fail (http://theoptimismbias.com/)

> *Ever have one of those days where you just can't win?*
> —Winnie the Pooh

Teach children to understand failure as a natural part of the developmental process. Teach children to overcome failure as a prerequisite for accomplishment. Children learn to avoid a fixed mind-set that expects success every time. They learn to develop a growth mind-set that associates accomplishment with persistent effort. They learn to use a growth mind-set to overcome obstacles.

Teach Children Grit (http://mindsetonline.com/)

> *You are braver than you believe, stronger than you seem, and smarter than you think.*
>
> —Winnie the Pooh

Teach children to pick themselves up after falling down, brush themselves off, and get back to work. Teach children resiliency so they bend and do not break. Children learn to be bold, take chances, and not to be afraid. They learn to put on their emotional lifejackets and jump back into the water because they are emotionally buoyant. They learn to try again and to try another way to accomplish the goal.

POSITIVE PSYCHOLOGY LESSON PLAN TEMPLATE

Use the template to design a project-based lesson plan that teaches the positive psychology teaching taxonomy. Identify what positive psychology benchmarks and indicators you will target and what positive psychology methods and techniques you will use.

Positive Psychology Standard _____

Positive Psychology Benchmark _____

Positive Psychology Indicator _____

Positive Psychology Method _____

Positive Psychology Technique _____

Guiding Question   What Feelings, Thoughts and Actions Expected?

Subject(s)   What Subject(s) Will You Teach?

Concept(s)   What Concept or Concepts Will You Teach?

Skill(s)   What Skill or Skills Will You Teach?

Project/Activity   What Is the Project, Problem, or Activity to Develop?

Materials/Resources   What Materials or Resources Will You Need?

Equipment	Is Any Special Equipment Needed?
Technology	Is Any Technology Needed?
Schedule	What Is the Schedule for the Lesson?
Universal Design	Affective, Cognitive, or Conative?
Curriculum Layers	How Will You Differentiate the Curriculum?
Adaptations	What Are the Accommodations/ Modifications, If Any?
Assessment	How Will You Access Accomplishment or Progress?
Home Follow-Up	How Will You Involve Parents/ Caregivers?

Notes

Chapter 1

1. The Positive Psychology Center. (2007). *Overview of positive psychology.* Philadelphia: University of Pennsylvania, p. 1. Retrieved from http://www.ppc.sas.upenn.edu/

2. Leckie, Robert. (1998). *The wars of America.* Minneapolis, MN: Castle Books (p. 537).

3. Rubenstein, G. (2009). Set up social emotional learning in your classroom, school, or school district. *Edutopia Schools that Work.* Retrieved from http://www.edutopia.org/stw-louisville-sel-replication-tips

4. Seligman, M. E. P. (2011). *Flourish: A visionary new understanding of happiness and well-being.* New York: Simon & Schuster.

5. Gottlieb, P. (2009). *The virtue of Aristotle's ethics.* Cambridge, UK: Cambridge University Press.

6. Kiefer, C. (1988). *The mantle of maturity: A history of ideas about character development.* New York: New York State University Press (p. 43).

7. Marinoff, L. (2007). *The middle way: Finding happiness in a world of extremes.* New York: Sterling.

8. Brett, J. (1996). *Goldilocks and the three bears.* New York: Puffin.

9. LeBlanc, G. (2008, March). Five things every happy person does. *O—The Oprah Magazine.*

10. King, L. A. (2001). The health benefits of writing about life goals. *Personality and Social Psychology Bulletin, 27,* 798–807.

11. Schwartz, B., & Sharpe, K. (2010). *Practical wisdom.* New York: Riverhead.

12. White, D. (2009). *Philosophy for kids.* Waco, TX: Prufrock Press (p. 13).

13. Taylor, E. (2001). Positive psychology and humanistic psychology: A reply to Seligman. *Journal of Humanistic Psychology, 41,* 13–29.

14. Rogers, C. (1961). *On becoming a person: Therapist's view of psychotherapy.* London: Constable and Robinson.

15. Ibid, 196.

16. Maslow, A., Frager, R., & Fadiman, J. (1987). *Motivation and personality*. New York: HarperCollins.

17. Ibid.

18. Ibid, p. 53.

19. Bandura, A. (1997). *Self-efficacy: The exercise of control*. New York: W. H. Freeman.

20. Bandura, A. (1977). *Social learning theory*. Englewood Cliffs, NJ: Prentice-Hall.

21. Erikson, E. [1950, 1963] (1993). *Childhood and society*. New York: W. W. Norton.

22. Dorfman, C. (2003). *I knew you could*. New York: Grosset and Dunlap/ Putnam Group.

23. Gardner, H. (2011). *Truth, beauty, and goodness reframed: Educating for the virtues in the 21st century*. New York: Basic Books.

24. Woolfolk, R. (2002). The power of negative thinking: Truth, melancholia, and the tragic sense of life. *Journal of Theoretical and Philosophical Psychology, 22*(1), 19–27.

25. Jung, C., & Hull, R. F. C. (1987). *Carl Jung speaking*. Princeton: Princeton University Press.

26. Cunningham, L. B. (2010). *The mandala's book: Patterns of the universe*. New York: Sterling.

27. Barnsley, Michael F., & Hawley, R. (1993). *Fractals everywhere*. Boston: Academic Press.

28. Wolfram, S. (2011). *Stephen Wolfram*. Retrieved from http://www .stephenwolfram.com/about-sw/

29. Jung, C. G. (1987). *Jung speaking: Interviews and encounters*. R. Hall (Ed.). Princeton, NJ: Princeton University Press.

30. Collaborative for Academic, Social, and Emotional Learning. (2011). *What is SEL?* Retrieved from http://casel.org/why-it-matters/what-is-sel/

31. Center for Positive Psychology (2007). *Overview*. Retrieved from http:// www.ppc.sas.upenn.edu/

32. Ibid.

33. U.S. Department of Education (2011). *Blueprint for reform*. Retrieved from http://www2.ed.gov/policy/elsec/leg/blueprint/index.html

34. U.S. Department of Education (2011). *Partnership for 21st century skills: A framework for twenty-first century education*. Retrieved from http:// www.p21.org/

35. Keyes, C. L. M., & Lopez, S. J. (2002). Toward a science of mental health: Positive directions in diagnosis and treatment. In C. R. Snyder & S. J. Lopez (Eds.), *The handbook of positive psychology*. New York: Oxford University Press.

36. Institute for Democratic Education (2012). *What is democratic education?* Retrieved from http://www.democraticeducation.org/

37. Bentham, S. (2002). *Applications of the humanistic approach*. Florence, KY: Routledge.

38. Schapiro, D. L. (1990). What if Montessori education is part of the answer? *Education Digest, 56*(1), 63.

39. Montessori, Maria. (1949). *The absorbent mind*. Claude A. Claremont (Trans., 1967 edition). New York: Delta (p. 17).

40. Progressive Education Network (PEN). (2011). *Progressive education*. Retrieved from http://www.progressiveed.org/

41. Carol, C. M. (1999). *Synergetic classroom: Joyful teaching and gentle discipline*. New York: Allyn & Bacon.

42. Association for Supervision and Curriculum Development (ASCD). (2007). *Whole child initiative*. Alexandria, VA. Retrieved from http://www.ascd.org/whole-child.aspx?

43. Seligman, M. E. P., Ernst, R., Gillham, J., Reivich, K., & Linkins, M. (2009). Positive education, positive psychology and classroom interventions. *Oxford Review of Education, 35*(3), 293–311.

44. White, M. (2009). Why teach positive education in schools? *Curriculum Leadership, 7*(7).

45. Journey North. (2012). *Migration: The monarch butterfly*. Retrieved from http://www.learner.org/

46. Who Moved My Cheese Book and Movie. (2010). *Who moved my cheese? for kids*. Retrieved from http://www.whomovedmycheese.com/

47. Seligman, M. E. P. (2011). *Flourish: A visionary new understanding of happiness and well-being*. New York: Simon & Schuster (pp. 3, 115, and 137).

48. Diener, E. (2000). Subjective well-being: The science of happiness and a proposal for national index. *American Psychologist, 55*(1), 34–43.

49. Csikszentmihalyi, M. (1990). *Flow: The psychology of optimal experience*. New York: Harper and Row (p. 6).

50. Duckworth, A., Peterson, C., Matthews, M., & Kelly, D. (2007). Grit, perseverance, and long-term passion. *Journal of Personality and Social Psychology*, in *Personality Processes and Individual Differences* (p. 1087).

51. Lehrer, J. (2009, May 18). The secrets of self-control. *The New Yorker*.

52. Stock Market Game. (n.d.). *Stock market game worldwide*. New York: Sifma Foundation. Retrieved from http://www.smgww.org/

53. Plutchik, R. (1980). A general psycho-evolutionary theory of emotion. In *Emotion: Theory, research, and experience*. New York: Academic Press (pp. 1, 3–33).

54. Salzberg, S. (2002). *Lovingkindness: The revolutionary art of happiness*. Boston, MA: Shambhala.

55. Story Time. (n.d.). On-line story-time for children. Retrieved from http://www.storylineonline.net/

56. American Library Association. (2012). Children's authors and illustrators. Retrieved from http://www.ala.org/gwstemplate.cfm?section=greatweb sites&template=/cfapps/gws/

57. Chart House (2011). *Fish! Philosophy*. Retrieved from http://www.chart house.com/

58. Fishful Thinking (2012). *Fishful thinking*. Retrieved from http://www .fishfulthinking.com/

59. Vygotsky, L. S. (1986). *Thought and language*. Cambridge: MIT Press.

60. Youngs, B. B. (1995). *Stress and your child: Helping kids cope with the strains and pressures of life*. New York: Fawcett Columbine.

61. Frankl, V. (1959). *Man's search for meaning*. Boston: Beacon Press (pp. 122–129).

62. Seligman, M. E. P. (2011). *Flourish: A visionary new understanding of happiness and well-being*. New York: Simon & Schuster (p. 293).

63. Ibid., p. 294.

64. Seligman, M. E. P., Reivich, K., Jaycox, L., & Gillham, J. (1995). *The optimistic child*. New York: Houghton Mifflin.

65. Seligman, M. E. P. (2011). *Flourish: A visionary new understanding of happiness and well-being*. New York: Simon & Schuster (p. 293).

66. Blum, R. W., McNeely, C.A., & Rinehart, P. M. (2002). *Improving the odds: The untapped power of schools to improve the health*. Division of General Pediatrics & Adolescent Health, Minneapolis: University of Minnesota Adolescent Health Program.

67. Payton, J., Weissberg, R.P., Durlak, J.A., Dymnicki, A.B., Taylor, R.D., Schellinger, K.B., & Pachan, M. (2008). *The positive impact of social and emotional learning for kindergarten to eighth-grade students: Findings from three scientific reviews*. Chicago: Collaborative for Academic, Social, and Emotional Learning.

68. Lyubomirsky, S. (2008). *The how of happiness: A scientific approach to getting the life you want*. New York: Penguin Press. Retrieved from http://www .faculty.ucr.edu/~sonja/index.html

69. 4-H Clubs (2012). *4-H history*. Retrieved from http://www.4-h.org/ about/4-h-history/faq/

70. Josephson Institute Center for Youth Ethics (2012). *Character counts*. Los Angeles, CA: Author. Retrieved from charactercounts.org/.

71. Hawkins, J. D., & Catalano, R. F. (2005). Doing prevention science: A response to Dennis M. Gorman and a brief history of the quasi-experimental study nested within the Seattle Social Development Project. *Journal of Experimental Criminology, 1*, 70–86.

72. Gottfredson, D. C., Gottfredson, G. D., & Hybl, L. G. (1993). Managing adolescent behavior: A multi-year, multi-school study. *American Educational Research Journal, 30*, 179–215.

73. Hawkins, J. D., Catalano, R. F., & Miller, J. Y. (1992). Risk and protective factors for alcohol and other drug problems in adolescence and early adulthood: Implications for substance abuse prevention. *Psychological Bulletin, 112*(1), 64–105.

74. Learning First Alliance, (2001). *Every child learning: Safe and supportive schools.* Washington, DC: LFA. Retrieved from http://www.learningfirst.org/publications/safeschools

75. Osterman, K. (2000). Students' need for belonging in the school community. *Review of Educational Research, 70*(3), 323–367.

76. Durlak, J. A., Weissberg, R. P., Dymnicki, A. B., Taylor, R. D., & Schellinger, K. B. (2011). The impact of enhancing students' social and emotional learning: A meta-analysis of school based universal interventions. *Child Development, 82*(1), 405–432.

77. Blum, R. W., McNeely, C. A., & Rinehart, P. M. (2002). *Improving the odds: The untapped power of schools to improve the health.* Division of General Pediatrics & Adolescent Health, Minneapolis, MN: University of Minnesota.

78. Weissbeg, R. P. (2000). Improving the lives of millions of school children. *American Psychologist, 55,* 1360–1373.

79. Flourishing Schools.org (2010). *The power of character strengths and emotions in American literature and culture.* Retrieved from http://www.flourishingschools.org/

80. Schaps, E., Battistich, V., & Solomon, D. (2004), Community in school as key to student growth: Findings from the Child Development Project. In J. Zins, R. Weissberg, M. Wang, & H. Walberg (Eds.), *Building academic success on social and emotional learning: What does the research say?* New York: Teachers College Press (pp. 89–205).

81. Seligman, M. E. P., Schulman, P., DeRubeis, R. J., & Hollon, S. D. (1999). The prevention of depression and anxiety. *Prevention and Treatment, 2(8), para.* 37.

82. Zins, J. E., Weissberg, R. P., Wang, M. C., & Walberg, H. J. (2004). *Building academic success on social and emotional learning: What does the research say?* New York: Teachers College Press.

83. Wang, M., Haertel, G., & Wallberg H. (1997). *What do we know: Widely implemented school improvement programs.* Philadelphia: Temple University Laboratory for Student Success.

84. Elias, M. J. (2004). *Promoting social and emotional learning: Guidelines for educators.* Alexandria, VA: Association for Supervision and Curriculum Development.

85. Weissbeg R. P. (2000). Improving the lives of millions of school children. *American Psychologist, 55,* 1360–1373.

86. Collaborative for Academic, Social, and Emotional Learning (2011). *What is SEL?* Retrieved from http://casel.org/why-it-matters/what-is-sel/

87. The Positive Psychology Center. (2007). *Overview of positive psychology.* Philadelphia: University of Pennsylvania. Retrieved from http://www.ppc.sas .upenn.edu/

88. Osher, D., Sprague, J., Weissberg, R. P., Axelrod, J., Keenan, S., Kendziora, K., & Zins, J. E. (2008). A comprehensive approach to promoting social, emotional, and academic growth in contemporary schools. In A. Thomas & J. Grimes (Eds.), *Best practices in school psychology.* Bethesda: National Association of School Psychologists (pp. 1263–1278).

89. Zins, J. E., Weissberg, R. P., Wang, M. C., & Walberg, H. J. (Eds.), (2004). *Building academic success on social and emotional learning: What does the research say?* New York: Teachers College Press.

90. Mayer, J. D., & Salovey, P. (1997). What is emotional intelligence? In P. Salovey & D. Sluyter (Eds.), *Emotional development and emotional intelligence: Implications for educators.* New York: Basic Books (pp. 3–31).

91. Peterson, C. (2006). *A primer in positive psychology.* Oxford: Oxford University Press (p. 6).

Chapter 2

1. Society for Neuroscience (2011). *What is neuroscience?* Washington, DC: Author. Retrieved from http://www.sfn.org/index.aspx?pagename= whatIsNeuroscience

2. Carter, R. (2010). *Mapping the mind.* Berkeley: University of California Press (p. 6).

3. Chudler, H. (2011). *Neuroscience for kids.* Retrieved from http://faculty .washington.edu/

4. Sacks, O. (2007). *Musicophilia: Tales of the music and the brain.* New York: Knopf.

5. Vaillant, G. (2009). *Spiritual evolution: How we are wired for faith, hope, and love.* New York: Three Rivers Press (p. 24).

6. Farrell, P. A. Gustafson, A. B., Garthwaite, T. L., Kalkoff, R. K., Cowley, A. W., & Morgan, W. P. (1986). Influence of endogenous opiates on the response of selected hormones to exercise in humans. *Journal of Applied Psychology, 61,* 1051–1057.

7. Society for Neuroscience (2011). *What is neuroscience?* Washington, DC: SfN. Retrieved from http://www.sfn.org/index.aspx?pagename=whatIsNeuro science

8. Bennett, M. R., & Hacker, P. M. S. (2007). *Philosophical foundations of neuroscience.* New York: Wiley-Blackwell.

9. Gioia, G. A., Esquith, P. K., Guy, S. C., & Kenworthy, L. (2000). Behavior rating inventory of executive functions. *Child Neuropsychology, 6*(3), 235–238.

10. Sousa, D. A. (2006). *How the brain works*. Thousand Oaks, CA: Corwin Press.

11. Ibid, p. 9.

12. Deng, W., Aimone, J., & Gage, F. (2010). New neurons and new memories: How does adult hippocampal neurogenesis affect learning and memory? *Nature Reviews Neuroscience 11*(5), 339–350.

13. Society for Neuroscience (2011). *Learning, memory, and language*. Retrieved from http://www.sfn.org/index.aspx?pagename=brainfacts

14. LeDoux, J. (1998). *The emotional brain: The mysterious underpinnings of emotional life*. New York: Simon & Schuster.

15. MacGuire, E., & Hassabis, D. (2011). Role of hippocampus in imagination and future. *National Academy of Science, 108*(11), E39.

16. Sharot, T., Riccardi, A. M., Raio, C. M., & Phelps, E. A. (2007). Neuro mechanism mediating optimism bias. *Nature, 102–105*.

17. Society for Neuroscience (2011). *Neuroscience core concepts: The essentials of principles of neuroscience*. Washington, DC: SfN. Retrieved from http://www.sfn.org/

18. Gazzaniga, M. S. (2009). *Human: The science of what makes us unique*. New York: Harper.

19. Siegel, D. J. (1999). *The developing mind*. New York: Guilford.

20. Nash, J. M. (1997). Fertile minds. *Time, 49*.

21. Society for Neuroscience (2005). *Neuron*. Washington, DC: SfN. http://www.sfn.org/

22. Ibid.

23. Fischer, K. W., & Bidell, T. R. (2006). Dynamic development of psychological structures in action and thought. In W. Damon & R. M. Lerner (Eds.), *Handbook of Child Psychology: Theoretical Models of Human Development*, 6th edition, Volume 1, New York: John Wiley (pp. 313–399).

24. Damasio, A. R. (1994). *Descartes' error: Emotion, reason and the human brain*. New York: Houghton Mifflin Harcourt (p. xii).

25. Society of Neuroscience (2011). *What are neuroscience core concepts?* Washington, DC. Retrieved from http://www.brainfacts.org/

26. Ibid.

27. Ibid.

28. Ibid.

29. Seligman, M. E. P. (2011). *Flourish: A revolutionary understanding of happiness and well-being*. New York: Simon & Schuster (pp. 3, 115, and 137).

30. Goleman, D. (1998). *Working with emotional intelligence*. New York: Bantam.

31. Ibid, back cover.

32. Rice University (2009). *Language and brain: Neurocognitive linguistics: An introduction*. Retrieved from http://www.ruf.rice.edu/~lngbrain/main.htm

33. Willis D., & Willis, J. (2007). *Doing task-based teaching.* Oxford: Oxford University Press.

34. Vaillaint, G. (2009). *Spiritual evolution: How we are wired for faith, hope, and love.* New York: Three Rivers Press (p. 24).

35. Sharot, T. (2011). *Optimism bias: Tour of the irrationally positive brain.* New York: Random House.

36. Sousa, D. (2003). *How the gifted brain learns.* New York: Corwin; Cooper, J. (2007). *Cognitive dissonance: Fifty years of a classic theory.* Thousand Oaks, CA: Sage.

37. Sharot, T. (2011). *Optimism bias: A tour of the irrationally positive brain.* New York: Pantheon, p. 4.

38. Dolan, R. J., & Sharot, T. (2012). *Neuroscience of preference and choice: Cognitive and neural mechanisms.* Waltham, MA: Academic Press.

39. Ibid.

40. Frankl, V. E. (1959). *Man's search for meaning.* Boston: Beacon (p. 104).

41. Frederickson, B. (2009). *Positivity: Groundbreaking research reveals how to embrace the hidden strength of positive emotions and negativity to thrive.* New York: Crown.

42. Ibid, p. 54.

43. Rizzolatti G., Fogassi L., & Gallese V. (2006). Mirrors of the mind. *Scientific American, 295,* 4–61.

44. Meltzoff, A. N. (2007). Like me: Social cognition. *Developmental Science, 10*(1), 126–134.

45. Miall, R. C. (2003). Connecting mirror neurons and forward models. *Neuro-report, 14*(17), 2135–2137.

46. Rizzolatti G., & Craighero L. (2004). The mirror neuron system. *Annual Review of Neuroscience, 27,* 169–192.

47. Society for Neuroscience (2005). *Neuron.* Washington, DC: SfN. Retrieved from www.sfn.org

48. Rizzolatti, G. (2005). The mirror neuron system and its function in humans. *Anatomical Embryology, 210*(5–6), 419–421.

49. Gallese, V., Keysers, C., & Rizzolatti, G. (2004). A unifying view of the basis of social cognition. *Trends in Cognitive Sciences, 8*(9), 396–403.

50. Ibid.

51. Society for Neuroscience (2005). *Neuron.* Washington, DC: SfN. Retrieved from sfn.org/index.

52. Kuehn, B. M. (2007). Scientists probe PTSD effects and treatment. *Journal of American Medical Association, 299*(1), 23–26.

53. Davidson, R. J. (2001). Toward a biology of personality and emotion. *Annals of the New York Academy of Science, 935,* 191–207.

54. Greenberg, M. (2006). Promoting resilience in children and youth: Preventive interventions and their interface with neuroscience. In Lester B. Mas-

ten & A. McEwen (Eds.), *Resilience in children*, New York: Annals of the New York Academies of Sciences (pp. 139–147).

55. Sapolsky, R. M. (2004). *Why zebras don't get ulcers*. New York: Holt Paperbacks.

56. Valliant, G. (2009). *Spiritual evolution: How we are wired for faith, hope, and love*. New York: Three Rivers Press (p. 35).

57. Damasio, A. (2000). *The feelings of what happens: Body and emotion in the making of consciousness*. New York: Mariner.

58. Davidson, R. J., & Van Reekum, C. (2005). Emotion is not one thing. *Psychological Inquiry, 1*(6), 16–18.

59. Damasio, A. (2003). *Looking for Spinoza: Joy, sorrow, and the feeling brain*. New York: Houghton Mifflin.

60. Society for Neuroscience (2005). *Neuron*. Washington, DC: SfN. Retrieved from www.sfn.org/

61. Begley, S. (2007). *Train your mind, change your brain: How a new science reveals our extraordinary ability to transform ourselves*. New York: Ballantine.

62. Kudulak, R. (1997). *Inside the brain: Revolutionary discoveries of how the mind works*. Riverside, NJ: Andrews McNeel.

63. Begley, S. (2007). *Train your mind, change your brain: How a new science reveals our extraordinary ability to transform ourselves*. New York: Ballantine (p. 9).

64. Siegel, D. J. (1999). *The developing mind: How relationships and the brain interact to shape who we are*. New York: Guilford.

65. Frankl, V. E. (1959). *Man's search for meaning*. Boston: Beacon (p. 104).

66. Doidge, N. (2007). *The brain that changes itself: Stories of personal triumph of brain science*. New York: Penguin.

67. Siegel, D. J., & Bryson, T. (2007). *The whole-brain child: 12 revolutionary strategies to nurture your child's developing mind, survive everyday parenting struggles, and help your family thrive*. New York: Guilford.

68. Blum, R. W. (2005). A case of school connectedness. *The Adolescent Learner, 62*(7), 16–20.

69. Schwartz, B., & Sharpe, K. (2010). *Practical wisdom*. New York: Riverhead (p. 51).

70. Ibid.

Chapter 3

1. Bloom, B. S. (1956). *Taxonomy of educational objective, handbook I: The cognitive domain*. New York: David McKay.

2. Krathwohl, D. R., Bloom, B. S., & Masia, B. B. (1964). *Taxonomy of educational objectives. The classification of educational goals, handbook II: The affective domain*. New York: David McKay (p. 35).

3. Wallace, B., & Adams, H. B. (1993). *TASC: Thinking actively in social context*. Oxford: Academic.

4. Seligman, Martin E. P. (2011). *Flourish: A visionary new understanding of happiness and well-being*. New York: Simon & Schuster.

5. Goleman, D. (1998). *Working with emotional intelligence*. New York: Bantam Books.

6. Peterson, C. (2006). *A primer in positive psychology*. Oxford: Oxford University Press.

7. Schwartz, B., & Sharpe, K. (2010). *Practical wisdom*. New York: Riverhead.

8. Park N., Huebner E. S., Laughlin J. E., Valois R. F., and Gilman R. (2004). A cross-cultural comparison of the dimensions of child and adolescent life satisfaction reports. *Social Indicators Research, 66*(1–2), *61–79*(19).

9. Csikszentmihalyi, M. (2000). *Beyond boredom and anxiety*. San Francisco: Jossey-Bass/Wiley.

10. Salzberg, S. (2002). *Lovingkindness: The revolutionary art of happiness*. Boston: Shambhala.

11. Valiente, C., Swanson, J., & Eisenberg, N. (2011). Linking students' emotions and academic achievement: When and why emotions matter. *Child Development Perspectives, 10*.

12. Rubenstein, G. (2011). *CARE for kids: Enhancing academic, social, emotional and ethical learning in Jefferson County Public Schools*. Retrieved from http://www.edutopia.org/stw-louisville-sel-care-for-kids-replication

13. Glasser, W. (1969). *Schools without failure*. New York: Harper and Row.

14. Hamilton, K. (2011). *Midnight rider virtual museums*. Retrieved from http://kidhistory.com/

15. Blecker, L. (2006). *Good in me from A–Z by Dottie*. Shoreham, VT: Discover Writing.

16. Tagg, J. (2003). *The learning paradigm college*. Bolton, MA: Anker (p. 70).

17. National Clearinghouse for Service Learning. (2012). *What is service learning?* Retrieved from http://www.servicelearning.org/what-is-service-learning

18. Eyler, J., & Giles, D. (1999). *Where is learning in service learning?* San Francisco: Jossey-Bass.

19. Lopez, S. J. (2009). *Encyclopedia of positive psychology*. New York: Wiley/Blackwell.

20. Annenberg Learner. (2011). *Journey north*. Retrieved from http://www.learner.org/jnorth/

21. Discovery Channel. (2011). *Human body learning experience puzzles*. Retrieved from http://dsc.discovery.com/tv/human-body/human-body.html

22. Seussville. (2011). *Seussville, the Sneetches writing activity*. Retrieved from http://www.seussville.com

23. Scholastic Learning. (2011). *Harry Potter learning, K–5.* Retrieved from http://harrypotter.scholastic.com/

24. Levitin, D. J. (2006). *This is your brain on music: The science of a human obsession.* New York: Dutton Adult.

25. Badcock, C. (2011). *The imprinted brain.* Psychology Today. Retrieved from http://www.psychologytoday.com/blog/the-imprinted-brain/201104/seeing-the-light-in-the-imprinted-brain

26. Gardner, H. (2011). *Truth, beauty, and goodness reframed.* New York: Basic Books.

27. Kincher, J., Bach, J.S., & Espeland, P. (1995). *Psychology for kids: 40 fun tests that help you understand yourself.* Minneapolis, MN: Free Spirit.

28. Berk, L. (1992). Children's private speech: An overview of theory and the status of research. In R. M. Diaz, & L. E. Berk (Eds.), *Private speech: From social interaction to self-regulation,* 101–122. Hillsdale, NJ: Lawrence Erlbaum.

29. Emerson. R. W. (1860). *Conduct of life.* Boston: Ticknor and Fields (p. 224).

Chapter 4

1. Mayer, J. D., & Salovey, P. (1997). What is emotional intelligence? In P. Salovey & D. Sluyter (Eds.), *Emotional development and emotional intelligence: Implications for educators* (3–31). New York: Basic Books.

2. Grille, R. (2011) *Heart to heart parenting: Foster emotional intelligence, personal empowerment through heartful parenting and loving relationships.* New York: Lifetime Media.

3. Ibid.

4. Bright Spots Catalog. (2011). *Emotion cards.* Rancho Santa Fe, CA: Bright Spots. Retrieved from http://www.brightspotsgames.com/

5. Six Seconds Catalog. (2011). *Choose to lose cards.* Watsonville, CA: Self-Science. Retrieved from http://www.6seconds.org/newstore/products/category/hands-on/page/2/

6. Wings for Kids Catalog. (2011). *Wings for Kids creed.* Charleston, SC: Author. Retrieved from http://www.wingsforkids.org/creed

7. Wings for Kids Catalog. (2011). *Wings for Kids pledge.* Charleston, SC: Author. Retrieved from http://www.wingsforkids.org/creed

8. Free Spirit Catalog. (2011). *Feelings in a Jar.* Minneapolis, MN: Free Spirit. Retrieved from http://www.freespirit.com/catalog/item_detail.cfm?ITEM_ID=318

9. Kimochis Catalog. (2011). *Toys with feelings inside.* San Anselmo, CA: Plushy Feely. Retrieved from http://kimochis.com/

10. Dr. Mac Music Catalog. (2010). Let 'em out song. Santa Barbara, CA: Dr. Mac Music. Retrieved from http://drmacmusic.com/

11. Developmental Studies Center Catalog. (2011). *Caring school community initiative, K–6*. Oakland, CA: Developmental Studies Center. Retrieved from http://www.devstu.org/caring-school-community

12. Six Seconds Catalog. (2011). *Self-science*. Watsonville, CA: Self-Science. Retrieved from http://www.6seconds.org

13. Center Source Systems. (2011). *Tribes learning community*. Windsor, CA: TribesTLC. Retrieved from http://tribes.com/

14. Plutchik, R. (1980). *Emotion: Psychoevolutionary synthesis*. New York: Harper and Row.

15. Plutchik, R. (1982). A psycho-evolutionary theory of emotions. Thousand Oaks: CA. Retrieved from http://ssi.sagepub.com/content/21/4-5/529.extract

16. Davidson, R. J., & Sutton, S. K. (1995). Affective neuroscience: The emergence of a discipline. *Current Opinions in Neurobiology, 5*, 217–224.

17. Davidson, R. J., Jackson, D. C., & Kalin, N. H. (2001). Emotion, plasticity, context and regulation. *Psychological Bulletin, 126*, 890–906.

18. Sacks, O. (2007). *Musicology: Tales of music and the brain*. New York: Knopf.

19. Curry, D. L. (2004). *How does your brain work*? New York: Children's Press; Ehrlich, F. (2005). *You can't use your brain if you are a jellyfish*. Maplewood, NJ: Blue Apple Books; Lennard, K., & Gulliksen, E. (2007). *Young genius: Brains*. Hauppauge, NY: Barrons; Rowan, P. (1998). *Big head! A book about your brain*. New York: Knopf.

20. Deak, J. (2010). *My fantastic elastic brain: Stretch it, shape it*. Belvedere, CA: Little Pickle Press.

21. Diamond, M. C., & Scheibel, A. B. (1985). *Human brain coloring book*. New York: HarperCollins Reference; Nettleton, H. & Shipe, P. (2006) *Think, think, think: Learning about your brain*. Bloomington, MN: Picture Window Books.

22. Chudler, E. H. (2010). *Neuroscience for kids*. Seattle, WA: National Center for Research Resources. Retrieved from http://www.dls.ym.edu.tw/chudler/neurok.html

23. Kid's Health. (2011). *Your brain and nervous system*. Wilmington, DE: The Nemours Center for Children's Health Media. Retrieved from http://kidshealth.org/kid/cancer_center/HTBW/brain.html

24. Chudler, E. H. X. (2005). *Brain board games*. Seattle, WA: Neuroscience for Kids. Retrieved from http://faculty.washington.edu/chudler/wwwbgame.html

25. Discovery Channel. (2011). *Anatomy of the brain interactive learning module: Emotions*. Silver Spring, MD: Discovery Communications. Retrieved from http://www.yourdiscovery.com/anatomiesof/brain/part_2.shtml

26. Public Broadcasting System. (2011). *Secret life of the brain: 3D brain anatomy*. Washington, DC: WBGH Educational Broadcasting Company. Re-

trieved from http://www.pbs.org/wnet/brain/; Nova Science Now. (2005). *Mirror Neurons.* Washington, DC: Public Broadcasting System. Retrieved from http://www.pbs.org/wgbh/nova/body/mirror-neurons.html

27. Brain Wise Program Catalog. (2011). *The 10 wise ways to stop and think.* Denver, CO: Brain Wise. Retrieved from http://brainwise-plc.org/story.htm

28. Brain Works Project. (2011). *Coping skills for kids.* Retrieved from http://www.copingskills4kids.net/

29. Rice, D. L. (2000). *Do animals have feelings, too?* Nevada City, CA: Dawn Publications.

30. Funston, S. (1998). *The secret life of animals.* Toronto: Maple Tree Press.

31. McCown, K., Jensen, A., Freedman, J., & Rideout, M. (2010). *Self-science: Getting started with social and emotional learning.* San Francisco, CA: Six Seconds. Retrieved from http://www.6seconds.org/

32. Bright Spots Catalog. (2011). *Bright spots games.* Rancho Santa Fe, CA: Bright Spots. Retrieved from http://www.brightspotsgames.com/home.html; Scholastic Catalog. (2009). *Harry Potter coloring book.* New York: Scholastic.

33. The Kindness Project. (n.d.). Retrieved from http://www.kindnessproject.com/home.php

34. Michaelson, D. (2009). *Classroom to community lesson plans.* Denver, CO: Random Acts of Kindness Foundation. Retrieved from www.randomactsofkindness.org/

35. Thorton, O. W. (2010). *The human kindness project enewsletter.* Retrieved from http://thehumankindnessproject.com

36. Brightspots Catalog (n.d.). *Card games.* Rancho Santa Fe, CA. Retrieved from http://www.brightspotsgames.com/home.html

37. TaliCor Aristo Play Catalog (n.d.). *Ungame.* Plainwell, MI: Toad Publishing. Retrieved from http://talicor.com/; TaliCor Aristo Play Catalog (n.d.). *Life stories.* Plainwell, MI: Toad Publishing. Retrieved from http://talicor.com/; Committee for Children Catalog (n.d.). *Peace town.* Seattle, WA: CfC. Retrieved from https://www.creativetherapystore.com/Anger-Control-Therapeutic-Games-and-Resources/Peacetown/W-362; HeartMath Catalog (n.d.). *Wild ride to heart.* Boulder City, CA: Heartmath Institute. Retrieved from http://www.heartmathstore.com/cgi-bin/category.cgi?item=5360; Black, C. (2004). *The stamp game: A game of feelings.* Bainbridge Island, WA: Mac-Publishing. Retrieved from www.themeadowsbookstore.com/p7/The_Stamp_Game/

38. Silverstein, S. (1964). *The giving tree.* New York: Harper and Row; Brumbeau, J. (2001). *The quilt maker's gift.* New York: Scholastic; Naylor, P. R. (2000). *Shiloh.* New York: Atheneum.

39. Lite. L. (2008). *The angry octopus: A relaxation story.* Marietta, GA: Stress-free kids. Retrieved from http://www.stressfreekids.com/; Mueller, P. B. (2007). *An angry drum echoed.* El Paso, TX: Pinata Publishing.

40. Namka, L. (2010). *Get your angries out for kids*. Retrieved from www.angriesout.com/

41. Geisel, T. (1996). *My many colored days*. New York: Knopf; Arts Education Ideas Catalog (n.d.). *Many colored days kit*. Norwalk, CT: Arts Education Ideas. Retrieved from http://www.toydirectory.com/monthly/toyshow/

42. Bang, M. (1999). *When Sophie gets angry . . . really, really angry*. New York: Blue Sky; Vail, R. (2005). *Sometimes I'm Bombaloo*. New York: Scholastic.

43. Covey, S. (2008). *The seven habits of happy kids*. New York: Simon & Schuster.

44. Covey, S. (2008). *The seven habits of happy kids website*. New York: Simon & Schuster. Retrieved from http://www.seancovey.com/kids.html

45. Columbia University. (2004). *Project ExSEL*. New York: Columbia University Teacher's College and New York City Public Schools. Retrieved from http://pd.ilt.columbia.edu/projects/exsel/

46. Keats, E. J. (1999). *My dog is lost*. New York: Puffin; Stevens, J. (1997). *Tops and bottoms*. New York: Harcourt.

47. Morningside Center for Teaching Social Responsibility. (2011). *4R's: Reading writing, and respect program*. New York: New York City Public Schools. Retrieved from http://www.morningsidecenter.org/programs_conflict.html

48. Morningside Center for Teaching Social Responsibility. (2011). *4R's bibliography*. New York: New York City Schools. Retrieved from www.morningsidecenter.org/

49. Torres, L. (1997). *Subway sparrow*. New York: Farrar, Straus, and Giroux.

50. Polacco, P. (2001). *The keeping quilt*. New York: Aladdin. Retrieved from http://www.serflo1.com/The Keeping Quilt.html

51. Lewis, Y. (2011). *So this is opera project*. Retrieved from http://www.operakids.com; Opening Minds through Arts. (OMA). (2012). *Why OMA works?* Tucson, Arizona: Tucson Unified School District. Retrieved from http://www.tusd1.org/contents/depart/finearts/omaworks.asp

52. Committee for Children Catalog. (2011). *Second step program: Skills for social and academic success*. Seattle, WA: Committee for Children. Retrieved from http://www.cfchildren.org/second-step.aspx

53. The Film Foundation (n.d.). *The story of movies*. Retrieved from http://www.storyofmovies.org/common/11041/default.cfm?clientID=11041

54. Niemiec, R.M., & Wedding, D. (2008). *Positive psychology at the movies: Using film to build virtues and character strengths*. Cambridge, MA: Hogrefe Publishing.

55. Rubin, G. (2011). *The happiness project: Or why I spent a year trying to sing in the morning, clean my closets, fight right, read Aristotle, and generally have more fun*. New York: Harper Perennial. Retrieved from http://happiness-project.com

56. Ibid.

57. Tel A Vision (2011). *It is your story*. Lake Elmo, MN: Tel-A-Vision. Retrieved from http://telavision.tv/

58. Rath, T., & Reckmeyer, M. (2009). *How full is your bucket? For kids*. Washington, DC: Gallup Press; Gosline, A. A., & Bossi, L. B. (2008). *The happiness tree: Celebrating the gifts of the trees we treasure*. New York: Macmillan/ Feiwel and Friends; Sakai, K. (1997). *Sachiko means happiness*. San Francisco: Children's Book Press; Thompson, C. (2008). *The big little book of happy sadness*. San Diego: Kane/Miller.

59. Frederickson, B. (2009). *Positivity: Discover the power of the 3–1 ratio*. Retrieved from http://www.positivityratio.com/

60. Levitin, D. J. (2009). The neural correlates of temporal structure in music. *Music and Medicine*, (1)1, 9–13.

61. Oden, B. (n.d.). *Songdrops: Funny songs for kids*. Retrieved from http://www.songdrops.com/

62. The Beatles (2011). *Yellow submarine*. Cupertino, CA: IBooks/Apple. Retrieved from http://itunes.apple.com/us/book/the-beatles-yellow-submarine/id479687204?mt=11

63. GreenStreets (2012). *Jeremy plays guitar: Use your words*. Boston: Green Streets, MP3. Retrieved from http://www.amazon.com/Use-Your-Words/dp/B0043UJJBY

64. Public Broadcasting Service Kids (PBS Kids). (2011). *Music pages*. Washington, DC: Educational Broadcasting Company. Retrieved from http://pbskids.org/music/; Songs, S. (n.d.). PBS *Music time*. Washington, DC: Education Broadcasting Company. Retrieved from http://www.stevesongs.com

65. Charles H. Dater Foundation (2011). *Classics for kids*. Retrieved from http://www.classicsforkids.com/

66. Armstrong, S. (2002). *The key to learning: A place of meaningful academic exploration*. Encinitas, CA: Edutopia. Retrieved from http://www.edutopia.org/key-learning-community

67. Singing fingers (2010). *Finger paint with your voice*. Cupertino, CA: IBooks/Apple. Retrieved from http://itunes.apple.com/us/app/singing-fingers/id381015280?mt=8

68. Bright Spots Catalog (2011). *Colorful garden: A feelings coloring book*. Rancho Santa Fe, CA: Bright Spots. Retrieved from http://www.brightspotsgames.com/home.html

69. HeartMath (2012). *Heart math software*. Boulder Creek, CA: HeartMath, LLC. Retrieved from http://www.heartmath.com/

70. White, D. (2000). *Philosophy for kids: 40 questions that help you wonder about everything*. Waco, TX: Prufrock Press.

71. Ibid., pp. 9, 24, 55, 86, 99, 108.

72. China Family Adventure (2011). *Who was Confucius?* Retrieved from chinadventure.com/.

73. Rowling, J. K. (2007). *Harry Potter and the order of the phoenix.* New York: Arthur Levine (p. 14).

74. Frankl, V. E. (1959). *Man's search for meaning.* Boston: Beacon (p. 104).

75. Bracket, M. (2005). *The RULER approach to social and emotional learning.* New Haven, CT: Health, Emotion, and Behavior Laboratory, Ruler Group, Yale University. Retrieved from http://therulerapproach.org/

76. Committee for Children. (2011). *Second steps program:* Skills for social and academic success, 4th ed. Seattle, WA: CfC. Retrieved from http://www.heartmath.com/technology-products/product-finder.html

77. Wellesley Center for Women. (1987). *Open circle curriculum.* Wellesley, MA: Wellesley College. Retrieved from http://www.open-circle.org/

78. HeartMath Catalog (n.d.). *HeartSmarts.* Boulder City, CA: Institute of Heartmath. Retrieved from http://store.heartmath.org/HeartSmarts-Grades3-5

79. Deerin, G. (1996). *Wings for kids program.* Charleston, SC: Wings for Kids. Retrieved from http://www.wingsforkids.org/

80. Gillen, L. & Gillen, J. (2008). *Yoga calm for children: Educating heart, mind, and body.* Portland, OR: Three Pebble Press.

81. Yoga 4 classrooms. (2011). *Yoga 4 classrooms cards deck.* Dover, NH: Child LightYoga. Retrieved from http://www.yoga4classrooms.com/

82. Yoga Kids. (2009). *Tools for schools.* Buffalo, MI: Yoga Kids International. Retrieved from http://yogakids.com/

83. Frankl, V. E. (1959). *Man's search for meaning.* Boston: Beacon (p. 104).

84. Silverstein, S. (1981). *A light in the attic: What if poem.* New York: HarperCollins (p. 90).

Chapter 5

1. Gardner, H. (2011). *Truth, beauty, and goodness reframed: Educating for virtues in the 21st century.* New York: Basic Books.

2. Vaillant, G. (2009). *Spiritual evolution: How we are hardwired for faith, hope, and love.* New York: Three Rivers Press.

3. Ibid, pp. 4–5.

4. Ibid., p. 35.

5. Virtues Project (n.d.). *The virtues project—education.* Victoria, BC: VP. Retrieved from http://www.virtuesproject.com/

6. Do2Learn Catalog (2012). *Social skills.* Raleigh, NC: Do2Learn. Retrieved from http://www.do2learn.com/SocialSkills/overview.htm

7. Peterson, C., & Seligman, M.P. (2004). *Character, strengths, and virtues: A handbook and classification.* New York: Oxford University Press.

8. Ibid., p. 13.

9. Seligman, M. E. P. (2011). *Flourish: A visionary new understanding of happiness and well-being.* New York: Simon & Schuster.

10. Ripley, A. (2008). *The unthinkable: Who survives when disaster strikes—and why.* New York: Crown.

11. Seligman, M. E. P. (2003). *Authentic happiness.* New York: Free Press (p. xi).

12. Dwek, C. (2006). *Mindset: New psychology of success.* New York: Random House.

13. Rath, T. (2007). *Strengths finder 2.0.* Washington, DC: Gallup Press. Retrieved from http://www.strengthsfinder.com/home.aspx

14. Ibid., p. iii.

15. McAdams, D. P. (2006). *Identity and story: Creating self-narrative: Self-narrative in the story of our lives.* Washington, DC: American Psychological Association.

16. Virtues Project (n.d.). *The virtues project - education.* Victoria, BC: The Virtues Project. Retrieved from http://www.virtuesproject.com/

17. Seligman, M. E. P. (2002). *Authentic happiness: Using the new positive psychology to realize your full potential.* New York: Simon & Schuster (p. xiv).

18. Peterson, C., & Seligman, M. P. (2004). Values in action: Inventory of strengths (VIA-IS). In *Character, strengths, and virtues: A handbook and classification.* New York: Oxford University Press. Retrieved from the VIA Institute on Character, www.viacharacter.org

19. Park, N., & Peterson, C. (2006). Moral strengths and character strengths in adolescents: The development and validation of the values in action inventory of strengths for youth. *Journal of Adolescence, 29*(6), 891–909.

20. Rath, T. (2007). *Strengths finder 2.0.* Washington, DC: Gallup Press. Retrieved from http://www.strengthsfinder.com/home.aspx

21. Gallup Youth Development Specialists. (2007). *Clifton strengths finder explorer for kids.* Washington, DC: Gallup Press. Retrieved from www.strengths-explorer.com/

22. Committee for Children Catalog (2011). *Second step program: Skills for social and academic success,* 4th ed. Seattle, WA: CfC. Retrieved from http://www.cfchildren.org/second-step.aspx; LeBuffe, P., Naglieri, J. A., & Shapiro, V. B. (2009). *Devereux student strengths assessment (DESSA).* Retrieved from http://www.devereux.org/site/

23. Kincher, J. (2008). *Psychology for kids: 40 fun tests that help you learn about yourself.* Minneapolis, MN: Free Spirit Publishing.

24. Virtues Project (n.d.). *The virtues project - education.* Victoria, BC: The Virtues Project. Retrieved from http://www.virtuesproject.com/

25. Virtue Toys Catalog (2008). *Virtue game.* Seattle, WA: Virtue Toys. Retrieved from http://www.virtuetoys.com/

26. Ibid.

27. Ibid.

28. Innovative Resources Catalog (2009). *Strength cards for kids.* Bendigo, Australia: Innovative Resources. Retrieved from http://www.innovative resources.org

29. Ibid.

30. Inspiration Software Catalog. (2012). *Inspiration and kidspiration.* Beaverton, OR: Inspiration Software, Inc. Retrieved from http://www.inspiration.com/

31. 4-H Pledge (1927). *National 4-H history preservation: 4-H pledge. project.* Chevy Chase, MD. Retrieved from http://4-hhistorypreservation.com/ Vision.asp

32. 4-H Creed (1918). Chevy Chase, MD: *National 4-H history preservation project: 4-H creed.* Retrieved from http://4-hhistorypreservation.com/Vision .asp

33. The Educational Pledge Partnership. (2010). *Educational pledge.* New York: TEEP. Retrieved from http://www.educationalpledge.com/

34. Ibid.

35. Ibid.

36. Anonymous. (n.d.). *Do not quit.* Retrieved from http://www.thedont quitpoem.com/

37. Kipling, R. (1910). If. In *Rewards and fairies.* New York: Doubleday (p. 115).

38. Library of Congress. (1997). *Favorite poem project.* Boston, MA: Boston University. Retrieved from http://www.favoritepoem.org/

39. Pinsky, Robert (1997). *39th Poet laureate of U.S.* Retrieved from http:// www.loc.gov/poetry/

40. Scholastic Writers Writing (2012). *Poetry writing.* New York: Scholastic. Retrieved from http://teacher.scholastic.com/writewit/poetry/index.htm

41. Animoto (2005). *Create videos.* New York: Animoto. Retrieved from http://animoto.com/

42. Tribes Learning Community (2012). *TLC creed.* Windsor, CA: Tribes Learning Community. Retrieved from http://tribes.com/about/

43. Fu, G., Evans, A. D., Wang, L., & Lee, K. (2008). Lying in the name of the collective good: A developmental study. *Developmental Science,* 11(4), 495–503.

44. Yeager, J. M., Fisher, S.W., & Shearon, D. N. (2011). *Smart strengths.* Albany, NY: Kravis/Whitson Publishing Company. Retrieved from http://www .flourishingschools.org/index.htm

45. My Hero Project (2010). *The my hero's teachers room.* Laguna Beach, CA: Author. Retrieved from http://myhero.com/go/home.asp

46. Giraffes Heroes Project (2012). *Teach Giraffe.* Langley, WA: Author. Retrieved from http://www.giraffe.org

47. Hallmark Hall of Fame. (2007). *The courageous heart of Irena Sendler.* Kansas City, MO: Hallmark, Inc. Retrieved from http://www.hallmark.com/online/hall-of-fame/resources.aspx

48. Rubin, S. G. (2011). *Irena Sendler and the children of the Warsaw ghetto.* New York: Holiday House.

49. Life in a Jar Project. (2006). *The Irena Sendler project.* Fort Scott, KA: Life in a Jar. Retrieved from http://www.irenasendler.com/

50. United States National Holocaust Memorial Museum (n.d.) *Education.* Washington, DC: United States National Holocaust Memorial Museum Council. Retrieved from http://www.ushmm.org/; Florida Center for Instructional Technology (2005). *USF Holocaust Teaching Guide.* Tampa, FL: University of South Florida. Retrieved from http://fcit.usf.edu/holocaust/

51. Kudlinski, K., & Diamond, D. (2001). *Helen Keller: A light for the blind.* New York: Puffin; Robinson, S. (2010). *Jackie's gift.* New York: Viking Children's Books.

52. Adler, D. A., & Wallner, J. (1992). *Helen Keller picture book.* New York: Holiday House Books; Adler, D. A., & Wasilla, R. (1997). *A picture book of Jackie Robinson.* New York: Holiday House Books.

53. Ries, L. (2007). *Super Sam.* Watertown, MA: Charlesbridge; Holub, J., & Lichtenheld, T. (2012). *Zero the hero.* New York: Henry Holt.

54. Treffinger, C. (1995). *Li Lun, lad of courage.* New York: Walker & Company; Crane, S. (2004). *Red badge of courage.* Mineola, NY: Dover Publications.

55. Learning for Life Program Catalog. (2011). *Character development.* Irving, TX: Learning for Life. Retrieved from http://www.learningforlife.org/

56. Project ExSEL. (2011). *Excellence in social and emotional learning.* New York: Columbia University. Retrieved from http://pd.ilt.columbia.edu/projects/

57. Keats, E. J. (1999). *My dog is lost.* New York: Puffin Books; Stevens, J. (1997), *Tops and bottoms.* New York: Harcourt Children's Books.

58. Heartwood Institute Catalog. (2012). *Teaching life lessons through literature.* Pittsburgh, PA: Heartwood Institute. Retrieved from http://www.heartwoodethics.org/

59. McKissack, P. C. (2003). *The honest to goodness truth.* New York: Atheneum Books for Young Readers; Alexander, L. (1989) *The king's fountain.* New York: Puffin Books; Stewart, S. H., & Steward, S. (2007). *The gardener.* Square Fish/Macmillan; Steig, W. (1988.) *Brave Irene.* New York: Farrar, Straus, and Giroux; Altman, L. J. (1995). *Amelia's road.* New York: Lee and Low Books; Bond, R. (1996). *Cherry tree.* Honesdale, PA: Boyds Mils Press.

60. McCully, E. A. (1992). *Mirette on the high wire.* New York: Putnam Juvenile.

61. Martin, B., & Archambault, J. (1987). *Knots on a counting rope.* New York: Square Fish.

62. Blecker, L. (2006). *Good in me from A–Z by Dottie.* Shoreham, VT: Discover Writing Press. Retrieved from http://www.discover-writing.com/; Blecker, L. (2010). *Dottie and me celebrate what makes us great.* Evanston, IN: Studio 9. Retrieved from http://studio9inc.com/games

63. Teach with Movies Organization (n.d.). *Lesson plans for films and movies.* Santa Monica, CA: Teach with Movies Inc.com. Retrieved from http://www.teachwithmovies.org/

64. Niemiec, R. M., & Wedding, D. (2008). *Positive psychology at the movies: Using film to build virtues and character strengths.* Cambridge, MA: Hogrefe.

65. Peterson, C., & Seligman, M.E. P. (2004). *Character, strengths, and virtues: A handbook and classification.* New York: Oxford University Press; Niemiec, R. M., & Wedding, D. (2008). *Positive psychology at the movies: Using film to build virtues and character strengths.* Cambridge, MA: Hogrefe.

66. Live Wire Media. (2010). *Character Counts.* Mill Valley, CA: Author. Retrieved from http://www.livewiremedia.com/catalog

67. Niemiec, R. M., & Wedding, D. (2008). *Positive psychology at the movies: Using film to build virtues and character strengths.* Cambridge, MA: Hogrefe (p. 5).

68. Day, J. (2006). *Creative visualization with children.* Rockport, MA: Element Books. Retrieved from http://www.thebeingeffect.com/

69. Dwek, C. (2006). *Mindset: The new psychology of success.* New York: Random House.

70. Salanova, M., Llorens, S., & Schaufeli, W. B. (2010). Yes, I can, I feel good, and I just do it! On gain cycles and spirals of efficacy beliefs, affect, and engagement. *Journal of Applied Psychology, 60*(2), 255–285.

71. Reznick, C. (2009). *The power of your child's imagination: How to transform stress and anxiety into joy and success.* Retrieved from http://www.imageryforkids.com

72. Usher, E. L. (2009). Sources of middle school students' self-efficacy in mathematics: A qualitative investigation of student, teacher, and parent perspectives. *American Educational Research Journal, 46,* 275–314.

73. Hayes, S., Hirsch, C.R., & Mathews, A. (2010). Facilitating a benign attentional bias reduces negative thought intrusions. *Journal of Abnormal Psychology, 119*(1), 235–240.

74. Gilbert, P. (Ed.). (2004). *Evolutionary theory and cognitive therapy.* New York: Springer; Norem, J., & Norem J. K (2002). *The positive power of negative thinking: Using defensive pessimism to harness anxiety and perform at peak.* New York: Basic Books.

75. University of Hertfordshire (2007). Resistance to thoughts of chocolate is futile. *Science Daily.* Retrieved from http://www.sciencedaily.com/releases/

76. Diaz, R., & Berk, L. (Eds.). (1992). *Private speech: From social interaction to self-regulation.* Hillsdale, NJ: Lawrence Erlbaum (p. 62).

77. Karpov, Y.V. (2006). *The neo-Vygotskian approach to child development.* Cambridge, UK: Cambridge University Press; Piaget, J., & Inhelder, B. (1972). *Psychology of child.* New York: Basic Books (p. 209).

78. Berk. L., & Diaz, R. M. (1992). *Private speech: From social interaction to self-regulation.* Hillsdale, NJ: Lawrence Erlbaum (pp. 17–53).

79. Gilbert, P. (Ed.). (2004). *Evolutionary theory and cognitive therapy.* New York: Springer (p. 198).

80. Denton, P. (2007). *The power of words: The teacher language that helps children learn.* Turners Fall, MA: Northeast Foundation for Children. Retrieved from http://www.responsiveclassroom.org/

81. Dwek, C. (2006). *Mindset: The psychology of success.* New York: Random House.

82. Ibid.

83. Red Tree Leadership & Development. (1998). *Who moved my cheese? An amazing way to deal with change in your work and life curriculum.* Orem, UT: Red Tree Leadership and Development. Retrieved from www.whomovedmy cheese.com/

84. Johnson, S., & Johnson, C. (2003). *Who moved my cheese? for kids.* New York: Putnam Juvenile.

85. McAdams, D. P. (1988). *Power, intimacy, and the life story: Personological inquiries into identity.* New York: Guilford.

86. Libby, L. K., & Eibach, R. P. (2007). How the self affects and reflects the content and subjective experience of autobiographical memory. In C. Sedikides & S. J. Spencer (Eds.), *The self,* 75–79. New York: Psychology Press.

87. Seligman, M. (2006). *Learned optimism: How to change your mind and your life.* New York: Random House (p. 44).

88. Hays, L. L. (2000). *Wisdom cards.* Carlsbad, CA: Hay House. Retrieved from www.hayhouse.com

89. Vision Makers. (2012). *Kids time affirmations.* Phoenix, AZ: Vision Makers, LLC. Retrieved from http://www.myvisionmakers.com/about/index.php

90. Hays, L. L., & Tracy, K. (2008). *I think, I am! Teaching kids the power of affirmations.* Carlsbad, CA: Hay House. Retrieved from http://www.louisehay.com/

91. Chopra, D., & Tracy, K. (2010). *On my way to a happy life.* Carlsbad, CA: Hay House. Retrieved from http://www.deepakchopra.com/

92. Lite, L. (1997). *The affirmation web: A believe-in-yourself adventure.* North Branch, MN: Specialty Press/A.D.D. Warehouse. http://www.stressfree kids.com/653/the-affirmation-web

93. Lazarus, R. S., & Folkman, S. (1984). *Stress, appraisal, and coping.* New York: Springer (p. 150).

94. Carver, C. S., Scheier, M. F., & Weintraub, J. K. (1989). Assessing coping strategies: A theoretically based approach. *Journal of Personality and Social Psychology, 56,* 267–283.

95. Compton, W. C. (2004). *An introduction to positive psychology*. Independence, KY: Wadsworth/Cengage, 4.

96. Carver, C. S., Scheier, M. F., & Weintraub, J. K. (1989). Assessing coping strategies: A theoretically based approach. *Journal of Personality and Social Psychology, 56*, 267–283.

97. Stanton, A. L., Parsa, A., & Austenfeld, J. L. (2002). The adaptive potential of coping through emotional approach. In C. R. Snyder & S. J. Lopez (Eds.), *Handbook of positive psychology*, 148–158. New York: Oxford University Press.

98. Frederickson, B. (2009). *Positivity: Ground-breaking research reveals how to embrace the hidden strengths of positive emotions, overcome negativity, and thrive*. New York: Crown Archetype.

99. Morrison, M. K. (2007). *Using humor to maximize learning: The links between positive emotions and education*. Lanham, MD: R&L Education Group.

100. Beecher, S, (1998), *Happiness is up to you*. NSW Australia: Logical happiness. Retrieved from http://www.logicalhappiness.com.au/

101. Efficacy Institute. (2012). *Student success program*. Waltham, MA: Efficacy Institute. Retrieved from http://www.efficacy.org/Home/tabid/220/Default.aspx

102. Epel, E. S., McEwan, B. S., & Ickovics, J. R. (1998). Embodying psychological thriving: Physical thriving in response to stress. *Journal of Social Issues, 54*(2), 301–322.

103. Mon-Williams, M., Tresilian, J. R., & Wann, J. P. (2003) Motor control and learning. In *Encyclopedia of Cognitive Science*. New York: Nature Publishing.

104. Weikart, P. S., & Carlton, Elizabeth. (2002). *85 engaging movement activities*. Ypsilanti, MI: High Scope Press. Retrieved from http://www.responsive classroom.org/

105. American Alliance for Health, Physical Education, Recreation, and Dance. (2012). *Let's move in schools*. Reston, VA: AAHPERD. Retrieved from www.aahperd.org/

106. Discover Wildlife. (2012). *Animals that dance*. Bristol, BS: Wildlife.com. Retrieved from http://www.discoverwildlife.com/animals/strictly-animals-dancing

107. Peterson, C. (2010). *Dogs do not dance/The good life*. New York: Psychology Today. Retrieved from http://www.psychologytoday.com/blog/; Payne, H. (2006). *Dance movement therapy: Theory, research, and practice*. New York: Routledge.

108. Activity TV. (2012). *Dance for kids*. Philadelphia, PA: Comcast. Retrieved from http://www.activitytv.com/dance-for-kids

109. World Cultural Dance. (2011). *Discover folk dances from around the world*. Oakville, ON: Fit for a Feast/Papcom. Retrieved from http://fitfora feast.com/dance_cultural.htm

110. Maclean, K. L. (2004). *Peaceful piggy meditation*. Park Ridge, IL: Albert Whitman & Company; Maclean, K. L. (2009). *Moody cow meditates*.

Somerville, MA: Wisdom; Alderfer, L. (2011). *Mindful monkey.* Somerville, MA: Wisdom; Lite, L. (1996). *A boy and a bear: The children's relaxation book.* North Branch, MN: Specialty Press.

111. Lite, L. (2005). *Indigo ocean dreams: Four children's stories.* Marietta, GA: Stress Free Kids. Retrieved from http://www.stressfreekids.com/168/indigo-dreams

112. Thich N. H. (2002). *A pebble for your pocket.* Eugene, OR: Plum Blossom. Retrieved from http://www.plumblossombooks.com/

113. Muth, J. J. (2002). *The three questions (based on a story by Leo Tolstoy).* New York: Scholastic Press.

114. Segerstrom, S.C. (2006). *Breaking Murphy's law: How optimists get what they want from life—and pessimists can too.* New York: Guilford.

115. Pfeifer, J. H., Masten, C. L., Borofsky, L. A., Dapretto, M., Fuligni, A. J., & Lieberman, M. D. (2009). Neural correlates of direct and reflected self-appraisals in adolescents and adults: When social perspective-taking informs self-perception. *Child Development, 80,* 1016–1038.

116. Hawn Foundation. *MindUP curriculum.* Dallas, Texas: Hawn Foundation. Retrieved from http://www.thehawnfoundation.org/mindup

117. Beecher, S. (1998). *Happiness is up to you.* NSW Australia: Logical Happiness. Retrieved from http://www.logicalhappiness.com.au/

118. Penn State University. *PATHS Curriculum.* State College, PA: The Prevention Research Center for the Promotion of Human Development. Retrieved from http://www.prevention.psu.edu/projects/PATHSCurriculum.html

119. Greenberg M. T., Kusche C. A., Cook, E. T., & Quamma, J. P. (1995). Promoting emotional competence in school-aged children: The effects of the PATHS curriculum. *Development and Psychopathology, 7,* 117–136.

120. Greenberg, M. T. (2006). Promoting resilience in children and youth: Preventive interventions and their interface with neuroscience. *The Annals of the New York Academy of Sciences, 1094,* 144.

121. Ibid., p. 146.

122. Klee, M. B. (2003). *Core virtues: A literature-based program in character education.* Claremont, NH: Core Virtues Program. Retrieved from http://www.amazon.com/Core-Virtues-Literature-Based-Character-Education/dp/0967962609

123. Innovative Resources Catalog (2009). *Cars-r-us.* Bendigo, Australia: Innovative Resources. Retrieved from http://www.innovativeresources.org/

124. Livewire Media Catalog (2010). *Auto-b-good.* Mill Valley, CA: Author. Retrieved from http://www.livewiremedia.com/catalog

125. Livewire Media Catalog (2010). *Popcorn park.* Mill Valley, CA: Author. Retrieved from http://www.livewiremedia.com/popcornpark/

126. Livewire Media Catalog (2010). *Character way.* Mill Valley, CA: Author. Retrieved from http://www.livewiremedia.com/CharacterWay/

127. Livewire Media Catalog (2010). *Groark's birthday surprise.* Mill Valley, CA: LWM. Retrieved from http://www.livewiremedia.com/GettingAlongwith Groark; Livewire Media Catalog (2010). *Angry?* Mill Valley, CA: LWM. Retrieved from http://www.livewiremedia.com/search?t=2&key=angry

128. Livewire Media Catalog (2010). *Character chronicles.* Mill Valley, CA: LWM. Retrieved from http://www.livewiremedia.com/TheCharacterChronicles

129. Columbia University (2011). *The comic book project.* New York: Teachers College Press. Retrieved from http://comicbookproject.org/

130. Zimmerman, B., & Bloom, T. (2012). *About us.* New York: MakeBeliefs Comix.com. Retrieved from http://www.makebeliefscomix.com/

131. Gownley, J. (2003). *Amelia rules book series.* New York: Simon & Schuster. Retrieved from http://www.ameliarules.com/

132. Saunders, N. (2007). *Twelve labors of Hercules.* New York: World Almanac Library; Grant, S., & Dumas, A. (2101). *Classics illustrated #8: The count of Monte Cristo.* New York: Papercutz. Retrieved from http://www.papercutz .com/index2.html

133. Vogel, T. (2008). *Use literary characters to teach emotional intelligence.* San Rafael, CA: Edutopia.

134. Katie, B., & Wilhelm, H. (2009). *Tiger, tiger is it true?* Carlsbad, CA: Hay House.

135. Jones, C. (1994). *Mistakes that worked.* New York: Doubleday for Young Readers.

136. Markle, S. (2008). *Animal heroes: True rescue stories.* Minneapolis, MN: Millbrook Press/Lerner Publishing.

137. Huss, S. (2011). *A boat full of animals.* La Jolla, CA: Happy Children Books. Retrieved from http://www.amazon.com/ANIMALS-Positive-Character-Year-Olds-ebook/dp/B006PN55F6

138. Whybrow, I. (2010). *Harry and his bucketful of dinosaurs.* Decorah, IA: Dragonfly Books; CCI Entertainment. (2007). *Harry and the bucketful full of dinosaurs.* Ontario, CA: CCI, Ltd. Retrieved from www.harryandhisbucketfullof dinosaurs.com/

139. Honeymoon, K. (n.d.). *Core samples.* Montgomery, AL: Teaching Tolerance/Southern Poverty Law Center. Retrieved from http://www.tolerance .org/activity/core-samples

140. Goedecke, A. (2006). *One fun thing.* Charleston, SC: Booksurge/ Amazon Group. Retrieved from http://onefunthing.com/

141. Judge, T. A., & Hurst, C. (2007). Capitalizing on one's advantages: Role of core self-evaluations. *Journal of Applied Psychology, 92*(5), 1212–1227.

Chapter 6

1. Blum, R. W. (2005). *School connectedness: Improving student lives.* Washington, DC: Military Child Initiative, U.S. Department of Defense.

2. Villarica, H. (2011). *Maslow 2.0: A new and improved theory of happiness*. Washington, DC: Atlantic Media.

3. Blum, R. W. (2005). *School connectedness: Improving student lives*. Washington, DC: Military Child Initiative, U.S. Department of Defense.

4. Pangle, L. S. (2002). *Aristotle and the philosophy of friendship*. Cambridge: Cambridge University Press.

5. Hruschka, D. J. (2010). *Friendship: Development, ecology, and evolution of a relationship*. Berkeley: University of California Press.

6. Ibid.

7. Ibid.

8. Ibid.

9. Collaborative for Academic, Social, and Emotional Learning (CASEL). (2011). *What is SEL?* Chicago, IL: Author.

10. Selman, R. L. (1993). *The promotion of social awareness: Powerful lessons from the partnership of developmental theory and classroom practice*. New York: Sage (p. 311).

11. Witkow, M. R., & Fuligni, A. J. (2010). In-school versus out-of-school friendships and academic achievement among an ethnically diverse sample of adolescents. *Journal of Research on Adolescence, 20*(3), 631–650.

12. Live Wire Media Catalog. (2010). *What does it mean to be a good friend?* Mill Valley, CA: Author. Retrieved from http://www.livewiremedia.com/goodfriend

13. Live Wire Media Catalog. (2010). *You can choose*. Mill Valley, CA: Author. Retrieved from http://www.livewiremedia.com/search

14. Botvin Life Skills Training. (1998). *Life skills training elementary*. White Plains, NY: National Health Promotion Associates. Retrieved from http://www.lifeskillstraining.com/

15. Southern Poverty Law Center. (2011). *Teaching tolerance*. Montgomery, AL: Author. Retrieved from http://www.tolerance.org/

16. Teaching Tolerance. (1997). *Start small training curriculum*. Montgomery, AL: Southern Poverty Law Center. Retrieved from http://www.tolerance.org/kit/starting-small

17. Eunice Kennedy Shriver Foundation for Community of Caring.(n.d.) *Community of caring: The framework*. Salt Lake City, UT: University of Utah. Retrieved from communityofcaring.org/.

18. Knudsen, M. (2011). *Argus*. Somerville, MA: Candlewick.

19. Tingle, T. (2006). *Crossing bok chitto: A Choctow tale of friendship and freedom*. El Paso, TX: Cinco Puntas.

20. Jazwierska, Z. (2012). *Laughter meditations*. Boulder, CO: Kids Relaxation.com. Retrieved from http://kidsrelaxation.com/?s=laughter; Smith, W. J. *Laughingtime*. Chicago, IL: Poetry Foundation. Retrieved from poetryfoundation.org; Fan Yang. (2012). *Gazillion bubbles show* video. New York: New World Stages. Retrieved from http://gazillionbubbleshow.com/

21. Eunice Kennedy Shriver National Center for Community of Caring Foundation. (n.d.) *Positive role models certificates*. Salt Lake City: University of Utah. Retrieved from http://www.communityofcaring.org/

22. Ohiya (2011). *The art of making friends*. Ripple Junction, OH: Ohiya. Retrieved from http://ohiyafriends.com/

23. Blue Mountain Arts. (2012). *Friendship magnets*. Boulder CO: BMA Holdings. Retrieved from http://www.sps.com/gifts/magnets.html

24. Valley, J. *Friendship train CD*. Gig Harbor, WA: Rainbow Planet. Retrieved from http://www.rainbowplanet.com/cd_train.php

25. Franklin Learning System (2005). *Play2Learn go fish: Hooked on friendship card game*. Westport, CT: FLS. Retrieved from http://www.franklinlearning.com/; Attainment Company Catalog. (2005). *Know the code card game*. Verona, CA: Author. Retrieved from http://www.attainmentcompany.com/

26. Franklin Learning System (2005). *The friendship island game*. Westport, CT: Author. Retrieved from http://www.franklinlearning.com/

27. Talicor (2012). *Ungame*. Plainwell, MI: Talicor-Aristoplay. Retrieved from http://talicor.com/

28. Hub World. (2012). *My little pony friendship magic games*. Pawtucket, RI: Hub Television Networks. Retrieved from http://www.hubworld.com/my-little-pony

29. Lionsgate Studios (2010). *Thomas & friends: Heroes of the Rails*. Santa Monica, CA: Lionsgate Entertainment. Retrieved from www.thomasandfriends.com/

30. Playing for Change Foundation. (2012). *The playing for change project*. Culver City, CA: Author. Retrieved from http://playingforchangeday.org/

31. Playing for Change Foundation. (2012). *Playing for the day project*. Culver City, CA: Author. Retrieved from http://playingforchangeday.org/

32. Coalition for Quality Children's Media. (2012). *Kids first film festival*. San Francisco: Author. Retrieved from http://www.kidsfirst.org/filmfestival/

33. New York International Kid's Film Festival (2012). *Watch online*. New York: Author.

34. Association of Waldorf Schools of North America (2012). *Why it works*, Chatham, NY: Author. Retrieved from http://www.whywaldorfworks.org/

35. Kindersley, A., & Kindersley, B. (1995). *Children just like me: Celebrations*. New York: DK Kids/UNICEF.

36. Jones, L. (1990). *Children around the world: The best feasts and festivals from many lands*. Thousand Oaks, CA: Jossey-Bass.

37. Heath, A. (1995). *Windows on the world: Multi-cultural festivals for schools and libraries*. New York: Scarecrow Press/Rowman and Littlefield.

38. Montanari, D. (2004). *Children around the world*. Tonawanda, NY: Kids Can Press.

39. Olympics of the Mind (2011). *Information.* Sewell, NJ: Creative Competitions. Retrieved from http://www.odysseyofthemind.com/; American Math Olympiads. (2011). *General information.* Lincoln, NB: Author. Retrieved from http://www.moems.org/

40. Charles. C. (1999). *Synergistic classroom: Joyful teaching and gentle classroom.* Upper Saddle River, NJ: Allyn & Bacon/Pearson.

41. Brown, L. K., & Brown, M. (2001). *How to be a friend.* New York: Little & Brown; Carlson, N. (1997). *How to lose all your friends.* New York: Penguin.

42. Moss, P., Tardiff, D. D., & Geis, A. I. (2011). *Friendship rules.* Gardiner, MA: Tilbury.

43. Kleven, E. (2011). *Friendship wish.* New York: Dutton Juvenile.

44. Hatkoff, I., Hatkoff, C., & Kahumba, P. (2006). *Owen and Myzee: The true story of a remarkable friendship.* New York: Scholastic; Owen and Myzee Foundation. (2008). *OMweb.* New York: Author. Retrieved from http://www.owenandmzee.com/omweb/

45. Antle, B. (2011). *Suryia and Roscoe: The true story of an unlikely friendship.* New York: Henry Holt.

46. Institute for Greatly Endangered & Rare Species Preservations Station (2010). *Suryia and Roscoe website.* Myrtle Beach, NC: T.I.G.E.R.S. Retrieved from www.suryiaandroscoe.com/ and www.myrtlebeachsafari.com/

47. Buckley, C. (2009). *Tarra and Bella: The elephant and dog who became friends.* New York: Putnam Juvenile.

48. Elephant Sanctuary (2011). *Meet our elephants* and *Bella's tribute page.* Hohenwald, TN: Elephant Sanctuary. Retrieved from http://www.elephants.com/meetElephants.php and http://www.elephants.com/Bella/Bella.php

49. Voices Literature and Character Education (2004). *Voices instructional plan and leveled library.* Columbus, OH: Zaner-Bloser. Retrieved from http://shop.zaner-bloser.com/c-205-zaner-bloser-voices-literature-character-education.aspx

50. Havill, J. (1987). *Jamaica's find.* San Anselmo, CA: Sandpiper.

51. Yashima, T. (1976). *Crow boy.* New York: Puffin.

52. Bruchac, J. (2001). *The heart of a chief.* New York: Puffin.

53. Wellesley Centers for Women. (2011). *Welcome to open circle.* Wellesley, MA: Wellesley College. Retrieved from http://www.open-circle.org/about_us/index.html

54. Wellesley Centers for Women. (2011). *What is open circle?* Wellesley, MA: Wellesley College. Retrieved from http://www.open-circle.org/about_us/index.html

55. Ibid.

56. Live Wire Media Catalog. (2010). *Being friends.* Mill Valley, CA: Author. Retrieved from http://www.goodcharacter.com/YCC/BeingFriends.html

57. Live Wire Media Catalog. (2010). *Getting along with Groark.* Mill Valley, CA: Author. Retrieved from http://www.livewiremedia.com/GettingAlong withGroark

58. Petersen, L. (2006). *Stop think do program.* Camberwell, VIC: ACER Press. Retrieved from http://www.stopthinkdo.com/

59. McCown, K., Anabel, J, Freedmand, J., & Rideout, M. (2010). *Self-Science: Getting started with social emotional learning* (3rd ed.). San Francisco, CA: Six Seconds. Retrieved from http://www.6seconds.org/tools/curriculum/

60. Six Seconds (2007). *Social emotional intelligence youth version* (SEI-YV). San Francisco, CA: Author. Retrieved from http://www.6seconds .org/tools/sei/

61. Educators for Social Responsibility Catalog. (2012). *Resolving conflict creatively program (RCCP).* Cambridge, MA: Author. Retrieved from http:// esrnational.org/professional-services/elementary-school/prevention/resolving-conflict-creatively-program-rccp/

62. Educators for Social Responsibility Catalog. (2012). *Connected and respected.* Cambridge, MA: Author. Retrieved from http://esrnational.org/ and http://www.esrnational.org/store/vol1/ and http://www.esrnational.org/store/vol2

63. Spiegel, C. (2010). *Book by book: An annotated guide to young people's literature with peace-making and conflict resolution themes.* Cambridge, MA: Educators for Social Responsibility. Retrieved from http://www.esrnational .org/store/; Lonberger, R., & Harrison, J. (2008). *Links to literature: Teaching tools to enhance literacy, character, and social skills.* Cambridge, MA: Educators for Social Responsibility. Retrieved from www.esrnational.org/ store/

64. Peace Partners Catalog (2012). *Peace builders creating safe, positive learning environments.* Long Beach, CA: Peace Partners. Retrieved from http:// www.peacebuilders.com/

65. Peace Education Foundation. (2010). *Fighting fair for kids: Dr. Martin Luther King Jr. curriculum.* Miami, FL: Author. Retrieved from http://store .peaceeducation.org/

66. Morningside Center for Social Responsibility. (2012). *Peace from A-Z: PAZ after-school program.* New York: Author. Retrieved from www.morning-sidecenter.org/; Morningside Center for Social Responsibility Catalog. (2012). After school: Adventures in peacemaking. New York: Author. Retrieved from http://esrnational.org/after-school/

67. Kreidler, W. J., & Furlong, L. (1995). *Adventures in peacemaking: A conflict resolution activity guide for school-age programs.* Beverly, MA: Project Adventure. Retrieved from http://www.pa.org/

68. Blum, R. W. (2005). *School connectedness: Improving student lives.* Washington, DC: Military Child Initiative, U.S. Department of Defense.

Chapter 7

1. Frankl, V. (1959). *Man's search for meaning.* Boston: Beacon Press.

2. Miller, D. (2009). *Book whisperer: Awakening the inner reader in every child.* Indianapolis, IN: Jossey-Bass (p. 37).

3. Swartz, B., & Sharpe, K. (2010). *Practical wisdom.* New York: Riverhead.

4. Ibid.

5. The Forum for Education and Democracy (2011). *Our mission.* Stewart, OH: Author. Retrieved from http://forumforeducation.org/

6. Rethinking Schools (2012). *About rethinking schools.* Milwaukee, WS: Author. Retrieved from http://www.rethinkingschools.org/index.shtml/

7. Ibid.

8. Glasser, W. (1999). *Choice theory: A new psychology of personal freedom.* New York: Harper Perennial. Retrieved from http://www.wglasser.com/; Glasser, W. (1997a). A new look at school failure and school success. *Phi Delta Kappan, 78,* 596–602.

9. Baraz, J., & Alexander, S. (2010). *Awakening joy: 10 steps putting you on the road to real happiness.* New York: Bantam.

10. Moll, J., Oliveira-Souza, R., & Eslinger, P. J. (2003). Morals and the human brain: A working model. *Neuroreport, 14*(3), 299–305.

11. Post, S. G. (2011). *The hidden gifts of helping: How the power of giving, compassion, and hope can get us through hard times.* Indianapolis, IN: Jossey-Bass (p. 127).

12. Onyx, J., & Bullen, P. (2000). Measuring social capital in five communities. *Journal of Applied Behavioral Science, 3*(1), 23–24.

13. NHCF (n.d.) *Social capital: Better together.* Retrieved from http://www.bettertogether.org/socialcapital.htm

14. Ibid.

15. Fischer, P., Sauer, A., Vogrincic, C., & Weisweiler, S. (2010). The ancestor effect: Thinking about our genetic origin enhances intellectual performance. *European Journal of Social Psychology, 41*(1), 11–16.

16. Brown, S., & Vaughn, C. (2009). *Play: How it shapes the brain, opens the imagination, and invigorates the soul.* New York: Avery. Retrieved from www.nifplay.org/

17. Parten, M. B. (1932). Social participation among pre-school children. *Journal of Abnormal and Social Psychology, 27*(3), 243–269.

18. Gray, P. (2009). Freedom to learn: Social play and the genesis of democracy. *Psychology Today.* Retrieved from http://www.psychologytoday.com/

19. Ibid.

20. Ibid., 1.

21. Andersen, L. (2010). Mind your body: Dance yourself happy. *Psychology Today.* Retrieved from http://www.psychologytoday.com/articles/

22. Schank, R. C. (1995). *Tell me a story: Narrative and intelligence theory.* Evanston, IL: Northwestern University Press (p. 15).

23. John F. Kennedy Center for the Performing Arts. (2012). *ArtsEdge.* Washington, DC: Author. Retrieved from http://artsedge.kennedy-center.org/educators.aspx

24. John F. Kennedy Center for the Performing Arts. (2012). *Listening doll.* Washington, DC: Author. http://artsedge.kennedy-center.org/storytelling+doll

25. Sports Feel Good Stories. (2012). *About us.* St. Paul, MN: Author. Retrieved from http://www.sportsfeelgoodstories.com/

26. Kagan, D. (2012). *Feel good stories.* Atlanta, GA: DarynKagan.com. Retrieved from http://www.darynkagan.com/index.html

27. Walker, C. (2009) *29 gifts: How a month of giving can change your life.* Boston, MA: Da Capo Lifelong Books. Retrieved from http://www.29gifts.org/

28. Walker, C. (2012). *29 day giving challenge.* Denver, CO: 29gift.org.

29. Silverstein, S. (1964). *The giving tree.* New York: Harper & Row; McGovern, A. (1986). *Stone soup.* New York: Scholastic.

30. Adopt a Classroom (2010). *Teachers.* Miami, FL: Author. Retrieved from http://www.adoptaclassroom.org/; DonorsChoose (2012). *Classrooms in need.* New York: Author. Retrieved from http://www.donorschoose.org/; School Family Media, Inc. (2012). *Teachers wish list.* Wrentham, MA: Author. Retrieved from http://www.teacherwishlist.com/

31. Rogers, F. (2000). *The giving box: Create a tradition of giving with your children.* Philadelphia: Running Press Kids.

32. Kids Care Clubs (2012). *About KCC.* Darien, CT: Author. Retrieved from http://www.kidscaring4kids.org/getinvolved/i_care_2_kit

33. Kids Caring 4 Kids (2008). *How we are making a difference.* Wheaton, IL: Author. Retrieved from http://www.kidscaring4kids.org/

34. KidsCaring4Kids (2008). *I-2-care.* Wheaton, IL: Author. Retrieved from http://www.kidscaring4kids.org/getinvolved/i_care_2_kit

35. Diener, E., Sandvik, E., & Pavot, W. (2009) Happiness is frequency, not the intensity, of positive versus negative affect. *Assessing Well-being: Social Indicators Research Series, 39,* 213–231.

36. Thomas, M., & Cerf, C. (2009). *Marlo Thomas and friends: Thanks and giving.* New York: Simon & Schuster; Wood, D. (2005). *The secret of saying thanks.* New York: Simon & Schuster; Lee, Q. B. (2005). *Care bears: Giving thanks.* New York: Scholastic; Berenstein, S., & Berenstein, J. (1999). *Berenstein Bears think of those in need first.* New York: Random House Books for Young Readers.

37. Sabin, E. *The giving book: Open the door to a lifetime of giving.* New York: Watering Can Press. Retrieved from http://www.wateringcanpress.com/index.html

38. Alex's Lemonade Stand Foundation (2012). *Our foundation.* Wynnewood, PA: Author. Retrieved from http://www.alexslemonade.org/

39. Charity: Water. (2012). *Water changes everything*. New York: Author. Retrieved from http://www.charitywater.org/

40. Boles, N. B. (2009). *How to be an everyday philanthropist: 330 ways to make a difference in your home, community, and world at no cost*. New York: Workman.

41. Humane Society of the United States. (2012). *Parents and educators*. Washington, DC: Author. Retrieved from http://www.humanesociety.org/; Goodrow, C. (2003). *Kids running*. New York: Breakaway Books. Retrieved from http://www.kidsrunning.com/ and http://www.carolgoodrow.com/; Association of Zoos and Aquariums. (2012). *Frog watch USA*. Silver Spring, MD: Author. Retrieved from http://www.aza.org/frogwatch/

42. National Wildlife Federation. (2012). *Citizen science programs*. Reston, VA: Author. http://www.nwf.org/

43. Nike. (2012). *Reuse a shoe*. Beaverton, OR: Author. Retrieved from nikereuseashoe.

44. ReCellular (2009). *Donate used cell phones*. Ann Arbor, MI: Author.

45. Care2Petition Site. (2012). *Petition site*. Redwood City, CA: Care2.com. Retrieved from http://www.thepetitionsite.com/

46. American Forests (2012). *Protecting and restoring forests for life*. Washington, DC: Author. Retrieved from http://www.americanforests.org/; Manuel, A. (2010). *Kids saving the rainforest*. Costa Rica: KSTR. Retrieved from www .kstr

47. American Institute for Philanthropy (2012). *Charity watch*. Chicago, IL: Charity Watch. Retrieved from http://www.charitywatch.org/

48. Africare. (2012). *Improving lives. Building futures*. Washington, DC: Africare. Retrieved from http://www.africare.org/; Blanket America. (2011). *About us*. New York: Author. Retrieved from http://www.blanketamerica.com/ about-us; The Dian Fossey Gorilla Fund International. (2012). *Helping people. Saving gorillas*. Atlanta, GA: Author. Retrieved from http://gorillafund.org/; International Gorillas Conservation Fund. (2012). *About the IGCP*. Washington, DC: African Wildlife Fund. Retrieved from http://www.igcp.org/; Give2theTroops. (2012). *Program and campaigns*. Rocky Hill, CT: Author. Retrieved from http://www.Give2TheTroops.org/default.htm; Guide Dogs of America. (2012). *Making a difference*. Sylmar, CA: Author. Retrieved from http://www.guidedogsofamerica.org/1/; Heifer Foundation International. (n.d.). *Classroom resources*. Little Rock, AK: Author. Retrieved from http:// www.heifer.org/?msource=kw2749; Helen Keller Foundation for Education and Research. (2008). *Helen Keller education*. Birmingham, AL: Author. Retrieved from http://www.helenkellerfoundation.org/; Hunger Project. (2012). World hunger 2012. New York: Author. Retrieved from http://www.thp.org/; Keep America Beautiful. (2006). Kid's zone. Stamford, CT: Author. Retrieved from http://www.kab.org/site/PageServer?pagename=index; Rainforest Alliance. (2012). *Kids corner*. New York: Author. Retrieved from http://www.rainforest-

alliance.org/; Save the Children. (2012). *Advocate for children.* Washington, DC: Author. Retrieved from http://www.savethechildren.org/site/; Share Our Strengths. (n.d.). *No child hungry.* Washington, DC: Author. Retrieved from http://www.strength.org/; Wildlife Conservation Society. (2012). *Take action.* New York: Author. Retrieved from http://www.wcs.org/take-action.aspx

49. National Service Learning Clearinghouse. (2012). *Work with K–12 youth.* Washington, DC: Author. Retrieved from http://www.servicelearning .org/

50. RMC Research Corporation (2009). *K–12 Service learning project planning toolkit.* National Service Learning Clearinghouse. Washington, DC: ETR Associates. Retrieved from http://www.servicelearning.org and http://www.etr.org/home

51. Learn and Serve America. (2012). *Educators.* Washington, DC: Author. Retrieved from http://www.servicelearning.org/what-you-do/educate-work-with-k-12-youth

52. Inagaki, T. K., & Eisenberger, N. I. (2012). Neural correlates of giving support to a loved one. *Psychosomatic Medicine, 74,* 3–7.

53. Warner, C. D. (1873). *Backlog Studies,* Central, Hong Kong: Forgotten Books (p. 108).

54. Barratt, N. (2006). *Family tree detective.* New York: Ebury Press.

55. Family Tree Kids (2012). *Making family history fun.* Cincinnati, OH: Family Tree Magazine. Retrieved from http://kids.familytreemagazine.com/kids/default.asp

56. Say, A. (1993). *My grandfather's journey.* New York: Houghton Mifflin.

57. Asgedom, M. (2002). *Beetles and Angels: A boy's remarkable journey from refugee camp to Harvard.* New York: Little, Brown.

58. Feder, P. K. (1995). *The feather bed journey.* New York: Albert Whitman & Company.

59. Wolfman, I. (2002) *Climbing your family tree: Online and offline genealogy for kids.* New York: Workman. Retrieved from www.workman.com/familytree/

60. PBS Colonial House. (2004). *Interactive learning.* Washington, DC: Educational Broadcasting System. Retrieved from http://www.pbs.org/wnet/colonialhouse/

61. Arbor Day Foundation. (n.d.). *Give a tree.* Nebraska City, NE: Author. Retrieved from http://www.arborday.org/shopping/Gifts.cfm

62. Bradbury, R. (2003) [1953]. *Fahrenheit 451: A novel.* New York: Simon & Schuster (p. 156).

63. Rohmer, H. (1999). *Honoring our ancestors.* New York: Children's Book Press.

64. The Legacy Project. (n.d.). *Create. connect. change.* Ontario, CA: Author. Retrieved from www.legacyproject.org/

65. The Legacy Project. (n.d.). *Life dreams.* Ontario, CA: Author. Retrieved from www.legacyproject.org/

66. The Legacy Project. (n.d.). *Across generations.* Ontario, CA: Author. Retrieved from www.legacyproject.org/

67. The Legacy Project. (n.d.). *For our world.* Ontario, CA: Author. Retrieved from www.legacyproject.org/

68. Grossman, R. D. (2006). *Global babies.* Watertown, MA: Charlesbridge Publishing/Global Children's Fund.

69. Grossman, R. D. (2009). *Carry me: Babies everywhere.* Cambridge, MA: Star Bright.

70. Focus Features. (2010). *Everybody loves babies.* New York: NBC/Universal. Retrieved from http://focusfeatures.com/babies

71. The Society for Safe and Caring Schools Community. (2003). *About Us.* Edmonton, CA: Author. Retrieved from http://www.sacsc.ca/students.htm

72. Global Education Project. (2004). *Wall chart.* BC, Canada: Author. Retrieved from http://www.theglobaleducationproject.org; The Society for Safe and Caring School. (2003). *Aboriginal students project.* Edmonton, CA: Author. Retrieved from http://www.sacsc.ca/Elementary_Unit_and_Lesson_Plans.htm# Aboriginal; The Society for Safe and Caring School. (2003). *Interfaith project.* Edmonton, CA: Author. Retrieved from http://www.sacsc.ca/Elementary_Unit_ and_Lesson_Plans.htm - InterfaithElementary

73. Heifer Foundation International. (n.d.). *Our work.* Little Rock, AK: Author. Retrieved from http://www.heifer.org/ourwork/our-work

74. Heifer Foundation International. (n.d.). *Read to feed.* Little Rock, AK: Author. Retrieved from http://www.heifer.org/ourwork/our-work

75. Global School Net (2011). *Global e-learning programs.* Encinitas, CA: Author. Retrieved from http://www.globalschoolnet.org/index.cfm?section= Programs

76. One World Classrooms (2010). *Programs and services.* Andover, MA: Author. Retrieved from http://www.ccph.com/programs.html

77. Sylvester, V. (October 26, 1929). What life means to Einstein. *Saturday Evening Post* (pp. 1, 17, 110, 113, 114, and 117).

78. Comstock, A. (1986). *The handbook of nature study.* New York: Comstock Publishing/Cornell University Press.

79. Ward, J. (2008). *I love dirt! 52 activities to help you and your kids discover the wonders of nature.* Boston, MA: Roost Books; Ward, J. (2011). *It's a jungle out there: 52 nature adventures for city kids.* Boston, MA: Roost Books.

80. Public Broadcasting System. (2012). *The nature channel.* Washington, DC: Educational Broadcasting Company. Retrieved from http://www.pbs.org/ wnet/nature/

81. National Geographic for Kids. (2012). *Dare to explore.* Washington, DC: National Geographic Society. Retrieved from http://kids.nationalgeographic .com/kids/

82. University of California Museum of Paleontology. (2005). *Natural history museums*. Berkeley, CA: Author. Retrieved from http://www.ucmp.berkeley.edu/subway/nathistmus.html

83. Kids Be Green.org. (n.d.). 3R's California Environmental Protection Agency. Retrieved from http://www.kidsbegreen.org/

84. Heinz, J. (2011). *Benefits of green space*. Chantilly, VA: Environmental Health Research Foundation. Retrieved from http://www.ehrf.info/

85. Cornell, J. (1998). *Sharing nature books*. Nevada City, CA: Dawn Publications. Retrieved from http://www.sharingnature.com/snwc1.html

86. Sharing Nature Worldwide. (2009). *Flow learning*. Nevada City, CA: Dawn Publications. Retrieved from http://www.sharingnature.com/flow-learning/

87. Sharing Nature Worldwide. (2009). *Nature activities*. Nevada City, CA: Sharing Nature Foundation. Retrieved from http://www.sharingnature.com/nature-activities/

88. Audubon. (2012). *Education*. New York: National Audubon Society. Retrieved from http://education.audubon.org/

89. Brandt, D. (1998). *Nature Log Kids: A kid's journal to record their nature experiences*. Cambridge, MA: Adventure Publications.

90. The Nature Conservancy. (2012). *Nature ecards*. Arlington, VA: Author. Retrieved from http://my.nature.org/ecards/

91. Kids Gardening (2012). *School gardening*. South Burlington, VT: National Gardening Association. Retrieved from http://www.kidsgardening.org/school-gardening

92. My First Garden. *A guide to the world of fun and clever gardening*. Urbana, IL: University of Illinois Extension. Retrieved from urbanext.illinois.edu/firstgarden/.

93. Wartenberg, T. E. (2009). *Big ideas for little kids: Teaching philosophy through literature*. R&L Education. Retrieved from www.teachingchildrenphilosophy.org/

94. Kids Philosophy Slam (2009). About us. Washington, DC: Retrieved from www.philosophyslam.org/ and http://kidsthinkaboutit.com/

95. Matthews, G. (2009). *Philosophy for kids*. Amherst, MA: University of Massachusetts Press.

96. Northwest Center Philosophy for Children (2008). *Lessons and activities*. Seattle, WA: University of Washington. Retrieved from dept.washington.edu/nwcenter/lessons.

97. Matthews, Gareth. (1980). *Philosophy and the young child*. Cambridge, MA: Harvard University Press.

98. Ibid., 1.

99. Geisel, T. (1954). *Horton hears a who*. New York: Random House for Young Readers.

100. Southern Poverty Law Center (2011). *Teaching tolerance.* Montgomery, AL: Author. Retrieved from http://www.tolerance.org/

101. Teaching Tolerance (2011). *Allies.* Montgomery, AL: Author. Retrieved from http://www.tolerance.org/search/apachesolr_search/allies

102. Center for Restorative Justice and Peacemaking (2011). *Our mission.* St. Paul, MN: Author. Retrieved from http://www.cehd.umn.edu/ssw/rjp/

103. The Society for Safe and Caring Schools Community. (2003). *About us.* Edmonton, CA: Author. Retrieved from http://www.sacsc.ca/students.htm

104. The Society for Safe and Caring Schools Community. (2003). *Restorative justice unit and lesson plans.* Edmonton, CA: Author. Retrieved from http://www.sacsc.ca/Elementary_Unit_and_Lesson_Plans.htm#Restorative Justice

105. Moorhead, J. (2011, September 4). 9/11 ten years on: The children left behind. *The Independent.* Retrieved from www.independent.co.uk/americas/

106. Smith Magazine (2011). *Six-word memoirs.* Brooklyn, NY: MagSmith. Retrieved from www.smithmag.net/sixwords/ and www.sixwordstories.net/

107. Berg, P. (2008). *Six-word stories.* Los Angeles, CA: Word Press. Retrieved from www.sixwordstories.net/

Chapter 8

1. Seligman, M. E. P. (2011). *Flourish: A visionary new understanding of happiness and well-being.* New York: Simon & Schuster.

2. Hu, W., & Gebeloff, R. (2012, February 27). Ratings throw spotlight on city's top teachers, *New York Times.*

3. Ibid.

4. Halfman, J. (2011). *Star of the sea: A day in the life of a starfish.* New York: Henry Holt.

5. Silverman, R. L. (2004). *Reaching your goals.* New York: Children's Press/ Scholastic.

6. Goal for It. (2012). *Success made easy.* New Port Richey, FL: Ascend Interactives. Retrieved from http://www.goalforit.com/

7. Learning for Life Catalog (2011). *Learning for life Pre-K–12 curriculum.* Irving, TX: Author. Retrieved from http://learning.learningforlife.org/programs/chardev-overview/

8. Kids.Gov (2012). *About kids.gov.* Washington, DC: Office of Citizen Services and Innovative Technologies, U.S General Services Administration. Retrieved from http://www.kids.gov/internal/about_site.shtml

9. Search Institute (2011). *What kids need: Developmental assets.* Minneapolis, MN: Author. Retrieved from http://www.search-institute.org/developmental-assets

10. The Georgetown Project (n.d.). *Developmental assets.* Georgetown, TX: Georgetown Developmental Assets Project Collaborative. Retrieved from http://www.georgetownproject.com/home/assets.htm

11. Search Institute (2011). *What kids need: Developmental assets.* Minneapolis, MN: Author. Retrieved from http://www.search-institute.org/developmental-assets

12. Espeland, P., & Verdick, E. (2006). *Developing assets series and teacher's guide.* Retrieved from www.freespirit.com/catalog/item and www.freespirit.com/developmental-assets/leaders-guide

13. Haberman, M. (1991). Pedagogy of poverty. *Phi Delta Kappan, 73*(4), 290–294.

14. Ibid., p. 291.

15. Ibid.

16. Ibid.

17. Baker, J. A., Dilly, L. J., Aupperlee, J. L., & Patil, S. A. (2003). The developmental context of school satisfaction: School as psychologically healthy environments. *School Psychology Quarterly, 18,* 296.

18. Graubard, A. (2012). *The free schools movement. Harvard Educational Review.* Boston, MA: Harvard Education Publishing Group; The League of Professional Schools (n.d.). *Vision for the future.* Athens, GA: University of Georgia. Retrieved from http://www.leagueschools.com/vision.html

19. The Forum for Education and Democracy (2011). *Creating a national culture of learning.* Stewart, OH: Author. Retrieved from http://forumforeducation.org/

20. Chaltain, S. (2012). *Democracy. Learning. Voice.* Washington, DC: Sam Chaltain. Retrieved from http://www.samchaltain.com/blog

21. Funderstanding (2011). *Inspiring and connecting people who care about learning.* Livingston, NJ: Author. Retrieved from http://www.funderstanding.com/slg/coaster/; Discovery Channel (2012). *Human body: Pushing the limits.* Silver Spring, MD: Author. Retrieved from http://dsc.discovery.com/tv/

22. Basman, M., & Ling, M. (2001) *Chess for kids.* New York: DK Publishing. Retrieved from http://www.chesskids.com/newcourse

23. O'Connor, S. D. (2009). *iCivics.* Washington, DC: iCivics.

24. The History Channel (2012). *Citizenship quiz and knowledge badges.* New York: History.com. Retrieved from http://www.history.com/interactives/citizenship-quiz

25. Public Broadcasting Service (2008). *Democracy project.* Washington, DC: Educational Broadcasting Company. Retrieved from http://pbskids.org/democracy/

26. Khan Academy (2012). *A world-class education for everyone.* Silicon Valley, CA: Author. Retrieved from http://www.khanacademy.org/

27. Hammond-Darling, L. (2011, March 23). U.S. versus highest achieving nations in education. In V. Strauss (Ed.), *The Answer Sheet*. Washington, DC: Washington Post. Retrieved from http://www.washingtonpost.com/answersheet

28. Global Chinese Positive Psychology Association. (2011). *Mission*. Beijing, China: Author. Retrieved from http://www.globalcppa.org/en/index.html

29. Zhao, Y. (2009). *Catching up or leading the way: American education in the age of globalization*. Alexandria, VA: Association for Supervision and Curriculum Development.

INDEX